The Editor

MICHAEL GORRA is the Mary Augusta Jordan Professor of English at Smith College, where he has taught since 1985. He is the recipient of fellowships from the National Endowment for the Humanities and the Guggenheim Foundation and, for his work as a reviewer, of the Balakian Award from the National Book Critics Circle. His books include *The Bells in Their Silence: Travels through Germany; After Empire: Scott, Naipaul, Rushdie; The English Novel at Mid-Century*; and, as editor, *The Portable Conrad*.

A NORTON CRITICAL EDITION

William Faulkner
AS I LAY DYING

AUTHORITATIVE TEXT
BACKGROUNDS AND CONTEXTS
CRITICISM

Edited by

MICHAEL GORRA
SMITH COLLEGE

W • W • NORTON & COMPANY • *New York* • *London*

W. W. Norton & Company has been independent since its founding in 1923, when William Warder Norton and Mary D. Herter Norton first published lectures delivered at the People's Institute, the adult education division of New York City's Cooper Union. The firm soon expanded its program beyond the Institute, publishing books by celebrated academics from America and abroad. By mid-century, the two major pillars of Norton's publishing program—trade books and college texts—were firmly established. In the 1950s, the Norton family transferred control of the company to its employees, and today—with a staff of four hundred and a comparable number of trade, college, and professional titles published each year—W. W. Norton & Company stands as the largest and oldest publishing house owned wholly by its employees.

This title is printed on permanent
paper containing 30 percent post-consumer
waste recycled fiber.

Book design by Antonina Krass
Production manager: Eric Pier-Hocking

Library of Congress Cataloging-in-Publication Data

Faulkner, William, 1897–1962.
As I lay dying : authoritative text, backgrounds and contexts,
criticism / William Faulkner ; edited by Michael Gorra.—1st ed.
p.   cm.—(A Norton critical edition)
This edition is based on the 1985 corrected text published by
The Library of America, and includes Valery Larbaud's never-before-
translated preface to the first French edition.
Includes bibliographical references.
ISBN: 978-0-393-93138-9 (pbk.)
1. Burial—Fiction. 2. Death—Fiction. 3. Mississippi—Fiction.
4. Stream of consciousness fiction. 5. Domestic fiction.
I. Gorra, Michael Edward. II. Title.
PS3511.A86A85 2010
813'.52—dc22   2009039276

W. W. Norton & Company, Inc., 500 Fifth Avenue, New York, N.Y. 10110
www.wwnorton.com

W. W. Norton & Company Ltd., Castle House, 75/76 Wells Street,
London W1T 3QT

3 4 5 6 7 8 9 0

Contents

Criticism   233

Introduction

The old power plant at the University of Mississippi sits in a hollow between the football stadium and the school of pharmacy, two stories of worn red brick surrounded by parking lots. The campus' needs have long since outstripped its capacity, and today the building houses the offices of the university's physical plant instead. Its location remains central—near the school's memorial to the Confederate dead, near the Grove where alumni tailgate on autumn weekends. It is central enough, and therefore valuable enough, to make one fear for the future of this half-forgotten structure. But for now the old plant still stands, a building as anonymous as any on campus. It seems an unlikely place to have played a role in the making of American literature, and yet that's exactly what happened here in the fall of 1929, when a local writer named William Faulkner took a job on the power plant's night shift, supervising the two African-American coal heavers who kept its boiler fired and its dynamo at work.

He had published four novels and written a fifth, which his publisher had rejected as indecent. The first of those books, *Soldiers' Pay*, had made him look promising, a young man to watch. The fourth of them, *The Sound and the Fury*, had appeared just that season, a novel that to some readers seemed a work of genius and to others willfully obscure. None of them had sold well, and Faulkner hadn't yet had any luck in placing his short stories in magazines. He was newly married and he needed money, and it wasn't the first time that the university, in his hometown of Oxford, had helped him out. He himself had spent just a year as a student there, but his father was the school's secretary, and in the early 1920s Faulkner had worked for three years as its postmaster. He had resigned from that job after he was accused of negligence—he threw some of the mail away and at times skipped out to play golf—and when he quit he told a friend that at least he wouldn't now "be at the beck and call of every son of a bitch who's got two cents to buy a stamp."[1] Faulkner had as little interest in the power plant as he did in the post office, and no particular talent for

---

1. Quoted in Joseph L. Blotner, *Faulkner: A Biography*, rev. ed. (New York: Random House, 1984), p. 118. Biographical information about Faulkner's work at the power plant is drawn from Blotner, pp. 247–52.

machinery. The position did, however, turn out to have a peculiar benefit.

He later wrote that he spent the first part of his twelve-hour shift shoveling "coal from the bunker into a wheelbarrow," and dumping it "where the fireman could put it into the boiler," but he was after all a storyteller and the physical work was done by others. His wife remembered him as leaving for work after dinner, his clothes spotless, and returning for breakfast, spotless still. He kept up the necessary level of power by reading gauges and pulling switches and telling the men he bossed when they should shovel some more, and toward midnight he turned to work of another kind. Each day when he left home he carried with him a sheaf of unlined onion-skin paper, its sheets rolled for convenience, and when the demand for power began to fall for the night he would spread those sheets on a table "he had invented . . . out of a wheelbarrow in the coal bunker." Around four in the morning "we would have to clean the fires and get up steam again," but in the small hours his time seems to have been his own, and he spent it with a pen in his hand, scratching his way through a new novel, working with steady confidence and apparently without any sense of heat or passion.[2]

He called the new book *As I Lay Dying* and claimed that before he "set down the first word, I knew what the last word would be."[3] He claimed too that he wrote it in six weeks and sent it off without changing a line. Those brags won't entirely hold up, but they are more nearly true than one might expect. He started on October 25, and in just forty-eight days had finished an entirely coherent draft. Both it and the typescript he completed a month later do show the signs of revision, and yet Faulkner's alterations are often little more than line editing: changing a word, clarifying a description, adjusting a character's voice. He had his plot from the start, and the ordering of the fifty-nine chapters in the manuscript is virtually identical with that in the finished book; if Faulkner had serious difficulties with this novel's structure, no trace of them survives. The story he told about the novel is true enough to justify his statement that *As I Lay Dying* was a deliberate attempt "to write a tour-de-force,"[4] a show of his strength, a display of his power. In the 1930s that was enough for him to describe the book as his favorite, even as his best. Later he used the same phrase to dismiss it. *The Sound and the Fury* had remained dear to him, as he told a Japanese interviewer in 1955, precisely because

2. Quotations in this paragraph drawn from William Faulkner, "Introduction" to *Sanctuary* (New York: Modern Library, 1932), p. vii. See pp. 184–85 of this Norton Critical Edition.
3. William Faulkner, "An Introduction for *The Sound and the Fury.*" Written 1933; first published in the *Southern Review*, n.s. 8.4 (October 1972): 709. See p. 186 of this Norton Critical Edition.
4. Ibid.

it was such a "gallant failure." But he had had no problems in writing *As I Lay Dying* and by then he liked it the least of all his books, simply because it had given him "no trouble . . . That's pure *tour de force*."[5]

That dismissal has had its effect. For fifty years and more *As I Lay Dying* has been one of Faulkner's most widely read novels, and yet it isn't often admired to the same degree as some of his other major books. Its different narrative voices do not have the monumental scale of those in *The Sound and the Fury*; it does not offer the same kind of meditation on the Southern past as do *Light in August* and *Absalom, Absalom*. It says virtually nothing about racial questions, and though it is the book in which Faulkner first named the mythical Mississippi county in which he set his best work, the story he tells about how Anse Bundren tried to bury his dead wife has little apparent connection with the Yoknapatawpha cycle as a whole. Some readers even find the book too easy, not properly hard; entry-level Faulkner. And maybe all that is true. *As I Lay Dying* isn't nearly so problematic as many of Faulkner's other great novels. It is merely perfect, as fine—as sublime—a job of verbal carpentry as one can imagine. So a reader may disagree with Faulkner's later judgment, and yet find that *tour de force* is exactly the right description for a book that can risk a five-word chapter and mixes comedy and horror indiscriminately; a novel in which one character provides an eyewitness account of events at which he was not present and another speaks from beyond the grave; a work whose fifteen first-person narrators offer the most disciplined and varied display of stream of consciousness in all of American fiction, a series of compressed lessons in the handling of voice and the management of point of view; a book that remains tight and taut and free of false steps in a way that makes it utterly singular in his *oeuvre*.

Faulkner never wrote a better scene than he did in the river-crossing episode at the center of this novel, with the water's "yellow surface dimpled monstrously into fading swirls travelling along the surface for an instant, silent, impermanent and profoundly significant" (82).[6] None of his other characters has a voice that cuts so deep as that of Addie Bundren in her compact and terrible soliloquy, a woman for whom "words dont ever fit even what they are trying to say at" (99). Then too, Faulkner does something here that no other modernist could; not Woolf, not Joyce. His exploration of the sharply differentiated inner lives of his characters serves to carry a plot that one follows with the same pleasure as that of a Victorian novel, the same desire to know what happens to the Bundrens next, as they move Addie's coffin over forty miles of washed-out roads to its resting place in the county seat of Jefferson. Yet to say that is to forget, or to under-play, the very real difficulties with which *As I Lay Dying* presents us. Take its opening page, headed by that single club of a word, "Darl." Few readers will have an immediate sense of its meaning. That sylla-ble looks something close to nonsense, and nothing in the novel's first chapter gives us the positive assurance that it is in fact a name, that of Anse and Addie's second son. (Faulkner would later define it as a regional pronunciation of "Darrell.") The word at the top of the next chapter—"Cora"—does make things easier, but there is still a long series of voices to which we must adjust, some of them belonging to characters whom we meet for the first time as they speak. That initial sense of dislocation never quite vanishes, and there are other confu-sions here as well.

So as Darl lies "beneath rain on a strange roof" (47), he plays with the tenses and forms of the verb "to be," with the difference between *is* and *was*, *are* and *am*, trying to conjugate himself into existence. Or take the way that in the novel's last pages the oldest Bundren boy, Cash, asks himself if "ere a man has the right to say what is crazy and what aint" (137). For whose judgment, whose version, can we trust? Some of this book's many narrators are more credible than others, but their sheer multitude makes the issue of reliability seem something close to irrelevant; the question of point of view leads us instead into a maze of dead ends and sudden open-ings, trick mirrors and startling perspectives. It is a radically unset-tling world, a world terrible and astonishing at once, in which "it aint none of us pure crazy and aint none of us pure sane until the bal-ance of us talks him that-a-way" (134). Moreover, the full truth of the Bundrens' family life remains forever unavailable to its surviv-ing members. The reader may come to understand it, but Anse doesn't, or Cash, or his sister Dewey Dell, and it is only the liberties Faulkner allows himself that makes us recognize the mystery at the heart of their lives.

Those complications endure on a second, a fifth, a tenth read-ing. For this reader, however, the most confusing thing about a *first* encounter with *As I Lay Dying* is the difficulty of determining just when its action takes place. At the Bundren farm time seems to be static, unmoving. The name "Vardaman"—that of a Mississippi politician active in the twentieth century's first decades—does help, but still the family appears to live in an outworn age, an age of hand-picked cotton and unsprung wagons, of mules and cedar buckets and cornshuck mattresses. It seems at first impossible to define their moment. Yet Faulkner is the best historian of any American novelist, a writer as acutely aware of flux and change as Balzac or Stendhal, and that frozen quality tells us something about the rural South in the stilled decades after the Civil War. By the end of the novel the Bundrens have moved out of stasis and into the world of automobiles and electric lights. Their odyssey covers a distance not only in space but also in time—or to borrow Darl's words from the river-crossing episode, "It is as though the space between us were time: an irrevocable quality" (85). So in reaching Jefferson they enter modernity as well. They step into history. It's no accident that the book's most decided reference to a date—an allusion to Darl's service in World War I—comes after they arrive in town; and the changes this trip brings to them will be irrevocable indeed.

Faulkner liked to re-use his people: to build a world out of our knowledge of what one book's characters have done in his other novels and stories. It's therefore surprising how solitary *As I Lay Dying* remains in his work, as cut off from his other books as the Bundren farm is from Jefferson itself. The novel is the third that Faulkner set in Yoknapatawpha County, a district based on his own Lafayette County in northern Mississippi, and many secondary figures from *As I Lay Dying* do apppear in Faulkner's other work—Vernon and Cora Tull, Doc Peabody, and even the soda jerk MacGowan. But the book has no stake in Faulkner's myths of race and historical memory, and it says nothing about the battle within Southern culture on which so much of his work depends, that between the social forces he calls "Sartoris" and "Snopes." This novel remains apart, and aside from a one-sentence reference in a story called "Uncle Willy" (1935), the Bundrens make no later appearance in his books. They stand alone—a family proud and often angry, its members sometimes hating one another and yet always and forever dependent upon each other in the face of the world around them. They survive—survive even if, like some fabled beast in a trap, they must gnaw off a leg to do so. It's perhaps no accident that a family so closed in upon itself could not reappear in his work; and no accident, either, that the book Faulkner wrote about them would be the tightest and most self-contained of all the Yoknapatawpha novels. The Bundrens may receive visitors from the rest of his books, but they will be no other story's beholden guest.

Still, if the major characters of *As I Lay Dying* have but the slightest of connections to Faulkner's other work, the novel has produced children of its own. It has inspired both a ballet and an opera, and a French illustrator has produced an edition that comes close to turning it into a graphic novel.[7] At least three other novelists have written

---

7. The ballet was a 1948 staging by Valerie Bettis; the 1988 opera was by David McKay, with a libretto drawn from Faulkner's text by Laura Jehn Menides. The comics artist Andre Juillard did the illustrations for a 1991 edition of *Tandis que j'agonise* (Paris: Futuropolis/Gallimard).

books that look stamped by it—Donald Barthelme in *The Dead Father* (1975), Suzan-Lori Parks in *Getting Mother's Body* (2003), and above all the British novelist Graham Swift. His Booker Prize–winning *Last Orders* (1996) borrows both Faulkner's plot and his multiple narrators, an act of homage that recasts the novel as a pub-crawl across the south of England, with four friends carrying the ashes of a fifth to his final resting place off Margate Pier. Addie Bundren has a less watery tomb, a filled hole in the ground of Jefferson's grave-yard. The one in Oxford sits a bit north of the town center, a few gently rolling hillsides where today the Bundrens' creator lies buried himself.

I have provided headnotes to each of the four sections of contextual and critical material that follow the text of *As I Lay Dying*, and will therefore say nothing here about their contents. It remains only to thank the people who have helped me with this edition: at Norton, Carol Bemis and Rivka Genesen; my research assistants Melina Moore and Catharina Gress-Wright; my colleagues at Smith College, Rick Millington, Michael Thurston, and David Ball; Pam Skinner and Martin Antonetti in Smith's wonderful Neilson Library, George Riser at the University of Virginia's Alderman Library, and special thanks to Tracy Carr Seabold of the Mississippi Library Commission in Jackson; and the scholars who patiently answered my questions: Christopher Benfey, Melanie Benson, Deborah Clarke, Deborah Cohn, Tom Ferraro, Minrose Gwin, Dori Hale, Don Kartiganer, Becky Mark, and Jay Parini.

Note on the Text

My introduction tells over the well-known legend of the writing of *As I Lay Dying*, the story of how, in the novelist's own phrase, he wrote the book "in six weeks, without changing a word."[1] Of course he did change words, and many of them. Still, there is more truth to that story than one might expect. Faulkner wrote by hand on large, unlined onion-skin pages—they measured 13"×8"—and he dated the first and the last of the manuscript's 107 sheets. He began on October 25, 1929—the day after the "Black Thursday" that started the Wall Street crash—and finished on December 11. He did his own typing, completing the job on January 12, 1930. Both the holograph manuscript and his ribbon typescript show the marks of revision; the manuscript suggests that most of his troubles lay in the

---

1. William Faulkner, "Introduction" to *Sanctuary* (New York: Modern Library, 1932), p. vii. See p. 185 of this Norton Critical Edition.

dialogue, in finding the precise register and diction for each individual character. But the quantity of Faulkner's blotted lines weighs as nothing in comparison to such obsessives as Joyce or Proust, or indeed to those in much of his other work. The novel's manuscript and carbon typescript are on deposit at the Alderman Library of the University of Virginia; the ribbon copy itself can be found at the Harry Ransom Humanities Research Center of the University of Texas. A facsimile of the holograph and carbon is available as *William Faulkner Manuscripts,* vol. 7, ed. Thomas L. McHaney (New York and London: Garland, 1987).

The authoritative text of *As I Lay Dying,* as indeed of Faulkner's work as a whole, has been established by Noel Polk. Polk's 1985 corrected text of the novel is based upon Faulkner's ribbon-setting copy, i.e., the pages he submitted to his publisher, in this case the New York firm of Cape and Smith. Copyediting on the first edition was minimal, though some attempt was made to regularize Faulkner's punctuation, and in returning his proofs the novelist noted that they looked "quite clean . . . I found few errors that could be called major ones."[2] These proofs do not appear to have survived. Nevertheless Polk's collation of the remaining materials has enabled him to track the changes Faulkner made upon them. Polk's stated goal in this work has been to produce a text as close as possible to the novelist's final intentions at the time of publication. His text emends the ribbon copy to include those revisions from the first edition that appear to be the result, not of editorial suggestion, but of Faulkner's own second thoughts; and to fix whatever other errors or inconsistencies (e.g., the novelist's erratic use of apostrophes) required correction. Interested readers may consult the Library of America edition of Faulkner's works for further details.

I have kept annotation to a minimum, and have drawn upon the following sources in tracing allusions and references and in supplying explanatory footnotes: *Faulkner: Novels 1930–1935,* eds. Joseph Blotner and Noel Polk (New York: Library of America, 1985); Calvin S. Brown, *A Glossary of Faulkner's South* (New Haven: Yale University Press, 1976); and Dianne C. Luce, *Annotations to* As I Lay Dying (New York and London: Garland, 1990).

---

2. Joseph Blotner, ed., *Selected Letters of William Faulkner* (New York: Random House, 1977), p. 48.

The Text of
AS I LAY DYING

AS I LAY DYING

WILLIAM
FAULKNER

NEW YORK

JONATHAN CAPE: HARRISON SMITH

Facsimile title page from the first edition. Courtesy of the Mortimer Rare Book Room, Smith College.

TO

HAL SMITH

When asked about the title Faulkner paraphrased the following lines from Book XI of the *Odyssey*. During his visit to Hades Odysseus learns from Agamemnon of the treachery of the dead king's wife, Clytemnestra:

> ". . . But in mine ears
> Most piteous rang the cry of Priam's daughter
> Cassandra, whom the treacherous Clytemnestra
> Slew at my side, while I, as I lay dying
> Upon the sword, raised up my hands to smite her;
> And shamelessly she turned away, and scorned
> To draw my eyelids down and close my mouth,
> Though I was on the road to Hades' house."

Homer's passage is not entirely apposite—it is, after all, the mother who lies dying in this book—and we shouldn't discount the possibility that Faulkner was first drawn to the phrase by its sound. Nevertheless there are some thematic links between the novel and the generations-long tragedy of the House of Atreus: betrayal, vengeance, the dissolution of familial bonds, and the visiting of the sins of the parents upon their children. See Carvel Collins, "The Pairing of *The Sound and the Fury* and *As I Lay Dying*," *Princeton University Library Chronicle* 18 (Spring 1957): 114–23, which identifies the translation Faulkner used as that of Sir Roger Marris' 1925 Oxford edition; and Dianne C. Luce, *Annotations to* As I Lay Dying (New York and London: Garland, 1990), pp. 1–4.

Faulkner dedicated the novel to Harrison Smith, the editor at Harcourt, Brace who in 1928 had accepted *Flags in the Dust*; it appeared the next year, in much abbreviated form, as *Sartoris*. Smith took Faulkner with him when he left Harcourt to become a partner in the new firm of Cape & Smith, and under that imprint published both *The Sound and the Fury* and *As I Lay Dying*.

Darl

■

Jewel and I come up from the field, following the path in single file. Although I am fifteen feet ahead of him, anyone watching us from the cottonhouse can see Jewel's frayed and broken straw hat a full head above my own.

The path runs straight as a plumb-line,[1] worn smooth by feet and baked brick-hard by July, between the green rows of laidby cotton,[2] to the cottonhouse in the center of the field, where it turns and circles the cottonhouse at four soft right angles and goes on across the field again, worn so by feet in fading precision.

The cottonhouse is of rough logs, from between which the chinking has long fallen. Square, with a broken roof set at a single pitch, it leans in empty and shimmering dilapidation in the sunlight, a single broad window in two opposite walls giving onto the approaches of the path. When we reach it I turn and follow the path which circles the house. Jewel, fifteen feet behind me, looking straight ahead, steps in a single stride through the window. Still staring straight ahead, his pale eyes like wood set into his wooden face, he crosses the floor in four strides with the rigid gravity of a cigar store Indian dressed in patched overalls and endued with life from the hips down, and steps in a single stride through the opposite window and into the path again just as I come around the corner. In single file and five feet apart and Jewel now in front, we go on up the path toward the foot of the bluff.

Tull's wagon stands beside the spring, hitched to the rail, the reins wrapped about the seat stanchion. In the wagon bed are two chairs. Jewel stops at the spring and takes the gourd from the willow branch and drinks. I pass him and mount the path, beginning to hear Cash's saw.

When I reach the top he has quit sawing. Standing in a litter of chips, he is fitting two of the boards together. Between the shadow spaces they are yellow as gold, like soft gold, bearing on their flanks in smooth undulations the marks of the adze blade: a good carpenter, Cash is. He holds the two planks on the trestle, fitted along the edges in a quarter of the finished box. He kneels and squints along the edge of them, then he lowers them and takes up the adze. A good carpenter.

---

1. A line or cord with a weight at one end, a builder's tool used for determining the vertical; a straight line.
2. Cotton is described as "laid by" in midsummer, when the plants have been cultivated for the last time before picking.

Addie Bundren could not want a better one, a better box to lie in. It will give her confidence and comfort. I go on to the house, followed by the

      Chuck.   Chuck.   Chuck.

of the adze.

Cora

■

So I saved out the eggs and baked yesterday. The cakes turned out right well. We depend a lot on our chickens. They are good layers, what few we have left after the possums and such. Snakes too, in the summer. A snake will break up a hen-house quicker than anything. So after they were going to cost so much more than Mr Tull thought, and after I promised that the difference in the number of eggs would make it up, I had to be more careful than ever because it was on my final say-so we took them. We could have stocked cheaper chickens, but I gave my promise as Miss Lawington said when she advised me to get a good breed, because Mr Tull himself admits that a good breed of cows or hogs pays in the long run. So when we lost so many of them we couldn't afford to use the eggs ourselves, because I could not have had Mr Tull chide me when it was on my say-so we took them. So when Miss Lawington told me about the cakes I thought that I could bake them and earn enough at one time to increase the net value of the flock the equivalent of two head. And that by saving the eggs out one at a time, even the eggs wouldn't be costing anything. And that week they laid so well that I not only saved out enough eggs above what we had engaged to sell, to bake the cakes with, I had saved enough so that the flour and the sugar and the stove wood would not be costing anything. So I baked yesterday, more careful than ever I baked in my life, and the cakes turned out right well. But when we got to town this morning Miss Lawington told me the lady had changed her mind and was not going to have the party after all.

"She ought to taken those cakes anyway," Kate says.

"Well," I say, "I reckon she never had no use for them now."

"She ought to taken them," Kate says. "But those rich town ladies can change their minds. Poor folks cant."

Riches is nothing in the face of the Lord, for He can see into the heart.[1] "Maybe I can sell them at the bazaar Saturday," I say. They turned out real well.

"You cant get two dollars a piece for them," Kate says.

"Well, it isn't like they cost me anything," I say. I saved them out and swapped a dozen of them for the sugar and flour. It isn't like the cakes

---

1. Cora's speech is larded with Biblical references, and at times she runs two verses together. Those given here are taken from the King James version, as are all subsequent Biblical citations. Proverbs 11.4: "Riches profit not in the day of wrath: but righteousness delivereth from death." 1 John 3.20: "For if our heart condemn us, God is greater than our heart, and knowest all things."

cost me anything, as Mr Tull himself realises that the eggs I saved
were over and beyond what we had engaged to sell, so it was like we
had found the eggs or they had been given to us.

"She ought to taken those cakes when she same as gave you her
word," Kate says. The Lord can see into the heart.[2] If it is His will
that some folks has different ideas of honesty from other folks, it is
not my place to question His decree.

"I reckon she never had any use for them," I say. They turned out
real well, too.

The quilt is drawn up to her chin, hot as it is, with only her two
hands and her face outside. She is propped on the pillow, with her
head raised so she can see out the window, and we can hear him every
time he takes up the adze or the saw. If we were deaf we could almost
watch her face and hear him, see him. Her face is wasted away so that
the bones draw just under the skin in white lines. Her eyes are like
two candles when you watch them gutter down into the sockets of
iron candle-sticks. But the eternal and the everlasting salvation and
grace is not upon her.

"They turned out real nice," I say. "But not like the cakes Addie used
to bake." You can see that girl's washing and ironing in the pillow-slip,
if ironed it ever was. Maybe it will reveal her blindness to her, laying
there at the mercy and the ministration of four men and a tom-boy
girl. "There's not a woman in this section could ever bake with Addie
Bundren," I say. "First thing we know she'll be up and baking again,
and then we wont have any sale for ours at all." Under the quilt she
makes no more of a hump than a rail would, and the only way you can
tell she is breathing is by the sound of the mattress shucks. Even the
hair at her cheek does not move, even with that girl standing right
over her, fanning her with the fan. While we watch she swaps the fan
to the other hand without stopping it.

"Is she sleeping?" Kate whispers.

"She's just watching Cash yonder," the girl says. We can hear the
saw in the board. It sounds like snoring. Eula turns on the trunk and
looks out the window. Her necklace looks real nice with her red hat.
You wouldn't think it only cost twenty-five cents.

"She ought to taken those cakes," Kate says.

I could have used the money real well. But it's not like they cost me
anything except the baking. I can tell him that anybody is likely to
make a miscue, but it's not all of them that can get out of it without
loss, I can tell him. It's not everybody can eat their mistakes, I can tell
him.

---

2. Cf. Psalm 139.23: "Search me, O God, and know my heart."

Someone comes through the hall. It is Darl. He does not look in as he passes the door. Eula watches him as he goes on and passes from sight again toward the back. Her hand rises and touches her beads lightly, and then her hair. When she finds me watching her, her eyes go blank.

Darl

■

Pa and Vernon are sitting on the back porch. Pa is tilting snuff from the lid of his snuff-box into his lower lip, holding the lip outdrawn between thumb and finger. They look around as I cross the porch and dip the gourd into the water bucket and drink.

"Where's Jewel?" pa says. When I was a boy I first learned how much better water tastes when it has set a while in a cedar bucket. Warmish-cool, with a faint taste like the hot July wind in cedar trees smells. It has to set at least six hours, and be drunk from a gourd. Water should never be drunk from metal.

And at night it is better still. I used to lie on the pallet in the hall, waiting until I could hear them all asleep, so I could get up and go back to the bucket. It would be black, the shelf black, the still surface of the water a round orifice in nothingness, where before I stirred it awake with the dipper I could see maybe a star or two in the bucket, and maybe in the dipper a star or two before I drank. After that I was bigger, older. Then I would wait until they all went to sleep so I could lie with my shirt-tail up, hearing them asleep, feeling myself without touching myself, feeling the cool silence blowing upon my parts and wondering if Cash was yonder in the darkness doing it too, had been doing it perhaps for the last two years before I could have wanted to or could have.

Pa's feet are badly splayed, his toes cramped and bent and warped, with no toenail at all on his little toes, from working so hard in the wet in homemade shoes when he was a boy. Beside his chair his brogans sit.[1] They look as though they had been hacked with a blunt axe out of pig-iron. Vernon has been to town. I have never seen him go to town in overalls. His wife, they say. She taught school too, once.

I fling the dipper dregs to the ground and wipe my mouth on my sleeve. It is going to rain before morning. Maybe before dark. "Down to the barn," I say. "Harnessing the team."

Down there fooling with that horse. He will go on through the barn, into the pasture. The horse will not be in sight: he is up there among the pine seedlings, in the cool. Jewel whistles, once and shrill. The horse snorts, then Jewel sees him, glinting for a gaudy instant among the blue shadows. Jewel whistles again; the horse comes dropping down the slope, stiff-legged, his ears cocking and flicking, his mis-matched eyes rolling, and fetches up twenty feet away, broadside on, watching Jewel over his shoulder in an attitude kittenish and alert.

---

1. High-topped lace-up shoes.

"Come here, sir," Jewel says. He moves. Moving that quick his coat, bunching, tongues swirling like so many flames. With tossing mane and tail and rolling eye the horse makes another short curvetting rush and stops again, feet bunched, watching Jewel. Jewel walks steadily toward him, his hands at his sides. Save for Jewel's legs they are like two figures carved for a tableau savage in the sun.

When Jewel can almost touch him, the horse stands on his hind legs and slashes down at Jewel. Then Jewel is enclosed by a glittering maze of hooves as by an illusion of wings; among them, beneath the upreared chest, he moves with the flashing limberness of a snake. For an instant before the jerk comes onto his arms he sees his whole body earth-free, horizontal, whipping snake-limber, until he finds the horse's nostrils and touches earth again. Then they are rigid, motionless, terrific, the horse back-thrust on stiffened, quivering legs, with lowered head; Jewel with dug heels, shutting off the horse's wind with one hand, with the other patting the horse's neck in short strokes myriad and caressing, cursing the horse with obscene ferocity.

They stand in rigid terrific hiatus, the horse trembling and groaning. Then Jewel is on the horse's back. He flows upward in a stooping swirl like the lash of a whip, his body in midair shaped to the horse. For another moment the horse stands spraddled, with lowered head, before it bursts into motion. They descend the hill in a series of spine-jolting jumps, Jewel high, leech-like on the withers, to the fence where the horse bunches to a scuttering halt again.

"Well," Jewel says, "you can quit now, if you got a-plenty."

Inside the barn Jewel slides running to the ground before the horse stops. The horse enters the stall, Jewel following. Without looking back the horse kicks at him, slamming a single hoof into the wall with a pistol-like report. Jewel kicks him in the stomach; the horse arches his neck back, crop-toothed; Jewel strikes him across the face with his fist and slides on to the trough and mounts upon it. Clinging to the hay-rack he lowers his head and peers out across the stall tops and through the doorway. The path is empty; from here he cannot even hear Cash sawing. He reaches up and drags down hay in hurried armsful and crams it into the rack.

"Eat," he says. "Get the goddamn stuff out of sight while you got a chance, you pussel-gutted bastard.[2] You sweet son of a bitch," he says.

---

2. Faulkner said that this common regionalism "means someone that is bloated, that has a tremendous belly that he shouldn't have." See p. 195 of this Norton Critical Edition.

Jewel

■

It's because he stays out there, right under the window, hammering and sawing on that goddamn box. Where she's got to see him. Where every breath she draws is full of his knocking and sawing where she can see him saying See. See what a good one I am making for you. I told him to go somewhere else. I said Good God do you want to see her in it. It's like when he was a little boy and she says if she had some fertilizer she would try to raise some flowers and he taken the bread pan and brought it back from the barn full of dung.

And now them others sitting there, like buzzards. Waiting, fanning themselves. Because I said If you wouldn't keep on sawing and nailing at it until a man cant sleep even and her hands laying on the quilt like two of them roots dug up and tried to wash and you couldn't get them clean. I can see the fan and Dewey Dell's arm. I said if you'd just let her alone. Sawing and knocking, and keeping the air always moving so fast on her face that when you're tired you cant breathe it, and that goddamn adze going One lick less. One lick less. One lick less until everybody that passes in the road will have to stop and see it and say what a fine carpenter he is. If it had just been me when Cash fell off of that church and if it had just been me when pa laid sick with that load of wood fell on him, it would not be happening with every bastard in the county coming in to stare at her because if there is a God what the hell is He for. It would just be me and her on a high hill and me rolling the rocks down the hill at their faces, picking them up and throwing them down the hill faces and teeth and all by God until she was quiet and not that goddamn adze going One lick less. One lick less and we could be quiet.

Darl

■

We watch him come around the corner and mount the steps. He does not look at us. "You ready?" he says.

"If you're hitched up," I say. I say "Wait." He stops, looking at pa. Vernon spits, without moving. He spits with decorous and deliberate precision into the pocked dust below the porch. Pa rubs his hands slowly on his knees. He is gazing out beyond the crest of the bluff, out across the land. Jewel watches him a moment, then he goes on to the pail and drinks again.

"I mislike undecision as much as ere a man," pa says.

"It means three dollars," I say. The shirt across pa's hump is faded lighter than the rest of it. There is no sweat stain on his shirt. I have never seen a sweat stain on his shirt. He was sick once from working in the sun when he was twenty-two years old, and he tells people that if he ever sweats, he will die. I suppose he believes it.

"But if she dont last until you get back," he says. "She will be disappointed."

Vernon spits into the dust. But it will rain before morning.

"She's counted on it," pa says. "She'll want to start right away. I know her. I promised her I'd keep the team here and ready, and she's counting on it."

"We'll need that three dollars then, sure," I say. He gazes out over the land, rubbing his hands on his knees. Since he lost his teeth his mouth collapses in slow repetition when he dips. The stubble gives his lower face that appearance that old dogs have. "You'd better make up your mind soon, so we can get there and get a load on before dark," I say.

"Ma aint that sick," Jewel says. "Shut up, Darl."

"That's right," Vernon says. "She seems more like herself today than she has in a week. Time you and Jewel get back, she'll be setting up."

"You ought to know," Jewel says. "You been here often enough looking at her. You or your folks." Vernon looks at him. Jewel's eyes look like pale wood in his high-blooded face. He is a head taller than any of the rest of us, always was. I told them that's why ma always whipped him and petted him more. Because he was peakling around the house more. That's why she named him Jewel I told them.[1]

"Shut up, Jewel," pa says, but as though he is not listening much. He gazes out across the land, rubbing his knees.

1. Cf. the character of Pearl in Nathaniel Hawthorne's *The Scarlet Letter*. For a further development of the comparison see Harold J. Douglas and Robert Daniel, "Faulkner and the Puritanism of the South," *Tennessee Studies in Literature* 2 (1957): 1–13. They write that both Pearl and Jewel are "passionate, impulsive, mercurial, and exotic"; they both vex their mothers and yet provide those women with their "sole link with humanity" (pg. 7).

"You could borrow the loan of Vernon's team and we could catch up with you," I say. "If she didn't wait for us."

"Ah, shut your goddamn mouth," Jewel says.

"She'll want to go in ourn," pa says. He rubs his knees. "Dont ere a man mislike it more."

"It's laying there, watching Cash whittle on that damn. . . . . ." Jewel says. He says it harshly, savagely, but he does not say the word. Like a little boy in the dark to flail his courage and suddenly aghast into silence by his own noise.

"She wanted that like she wants to go in our own wagon," pa says. "She'll rest easier for knowing it's a good one, and private. She was ever a private woman. You know it well."

"Then let it be private," Jewel says. "But how the hell can you expect it to be——" he looks at the back of pa's head, his eyes like pale wooden eyes.

"Sho," Vernon says, "she'll hold on till it's finished. She'll hold on till everything's ready, till her own good time. And with the roads like they are now, it wont take you no time to get her to town."

"It's fixing up to rain," pa says. "I am a luckless man. I have ever been." He rubs his hands on his knees. "It's that durn doctor, liable to come at any time. I couldn't get word to him till so late. If he was to come tomorrow and tell her the time was nigh, she wouldn't wait. I know her. Wagon or no wagon, she wouldn't wait. Then she'd be upset, and I wouldn't upset her for the living world. With that family burying-ground in Jefferson and them of her blood waiting for her there, she'll be impatient.[2] I promised my word me and the boys would get her there quick as mules could walk it, so she could rest quiet." He rubs his hands on his knees. "No man ever misliked it more."

"If everybody wasn't burning hell to get her there," Jewel says in that harsh, savage voice. "With Cash all day long right under the window, hammering and sawing at that——"

"It was her wish," pa says. "You got no affection nor gentleness for her. You never had. We would be beholden to no man," he says, "me and her. We have never yet been, and she will rest quieter for knowing it and that it was her own blood sawed out the boards and drove the nails. She was ever one to clean up after herself."

"It means three dollars," I say. "Do you want us to go, or not?" Pa rubs his knees. "We'll be back by tomorrow sundown."

"Well. . . . . . ." pa says. He looks out over the land, awry-haired, mouthing the snuff slowly against his gums.

"Come on," Jewel says. He goes down the steps. Vernon spits neatly into the dust.

2. The county seat of Faulkner's mythical Yoknapatawpha County, based largely upon Oxford in Lafayette County, Mississippi, though it incorporates aspects of other towns in the northern part of that state as well.

"By sundown, now," pa says. "I would not keep her waiting."

Jewel glances back, then he goes on around the house. I enter the hall, hearing the voices before I reach the door. Tilting a little down the hill, as our house does, a breeze draws through the hall all the time, upslanting. A feather dropped near the front door will rise and brush along the ceiling, slanting backward, until it reaches the down-turning current at the back door: so with voices. As you enter the hall, they sound as though they were speaking out of the air about your head.

Cora

■

It was the sweetest thing I ever saw. It was like he knew he would never see her again, that Anse Bundren was driving him from his mother's death bed, never to see her in this world again. I always said Darl was different from those others. I always said he was the only one of them that had his mother's nature, had any natural affection. Not that Jewel, the one she labored so to bear and coddled and petted so and him flinging into tantrums or sulking spells, inventing devilment to devil her until I would have frailed him time and time. Not him to come and tell her goodbye. Not him to miss a chance to make that extra three dollars at the price of his mother's goodbye kiss. A Bundren through and through, loving nobody, caring for nothing except how to get something with the least amount of work. Mr Tull says Darl asked them to wait. He said Darl almost begged them on his knees not to force him to leave her in her condition. But nothing would do but Anse and Jewel must make that three dollars. Nobody that knows Anse could have expected different, but to think of that boy, that Jewel, selling all those years of self-denial and down-right partiality—they couldn't fool me: Mr Tull says Mrs Bundren liked Jewel the least of all, but I knew better. I knew she was partial to him, to the same quality in him that let her put up with Anse Bundren when Mr Tull said she ought to poisoned him— for three dollars, denying his dying mother the goodbye kiss.

Why, for the last three weeks I have been coming over every time I could, coming sometimes when I shouldn't have, neglecting my own family and duties so that somebody would be with her in her last moments and she would not have to face the Great Unknown without one familiar face to give her courage. Not that I deserve credit for it: I will expect the same for myself. But thank God it will be the faces of my loved kin, my blood and flesh, for in my husband and children I have been more blessed than most, trials though they have been at times.

She lived, a lonely woman, lonely with her pride, trying to make folks believe different, hiding the fact that they just suffered her, because she was not cold in the coffin before they were carting her forty miles away to bury her, flouting the will of God to do it. Refusing to let her lie in the same earth with those Bundrens.

"But she wanted to go," Mr Tull said. "It was her own wish to lie among her own people."

"Then why didn't she go alive?" I said. "Not one of them would have stopped her, with even that little one almost old enough now to be selfish and stone-hearted like the rest of them."

"It was her own wish," Mr Tull said. "I heard Anse say it was."

"And you would believe Anse, of course," I said. "A man like you would. Dont tell me."

"I'd believe him about something he couldn't expect to make anything off of me by not telling," Mr Tull said.

"Dont tell me," I said. "A woman's place is with her husband and children, alive or dead. Would you expect me to want to go back to Alabama and leave you and the girls when my time comes, that I left of my own will to cast my lot with yours for better and worse, until death and after?"

"Well, folks are different," he said.

I should hope so. I have tried to live right in the sight of God and man, for the honor and comfort of my Christian husband and the love and respect of my Christian children. So that when I lay me down in the consciousness of my duty and reward I will be surrounded by loving faces, carrying the farewell kiss of each of my loved ones into my reward. Not like Addie Bundren dying alone, hiding her pride and her broken heart. Glad to go. Lying there with her head propped up so she could watch Cash building the coffin, having to watch him so he would not skimp on it, like as not, with those men not worrying about anything except if there was time to earn another three dollars before the rain come and the river got too high to get across it. Like as not, if they hadn't decided to make that last load, they would have loaded her into the wagon on a quilt and crossed the river first and then stopped and give her time to die what Christian death they would let her.

Except Darl. It was the sweetest thing I ever saw. Sometimes I lose faith in human nature for a time; I am assailed by doubt. But always the Lord restores my faith and reveals to me His bounteous love for His creatures. Not Jewel, the one she had always cherished, not him. He was after that three extra dollars. It was Darl, the one that folks say is queer, lazy, pottering about the place no better than Anse, with Cash a good carpenter and always more building than he can get around to, and Jewel always doing something that made him some money or got him talked about, and that near-naked girl always standing over Addie with a fan so that every time a body tried to talk to her and cheer her up, would answer for her right quick, like she was trying to keep anybody from coming near her at all.

It was Darl. He come to the door and stood there, looking at his dying mother. He just looked at her, and I felt the bounteous love of the Lord again and His mercy. I saw that with Jewel she had just been pretending, but that it was between her and Darl that the understanding and the true love was. He just looked at her, not even coming in where she could see him and get upset, knowing that Anse was driving him away and he would never see her again. He said nothing, just looking at her.

"What you want, Darl?" Dewey Dell said, not stopping the fan, speaking up quick, keeping even him from her. He didn't answer. He just stood and looked at his dying mother, his heart too full for words.

Dewey Dell

■

The first time me and Lafe picked on down the row. Pa dassent sweat because he will catch his death from the sickness so everybody that comes to help us. And Jewel dont care about anything he is not kin to us in caring, not care-kin. And Cash like sawing the long hot sad yellow days up into planks and nailing them to something. And pa thinks because neighbors will always treat one another that way because he has always been too busy letting neighbors do for him to find out. And I did not think that Darl would, that sits at the supper table with his eyes gone further than the food and the lamp, full of the land dug out of his skull and the holes filled with distance beyond the land.

We picked on down the row, the woods getting closer and closer and the secret shade, picking on into the secret shade with my sack and Lafe's sack. Because I said will I or wont I when the sack was half full because I said if the sack is full when we get to the woods it wont be me. I said if it dont mean for me to do it the sack will not be full and I will turn up the next row but if the sack is full, I cannot help it. It will be that I had to do it all the time and I cannot help it. And we picked on toward the secret shade and our eyes would drown together touching on his hands and my hands and I didn't say anything. I said "What are you doing?" and he said "I am picking into your sack." And so it was full when we came to the end of the row and I could not help it.

And so it was because I could not help it. It was then, and then I saw Darl and he knew. He said he knew without the words like he told me that ma is going to die without words, and I knew he knew because if he had said he knew with the words I would not have believed that he had been there and saw us. But he said he did know and I said "Are you going to tell pa are you going to kill him?" without the words I said it and he said "Why?" without the words. And that's why I can talk to him with knowing with hating because he knows.

He stands in the door, looking at her.

"What you want, Darl?" I say.

"She is going to die," he says. And old turkey-buzzard Tull coming to watch her die but I can fool them.

"When is she going to die?" I say.

"Before we get back," he says.

"Then why are you taking Jewel?" I say.

"I want him to help me load," he says.

Tull

■

Anse keeps on rubbing his knees. His overalls are faded; on one knee a serge patch cut out of a pair of Sunday pants, wore iron-slick. "No man mislikes it more than me," he says.

"A fellow's got to guess ahead now and then," I say. "But, come long and short, it wont be no harm done neither way."

"She'll want to get started right off," he says. "It's far enough to Jefferson at best."

"But the roads is good now," I say. It's fixing to rain tonight, too. His folks buries at New Hope, too, not three miles away. But it's just like him to marry a woman born a day's hard ride away and have her die on him.

He looks out over the land, rubbing his knees. "No man so mislikes it," he says.

"They'll get back in plenty of time," I say. "I wouldn't worry none."

"It means three dollars," he says.

"Might be it wont be no need for them to rush back, no ways," I say. "I hope it."

"She's a-going," he says. "Her mind is set on it."

It's a hard life on women, for a fact. Some women. I mind my mammy lived to be seventy and more. Worked every day, rain or shine; never a sick day since her last chap was born until one day she kind of looked around her and then she went and taken that lace-trimmed night gown she had had forty-five years and never wore out of the chest and put it on and laid down on the bed and pulled the covers up and shut her eyes. "You all will have to look out for pa the best you can," she said. "I'm tired."

Anse rubs his hands on his knees. "The Lord giveth," he says. We can hear Cash a-hammering and sawing beyond the corner.

It's true. Never a truer breath was ever breathed. "The Lord giveth," I say.[1]

That boy comes up the hill. He is carrying a fish nigh long as he is. He slings it to the ground and grunts "Hah" and spits over his shoulder like a man. Durn nigh long as he is.

"What's that?" I say. "A hog? Where'd you get it?"

"Down to the bridge," he says. He turns it over, the under side caked over with dust where it is wet, the eye coated over, humped under the dirt.

---

1. Cf. Job 1.21: "And [Job] said, Naked came I out of my mother's womb, and naked shall I return thither: the Lord gave, and the Lord hath taken away; blessed be the name of the Lord."

"Are you aiming to leave it laying there?" Anse says.

"I aim to show it to ma," Vardaman says.[2] He looks toward the door. We can hear the talking, coming out on the draft. Cash too, knocking and hammering at the boards. "There's company in there," he says.

"Just my folks," I say. "They'd enjoy to see it too."

He says nothing, watching the door. Then he looks down at the fish laying in the dust. He turns it over with his foot and prods at the eye-bump with his toe, gouging at it. Anse is looking out over the land. Vardaman looks at Anse's face, then at the door. He turns, going toward the corner of the house, when Anse calls him without looking around.

"You clean that fish," Anse says.

Vardaman stops. "Why cant Dewey Dell clean it?" he says.

"You clean that fish," Anse says.

"Aw, pa," Vardaman says.

"You clean it," Anse says. He dont look around. Vardaman comes back and picks up the fish. It slides out of his hands, smearing wet dirt onto him, and flops down, dirtying itself again, gapmouthed, goggle-eyed, hiding into the dust like it was ashamed of being dead, like it was in a hurry to get back hid again. Vardaman cusses it. He cusses it like a grown man, standing a-straddle of it. Anse dont look around. Vardaman picks it up again. He goes on around the house, toting it in both arms like a armful of wood, it overlapping him on both ends, head and tail. Durn nigh big as he is.

Anse's wrists dangle out of his sleeves: I never see him with a shirt on that looked like it was his in all my life. They all looked like Jewel might have give him his old ones. Not Jewel, though. He's long-armed, even if he is spindling. Except for the lack of sweat. You could tell they aint been nobody else's but Anse's that way without no mistake. His eyes look like pieces of burnt-out cinder fixed in his face, looking out over the land.

When the shadow touches the steps he says "It's five oclock."

Just as I get up Cora comes to the door and says it's time to get on. Anse reaches for his shoes. "Now, Mr Bundren," Cora says, "dont you get up now." He puts his shoes on, stomping into them, like he does everything, like he is hoping all the time he really cant do it and can quit trying to. When we go up the hall we can hear them clumping on

---

2. In 1957 Faulkner told an audience at the University of Virginia that "Vardaman, Bilbo— they are very popular with country people in Mississippi to name their children after governors and senators and the politicians that come out and shake their hands and say, I'm one of you all . . ." See p. 194 of this Norton Critical Edition. Governor and Senator James K. Vardaman (1861–1930) was a charismatic politician especially popular with small farmers in Mississippi, and a man who advocated lynching as a way to maintain white supremacy.

the floor like they was iron shoes. He comes toward the door where she is, blinking his eyes, kind of looking ahead of hisself before he sees, like he is hoping to find her setting up, in a chair maybe or maybe sweeping, and looks into the door in that surprised way like he looks in and finds her still in bed every time and Dewey Dell still a-fanning her with the fan. He stands there, like he dont aim to move again nor nothing else.

"Well, I reckon we better get on," Cora says. "I got to feed the chickens." It's fixing to rain, too. Clouds like that dont lie, and the cotton making every day the Lord sends. That'll be something else for him. Cash is still trimming at the boards. "If there's ere a thing we can do," Cora says.

"Anse'll let us know," I say.

Anse dont look at us. He looks around, blinking, in that surprised way, like he had wore hisself down being surprised and was even surprised at that. If Cash just works that careful on my barn.

"I told Anse it likely wont be no need," I say. "I so hope it."

"Her mind is set on it," he says. "I reckon she's bound to go."

"It comes to all of us," Cora says. "Let the Lord comfort you."

"About that corn," I say. I tell him again I will help him out if he gets into a tight, with her sick and all. Like most folks around here, I done holp him so much already I cant quit now.

"I aimed to get to it today," he says. "Seems like I cant get my mind on nothing."

"Maybe she'll hold out till you are laid-by," I say.

"If God wills it," he says.

"Let Him comfort you," Cora says.

If Cash just works that careful on my barn. He looks up when we pass. "Dont reckon I'll get to you this week," he says.

"'Taint no rush," I say. "Whenever you get around to it."

We get into the wagon. Cora sets the cake box on her lap. It's fixing to rain, sho.

"I dont know what he'll do," Cora says. "I just dont know."

"Poor Anse," I say. "She kept him at work for thirty-odd years. I reckon she is tired."

"And I reckon she'll be behind him for thirty years more," Kate says. "Or if it aint her, he'll get another one before cotton-picking."

"I reckon Cash and Darl can get married now," Eula says.

"That poor boy," Cora says. "The poor little tyke."

"What about Jewel?" Kate says.

"He can, too," Eula says.

"Hmph," Kate says. "I reckon he will. I reckon so. I reckon there's more gals than one around here that dont want to see Jewel tied down. Well, they needn't to worry."

"Why, Kate!" Cora says. The wagon begins to rattle. "The poor little tyke," Cora says.

It's fixing to rain this night. Yes, sir. A rattling wagon is mighty dry weather, for a Birdsell.[3] But that'll be cured. It will for a fact.

"She ought to taken them cakes after she said she would," Kate says.

3. The Indiana-based Birdsell Manufacturing Company made farm wagons.

Anse

∎

Durn that road. And it fixing to rain, too. I can stand here and same as see it with second-sight, a-shutting down behind them like a wall, shutting down betwixt them and my given promise. I do the best I can, much as I can get my mind on anything, but durn them boys.

A-laying there, right up to my door, where every bad luck that comes and goes is bound to find it. I told Addie it want any luck living on a road when it come by here, and she said, for the world like a woman, "Get up and move, then." But I told her it want no luck in it, because the Lord put roads for travelling: why He laid them down flat on the earth. When He aims for something to be always a-moving, He makes it long ways, like a road or a horse or a wagon, but when He aims for something to stay put, He makes it up-and-down ways, like a tree or a man. And so He never aimed for folks to live on a road, because which gets there first, I says, the road or the house? Did you ever know Him to set a road down by a house? I says. No you never, I says, because it's always men cant rest till they gets the house set where everybody that passes in a wagon can spit in the doorway, keeping the folks restless and wanting to get up and go somewheres else when He aimed for them to stay put like a tree or a stand of corn. Because if He'd a aimed for man to be always a-moving and going somewheres else, wouldn't He a put him longways on his belly, like a snake? It stands to reason He would.

Putting it where every bad luck prowling can find it and come straight to my door, charging me taxes on top of it. Making me pay for Cash having to get them carpenter notions when if it hadn't been no road come there, he wouldn't a got them; falling off of churches and lifting no hand in six months and me and Addie slaving and a-slaving, when there's plenty of sawing on this place he could do if he's got to saw.

And Darl too. Talking me out of him, durn them. It aint that I am afraid of work; I always is fed me and mine and kept a roof above us: it's that they would short-hand me just because he tends to his own business, just because he's got his eyes full of the land all the time. I says to them, he was alright at first, with his eyes full of the land, because the land laid up-and-down ways then; it wasn't till that ere road come and switched the land around longways and his eyes still full of the land, that they begun to threaten me out of him, trying to short-hand me with the law.

Making me pay for it. She was well and hale as ere a woman ever were, except for that road. Just laying down, resting herself in her own bed, asking naught of none. "Are you sick, Addie?" I said.

"I am not sick," she said.

"You lay you down and rest you," I said. "I knowed you are not sick. You're just tired. You lay you down and rest."

"I am not sick," she said. "I will get up."

"Lay still and rest," I said. "You are just tired. You can get up tomorrow." And she was laying there, well and hale as ere a woman ever were, except for that road.

"I never sent for you," I said. "I take you to witness I never sent for you."

"I know you didn't," Peabody said. "I bound that. Where is she?"

"She's a-laying down," I said. "She's just a little tired, but she'll——"

"Get outen here, Anse," he said. "Go set on the porch a while."

And now I got to pay for it, me without a tooth in my head, hoping to get ahead enough so I could get my mouth fixed where I could eat God's own victuals as a man should, and her hale and well as ere a woman in the land until that day. Got to pay for being put to the need of that three dollars. Got to pay for the way for them boys to have to go away to earn it. And now I can see same as second sight the rain shutting down betwixt us, a-coming up that road like a durn man, like it want ere a other house to rain on in all the living land.

I have heard men cuss their luck, and right, for they were sinful men. But I do not say it's a curse on me, because I have done no wrong to be cussed by. I am not religious, I reckon. But peace is in my heart: I know it is. I have done things but neither better nor worse than them that pretend otherlike, and I know that Old Marster will care for me as for ere a sparrow that falls.[1] But it seems hard that a man in his need could be so flouted by a road.

Vardaman comes around the house, bloody as a hog to his knees, and that ere fish chopped up with the axe like as not, or maybe throwed away for him to lie about the dogs et it. Well, I reckon I aint no call to expect no more of him than of his man-growed brothers. He comes along, watching the house, quiet, and sits on the steps. "Whew," he says, "I'm pure tired."

"Go wash them hands," I say. But couldn't no woman strove harder than Addie to make them right, man and boy: I'll say that for her.

"It was full of blood and guts as a hog," he says. But I just cant seem to get no heart into anything, with this here weather sapping me, too. "Pa," he says, "is ma sick some more?"

"Go wash them hands," I say. But I just cant seem to get no heart into it.

---

1. Cf. Matthew 10.29–31: "Are not two sparrows sold for a farthing? and one of them shall not fall on the ground without your Father. But the very hairs of your head are all numbered. Fear ye not therefore, ye are of more value than many sparrows."

Darl

■

He has been to town this week: the back of his neck is trimmed close, with a white line between hair and sunburn like a joint of white bone. He has not once looked back.

"Jewel," I say. Back running, tunnelled between the two sets of bobbing mule ears, the road vanishes beneath the wagon as though it were a ribbon and the front axle were a spool. "Do you know she is going to die, Jewel?"

It takes two people to make you, and one people to die. That's how the world is going to end.

I said to Dewey Dell: "You want her to die so you can get to town: is that it?" She wouldn't say what we both knew. "The reason you will not say it is, when you say it, even to yourself, you will know it is true: is that it? But you know it is true now. I can almost tell you the day when you knew it is true. Why wont you say it, even to yourself?" She will not say it. She just keeps on saying Are you going to tell pa? Are you going to kill him? "You cannot believe it is true because you cannot believe that Dewey Dell, Dewey Dell Bundren, could have such bad luck: is that it?"

The sun, an hour above the horizon, is poised like a bloody egg upon a crest of thunderheads; the light has turned copper: in the eye portentous, in the nose sulphurous, smelling of lightning. When Peabody comes, they will have to use the rope. He has pussel-gutted himself eating cold greens. With the rope they will haul him up the path, balloon-like up the sulphurous air.

"Jewel," I say, "do you know that Addie Bundren is going to die? Addie Bundren is going to die?"

Peabody

∎

When Anse finally sent for me of his own accord, I said "He has wore her out at last." And I said a damn good thing, and at first I would not go because there might be something I could do and I would have to haul her back, by God. I thought maybe they have the same sort of fool ethics in heaven they have in the Medical College and that it was maybe Vernon Tull sending for me again, getting me there in the nick of time, as Vernon always does things, getting the most for Anse's money like he does for his own. But when it got far enough into the day for me to read weather sign I knew it couldn't have been anybody but Anse that sent. I knew that nobody but a luckless man could ever need a doctor in the face of a cyclone. And I knew that if it had finally occurred to Anse himself that he needed one, it was already too late.

When I reach the spring and get down and hitch the team, the sun has gone down behind a bank of black cloud like a topheavy mountain range, like a load of cinders dumped over there, and there is no wind. I could hear Cash sawing for a mile before I got there. Anse is standing at the top of the bluff above the path.

"Where's the horse?" I say.

"Jewel's taken and gone," he says. "Cant nobody else ketch hit. You'll have to walk up, I reckon."

"Me, walk up, weighing two hundred and twenty-five pounds?" I say. "Walk up that durn wall?" He stands there beside a tree. Too bad the Lord made the mistake of giving trees roots and giving the Anse Bundrens He makes feet and legs. If He'd just swapped them, there wouldn't ever be a worry about this country being deforested some-day. Or any other country. "What do you aim for me to do?" I say. "Stay here and get blowed clean out of the county when that cloud breaks?" Even with the horse it would take me fifteen minutes to ride up across the pasture to the top of the ridge and reach the house. The path looks like a crooked limb blown against the bluff. Anse has not been in town in twelve years. And how his mother ever got up there to bear him, he being his mother's son.

"Vardaman's gittin the rope," he says.

After a while Vardaman appears with the plowline. He gives the end of it to Anse and comes down the path, uncoiling it.

"You hold it tight," I say. "I done already wrote this visit onto my books, so I'm going to charge you just the same, whether I get there or not."

"I got hit," Anse says. "You kin come on up."

I'll be damned if I can see why I dont quit. A man seventy years old, weighing two hundred and odd pounds, being hauled up and down a damn mountain on a rope. I reckon it's because I must reach the fifty thousand dollar mark of dead accounts on my books before I can quit. "What the hell does your wife mean," I say, "taking sick on top of a durn mountain?"

"I'm right sorry," he says. He let the rope go, just dropped it, and he has turned toward the house. There is a little daylight up here still, of the color of sulphur matches. The boards look like strips of sulphur. Cash does not look back. Vernon Tull says he brings each board up to the window for her to see it and say it is all right. The boy overtakes us. Anse looks back at him. "Wher's the rope?" he says.

"It's where you left it," I say. "But never you mind that rope. I got to get back down that bluff. I dont aim for that storm to catch me up here. I'd blow too durn far once I got started."

The girl is standing by the bed, fanning her. When we enter she turns her head and looks at us. She has been dead these ten days. I suppose it's having been a part of Anse for so long that she cannot even make that change, if change it be. I can remember how when I was young I believed death to be a phenomenon of the body; now I know it to be merely a function of the mind—and that of the minds of the ones who suffer the bereavement. The nihilists say it is the end; the fundamentalists, the beginning; when in reality it is no more than a single tenant or family moving out of a tenement or a town.

She looks at us. Only her eyes seem to move. It's like they touch us, not with sight or sense, but like the stream from a hose touches you, the stream at the instant of impact as dissociated from the nozzle as though it had never been there. She does not look at Anse at all. She looks at me, then at the boy. Beneath the quilt she is no more than a bundle of rotten sticks.

"Well, Miss Addie," I say. The girl does not stop the fan. "How are you, sister?" I say. Her head lies gaunt on the pillow, looking at the boy. "You picked out a fine time to get me out here and bring up a storm." Then I send Anse and the boy out. She watches the boy as he leaves the room. She has not moved save her eyes.

He and Anse are on the porch when I come out, the boy sitting on the steps, Anse standing by a post, not even leaning against it, his arms dangling, the hair pushed and matted up on his head like a dipped rooster. He turns his head, blinking at me.

"Why didn't you send for me sooner?" I say.

"Hit was jest one thing and then another," he says. "That ere corn me and the boys was aimin to git up with, and Dewey Dell a-takin good keer of her, and folks comin in, a-offerin to help and sich, till I jest thought. . . . . . ."

"Damn the money," I say. "Did you ever hear of me worrying a fellow before he was ready to pay?"

"Hit aint begrudgin the money," he says. "I jest kept a-thinkin. . . .
. . . She's goin, is she?" The durn little tyke is sitting on the top step,
looking smaller than ever in the sulphur-colored light. That's the
one trouble with this country: everything, weather, all, hangs on too
long. Like our rivers, our land: opaque, slow, violent; shaping and
creating the life of man in its implacable and brooding image. "I
knowed hit," Anse says. "All the while I made sho. Her mind is sot
on hit."

"And a damn good thing, too," I say. "With a trifling——" He sits
on the top step, small, motionless in faded overalls. When I came
out he looked up at me, then at Anse. But now he has stopped looking at us. He just sits there.

"Have you told her yit?" Anse says.

"What for?" I say. "What the devil for?"

"She'll know hit. I knowed that when she see you she would know
hit, same as writing. You wouldn't need to tell her. Her mind——"

Behind us the girl says, "Paw." I look at her, at her face.

"You better go quick," I say.

When we enter the room she is watching the door. She looks at
me. Her eyes look like lamps blaring up just before the oil is gone.
"She wants you to go out," the girl says.

"Now, Addie," Anse says, "when he come all the way from Jefferson to git you well?" She watches me: I can feel her eyes. It's like she
was shoving at me with them. I have seen it before in women. Seen
them drive from the room them coming with sympathy and pity, with
actual help, and clinging to some trifling animal to whom they never
were more than pack-horses. That's what they mean by the love that
passeth understanding:[1] that pride, that furious desire to hide that
abject nakedness which we bring here with us, carry with us into
operating rooms, carry stubbornly and furiously with us into the earth
again.[2] I leave the room. Beyond the porch Cash's saw snores steadily
into the board. A minute later she calls his name, her voice harsh and
strong.

"Cash," she says; "you, Cash!"

---

1. Cf. Phillipians 4.7: "And the peace of God, which passeth all understanding, shall keep
   your hearts and minds through Christ Jesus."
2. Cf. Job 1.21. See p. 18 of this Norton Critical Edition.

Darl

■

Pa stands beside the bed. From behind his leg Vardaman peers, with his round head and his eyes round and his mouth beginning to open. She looks at pa; all her failing life appears to drain into her eyes, urgent, irremediable. "It's Jewel she wants," Dewey Dell says.

"Why, Addie," pa says, "him and Darl went to make one more load. They thought there was time. That you would wait for them, and that three dollars and all. . . . . . ." He stoops laying his hand on hers. For a while yet she looks at him, without reproach, without anything at all, as if her eyes alone are listening to the irrevocable cessation of his voice. Then she raises herself, who has not moved in ten days. Dewey Dell leans down, trying to press her back.

"Ma," she says; "ma."

She is looking out the window, at Cash stooping steadily at the board in the failing light, laboring on toward darkness and into it as though the stroking of the saw illumined its own motion, board and saw engendered.

"You, Cash," she shouts, her voice harsh, strong, and unimpaired. "You, Cash!"

He looks up at the gaunt face framed by the window in the twilight. It is a composite picture of all time since he was a child. He drops the saw and lifts the board for her to see, watching the window in which the face has not moved. He drags a second plank into position and slants the two of them into their final juxtaposition, gesturing toward the ones yet on the ground, shaping with his empty hand in pantomime the finished box. For a while still she looks down at him from the composite picture, neither with censure nor approbation. Then the face disappears.

She lies back and turns her head without so much as glancing at pa. She looks at Vardaman; her eyes, the life in them, rushing suddenly upon them; the two flames glare up for a steady instant. Then they go out as though someone had leaned down and blown upon them.

"Ma," Dewey Dell says; "ma!" Leaning above the bed, her hands lifted a little, the fan still moving like it has for ten days, she begins to keen. Her voice is strong, young, tremulous and clear, rapt with its own timbre and volume, the fan still moving steadily up and down, whispering the useless air. Then she flings herself across Addie Bundren's knees, clutching her, shaking her with the furious strength of the young before sprawling suddenly across the handful of rotten bones that Addie Bundren left, jarring the whole bed into a chattering sibilance of mattress shucks, her arms outflung and the fan in one hand still beating with expiring breath into the quilt.

From behind pa's leg Vardaman peers, his mouth full open and all color draining from his face into his mouth, as though he has by some means fleshed his own teeth in himself, sucking. He begins to move slowly backward from the bed, his eyes round, his pale face fading into the dusk like a piece of paper pasted on a failing wall, and so out of the door.

Pa leans above the bed in the twilight, his humped silhouette partaking of that owl-like quality of awry-feathered, disgruntled outrage within which lurks a wisdom too profound or too inert for even thought.

"Durn them boys," he says.

Jewel, I say. Overhead the day drives level and gray, hiding the sun by a flight of gray spears. In the rain the mules smoke a little, splashed yellow with mud, the off one clinging in sliding lunges to the side of the road above the ditch. The tilted lumber gleams dull yellow, water-soaked and heavy as lead, tilted at a steep angle into the ditch above the broken wheel; about the shattered spokes and about Jewel's ankles a runnel of yellow neither water nor earth swirls, curving with the yellow road neither of earth nor water, down the hill dissolving into a streaming mass of dark green neither of earth nor sky. Jewel, I say

Cash comes to the door, carrying the saw. Pa stands beside the bed, humped, his arms dangling. He turns his head, his shabby profile, his chin collapsing slowly as he works the snuff against his gums.

"She's gone," Cash says.

"She taken and left us," pa says. Cash does not look at him. "How nigh are you done?" pa says. Cash does not answer. He enters, carrying the saw. "I reckon you better get at it," pa says. "You'll have to do the best you can, with them boys gone off that-a-way." Cash looks down at her face. He is not listening to pa at all. He does not approach the bed. He stops in the middle of the floor, the saw against his leg, his sweating arms powdered lightly with sawdust, his face composed. "If you get in a tight, maybe some of them'll get here tomorrow and help you," pa says. "Vernon could." Cash is not listening. He is looking down at her peaceful, rigid face fading into the dusk as though darkness were a precursor of the ultimate earth, until at last the face seems to float detached upon it, lightly as the reflection of a dead leaf. "There is Christians enough to help you," pa says. Cash is not listening. After a while he turns without looking at pa and leaves the room. Then the saw begins to snore again. "They will help us in our sorrow," pa says.

The sound of the saw is steady, competent, unhurried, stirring the dying light so that at each stroke her face seems to wake a little into an expression of listening and of waiting, as though she were counting the strokes. Pa looks down at the face, at the black sprawl of Dewey Dell's hair, the outflung arms, the clutched fan now motionless on the fading quilt. "I reckon you better get supper on," he says.

Dewey Dell does not move.

"Git up, now, and put supper on," pa says. "We got to keep our strength up. I reckon Doctor Peabody's right hungry, coming all this way. And Cash'll need to eat quick and get back to work so he can finish it in time."

Dewey Dell rises, heaving to her feet. She looks down at the face. It is like a casting of fading bronze upon the pillow, the hands alone still with any semblance of life: a curled, gnarled inertness; a spent yet alert quality from which weariness, exhaustion, travail has not yet departed, as though they doubted even yet the actuality of rest, guarding with horned and penurious alertness the cessation which they know cannot last.

Dewey Dell stoops and slides the quilt from beneath them and draws it up over them to the chin, smoothing it down, drawing it smooth. Then without looking at pa she goes around the bed and leaves the room.

She will go out where Peabody is, where she can stand in the twilight and look at his back with such an expression that, feeling her eyes and turning, he will say: I would not let it grieve me, now. She was old, and sick too. Suffering more than we knew. She couldn't have got well. Vardaman's getting big now, and with you to take good care of them all. I would try not to let it grieve me. I expect you'd better go and get some supper ready. It dont have to be much. But they'll need to eat, and she looking at him, saying You could do so much for me if you just would. If you just knew. I am I and you are you and I know it and you dont know it and you could do so much for me if you just would and if you just would then I could tell you and then nobody would have to know it except you and me and Darl

Pa stands over the bed, dangle-armed, humped, motionless. He raises his hand to his head, scouring his hair, listening to the saw. He comes nearer and rubs his hand, palm and back, on his thigh and lays it on her face and then on the hump of quilt where her hands are. He touches the quilt as he saw Dewey Dell do, trying to smoothe it up to the chin, but disarranging it instead. He tries to smoothe it again, clumsily, his hand awkward as a claw, smoothing at the wrinkles which he made and which continue to emerge beneath his hand with perverse ubiquity, so that at last he desists, his hand falling to his side and stroking itself again, palm and back, on his thigh. The sound of the saw snores steadily into the room. Pa breathes with a quiet, rasping sound, mouthing the snuff against his gums. "God's will be done," he says. "Now I can get them teeth."

Jewel's hat droops limp about his neck, channelling water onto the soaked towsack tied about his shoulders as, ankle-deep in the running ditch, he pries with a slipping two-by-four, with a piece of rotting log for fulcrum, at the axle. Jewel, I say, she is dead, Jewel. Addie Bundren is dead

Vardaman

■

Then I begin to run. I run toward the back and come to the edge of the porch and stop. Then I begin to cry. I can feel where the fish was in the dust. It is cut up into pieces of not-fish now, not-blood on my hands and overalls. Then it wasn't so. It hadn't happened then. And now she is getting so far ahead I cannot catch her.

The trees look like chickens when they ruffle out into the cool dust on the hot days. If I jump off the porch I will be where the fish was, and it all cut up into not-fish now. I can hear the bed and her face and them and I can feel the floor shake when he walks on it that came and did it. That came and did it when she was all right but he came and did it.

"The fat son of a bitch."

I jump from the porch, running. The top of the barn comes swooping up out of the twilight. If I jump I can go through it like the pink lady in the circus, into the warm smelling, without having to wait. My hands grab at the bushes; beneath my feet the rocks and dirt go rubbling down.

Then I can breathe again, in the warm smelling. I enter the stall, trying to touch him, and then I can cry then I vomit the crying. As soon as he gets through kicking I can and then I can cry, the crying can.

"He kilt her. He kilt her."

The life in him runs under the skin, under my hand, running through the splotches, smelling up into my nose where the sickness is beginning to cry, vomiting the crying, and then I can breathe, vomiting it. It makes a lot of noise. I can smell the life running up from under my hands, up my arms, and then I can leave the stall.

I cannot find it. In the dark, along the dust, the walls I cannot find it. The crying makes a lot of noise. I wish it wouldn't make so much noise. Then I find it in the wagon shed, in the dust, and I run across the lot and into the road, the stick jouncing on my shoulder.

They watch me as I run up, beginning to jerk back, their eyes rolling, snorting, jerking back on the hitch-rein. I strike. I can hear the stick striking; I can see it hitting their heads, the breast-yoke, missing altogether sometimes as they rear and plunge, but I am glad.

"You kilt my maw!"

The stick breaks, they rearing and snorting, their feet popping loud on the ground; loud because it is going to rain and the air is empty for the rain. But it is still long enough. I run this way and that as they rear and jerk at the hitch-rein, striking.

"You kilt her!"

I strike at them, striking, they wheeling in a long lunge, the buggy wheeling onto two wheels and motionless like it is nailed to the ground and the horses motionless like they are nailed by the hind feet to the center of a whirling plate.

I run in the dust. I cannot see, running in the sucking dust where the buggy vanishes tilted on two wheels. I strike, the stick hitting into the ground, bouncing, striking into the dust and then into the air again and the dust sucking on down the road faster than if a car was in it. And then I can cry, looking at the stick. It is broken down to my hand, not longer than stove wood that was a long stick. I throw it away and I can cry. It does not make so much noise now.

The cow is standing in the barn door, chewing. When she sees me come into the lot she lows, her mouth full of flopping green, her tongue flopping.

"I aint a-goin to milk you. I aint a-goin to do nothing for them."

I hear her turn when I pass. When I turn she is just behind me with her sweet, hot, hard breath.

"Didn't I tell you I wouldn't?"

She nudges me, snuffing. She moans deep inside, her mouth closed. I jerk my hand, cursing her like Jewel does.

"Git, now."

I stoop my hand to the ground and run at her. She jumps back and whirls away and stops, watching me. She moans. She goes on to the path and stands there, looking up the path.

It is dark in the barn, warm, smelling, silent. I can cry quietly, watching the top of the hill.

Cash comes to the hill, limping where he fell off of the church. He looks down at the spring, then up the road and back toward the barn. He comes down the path stiffly and looks at the broken hitch-rein and at the dust in the road and then up the road, where the dust is gone.

"I hope they've got clean past Tull's by now. I so hope hit."

Cash turns and limps up the path.

"Durn him. I showed him. Durn him."

I am not crying now. I am not anything. Dewey Dell comes to the hill and calls me. Vardaman. I am not anything. I am quiet. You, Vardaman. I can cry quiet now, feeling and hearing my tears.

"Then hit want. Hit hadn't happened then. Hit was a-layin right there on the ground. And now she's gittin ready to cook hit."

It is dark. I can hear wood, silence: I know them. But not living sounds, not even him. It is as though the dark were resolving him out of his integrity, into an unrelated scattering of components— snuffings and stampings; smells of cooling flesh and ammoniac hair; an illusion of a coordinated whole of splotched hide and strong bones within which, detached and secret and familiar, an *is* different from my *is*. I see him dissolve—legs, a rolling eye, a gaudy splotching like cold flames—and float upon the dark in fading solution; all one yet neither; all either yet none. I can see hearing coil toward him, caressing, shaping his hard shape—fetlock, hip, shoulder and head; smell and sound. I am not afraid.

"Cooked and et. Cooked and et."

Dewey Dell

■

He could do so much for me if he just would. He could do everything for me. It's like everything in the world for me is inside a tub full of guts, so that you wonder how there can be any room in it for anything else very important. He is a big tub of guts and I am a little tub of guts and if there is not any room for anything else important in a big tub of guts, how can it be room in a little tub of guts. But I know it is there because God gave women a sign when something has happened bad.

It's because I am alone. If I could just feel it, it would be different, because I would not be alone. But if I were not alone, everybody would know it. And he could do so much for me, and then I would not be alone. Then I could be all right alone.

I would let him come in between me and Lafe, like Darl came in between me and Lafe, and so Lafe is alone too. He is Lafe and I am Dewey Dell, and when mother died I had to go beyond and outside of me and Lafe and Darl to grieve because he could do so much for me and he dont know it. He dont even know it.

From the back porch I cannot see the barn. Then the sound of Cash's sawing comes in from that way. It is like a dog outside the house, going back and forth around the house to whatever door you come to, waiting to come in. He said I worry more than you do and I said You dont know what worry is so I cant worry. I try to but I cant think long enough to worry.

I light the kitchen lamp. The fish, cut into jagged pieces, bleeds quietly in the pan. I put it into the cupboard quick, listening into the hall, hearing. It took her ten days to die; maybe she dont know it is yet. Maybe she wont go until Cash. Or maybe until Jewel. I take the dish of greens from the cupboard and the bread pan from the cold stove, and I stop, watching the door.

"Where's Vardaman?" Cash says. In the lamp his sawdusted arms look like sand.

"I dont know. I aint seen him."

"Peabody's team run away. See if you can find Vardaman. The horse will let him catch him."

"Well. Tell them to come to supper."

I cannot see the barn. I said, I dont know how to worry. I dont know how to cry. I tried, but I cant. After a while the sound of the saw comes around, coming dark along the ground in the dust-dark. Then I can see him, going up and down above the plank.

"You come in to supper," I say. "Tell him." He could do everything for me. And he dont know it. He is his guts and I am my guts. And I

am Lafe's guts. That's it. I dont see why he didn't stay in town. We
are country people, not as good as town people. I dont see why he
didn't. Then I can see the top of the barn. The cow stands at the foot
of the path, lowing. When I turn back, Cash is gone.

I carry the buttermilk in. Pa and Cash and he are at the table.

"Where's that big fish Bud caught, sister?" he says.

I set the milk on the table. "I never had no time to cook it."

"Plain turnip greens is mighty spindling eating for a man my size,"
he says. Cash is eating. About his head the print of his hat is sweated
into his hair. His shirt is blotched with sweat. He has not washed his
hands and arms.

"You ought to took time," pa says. "Where's Vardaman?"

I go toward the door. "I cant find him."

"Here, sister," he says; "never mind about the fish. It'll save, I
reckon. Come on and sit down."

"I aint minding it," I say. "I'm going to milk before it sets in to rain."

Pa helps himself and pushes the dish on. But he does not begin
to eat. His hands are halfclosed on either side of his plate, his head
bowed a little, his awry hair standing into the lamplight. He looks
like right after the maul hits the steer and it no longer alive and dont
yet know that it is dead.

But Cash is eating, and he is too. "You better eat something," he
says. He is looking at pa. "Like Cash and me. You'll need it."

"Ay," pa says. He rouses up, like a steer that's been kneeling in a
pond and you run at it. "She would not begrudge me it."

When I am out of sight of the house, I go fast. The cow lows at
the foot of the bluff. She nuzzles at me, snuffing, blowing her breath
in a sweet, hot blast, through my dress, against my hot nakedness,
moaning. "You got to wait a little while. Then I'll tend to you." She
follows me into the barn where I set the bucket down. She breathes
into the bucket, moaning. "I told you. You just got to wait, now. I got
more to do than I can tend to." The barn is dark. When I pass, he
kicks the wall a single blow. I go on. The broken plank is like a pale
plank standing on end. Then I can see the slope, feel the air moving
on my face again, slow, pale with lesser dark and with empty seeing,
the pine clumps blotched up the tilted slope, secret and waiting.

The cow in silhouette against the door nuzzles at the silhouette of
the bucket, moaning.

Then I pass the stall. I have almost passed it. I listen to it saying for
a long time before it can say the word and the listening part is afraid
that there may not be time to say it. I feel my body, my bones and
flesh beginning to part and open upon the alone, and the process
of coming unalone is terrible. Lafe. Lafe. "Lafe" Lafe. Lafe. I lean a
little forward, one foot advanced with dead walking. I feel the darkness rushing past my breast, past the cow; I begin to rush upon the

darkness but the cow stops me and the darkness rushes on upon the sweet blast of her moaning breath, filled with wood and with silence.

"Vardaman. You, Vardaman."

He comes out of the stall. "You durn little sneak! You durn little sneak!"

He does not resist; the last of rushing darkness flees whistling away. "What? I aint done nothing."

"You durn little sneak!" My hands shake him, hard. Maybe I couldn't stop them. I didn't know they could shake so hard. They shake both of us, shaking.

"I never done it," he says. "I never touched them."

My hands stop shaking him, but I still hold him. "What are you doing here? Why didn't you answer when I called you?"

"I aint doing nothing."

"You go on to the house and get your supper."

He draws back. I hold him. "You quit now. You leave me be."

"What were you doing down here? You didn't come down here to sneak after me?"

"I never. I never. You quit, now. I didn't even know you was down here. You leave me be."

I hold him, leaning down to see his face, feel it with my eyes. He is about to cry. "Go on, now. I done put supper on and I'll be there soon as I milk. You better go on before he eats everything up. I hope that team runs clean back to Jefferson."

"He kilt her," he says. He begins to cry.

"Hush."

"She never hurt him and he come and kilt her."

"Hush." He struggles. I hold him. "Hush."

"He kilt her." The cow comes up behind us, moaning. I shake him again.

"You stop it, now. Right this minute. You're fixing to make yourself sick and then you cant go to town. You go on to the house and eat your supper."

"I dont want no supper. I dont want to go to town."

"We'll leave you here, then. Lessen you behave, we will leave you. Go on, now, before that old green-eating tub of guts eats everything up from you." He goes on, disappearing slowly into the hill. The crest, the trees, the roof of the house stand against the sky. The cow nuzzles at me, moaning. "You'll just have to wait. What you got in you aint nothing to what I got in me, even if you are a woman too." She follows me, moaning. Then the dead, hot, pale air breathes on my face again. He could fix it all right, if he just would. And he dont even know it. He could do everything for me if he just knowed it. The cow breathes upon my hips and back, her breath warm, sweet, ster-torous, moaning. The sky lies flat down the slope, upon the secret clumps. Beyond the hill sheet-lightning stains upward and fades. The dead air shapes the dead earth in the dead darkness, further away than seeing shapes the dead earth. It lies dead and warm upon me, touching me naked through my clothes. I said You dont know what worry is. I dont know what it is. I dont know whether I am worrying or not. Whether I can or not. I dont know whether I can cry or not. I dont know whether I have tried to or not. I feel like a wet seed wild in the hot blind earth.

Vardaman

■

When they get it finished they are going to put her in it and then for a long time I couldn't say it. I saw the dark stand up and go whirling away and I said "Are you going to nail her up in it, Cash? Cash? Cash?" I got shut up in the crib the new door it was too heavy for me it went shut I couldn't breathe because the rat was breathing up all the air. I said "Are you going to nail it shut, Cash? Nail it? *Nail* it?"

Pa walks around. His shadow walks around, over Cash going up and down above the saw, at the bleeding plank.

Dewey Dell said we will get some bananas. The train is behind the glass, red on the track. When it runs the track shines on and off. Pa said flour and sugar and coffee costs so much. Because I am a country boy because boys in town. Bicycles. Why do flour and sugar and coffee cost so much when he is a country boy. "Wouldn't you ruther have some bananas instead?" Bananas are gone, eaten. Gone. When it runs on the track shines again. "Why aint I a town boy, pa?" I said. God made me. I did not said to God to made me in the country. If He can make the train, why cant He make them all in the town because flour and sugar and coffee. "Wouldn't you ruther have bananas?"

He walks around. His shadow walks around.

It was not her. I was there, looking. I saw. I thought it was her, but it was not. It was not my mother. She went away when the other one laid down in her bed and drew the quilt up. She went away. "Did she go as far as town?" "She went further than town." "Did all those rabbits and possums go further than town?" God made the rabbits and possums. He made the train. Why must He make a different place for them to go if she is just like the rabbit.

Pa walks around. His shadow does. The saw sounds like it is asleep.

And so if Cash nails the box up, she is not a rabbit. And so if she is not a rabbit I couldn't breathe in the crib and Cash is going to nail it up. And so if she lets him it is not her. I know. I was there. I saw when it did not be her. I saw. They think it is and Cash is going to nail it up.

It was not her because it was laying right yonder in the dirt. And now it's all chopped up. I chopped it up. It's laying in the kitchen in the bleeding pan, waiting to be cooked and et. Then it wasn't and she was, and now it is and she wasn't. And tomorrow it will be cooked and et and she will be him and pa and Cash and Dewey Dell and there wont be anything in the box and so she can breathe. It was laying right yonder on the ground. I can get Vernon. He was there and he seen it, and with both of us it will be and then it will not be.

Tull

It was nigh to midnight and it had set in to rain when he woke us. It had been a misdoubtful night, with the storm making; a night when a fellow looks for most anything to happen before he can get the stock fed and himself to the house and supper et and in bed with the rain starting, and when Peabody's team come up, lathered, with the broke harness dragging and the neck-yoke betwixt the off critter's legs, Cora says "It's Addie Bundren. She's gone at last."

"Peabody mought have been to ere a one of a dozen houses hereabouts," I says. "Besides, how do you know it's Peabody's team?"

"Well, aint it?" she says. "You hitch up, now."

"What for?" I says. "If she is gone, we cant do nothing till morning. And it fixing to storm, too."

"It's my duty," she says. "You put the team in."

But I wouldn't do it. "It stands to reason they'd send for us if they needed us. You dont even know she's gone yet."

"Why, dont you know that's Peabody's team? Do you claim it aint? Well, then." But I wouldn't go. When folks wants a fellow, it's best to wait till they sends for him, I've found. "It's my Christian duty," Cora says. "Will you stand between me and my Christian duty?"

"You can stay there all day tomorrow, if you want," I says.

So when Cora waked me it had set in to rain. Even while I was going to the door with the lamp and it shining on the glass so he could see I am coming, it kept on knocking. Not loud, but steady, like he might have gone to sleep thumping, but I never noticed how low down on the door the knocking was till I opened it and never seen nothing. I held the lamp up, with the rain sparkling across it and Cora back in the hall saying "Who is it, Vernon?" but I couldn't see nobody a-tall at first until I looked down and around the door, lowering the lamp.

He looked like a drownded puppy, in them overalls, without no hat, splashed up to his knees where he had walked them four miles in the mud. "Well, I'll be durned," I says.

"Who is it, Vernon?" Cora says.

He looked at me, his eyes round and black in the middle like when you throw a light in a owl's face. "You mind that ere fish," he says.

"Come in the house," I says. "What is it? Is your maw——"

"Vernon," Cora says.

He stood kind of around behind the door, in the dark. The rain was blowing onto the lamp, hissing on it so I am scared every minute it'll break. "You was there," he says. "You seen it."

Then Cora come to the door. "You come right in outen the rain," she says, pulling him in and him watching me. He looked just like a drownded puppy. "I told you," Cora says. "I told you it was a-happening. You go and hitch."

"But he aint said——" I says.

He looked at me, dripping onto the floor. "He's a-ruining the rug," Cora says. "You go get the team while I take him to the kitchen."

But he hung back, dripping, watching me with them eyes. "You was there. You seen it laying there. Cash is fixing to nail her up, and it was a-laying right there on the ground. You seen it. You seen the mark in the dirt. The rain never come up till after I was a-coming here. So we can get back in time."

I be durn if it didn't give me the creeps, even when I didn't know yet. But Cora did. "You get that team quick as you can," she says. "He's outen his head with grief and worry."

I be durn if it didn't give me the creeps. Now and then a fellow gets to thinking. About all the sorrow and afflictions in this world; how it's liable to strike anywhere, like lightning. I reckon it does take a powerful trust in the Lord to guard a fellow, though sometimes I think that Cora's a mite over-cautious, like she was trying to crowd the other folks away and get in closer than anybody else. But then, when something like this happens, I reckon she is right and you got to keep after it and I reckon I am blessed in having a wife that ever strives for sanctity and well-doing like she says I am.

Now and then a fellow gets to thinking about it. Not often, though. Which is a good thing. For the Lord aimed for him to do and not to spend too much time thinking, because his brain it's like a piece of machinery: it wont stand a whole lot of racking. It's best when it all runs along the same, doing the day's work and not no one part used no more than needful. I have said and I say again, that's ever living thing the matter with Darl: he just thinks by himself too much. Cora's right when she says all he needs is a wife to straighten him out. And when I think about that, I think that if nothing but being married will help a man, he's durn nigh hopeless. But I reckon Cora's right when she says the reason the Lord had to create women is because man dont know his own good when he sees it.

When I come back to the house with the team, they was in the kitchen. She was dressed on top of her nightgownd, with a shawl over her head and her umbrella and her bible wrapped up in the oilcloth, and him sitting on a up-turned bucket on the stove-zinc where she had put him, dripping onto the floor. "I cant get nothing outen him except about a fish," she says. "It's a judgment on them. I see the hand of the Lord upon this boy for Anse Bundren's judgment and warning."

"The rain never come up till after I left," he says. "I had done left. I was on the way. And so it was there in the dust. You seen it. Cash is fixing to nail her, but you seen it."

When we got there it was raining hard, and him sitting on the seat between us, wrapped up in Cora's shawl. He hadn't said nothing else, just sitting there with Cora holding the umbrella over him. Now and then Cora would stop singing long enough to say "It's a judgment on Anse Bundren. May it show him the path of sin he is a-trodding." Then she would sing again, and him sitting there between us, leaning forward a little like the mules couldn't go fast enough to suit him.

"It was laying right yonder," he says, "but the rain come up after I taken and left. So I can go and open the windows, because Cash aint nailed her yet."

It was long a-past midnight when we drove the last nail, and almost dust-dawn when I got back home and taken the team out and got back in bed, with Cora's nightcap laying on the other pillow. And be durned if even then it wasn't like I could still hear Cora singing and feel that boy leaning forward between us like he was ahead of the mules, and still see Cash going up and down with that saw, and Anse standing there like a scarecrow, like he was a steer standing knee-deep in a pond and somebody come by and set the pond up on edge and he aint missed it yet.

It was nigh toward daybreak when we drove the last nail and toted it into the house, where she was laying on the bed with the window open and the rain blowing on her again. Twice he did it, and him so dead for sleep that Cora says his face looked like one of these here Christmas masts[1] that had done been buried a while and then dug up, until at last they put her into it and nailed it down so he couldn't open the window on her no more. And the next morning they found him in his shirt tail, laying asleep on the floor like a felled steer, and the top of the box bored clean full of holes and Cash's new auger broke off in the last one. When they taken the lid off they found that two of them had bored on into her face.

If it's a judgment, it aint right. Because the Lord's got more to do than that. He's bound to have. Because the only burden Anse Bundren's ever had is himself. And when folks talks him low, I think to myself he aint that less of a man or he couldn't a bore himself this long.

It aint right. I be durn if it is. Because He said Suffer little children to come unto Me dont make it right, neither.[2] Cora said, "I have bore you what the Lord God sent me. I faced it without fear nor terror because my faith was strong in the Lord, a-bolstering and sustaining me. If you have no son, it's because the Lord has decreed otherwise in His wisdom. And my life is and has ever been a open book to ere a

---

1. Masks.
2. Matthew 19.14: "But Jesus said, Suffer little children, and forbid them not, to come unto me: for of such is the kingdom of heaven."

man or woman among His creatures because I trust in my God and my reward."

I reckon she's right. I reckon if there's ere a man or woman anywhere that He could turn it all over to and go away with His mind at rest, it would be Cora. And I reckon she would make a few changes, no matter how He was running it. And I reckon they would be for man's good. Leastways, we would have to like them. Leastways, we might as well go on and make like we did.

Darl

■

The lantern sits on a stump. Rusted, grease-fouled, its cracked chimney smeared on one side with a soaring smudge of soot, it sheds a feeble and sultry glare upon the trestles and the boards and the adjacent earth. Upon the dark ground the chips look like random smears of soft pale paint on a black canvas. The boards look like long smooth tatters torn from the flat darkness and turned backside out.

Cash labors about the trestles, moving back and forth, lifting and placing the planks with long clattering reverberations in the dead air as though he were lifting and dropping them at the bottom of an invisible well, the sounds ceasing without departing, as if any movement might dislodge them from the immediate air in reverberant repetition. He saws again, his elbow flashing slowly, a thin thread of fire running along the edge of the saw, lost and recovered at the top and bottom of each stroke in unbroken elongation, so that the saw appears to be six feet long, into and out of pa's shabby and aimless silhouette. "Give me that plank," Cash says. "No; the other one." He puts the saw down and comes and picks up the plank he wants, sweeping pa away with the long swinging gleam of the balanced board.

The air smells like sulphur. Upon the impalpable plane of it their shadows form as upon a wall, as though like sound they had not gone very far away in falling but had merely congealed for a moment, immediate and musing. Cash works on, half turned into the feeble light, one thigh and one pole-thin arm braced, his face sloped into the light with a rapt, dynamic immobility above his tireless elbow. Below the sky sheet-lightning slumbers lightly; against it the trees, motionless, are ruffled out to the last twig, swollen, increased as though quick with young.

It begins to rain. The first harsh, sparse, swift drops rush through the leaves and across the ground in a long sigh, as though of relief from intolerable suspense. They are big as buckshot, warm as though fired from a gun; they sweep across the lantern in a vicious hissing. Pa lifts his face, slack-mouthed, the wet black rim of snuff plastered close along the base of his gums; from behind his slack-faced astonishment he muses as though from beyond time, upon the ultimate outrage. Cash looks once at the sky, then at the lantern. The saw has not faltered, the running gleam of its pistoning edge unbroken. "Get something to cover the lantern," he says.

Pa goes to the house. The rain rushes suddenly down, without thunder, without warning of any sort; he is swept onto the porch upon the edge of it and in an instant Cash is wet to the skin. Yet the motion of the saw has not faltered, as though it and the arm functioned in a tranquil conviction that rain was an illusion of the mind. Then he puts down the saw and goes and crouches above the lantern, shielding it with his body, his back shaped lean and scrawny by his wet shirt as though he had been abruptly turned wrong-side out, shirt and all.

Pa returns. He is wearing Jewel's raincoat and carrying Dewey Dell's. Squatting over the lantern, Cash reaches back and picks up four sticks and drives them into the earth and takes Dewey Dell's raincoat from pa and spreads it over the sticks, forming a roof above the lantern. Pa watches him. "I dont know what you'll do," he says. "Darl taken his coat with him."

"Get wet," Cash says. He takes up the saw again; again it moves up and down, in and out of that unhurried imperviousness as a piston moves in the oil; soaked, scrawny, tireless, with the lean light body of a boy or an old man. Pa watches him, blinking, his face streaming; again he looks up at the sky with that expression of dumb and brooding outrage and yet of vindication, as though he had expected no less; now and then he stirs, moves, gaunt and streaming, picking up a board or a tool and then laying it down. Vernon Tull is there now, and Cash is wearing Mrs Tull's raincoat and he and Vernon are hunting the saw. After a while they find it in pa's hand.

"Why dont you go on to the house, out of the rain?" Cash says. Pa looks at him, his face streaming slowly. It is as though upon a face carved by a savage caricaturist a monstrous burlesque of all bereavement flowed. "You go on in," Cash says. "Me and Vernon can finish it."

Pa looks at them. The sleeves of Jewel's coat are too short for him. Upon his face the rain streams, slow as cold glycerin. "I dont begrudge her the wetting," he says. He moves again and falls to shifting the planks, picking them up, laying them down again carefully, as though they are glass. He goes to the lantern and pulls at the propped raincoat until he knocks it down and Cash comes and fixes it back.

"You get on to the house," Cash says. He leads pa to the house and returns with the raincoat and folds it and places it beneath the shelter where the lantern sits. Vernon has not stopped. He looks up, still sawing.

"You ought to done that at first," he says. "You knowed it was fixing to rain."

"It's his fever," Cash says. He looks at the board.

"Ay," Vernon says. "He'd a come, anyway."

Cash squints at the board. On the long flank of it the rain crashes steadily, myriad, fluctuant. "I'm going to bevel it," he says.

"It'll take more time," Vernon says. Cash sets the plank on edge; a moment longer Vernon watches him, then he hands him the plane.

Vernon holds the board steady while Cash bevels the edge of it with the tedious and minute care of a jeweler. Mrs Tull comes to the edge of the porch and calls Vernon. "How near are you done?" she says.

Vernon does not look up. "Not long. Some, yet."

She watches Cash stooping at the plank, the turgid savage gleam of the lantern slicking on the raincoat as he moves. "You go down and get some planks off the barn and finish it and come in out of the rain," she says. "You'll both catch your death." Vernon does not move. "Vernon," she says.

"We wont be long," he says. "We'll be done after a spell." Mrs Tull watches them a while. Then she reenters the house.

"If we get in a tight, we could take some of them planks," Vernon says. "I'll help you put them back."

Cash ceases the plane and squints along the plank, wiping it with his palm. "Give me the next one," he says.

Some time toward dawn the rain ceases. But it is not yet day when Cash drives the last nail and stands stiffly up and looks down at the finished coffin, the others watching him. In the lantern light his face is calm, musing; slowly he strokes his hands on his raincoated thighs in a gesture deliberate, final and composed. Then the four of them—Cash and pa and Vernon and Peabody—raise the coffin to their shoulders and turn toward the house. It is light, yet they move slowly; empty, yet they carry it carefully; lifeless, yet they move with hushed precautionary words to one another, speaking of it as though, complete, it now slumbered lightly alive, waiting to come awake. On the dark floor their feet clump awkwardly, as though for a long time they have not walked on floors.

They set it down by the bed. Peabody says quietly: "Let's eat a snack. It's almost daylight. Where's Cash?"

He has returned to the trestles, stooped again in the lantern's feeble glare as he gathers up his tools and wipes them on a cloth carefully and puts them into the box with its leather sling to go over the shoulder. Then he takes up box, lantern and raincoat and returns to the house, mounting the steps into faint silhouette against the paling east.

In a strange room you must empty yourself for sleep. And before you are emptied for sleep, what are you. And when you are emptied for sleep, you are not. And when you are filled with sleep, you never were. I dont know what I am. I dont know if I am or not. Jewel knows he is, because he does not know that he does not know whether he is or not. He cannot empty himself for sleep because he is not what he is and he is what he is not. Beyond the unlamped wall I can hear the rain shaping the wagon that is ours, the load that is no longer theirs that felled and sawed it nor yet theirs that bought it and which is not ours either, lie on our wagon though it does, since only the wind and the rain shape it only to Jewel and me, that are not asleep. And since sleep is is-not and rain and wind are *was*, it is not. Yet the wagon *is*, because when the wagon is *was*, Addie Bundren will not be. And Jewel *is*, so Addie Bundren must be. And then I must be, or I could not empty myself for sleep in a strange room. And so if I am not emptied yet, I am *is*.

How often have I lain beneath rain on a strange roof, thinking of home.

Cash

■

I made it on the bevel.

1. There is more surface for the nails to grip.
2. There is twice the gripping-surface to each seam.
3. The water will have to seep into it on a slant. Water moves easiest up and down or straight across.
4. In a house people are upright two thirds of the time. So the seams and joints are made up-and-down. Because the stress is up-and-down.
5. In a bed where people lie down all the time, the joints and seams are made sideways, because the stress is sideways.
6. Except.
7. A body is not square like a crosstie.[1]
8. Animal magnetism.
9. The animal magnetism of a dead body makes the stress come slanting, so the seams and joints of a coffin are made on the bevel.
10. You can see by an old grave that the earth sinks down on the bevel.
11. While in a natural hole it sinks by the center, the stress being up-and-down.
12. So I made it on the bevel.
13. It makes a neater job.

---

1. A transverse beam supporting and connecting the rails on a train track.

Vardaman

■

My mother is a fish.

Tull

■

It was ten oclock when I got back, with Peabody's team hitched on to the back of the wagon. They had already dragged the buckboard back from where Quick found it upside down straddle of the ditch about a mile from the spring. It was pulled out of the road at the spring, and about a dozen wagons was already there. It was Quick found it. He said the river was up and still rising. He said it had already covered the highest water-mark on the bridge-piling he had ever seen. "That bridge wont stand a whole lot of water," I said. "Has somebody told Anse about it?"

"I told him," Quick said. "He says he reckons them boys has heard and unloaded and are on the way back by now. He says they can load up and get across."

"He better go on and bury her at New Hope," Armstid said. "That bridge is old. I wouldn't monkey with it."

"His mind is set on taking her to Jefferson," Quick said.

"Then he better get at it soon as he can," Armstid said.

Anse meets us at the door. He has shaved, but not good. There is a long cut on his jaw, and he is wearing his Sunday pants and a white shirt with the neckband buttoned. It is drawn smooth over his hump, making it look bigger than ever, like a white shirt will, and his face is different too. He looks folks in the eye now, dignified, his face tragic and composed, shaking us by the hand as we walk up onto the porch and scrape our shoes, a little stiff in our Sunday clothes, our Sunday clothes rustling, not looking full at him as he meets us.

"The Lord giveth," we say.

"The Lord giveth."

That boy is not there. Peabody told about how he come into the kitchen, hollering, swarming and clawing at Cora when he found her cooking that fish, and how Dewey Dell taken him down to the barn. "My team all right?" Peabody says.

"All right," I tell him. "I give them a bait this morning. Your buggy seems all right too. It aint hurt."

"And no fault of somebody's," he says. "I'd give a nickel to know where that boy was when that team broke away."

"If it's broke anywhere, I'll fix it," I say.

The women folks go on into the house. We can hear them, talking and fanning. The fans go whish. whish. whish and them talking, the talking sounding kind of like bees murmuring in a water bucket. The men stop on the porch, talking some, not looking at one another.

"Howdy, Vernon," they say. "Howdy, Tull."

"Looks like more rain."

"It does for a fact."

"Yes, sir. It will rain some more."

"It come up quick."

"And going away slow. It dont fail."

I go around to the back. Cash is filling up the holes he bored in the top of it. He is trimming out plugs for them, one at a time, the wood wet and hard to work. He could cut up a tin can and hide the holes and nobody wouldn't know the difference. Wouldn't mind, anyway. I have seen him spend a hour trimming out a wedge like it was glass he was working, when he could have reached around and picked up a dozen sticks and drove them into the joint and made it do.

When we finished I go back to the front. The men have gone a little piece from the house, sitting on the ends of the boards and on the saw-horses where we made it last night, some sitting and some squatting. Whitfield aint come yet.

They look up at me, their eyes asking.

"It's about," I say. "He's ready to nail."

While they are getting up Anse comes to the door and looks at us and we return to the porch. We scrape our shoes again, careful, waiting for one another to go in first, milling a little at the door. Anse stands inside the door, dignified, composed. He waves us in and leads the way into the room.

They had laid her in it reversed. Cash made it clock-shape, like this with every joint and seam bevelled and scrubbed with the plane, tight as a drum and neat as a sewing basket, and they had laid her in it head to foot so it wouldn't crush her dress. It was her wedding dress and it had a flare-out bottom, and they had laid her head to foot in it so the dress could spread out, and they had made her a veil out of a mosquito bar so the auger holes in her face wouldn't show.

When we are going out, Whitfield comes. He is wet and muddy to the waist, coming in. "The Lord comfort this house," he says. "I was late because the bridge has gone. I went down to the old ford and swum my horse over, the Lord protecting me. His grace be upon this house."

We go back to the trestles and plank-ends and sit or squat.

"I knowed it would go," Armstid says.

"It's been there a long time, that ere bridge," Quick says.

"The Lord has kept it there, you mean," Uncle Billy says. "I dont know ere a man that's touched hammer to it in twenty-five years."

"How long has it been there, Uncle Billy?" Quick says.

"It was built in. . . . . . .let me see. . . . . . . It was in the year 1888," Uncle Billy says. "I mind it because the first man to cross it was Peabody coming to my house when Jody was born."

"If I'd a crossed it every time your wife littered since, it'd a been wore out long before this, Billy," Peabody says.

We laugh, suddenly loud, then suddenly quiet again. We look a little aside at one another.

"Lots of folks has crossed it that wont cross no more bridges," Houston says.

"It's a fact," Littlejohn says. "It's so."

"One more aint, no ways," Armstid says. "It'd taken them two-three days to got her to town in the wagon. They'd be gone a week, getting her to Jefferson and back."

"What's Anse so itching to take her to Jefferson for, anyway?" Houston says.

"He promised her," I say. "She wanted it. She come from there. Her mind was set on it."

"And Anse is set on it, too," Quick says.

"Ay," Uncle Billy says. "It's like a man that's let everything slide all his life to get set on something that will make the most trouble for everybody he knows."

"Well, it'll take the Lord to get her over that river now," Peabody says. "Anse cant do it."

"And I reckon He will," Quick says. "He's took care of Anse a long time, now."

"It's a fact," Littlejohn says.

"Too long to quit now," Armstid says.

"I reckon He's like everybody else around here," Uncle Billy says. "He's done it so long now He cant quit."

Cash comes out. He has put on a clean shirt; his hair, wet, is combed smooth down on his brow, smooth and black as if he had painted it onto his head. He squats stiffly among us, we watching him.

"You feeling this weather, aint you?" Armstid says.

Cash says nothing.

"A broke bone always feels it," Littlejohn says. "A fellow with a broke bone can tell it a-coming."

"Lucky Cash got off with just a broke leg," Armstid says. "He might have hurt himself bed-rid. How far'd you fall, Cash?"

"Twenty-eight foot, four and a half inches, about," Cash says. I move over beside him.

"A fellow can sho slip quick on wet planks," Quick says.

"It's too bad," I say. "But you couldn't a holp it."

"It's them durn women," he says. "I made it to balance with her. I made it to her measure and weight."

If it takes wet boards for folks to fall, it's fixing to be lots of falling before this spell is done.

"You couldn't have holp it," I say.

I dont mind the folks falling. It's the cotton and corn I mind.

Neither does Peabody mind the folks falling. How bout it, Doc?

It's a fact. Washed clean outen the ground it will be. Seems like something is always happening to it.

Course it does. That's why it's worth anything. If nothing didn't happen and everybody made a big crop, do you reckon it would be worth the raising?

Well, I be durn if I like to see my work washed outen the ground, work I sweat over.

It's a fact. A fellow wouldn't mind seeing it washed up if he could just turn on the rain himself.

Who is that man can do that? Where is the color of his eyes?[1]

Ay. The Lord made it to grow. It's Hisn to wash up if He sees it fitten so.

"You couldn't have holp it," I say.

"It's them durn women," he says.

In the house the women begin to sing. We hear the first line commence, beginning to swell as they take hold, and we rise and move toward the door, taking off our hats and throwing our chews away. We do not go in. We stop at the steps, clumped, holding our hats between our lax hands in front or behind, standing with one foot advanced and our heads lowered, looking aside, down at our hats in our hands and at the earth or now and then at the sky and at one another's grave, composed face.

The song ends; the voices quaver away with a rich and dying fall. Whitfield begins. His voice is bigger than him. It's like they are not the same. It's like he is one, and his voice is one, swimming on two horses side by side across the ford and coming into the house, the mud-splashed one and the one that never even got wet, triumphant and sad. Somebody in the house begins to cry. It sounds like her eyes and her voice were turned back inside her, listening; we move, shifting to the other leg, meeting one another's eye and making like they hadn't touched.

Whitfield stops at last. The women sing again. In the thick air it's like their voices come out of the air, flowing together and on in the sad, comforting tunes. When they cease it's like they hadn't gone away. It's like they had just disappeared into the air and when we moved we would loose them again out of the air around us, sad and comforting. Then they finish and we put on our hats, our movements stiff, like we hadn't never wore hats before.

On the way home Cora is still singing. "I am bounding toward my God and my reward," she sings, sitting on the wagon, the shawl around her shoulders and the umbrella open over her, though it is not raining.

"She has hern," I say. "Wherever she went, she has her reward in being free of Anse Bundren." *She laid there three days in that box, waiting for Darl and Jewel to come clean back home and get a new*

---

1. Cf. Job 38.25–26: "Who hath divided the watercourse for the overflowing of waters, or a way for the lightning of thunder; To cause it to rain on the earth, where no man is; on the wilderness, wherein there is no man."

wheel and go back to where the wagon was in the ditch. Take my team, Anse, I said.

We'll wait for ourn, he said. She'll want it so. She was ever a particular woman.

On the third day they got back and they loaded her into the wagon and started and it already too late.[2] You'll have to go all the way round by Samson's bridge. It'll take you a day to get there. Then you'll be forty miles from Jefferson. Take my team, Anse.

We'll wait for ourn. She'll want it so.

It was about a mile from the house we saw him, sitting on the edge of the slough. It hadn't had a fish in it never that I knowed. He looked around at us, his eyes round and calm, his face dirty, the pole across his knees. Cora was still singing.

"This aint no good day to fish," I said. "You come on home with us and me and you'll go down to the river first thing in the morning and catch some fish."

"It's one in here," he said. "Dewey Dell seen it."

"You come on with us. The river's the best place."

"It's in here," he said. "Dewey Dell seen it."

"I'm bounding toward my God and my reward," Cora sung.

2. Cf. Luke 24.6–7: "He is not here, but is risen: remember how he spake unto you when he was yet in Galilee, Saying, The Son of man must be delivered into the hands of sinful men, and be crucified, and the third day rise again."

Darl

■

It's not your horse that's dead, Jewel," I say. He sits erect on the seat, leaning a little forward, wooden-backed. The brim of his hat has soaked free of the crown in two places, drooping across his wooden face so that, head lowered, he looks through it like through the visor of a helmet, looking long across the valley to where the barn leans against the bluff, shaping the invisible horse. "See them?" I say. High above the house, against the quick thick sky, they hang in narrowing circles. From here they are no more than specks, implacable, patient, portentous. "But it's not your horse that's dead."

"Goddamn you," he says. "Goddamn you."

I cannot love my mother because I have no mother. Jewel's mother is a horse.

Motionless, the tall buzzards hang in soaring circles, the clouds giving them an illusion of retrograde.

Motionless, wooden-backed, wooden-faced, he shapes the horse in a rigid stoop like a hawk, hook-winged. They are waiting for us, ready for the moving of it, waiting for him. He enters the stall and waits until it kicks at him so that he can slip past and mount onto the trough and pause, peering out across the intervening stall-tops toward the empty path, before he reaches into the loft.

"Goddamn him. Goddamn him."

Cash

■

It wont balance. If you want it to tote and ride on a balance, we will have——"

"Pick up. Goddamn you, pick up."

"I'm telling you it wont tote and it wont ride on a balance unless——"

"Pick up! Pick up, goddamn your thick-nosed soul to hell, pick up!"

It wont balance. If they want it to tote and ride on a balance, they will have

Darl

■

He stoops among us above it, two of the eight hands. In his face the blood goes in waves. In between them his flesh is greenish looking, about that smooth, thick, pale green of cow's cud; his face suffocated, furious, his lip lifted upon his teeth. "Pick up!" he says. "Pick up, goddamn your thick-nosed soul!"

He heaves, lifting one whole side so suddenly that we all spring into the lift to catch and balance it before he hurls it completely over. For an instant it resists, as though volitional, as though within it her pole-thin body clings furiously, even though dead, to a sort of modesty, as she would have tried to conceal a soiled garment that she could not prevent her body soiling. Then it breaks free, rising suddenly as though the emaciation of her body had added buoyancy to the planks or as though, seeing that the garment was about to be torn from her, she rushes suddenly after it in a passionate reversal that flouts its own desire and need. Jewel's face goes completely green and I can hear teeth in his breath.

We carry it down the hall, our feet harsh and clumsy on the floor, moving with shuffling steps, and through the door.

"Steady it a minute, now," pa says, letting go. He turns back to shut and lock the door, but Jewel will not wait.

"Come on," he says in that suffocating voice. "Come on."

We lower it carefully down the steps. We move, balancing it as though it were something infinitely precious, our faces averted, breathing through our teeth to keep our nostrils closed. We go down the path, toward the slope.

"We better wait," Cash says. "I tell you it aint balanced now. We'll need another hand on that hill."

"Then turn loose," Jewel says. He will not stop. Cash begins to fall behind, hobbling to keep up, breathing harshly; then he is distanced and Jewel carries the entire front end alone, so that, tilting as the path begins to slant, it begins to rush away from me and slip down the air like a sled upon invisible snow, smoothly evacuating atmosphere in which the sense of it is still shaped.

"Wait, Jewel," I say. But he will not wait. He is almost running now and Cash is left behind. It seems to me that the end which I now carry alone has no weight, as though it coasts like a rushing straw upon the furious tide of Jewel's despair. I am not even touching it when, turning, he lets it overshoot him, swinging, and stops it and sloughs it into the wagon bed in the same motion and looks back at me, his face suffused with fury and despair.

"Goddamn you. Goddamn you."

Vardaman

■

We are going to town. Dewey Dell says it wont be sold because it belongs to Santa Claus and he taken it back with him until next Christmas. Then it will be behind the glass again, shining with waiting.

Pa and Cash are coming down the hill, but Jewel is going to the barn. "Jewel," pa says. Jewel does not stop. "Where you going?" pa says. But Jewel does not stop. "You leave that horse here," pa says. Jewel stops and looks at pa. Jewel's eyes look like marbles. "You leave that horse here," pa says. "We'll all go in the wagon with ma, like she wanted."

But my mother is a fish. Vernon seen it. He was there.

"Jewel's mother is a horse," Darl said.

"Then mine can be a fish, cant it, Darl?" I said.

Jewel is my brother.

"Then mine will have to be a horse, too," I said.

"Why?" Darl said. "If pa is your pa, why does your ma have to be a horse just because Jewel's is?"

"Why does it?" I said. "Why does it, Darl?"

Darl is my brother.

"Then what is your ma, Darl?" I said.

"I haven't got ere one," Darl said. "Because if I had one, it is *was*. And if it is was, it cant be *is*. Can it?"

"No," I said.

"Then I am not," Darl said. "Am I?"

"No," I said.

I am. Darl is my brother.

"But you *are*, Darl," I said.

"I know it," Darl said. "That's why I am not *is*. *Are* is too many for one woman to foal."

Cash is carrying his tool box. Pa looks at him. "I'll stop at Tull's on the way back," Cash says. "Get on that barn roof."

"It aint respectful," pa says. "It's a deliberate flouting of her and of me."

"Do you want him to come all the way back here and carry them up to Tull's afoot?" Darl says. Pa looks at Darl, his mouth chewing. Pa shaves every day now because my mother is a fish.

"It aint right," pa says.

Dewey Dell has the package in her hand. She has the basket with our dinner too.

"What's that?" pa says.

"Mrs Tull's cakes," Dewey Dell says, getting into the wagon. "I'm taking them to town for her."

"It aint right," pa says. "It's a flouting of the dead."

It'll be there. It'll be there come Christmas, she says, shining on the track. She says he wont sell it to no town boys.

Darl

■

He goes on toward the barn, entering the lot, wooden-backed.

Dewey Dell carries the basket on one arm, in the other hand something wrapped square in a newspaper. Her face is calm and sullen, her eyes brooding and alert; within them I can see Peabody's back like two round peas in two thimbles: perhaps in Peabody's back two of those worms which work surreptitious and steady through you and out the other side and you waking suddenly from sleep or from waking, with on your face an expression sudden, intent, and concerned. She sets the basket into the wagon and climbs in, her leg coming long from beneath her tightening dress: that lever which moves the world;[1] one of that caliper which measures the length and breadth of life. She sits on the seat beside Vardaman and sets the parcel on her lap.

Then he enters the barn. He has not looked back.

"It aint right," pa says. "It's little enough for him to do for her."

"Go on," Cash says. "Leave him stay if he wants. He'll be all right here. Maybe he'll go up to Tull's and stay."

"He'll catch us," I say. "He'll cut across and meet us at Tull's lane."

"He would have rid that horse, too," pa says, "if I hadn't a stopped him. A durn spotted critter wilder than a cattymount. A deliberate flouting of her and of me."

The wagon moves; the mules' ears begin to bob. Behind us, above the house, motionless in tall and soaring circles, they diminish and disappear.

---

1. Archimedes (c. 287–212 B.C.E.), Greek mathematician and physicist, supposedly once boasted to King Hieron II of Syracuse that if he were only given a long enough lever he could move the earth.

Anse

■

I told him not to bring that horse out of respect for his dead ma, because it wouldn't look right, him prancing along on a durn circus animal and her wanting us all to be in the wagon with her that sprung from her flesh and blood, but we hadn't no more than passed Tull's lane when Darl begun to laugh. Setting back there on the plank seat with Cash, with his dead ma laying in her coffin at his feet, laughing. How many times I told him it's doing such things as that that makes folks talk about him, I dont know. I says I got some regard for what folks says about my flesh and blood even if you haven't, even if I have raised such a durn passel of boys, and when you fixes it so folks can say such about you, it's a reflection on your ma, I says, not me: I am a man and I can stand it; it's on your womenfolks, your ma and sister that you should care for, and I turned and looked back at him and him setting there, laughing.

"I dont expect you to have no respect for me," I says. "But with your own ma not cold in her coffin yet."

"Yonder," Cash says, jerking his head toward the lane. The horse is still a right smart piece away, coming up at a good pace, but I dont have to be told who it is. I just looked back at Darl, setting there laughing.

"I done my best," I says. "I tried to do as she would wish it. The Lord will pardon me and excuse the conduct of them He sent me." And Darl setting on the plank seat right above her where she was laying, laughing.

Darl

■

He comes up the lane fast, yet we are three hundred yards beyond the mouth of it when he turns into the road, the mud flying beneath the flicking drive of the hooves. Then he slows a little, light and erect in the saddle, the horse mincing through the mud.

Tull is in his lot. He looks at us, lifts his hand. We go on, the wagon creaking, the mud whispering on the wheels. Vernon still stands there. He watches Jewel as he passes, the horse moving with a light, high-kneed driving gait, three hundred yards back. We go on, with a motion so soporific, so dreamlike as to be uninferant of progress, as though time and not space were decreasing between us and it.

It turns off at right angles, the wheel-marks of last Sunday healed away now: a smooth, red scoriation curving away into the pines; a white signboard with faded lettering: New Hope Church. 3 mi. It wheels up like a motionless hand lifted above the profound desolation of the ocean; beyond it the red road lies like a spoke of which Addie Bundren is the rim. It wheels past, empty, unscarred, the white signboard turns away its fading and tranquil assertion. Cash looks up the road quietly, his head turning as we pass it like an owl's head, his face composed. Pa looks straight ahead, humped. Dewey Dell looks at the road too, then she looks back at me, her eyes watchful and repudiant, not like that question which was in those of Cash, for a smoldering while. The signboard passes; the unscarred road wheels on. Then Dewey Dell turns her head. The wagon creaks on.

Cash spits over the wheel. "In a couple of days now it'll be smelling," he says.

"You might tell Jewel that," I say.

He is motionless now, sitting the horse at the junction, upright, watching us, no less still than the signboard that lifts its fading capitulation opposite him.

"It aint balanced right for no long ride," Cash says.

"Tell him that, too," I say. The wagon creaks on.

A mile further along he passes us, the horse, archnecked, reined back to a swift singlefoot. He sits lightly, poised, upright, wooden-faced in the saddle, the broken hat raked at a swaggering angle. He passes us swiftly, without looking at us, the horse driving, its hooves hissing in the mud. A gout of mud, backflung, plops onto the box. Cash leans forward and takes a tool from his box and removes it carefully. When the road crosses Whiteleaf, the willows leaning near enough, he breaks off a branch and scours at the stain with the wet leaves.

Anse

∎

It's a hard country on man; it's hard. Eight miles of the sweat of his body washed up outen the Lord's earth, where the Lord Himself told him to put it. Nowhere in this sinful world can a honest, hardworking man profit. It takes them that runs the stores in the towns, doing no sweating, living off of them that sweats. It aint the hardworking man, the farmer. Sometimes I wonder why we keep at it. It's because there is a reward for us above, where they cant take their autos and such. Every man will be equal there and it will be taken from them that have and give to them that have not by the Lord.

But it's a long wait, seems like. It's bad that a fellow must earn the reward of his right-doing by flouting hisself and his dead. We drove all the rest of the day and got to Samson's at dust-dark and then that bridge was gone, too. They hadn't never see the river so high, and it not done raining yet. There was old men that hadn't never see nor hear of it being so in the memory of man. I am the chosen of the Lord, for who He loveth, so doeth He chastiseth.[1] But I be durn if He dont take some curious ways to show it, seems like.

But now I can get them teeth. That will be a comfort. It will.

---

1. Cf. Hebrews 12.6–8: "For whom the Lord loveth he chasteneth, and scourgeth every son whom he receiveth. If ye endure chastening, God dealeth with you as with sons; for what son is he whom the father chasteneth not? But if ye be without chastisement, whereof all are partakers, then are ye bastards, and not sons."

Samson

■

It was just before sundown. We were sitting on the porch when the wagon came up the road with the five of them in it and the other one on the horse behind. One of them raised his hand, but they was going on past the store without stopping.

"Who's that?" MacCallum says: I cant think of his name: Rafe's twin; that one it was.

"It's Bundren, from down beyond New Hope," Quick says. "There's one of them Snopes horses Jewel's riding."[1]

"I didn't know there was ere a one of them horses left," MacCallum says. "I thought you folks down there finally contrived to give them all away."

"Try and get that one," Quick says. The wagon went on.

"I bet old man Lon never gave it to him," I says.

"No," Quick says. "He bought it from pappy." The wagon went on. "They must not a heard about the bridge," he says.

"What're they doing up here, anyway?" MacCallum says.

"Taking a holiday since he got his wife buried, I reckon," Quick says. "Heading for town, I reckon, with Tull's bridge gone too. I wonder if they aint heard about the bridge."

"They'll have to fly, then," I says. "I dont reckon there's ere a bridge between here and Mouth of Ishatawa."

They had something in the wagon. But Quick had been to the funeral three days ago and we naturally never thought anything about it except that they were heading away from home mighty late and that they hadn't heard about the bridge. "You better holler at them," MacCallum says. Durn it, the name is right on the tip of my tongue. So Quick hollered and they stopped and he went to the wagon and told them.

He come back with them. "They're going to Jefferson," he says. "The bridge at Tull's is gone, too." Like we didn't know it, and his face looked funny, around the nostrils, but they just sat there, Bundren and the girl and the chap on the seat, and Cash and the second one, the one folks talks about, on a plank across the tail-gate, and the other one on that spotted horse. But I reckon they was used to it by

---

1. A family in Faulkner's fictional Yoknapatawpha County. Flem Snopes is the principal character in the trilogy comprised of *The Hamlet* (1940), *The Town* (1957), and *The Mansion* (1959). Members of the family appear throughout Faulkner's work, in e.g., *Sartoris* (1929) and *The Unvanquished* (1938), and indeed they figure in his first attempt at a Yoknapatawpha story, the unfinished 1926 *Father Abraham* (published posthumously in an edition edited by James B. Meriwether [New York: Random House, 1983]). The family is persistently depicted as unscrupulous, rapacious, and all-devouring; a white-trash, New South threat to the social order.

then, because when I said to Cash that they'd have to pass by New Hope again and what they'd better do, he just says,

"I reckon we can get there."

I aint much for meddling. Let every man run his own business to suit himself, I say. But after I talked to Rachel about them not having a regular man to fix her and it being July and all, I went back down to the barn and tried to talk to Bundren about it.

"I give her my promise," he says. "Her mind was set on it."

I notice how it takes a lazy man, a man that hates moving, to get set on moving once he does get started off, the same as he was set on staying still, like it aint the moving he hates so much as the starting and the stopping. And like he would be kind of proud of whatever come up to make the moving or the setting still look hard. He set there on the wagon, hunched up, blinking, listening to us tell about how quick the bridge went and how high the water was, and I be durn if he didn't act like he was proud of it, like he had made the river rise himself.

"You say it's higher than you ever see it before?" he says. "God's will be done," he says. "I reckon it wont go down much by morning, neither," he says.

"You better stay here tonight," I says, "and get a early start for New Hope tomorrow morning." I was just sorry for them bone-gaunted mules. I told Rachel, I says, "Well, would you have had me turn them away at dark, eight miles from home? What else could I do," I says. "It wont be but one night, and they'll keep it in the barn, and they'll sholy get started by daylight." And so I says, "You stay here tonight and early tomorrow you can go back to New Hope. I got tools enough, and the boys can go on right after supper and have it dug and ready if they want" and then I found that girl watching me. If her eyes had a been pistols, I wouldn't be talking now. I be dog if they didn't blaze at me. And so when I went down to the barn I come on them, her talking so she never noticed when I come up.

"You promised her," she says. "She wouldn't go until you promised. She thought she could depend on you. If you dont do it, it will be a curse on you."

"Cant no man say I dont aim to keep my word," Bundren says. "My heart is open to ere a man."

"I dont care what your heart is," she says. She was whispering, kind of, talking fast. "You promised her. You've got to. You——" then she seen me and quit, standing there. If they'd been pistols, I wouldn't be talking now. So when I talked to him about it, he says,

"I give her my promise. Her mind is set on it."

"But seems to me she'd rather have her ma buried close by, so she could——"

"It's Addie I give the promise to," he says. "Her mind is set on it."

So I told them to drive it into the barn, because it was threatening rain again, and that supper was about ready. Only they didn't want to come in.

"I thank you," Bundren says. "We wouldn't discommode you. We got a little something in the basket. We can make out."

"Well," I says, "since you are so particular about your womenfolks, I am too. And when folks stops with us at meal time and wont come to the table, my wife takes it as a insult."

So the girl went on to the kitchen to help Rachel. And then Jewel come to me.

"Sho," I says. "Help yourself outen the loft. Feed him when you bait the mules."

"I rather pay you for him," he says.

"What for?" I says. "I wouldn't begrudge no man a bait for his horse."

"I rather pay you," he says; I thought he said extra.

"Extra for what?" I says. "Wont he eat hay and corn?"

"Extra feed," he says. "I feed him a little extra and I dont want him beholden to no man."

"You cant buy no feed from me, boy," I says. "And if he can eat that loft clean, I'll help you load the barn onto the wagon in the morning."

"He aint never been beholden to no man," he says. "I rather pay you for it."

And if I had my rathers, you wouldn't be here a-tall, I wanted to say. But I just says, "Then it's high time he commenced. You cant buy no feed from me."

When Rachel put supper on, her and the girl went and fixed some beds. But wouldn't any of them come in. "She's been dead long enough to get over that sort of foolishness," I says. Because I got just as much respect for the dead as ere a man, but you've got to respect the dead themselves, and a woman that's been dead in a box four days, the best way to respect her is to get her into the ground as quick as you can. But they wouldn't do it.

"It wouldn't be right," Bundren says. "Course, if the boys wants to go to bed, I reckon I can set up with her. I dont begrudge her it."

So when I went back down there they were squatting on the ground around the wagon, all of them. "Let that chap come to the house and get some sleep, anyway," I says. "And you better come too," I says to the girl. I wasn't aiming to interfere with them. And I sholy hadn't done nothing to her that I knowed.

"He's done already asleep," Bundren says. They had done put him to bed in the trough in a empty stall.

"Well, you come on, then," I says to her. But still she never said nothing. They just squatted there. You couldn't hardly see them.

"How about you boys?" I says. "You got a full day tomorrow." After a while Cash says,

"I thank you. We can make out."

"We wouldn't be beholden," Bundren says. "I thank you kindly."

So I left them squatting there. I reckon after four days they was used to it. But Rachel wasn't.

"It's a outrage," she says. "A outrage."

"What could he a done?" I says. "He give her his promised word."

"Who's talking about him?" she says. "Who cares about him?" she says, crying. "I just wish that you and him and all the men in the world that torture us alive and flout us dead, dragging us up and down the country——"

"Now, now," I says. "You're upset."

"Dont you touch me!" she says. "Dont you touch me!"

A man cant tell nothing about them. I lived with the same one fifteen years and I be durn if I can. And I imagined a lot of things coming up between us, but I be durn if I ever thought it would be a body four days dead and that a woman. But they make life hard on them, not taking it as it comes up, like a man does.

So I laid there, hearing it commence to rain, thinking about them down there, squatting around the wagon and the rain on the roof, and thinking about Rachel crying there until after a while it was like I could still hear her crying even after she was asleep, and smelling it even when I knowed I couldn't. I couldn't decide even then whether I could or not, or if it wasn't just knowing it was what it was.

So next morning I never went down there. I heard them hitching up and then when I knowed they must be about ready to take out, I went out the front and went down the road toward the bridge until I heard the wagon come out of the lot and go back toward New Hope. And then when I come back to the house, Rachel jumped on me because I wasn't there to make them come in to breakfast. You cant tell about them. Just about when you decide they mean one thing, I be durn if you not only haven't got to change your mind, like as not you got to take a rawhiding for thinking they meant it.

But it was still like I could smell it. And so I decided then that it wasn't smelling it, but it was just knowing it was there, like you will get fooled now and then. But when I went to the barn I knew different. When I walked into the hallway I saw something. It kind of hunkered up when I come in and I thought at first it was one of them got left, then I saw what it was. It was a buzzard. It looked around and saw me and went on down the hall, spraddle-legged, with its wings kind of hunkered out, watching me first over one shoulder and then over the other, like a old baldheaded man. When it got outdoors it begun to fly. It had to fly a long time before it ever got up into the air, with it thick and heavy and full of rain like it was.

If they was bent on going to Jefferson, I reckon they could have gone around up by Mount Vernon, like MacCallum did. He'll get home about day after tomorrow, horseback. Then they'd be just eighteen miles from town. But maybe this bridge being gone too has learned him the Lord's sense and judgment.

That MacCallum. He's been trading with me off and on for twelve years. I have known him from a boy up; know his name as well as I do my own. But be durn if I can say it.

Dewey Dell

∎

The signboard comes in sight. It is looking out at the road now, because it can wait. New Hope. 3 mi. it will say. New Hope. 3 mi. New Hope. 3 mi. And then the road will begin curving away into the trees, empty with waiting, saying New Hope three miles.

I heard that my mother is dead. I wish I had time to let her die. I wish I had time to wish I had. It is because in the wild and outraged earth too soon too soon too soon. It's not that I wouldn't and will not it's that it is too soon too soon too soon.

Now it begins to say it. New Hope three miles. New Hope three miles. *That's what they mean by the womb of time:*[1] *the agony and the despair of spreading bones, the hard girdle in which lie the outraged entrails of events* Cash's head turns slowly as we approach, his pale empty sad composed and questioning face following the red and empty curve; beside the back wheel Jewel sits the horse, gazing straight ahead.

The land runs out of Darl's eyes; they swim to pin points. They begin at my feet and rise along my body to my face, and then my dress is gone: I sit naked on the seat above the unhurrying mules, above the travail. *Suppose I tell him to turn. He will do what I say. Dont you know he will do what I say?* Once I waked with a black void rushing under me. I could not see. I saw Vardaman rise and go to the window and strike the knife into the fish, the blood gushing, hissing like steam but I could not see. *He'll do as I say. He always does. I can persuade him to anything. You know I can. Suppose I say Turn here.* That was when I died that time. *Suppose I do. We'll go to New Hope. We wont have to go to town.* I rose and took the knife from the streaming fish still hissing and I killed Darl.

When I used to sleep with Vardaman I had a nightmare once I thought I was awake but I couldn't see and couldn't feel I couldn't feel the bed under me and I couldn't think what I was I couldn't think of my name I couldn't even think I am a girl I couldn't even think I nor even think I want to wake up nor remember what was opposite to awake so I could do that I knew that something was passing but I couldn't even think of time then all of a sudden I knew that something was it was wind blowing over me it was like the wind came and blew me back from where it was I was not blowing the room and Vardaman asleep and all of them back under me again and going on like a piece of cool silk dragging across my naked legs

---

1. Cf. *Othello* 1.3.365–66. Iago says, "There are many events in the womb of time which will be delivered."

It blows cool out of the pines, a sad steady sound. New Hope. Was 3 mi. Was 3 mi. I believe in God I believe in God.

"Why didn't we go to New Hope, pa?" Vardaman says. "Mr Samson said we was, but we done passed the road."

Darl says, "Look, Jewel." But he is not looking at me. He is looking at the sky. The buzzard is as still as if he were nailed to it.

We turn into Tull's lane. We pass the barn and go on, the wheels whispering in the mud, passing the green rows of cotton in the wild earth, and Vernon little across the field behind the plow. He lifts his hand as we pass and stands there looking after us for a long while.

"Look, Jewel," Darl says. Jewel sits on his horse like they were both made out of wood, looking straight ahead.

I believe in God, God. God, I believe in God.

Tull

■

After they passed I taken the mule out and looped up the trace chains and followed. They was setting in the wagon at the end of the levee. Anse was setting there, looking at the bridge where it was swagged down into the river with just the two ends in sight. He was looking at it like he had believed all the time that folks had been lying to him about it being gone, but like he was hoping all the time it really was. Kind of pleased astonishment he looked, setting on the wagon in his Sunday pants, mumbling his mouth. Looking like a uncurried horse dressed up: I dont know.

The boy was watching the bridge where it was mid-sunk and logs and such drifted up over it and it swagging and shivering like the whole thing would go any minute, big-eyed he was watching it, like he was to a circus. And the gal too. When I come up she looked around at me, her eyes kind of blaring up and going hard like I had made to touch her. Then she looked at Anse again and then back at the water again.

It was nigh up to the levee on both sides, the earth hid except for the tongue of it we was on going out to the bridge and then down into the water, and except for knowing how the road and the bridge used to look, a fellow couldn't tell where was the river and where the land. It was just a tangle of yellow and the levee not less wider than a knife-back kind of, with us setting in the wagon and on the horse and the mule.

Darl was looking at me, and then Cash turned and looked at me with that look in his eyes like when he was figuring on whether the planks would fit her that night, like he was measuring them inside of him and not asking you to say what you thought and not even letting on he was listening if you did say it, but listening all right. Jewel hadn't moved. He sat there on the horse, leaning a little forward, with that same look on his face when him and Darl passed the house yesterday, coming back to get her.

"If it was just up, we could drive across," Anse says. "We could drive right on across it."

Sometimes a log would get shoved over the jam and float on, rolling and turning, and we could watch it go on to where the ford used to be. It would slow up and whirl crossways and hang out of water for a minute, and you could tell by that that the ford used to be there.

"But that dont show nothing," I say. "It could be a bar of quicksand built up there." We watch the log. Then the gal is looking at me again.

"Mr Whitfield crossed it," she says.

"He was a horse-back," I say. "And three days ago. It's riz five foot since."

"If the bridge was just up," Anse says.

The log bobs up and goes on again. There is a lot of trash and foam, and you can hear the water.

"But it's down," Anse says.

Cash says, "A careful fellow could walk across yonder on the planks and logs."

"But you couldn't tote nothing," I say. "Likely time you set foot on that mess, it'll all go, too. What you think, Darl?"

He is looking at me. He dont say nothing; just looks at me with them queer eyes of hisn that makes folks talk. I always say it aint never been what he done so much or said or anything so much as how he looks at you. It's like he had got into the inside of you, someway. Like somehow you was looking at yourself and your doings outen his eyes. Then I can feel that gal watching me like I had made to touch her. She says something to Anse. ". . . . . . . Mr Whitfield. . . ." she says.

"I give her my promised word in the presence of the Lord," Anse says. "I reckon it aint no need to worry."

But still he does not start the mules. We set there above the water. Another log bobs up over the jam and goes on; we watch it check up and swing slow for a minute where the ford used to be. Then it goes on.

"It might start falling tonight," I say. "You could lay over one more day."

Then Jewel turns sideways on the horse. He has not moved until then, and he turns and looks at me. His face is kind of green, then it would go red and then green again. "Get to hell on back to your damn plowing," he says. "Who the hell asked you to follow us here?"

"I never meant no harm," I say.

"Shut up, Jewel," Cash says. Jewel looks back at the water, his face gritted, going red and green and then red. "Well," Cash says after a while, "what you want to do?"

Anse dont say nothing. He sets humped up, mumbling his mouth. "If it was just up, we could drive across it," he says.

"Come on," Jewel says, moving the horse.

"Wait," Cash says. He looks at the bridge. We look at him, except Anse and the gal. They are looking at the water. "Dewey Dell and Vardaman and pa better walk across on the bridge," Cash says.

"Vernon can help them," Jewel says. "And we can hitch his mule ahead of ourn."

"You aint going to take my mule into that water," I say.

Jewel looks at me. His eyes look like pieces of a broken plate. "I'll pay for your damn mule. I'll buy it from you right now."

"My mule aint going into that water," I say.

"Jewel's going to use his horse," Darl says. "Why wont you risk your mule, Vernon?"

"Shut up, Darl," Cash says. "You and Jewel both."

"My mule aint going into that water," I say.

Darl

■

He sits the horse, glaring at Vernon, his lean face suffused up to and beyond the pale rigidity of his eyes. The summer when he was fifteen, he took a spell of sleeping. One morning when I went to feed the mules the cows were still in the tie-up and then I heard pa go back to the house and call him. When we came on back to the house for breakfast he passed us, carrying the milk buckets, stumbling along like he was drunk, and he was milking when we put the mules in and went on to the field without him. We had been there an hour and still he never showed up. When Dewey Dell came with our lunch, pa sent her back to find Jewel. They found him in the tie-up, sitting on the stool, asleep.

After that, every morning pa would go in and wake him. He would go to sleep at the supper table and soon as supper was finished he would go to bed, and when I came in to bed he would be lying there like a dead man. Yet still pa would have to wake him in the morning. He would get up, but he wouldn't hardly have half sense: he would stand for pa's jawing and complaining without a word and take the milk buckets and go to the barn, and once I found him asleep at the cow, the bucket in place and half full and his hands up to the wrists in the milk and his head against the cow's flank.

After that Dewey Dell had to do the milking. He still got up when pa waked him, going about what we told him to do in that dazed way. It was like he was trying hard to do them; that he was as puzzled as anyone else.

"Are you sick?" ma said. "Dont you feel all right?"

"Yes," Jewel said. "I feel all right."

"He's just lazy, trying me," pa said, and Jewel standing there, asleep on his feet like as not. "Aint you?" he said, waking Jewel up again to answer.

"No," Jewel said.

"You take off and stay in the house today," ma said.

"With that whole bottom piece to be busted out?" pa said. "If you aint sick, what's the matter with you?"

"Nothing," Jewel said. "I'm all right."

"All right?" pa said. "You're asleep on your feet this minute."

"No," Jewel said. "I'm all right."

"I want him to stay at home today," ma said.

"I'll need him," pa said. "It's tight enough, with all of us to do it."

"You'll just have to do the best you can with Cash and Darl," ma said. "I want him to stay in today."

But he wouldn't do it. "I'm all right," he said, going on. But he wasn't all right. Anybody could see it. He was losing flesh, and I have seen him go to sleep chopping; watched the hoe going slower and slower up and down, with less and less of an arc, until it stopped and he leaning on it motionless in the hot shimmer of the sun.

Ma wanted to get the doctor, but pa didn't want to spend the money without it was needful, and Jewel did seem all right except for his thinness and his way of dropping off to sleep at any moment. He ate hearty enough, except for his way of going to sleep in his plate, with a piece of bread half way to his mouth and his jaws still chewing. But he swore he was all right.

It was ma that got Dewey Dell to do his milking, paid her somehow, and the other jobs around the house that Jewel had been doing before supper she found some way for Dewey Dell and Vardaman to do them. And doing them herself when pa wasn't there. She would fix him special things to eat and hide them for him. And that may have been when I first found it out, that Addie Bundren should be hiding anything she did, who had tried to teach us that deceit was such that, in a world where it was, nothing else could be very bad or very important, not even poverty. And at times when I went in to go to bed she would be sitting in the dark by Jewel where he was asleep. And I knew that she was hating herself for that deceit and hating Jewel because she had to love him so that she had to act the deceit.

One night she was taken sick and when I went to the barn to put the team in and drive to Tull's, I couldn't find the lantern. I remembered noticing it on the nail the night before, but it wasn't there now at midnight. So I hitched in the dark and went on and came back with Mrs Tull just after daylight. And there the lantern was, hanging on the nail where I remembered it and couldn't find it before. And then one morning while Dewey Dell was milking just before sunup, Jewel came into the barn from the back, through the hole in the back wall, with the lantern in his hand.

I told Cash, and Cash and I looked at one another.

"Rutting," Cash said.

"Yes," I said. "But why the lantern? And every night, too. No wonder he's losing flesh. Are you going to say anything to him?"

"Wont do any good," Cash said.

"What he's doing now wont do any good, either."

"I know. But he'll have to learn that himself. Give him time to realise that it'll save, that there'll be just as much more tomorrow, and he'll be all right. I wouldn't tell anybody, I reckon."

"No," I said. "I told Dewey Dell not to. Not ma, anyway."

"No. Not ma."

After that I thought it was right comical: he acting so bewildered and willing and dead for sleep and gaunt as a bean-pole, and thinking he was so smart with it. And I wondered who the girl was. I thought of all I knew that it might be, but I couldn't say for sure.

"'Taint any girl," Cash said. "It's a married woman somewhere. Aint any young girl got that much daring and staying power. That's what I dont like about it."

"Why?" I said. "She'll be safer for him than a girl would. More judgment."

He looked at me, his eyes fumbling, the words fumbling at what he was trying to say. "It aint always the safe things in this world that a fellow. . . . . . ."

"You mean, the safe things are not always the best things?"

"Ay; best," he said, fumbling again. "It aint the best things, the things that are good for him. . . . . . . A young boy. A fellow kind of hates to see. . . . . . .wallowing in somebody else's mire. . . . . . ." That's what he was trying to say. When something is new and hard and bright, there ought to be something a little better for it than just being safe, since the safe things are just the things that folks have been doing so long they have worn the edges off and there's nothing to the doing of them that leaves a man to say, That was not done before and it cannot be done again.

So we didn't tell, not even when after a while he'd appear suddenly in the field beside us and go to work, without having had time to get home and make out he had been in bed all night. He would tell ma that he hadn't been hungry at breakfast or that he had eaten a piece of bread while he was hitching up the team. But Cash and I knew that he hadn't been home at all on those nights and he had come up out of the woods when we got to the field. But we didn't tell. Summer was almost over then; we knew that when the nights began to get cool, she would be done if he wasn't.

But when fall came and the nights began to get longer, the only difference was that he would always be in bed for pa to wake him, getting him up at last in that first state of semi-idiocy like when it first started, worse than when he had stayed out all night.

"She's sure a stayer," I told Cash. "I used to admire her, but I downright respect her now."

"It aint a woman," he said.

"You know," I said. But he was watching me. "What is it, then?"

"That's what I aim to find out," he said.

"You can trail him through the woods all night if you want to," I said. "I'm not."

"I aint trailing him," he said.

"What do you call it, then?"

"I aint trailing him," he said. "I dont mean it that way."

And so a few nights later I heard Jewel get up and climb out the window, and then I heard Cash get up and follow him. The next morning when I went to the barn, Cash was already there, the mules fed, and he was helping Dewey Dell milk. And when I saw him I knew that he knew what it was. Now and then I would catch him watching Jewel with a queer look, like having found out where Jewel went and what he was doing had given him something to really think about at last. But it was not a worried look; it was the kind of look I would see on him when I would find him doing some of Jewel's work around the house, work that pa still thought Jewel was doing and that ma thought Dewey Dell was doing. So I said nothing to him, believing that when he got done digesting it in his mind, he would tell me. But he never did.

One morning—it was November then, five months since it started—Jewel was not in bed and he didn't join us in the field. That was the first time ma learned anything about what had been going on. She sent Vardaman down to find where Jewel was, and after a while she came down too. It was as though, so long as the deceit ran along quiet and monotonous, all of us let ourselves be deceived, abetting it unawares or maybe through cowardice, since all people are cowards and naturally prefer any kind of treachery because it has a bland outside. But now it was like we had all—and by a kind of telepathic agreement of admitted fear—flung the whole thing back like covers on the bed and we all sitting bolt upright in our nakedness, staring at one another and saying "Now is the truth. He hasn't come home. Something has happened to him. We let something happen to him."

Then we saw him. He came up along the ditch and then turned straight across the field, riding the horse. Its mane and tail were going, as though in motion they were carrying out the splotchy pattern of its coat: he looked like he was riding on a big pinwheel, barebacked, with a rope bridle, and no hat on his head. It was a descendant of those Texas ponies[1] Flem Snopes brought here twenty-five years ago and auctioned off for two dollars a head and nobody but old Lon Quick ever caught his and still owned some of the blood because he could never give it away.

He galloped up and stopped, his heels in the horse's ribs and it dancing and swirling like the shape of its mane and tail and the splotches of its coat had nothing whatever to do with the flesh-and-bone horse inside them, and he sat there, looking at us.

"Where did you get that horse?" pa said.

"Bought it," Jewel said. "From Mr Quick."

"Bought it?" pa said. "With what? Did you buy that thing on my word?"

"It was my money," Jewel said. "I earned it. You wont need to worry about it."

---

1. Those horses figure in *Father Abraham, The Hamlet,* and the early unpublished story "As I Lay Dying," pp. 173–83 in this Norton Critical Edition. See my headnote to that section, "The Writer and His Work."

"Jewel," ma said; "Jewel."

"It's all right," Cash said. "He earned the money. He cleaned up that forty acres of new ground Quick laid out last spring. He did it single handed, working at night by lantern. I saw him. So I dont reckon that horse cost anybody anything except Jewel. I dont reckon we need worry."

"Jewel," ma said. "Jewel——" Then she said: "You come right to the house and go to bed."

"Not yet," Jewel said. "I aint got time. I got to get me a saddle and bridle. Mr Quick says he——"

"Jewel," ma said, looking at him. "I'll give——I'll give——give——" Then she began to cry. She cried hard, not hiding her face, standing there in her faded wrapper, looking at him and him on the horse, looking down at her, his face growing cold and a little sick looking, until he looked away quick and Cash came and touched her.

"You go on to the house," Cash said. "This here ground is too wet for you. You go on, now." She put her hands to her face then and after a while she went on, stumbling a little on the plow-marks. But pretty soon she straightened up and went on. She didn't look back. When she reached the ditch she stopped and called Vardaman. He was looking at the horse, kind of dancing up and down by it.

"Let me ride, Jewel," he said. "Let me ride, Jewel."

Jewel looked at him, then he looked away again, holding the horse reined back. Pa watched him, mumbling his lip.

"So you bought a horse," he said. "You went behind my back and bought a horse. You never consulted me; you know how tight it is for us to make by, yet you bought a horse for me to feed. Taken the work from your flesh and blood and bought a horse with it."

Jewel looked at pa, his eyes paler than ever. "He wont never eat a mouthful of yours," he said. "Not a mouthful. I'll kill him first. Dont you never think it. Dont you never."

"Let me ride, Jewel," Vardaman said. "Let me ride, Jewel." He sounded like a cricket in the grass, a little one. "Let me ride, Jewel."

That night I found ma sitting beside the bed where he was sleeping, in the dark. She cried hard, maybe because she had to cry so quiet; maybe because she felt the same way about tears she did about deceit, hating herself for doing it, hating him because she had to. And then I knew that I knew. I knew that as plain on that day as I knew about Dewey Dell on that day.

Tull

■

So they finally got Anse to say what he wanted to do, and him and the gal and the boy got out of the wagon. But even when we were on the bridge Anse kept on looking back, like he thought maybe, once he was outen the wagon, the whole thing would kind of blow up and he would find himself back yonder in the field again and her laying up there in the house, waiting to die and it to do all over again.

"You ought to let them taken your mule," he says, and the bridge shaking and swaying under us, going down into the moiling water like it went clean through to the other side of the earth, and the other end coming up outen the water like it wasn't the same bridge a-tall and that them that would walk up outen the water on that side must come from the bottom of the earth. But it was still whole; you could tell that by the way when this end swagged, it didn't look like the other end swagged at all: just like the other trees and the bank yonder were swinging back and forth slow like on a big clock. And them logs scraping and bumping at the sunk part and tilting end-up and shooting clean outen the water and tumbling on toward the ford and the waiting, slick, whirling, and foamy.

"What good would that a done?" I says. "If your team cant find the ford and haul it across, what good would three mules or even ten mules do?"

"I aint asking it of you," he says. "I can always do for me and mine. I aint asking you to risk your mule. It aint your dead; I am not blaming you."

"They ought to went back and laid over until tomorrow," I says. The water was cold. It was thick, like slush ice. Only it kind of lived. One part of you knowed it was just water, the same thing that had been running under this same bridge for a long time, yet when them logs would come spewing up outen it, you were not surprised, like they was a part of water, of the waiting and the threat.

It was like when we was across, up out of the water again and the hard earth under us, that I was surprised. It was like we hadn't expected the bridge to end on the other bank, on something tame like the hard earth again that we had tromped on before this time and knowed well. Like it couldn't be me here, because I'd have had better sense than to done what I just done. And when I looked back and saw the other bank and saw my mule standing there where I used to be and knew that I'd have to get back there someway, I knew it couldn't be, because I just couldn't think of anything that could make me cross that bridge ever even once. Yet here I was, and the fellow that could make himself cross it twice, couldn't be me, not even if Cora told him to.

It was that boy. I said "Here; you better take a holt of my hand" and he waited and held to me. I be durn if it wasn't like he come back and got me; like he was saying They wont nothing hurt you. Like he was saying about a fine place he knowed where Christmas come twice with Thanksgiving and lasts on through the winter and the spring and the summer, and if I just stayed with him I'd be all right too.

When I looked back at my mule it was like he was one of these here spy-glasses and I could look at him standing there and see all the broad land and my house sweated outen it like it was the more the sweat, the broader the land; the more the sweat, the tighter the house because it would take a tight house for Cora, to hold Cora like a jar of milk in the spring: you've got to have a tight jar or you'll need a powerful spring, so if you have a big spring, why then you have the incentive to have tight, wellmade jars, because it is your milk, sour or not, because you would rather have milk that will sour than to have milk that wont, because you are a man.

And him holding to my hand, his hand that hot and confident, so that I was like to say: Look-a-here. Cant you see that mule yonder? He never had no business over here, so he never come, not being nothing but a mule. Because a fellow can see ever now and then that children have more sense than him. But he dont like to admit it to them until they have beards. After they have a beard, they are too busy because they dont know if they'll ever quite make it back to where they were in sense before they was haired, so you dont mind admitting then to folks that are worrying about the same thing that aint worth the worry that you are yourself.

Then we was over and we stood there, looking at Cash turning the wagon around. We watched them drive back down the road to where the trail turned off into the bottom. After a while the wagon was out of sight.

"We better get on down to the ford and git ready to help," I said.

"I give her my word," Anse says. "It is sacred on me. I know you begrudge it, but she will bless you in heaven."

"Well, they got to finish circumventing the land before they can dare the water," I said. "Come on."

"It's the turning back," he said. "It aint no luck in turning back."

He was standing there, humped, mournful, looking at the empty road beyond the swagging and swaying bridge. And that gal, too, with the lunch basket on one arm and that package under the other.

Just going to town. Bent on it. They would risk the fire and the earth and the water and all just to eat a sack of bananas. "You ought to laid over a day," I said. "It would a fell some by morning. It mought not a rained tonight. And it cant get no higher."

"I give my promise," he says. "She is counting on it."

Darl

■

Before us the thick dark current runs. It talks up to us in a murmur become ceaseless and myriad, the yellow surface dimpled monstrously into fading swirls travelling along the surface for an instant, silent, impermanent and profoundly significant, as though just beneath the surface something huge and alive waked for a moment of lazy alertness out of and into light slumber again.[1]

It clucks and murmurs among the spokes and about the mules' knees, yellow, skummed with flotsam and with thick soiled gouts of foam as though it had sweat, lathering, like a driven horse. Through the undergrowth it goes with a plaintive sound, a musing sound; in it the unwinded cane and saplings lean as before a little gale, swaying without reflections as though suspended on invisible wires from the branches overhead. Above the ceaseless surface they stand—trees, cane, vines—rootless, severed from the earth, spectral above a scene of immense yet circumscribed desolation filled with the voice of the waste and mournful water.

Cash and I sit in the wagon; Jewel sits the horse at the off rear wheel. The horse is trembling, its eye rolling wild and baby-blue in its long pink face, its breathing stertorous like groaning. He sits erect, poised, looking quietly and steadily and quickly this way and that, his face calm, a little pale, alert. Cash's face is also gravely composed; he and I look at one another with long probing looks, looks that plunge unimpeded through one another's eyes and into the ultimate secret place where for an instant Cash and Darl crouch flagrant and unabashed in all the old terror and the old foreboding, alert and secret and without shame. When we speak our voices are quiet, detached.

"I reckon we're still in the road, all right."

"Tull taken and cut them two big whiteoaks. I heard tell how at high water in the old days they used to line up the ford by them trees."

"I reckon he did that two years ago when he was logging down here. I reckon he never thought that anybody would ever use this ford again."

"I reckon not. Yes, it must have been then. He cut a sight of timber outen here then. Payed off that mortgage with it, I hear tell."

1. Cf. William Butler Yeats, "The Second Coming":

> . . . but now I know,
> That twenty centuries of stony sleep
> Were vexed to nightmare by a rocking cradle,
> And what rough beast, its hour come round at last,
> Slouches towards Bethlehem to be born?

Both Yeats and Faulkner evoke Revelations 13.1: "And I stood upon the sand of the sea, and saw a beast rise up out of the sea, having seven heads and ten horns, and upon his horns ten crowns, and upon his heads the name of blasphemy."

"Yes. Yes, I reckon so. I reckon Vernon could have done that."

"That's a fact. Most folks that logs in this here country, they need a durn good farm to support the sawmill. Or maybe a store. But I reckon Vernon could."

"I reckon so. He's a sight."

"Ay. Vernon is. Yes, it must still be here. He never would have got that timber out of here if he hadn't cleaned out that old road. I reckon we are still on it." He looks about quietly, at the position of the trees, leaning this way and that, looking back along the floorless road shaped vaguely high in air by the position of the lopped and felled trees, as if the road too had been soaked free of earth and floated upward, to leave in its spectral tracing a monument to a still more profound desolation than this above which we now sit, talking quietly of old security and old trivial things. Jewel looks at him, then at me, then his face turns in in that quiet, constant, questing about the scene, the horse trembling quietly and steadily between his knees.

"He could go on ahead slow and sort of feel it out," I say.

"Yes," Cash says, not looking at me. His face is in profile as he looks forward where Jewel has moved on ahead.

"He cant miss the river," I say. "He couldn't miss seeing it fifty yards ahead."

Cash does not look at me, his face in profile. "If I'd just suspicioned it, I could a come down last week and taken a sight on it."

"The bridge was up then," I say. He does not look at me. "Whitfield crossed it a-horseback."

Jewel looks at us again, his expression sober and alert and subdued. His voice is quiet. "What you want me to do?"

"I ought to come down last week and taken a sight on it," Cash says.

"We couldn't have known," I say. "There wasn't any way for us to know."

"I'll ride on ahead," Jewel says. "You can follow where I am." He lifts the horse. It shrinks, bowed; he leans to it, speaking to it, lifting it forward almost bodily, it setting its feet down with gingerly splashings, trembling, breathing harshly. He speaks to it, murmurs to it. "Go on," he says. "I aint going to let nothing hurt you. Go on, now."

"Jewel," Cash says. Jewel does not look back. He lifts the horse on.

"He can swim," I say. "If he'll just give the horse time, anyhow. . . . ." When he was born, he had a bad time of it. Ma would sit in the lamp-light, holding him on a pillow on her lap. We would wake and find her so. There would be no sound from them.

"That pillow was longer than him," Cash says. He is leaning a little forward. "I ought to come down last week and sighted. I ought to done it."

"That's right," I say. "Neither his feet nor his head would reach the end of it. You couldn't have known," I say.

"I ought to done it," he says. He lifts the reins. The mules move, into the traces; the wheels murmur alive in the water. He looks back and down at Addie. "It aint on a balance," he says.

At last the trees open; against the open river Jewel sits the horse, half turned, it belly deep now. Across the river we can see Vernon and pa and Vardaman and Dewey Dell. Vernon is waving at us, waving us further down stream.

"We are too high up," Cash says. Vernon is shouting too, but we cannot make out what he says for the noise of the water. It runs steady and deep now, unbroken, without sense of motion until a log comes along, turning slowly. "Watch it," Cash says. We watch it and see it falter and hang for a moment, the current building up behind it in a thick wave, submerging it for an instant before it shoots up and tumbles on.

"There it is," I say.

"Ay," Cash says. "It's there." We look at Vernon again. He is now flapping his arms up and down. We move on down stream, slowly and carefully, watching Vernon. He drops his hands. "This is the place," Cash says.

"Well, goddamn it, let's get across, then," Jewel says. He moves the horse on.

"You wait," Cash says. Jewel stops again.

"Well, by God——" he says. Cash looks at the water, then he looks back at Addie. "It aint on a balance," he says.

"Then go on back to the goddamn bridge and walk across," Jewel says. "You and Darl both. Let me on that wagon."

Cash does not pay him any attention. "It aint on a balance," he says. "Yes, sir. We got to watch it."

"Watch it, hell," Jewel says. "You get out of that wagon and let me have it. By God, if you're afraid to drive it over. . . . . . ." His eyes are pale as two bleached chips in his face. Cash is looking at him.

"We'll get it over," he says. "I tell you what you do. You ride on back and walk across the bridge and come down the other bank and meet us with the rope. Vernon'll take your horse home with him and keep it till we get back."

"You go to hell," Jewel says.

"You take the rope and come down the bank and be ready with it," Cash says. "Three cant do no more than two can—one to drive and one to steady it."

"Goddamn you," Jewel says.

"Let Jewel take the end of the rope and cross upstream of us and brace it," I say. "Will you do that, Jewel?"

Jewel watches me, hard. He looks quick at Cash, then back at me, his eyes alert and hard. "I dont give a damn. Just so we do something. Setting here, not lifting a goddamn hand. . . ."

"Let's do that, Cash," I say.

"I reckon we'll have to," Cash says.

The river itself is not a hundred yards across, and pa and Vernon and Vardaman and Dewey Dell are the only things in sight not of that single monotony of desolation leaning with that terrific quality a little from right to left, as though we had reached the place where the motion of the wasted world accelerates just before the final precipice. Yet they appear dwarfed. It is as though the space between us were time: an irrevocable quality. It is as though time, no longer running straight before us in a diminishing line, now runs parallel between us like a looping string, the distance being the doubling accretion of the thread and not the interval between. The mules stand, their fore quarters already sloped a little, their rumps high. They too are breathing now with a deep groaning sound; looking back once, their gaze sweeps across us with in their eyes a wild, sad, profound and despairing quality as though they had already seen in the thick water the shape of the disaster which they could not speak and we could not see.

Cash turns back into the wagon. He lays his hands flat on Addie, rocking her a little. His face is calm, down-sloped, calculant, concerned. He lifts his box of tools and wedges it forward under the seat; together we shove Addie forward, wedging her between the tools and the wagon bed. Then he looks at me.

"No," I say. "I reckon I'll stay. Might take both of us."

From the tool box he takes his coiled rope and carries the end twice around the seat stanchion and passes the end to me without tying it. The other end he pays out to Jewel, who takes a turn about his saddle horn.

He must force the horse down into the current. It moves, high-kneed, archnecked, boring and chafing. Jewel sits lightly forward, his knees lifted a little; again his swift alert calm gaze sweeps upon us and on. He lowers the horse into the stream, speaking to it in a soothing murmur. The horse slips, goes under to the saddle, surges to its feet again, the current building up against Jewel's thighs.

"Watch yourself," Cash says.

"I'm on it now," Jewel says. "You can come ahead now."

Cash takes the reins and lowers the team carefully and skillfully into the stream.

I felt the current take us and I knew we were on the ford by that reason, since it was only by means of that slipping contact that we could tell that we were in motion at all. What had once been a flat surface was now a succession of troughs and hillocks lifting and falling about us, shoving at us, teasing at us with light lazy touches in the vain instants of solidity underfoot. Cash looked back at me, and then I knew that we were gone. But I did not realise the reason for the rope until I saw the log. It surged up out of the water and stood for an instant upright upon that surging and heaving desolation like Christ. Get out and let the current take you down to the bend, Cash said, You can make it all right. No, I said, I'd get just as wet that way as this

The log appears suddenly between two hills, as if it had rocketed suddenly from the bottom of the river. Upon the end of it a long gout of foam hangs like the beard of an old man or a goat. When Cash speaks to me I know that he has been watching it all the time, watching it and watching Jewel ten feet ahead of us. "Let the rope go," he says. With his other hand he reaches down and reeves the two turns from the stanchion. "Ride on, Jewel," he says; "see if you can pull us ahead of the log."

Jewel shouts at the horse; again he appears to lift it bodily between his knees. He is just above the top of the ford and the horse has a purchase of some sort for it surges forward, shining wetly half out of water, crashing on in a succession of lunges. It moves unbelievably fast; by that token Jewel realises at last that the rope is free, for I can see him sawing back on the reins, his head turned, as the log rears in a long sluggish lunge between us, bearing down upon the team. They see it too; for a moment they also shine black out of water. Then the downstream one vanishes, dragging the other with him; the wagon sheers crosswise, poised on the crest of the ford as the log strikes it, tilting it up and on. Cash is half turned, the reins running taut from his hand and disappearing into the water, the other hand reached back upon Addie, holding her jammed over against the high side of the wagon. "Jump clear," he says quietly. "Stay away from the team and dont try to fight it. It'll swing you into the bend all right."

"You come too," I say. Vernon and Vardaman are running along the bank, pa and Dewey Dell stand watching us, Dewey Dell with the basket and the package in her arms. Jewel is trying to fight the horse back. The head of one mule appears, its eyes wide; it looks back at us for an instant, making a sound almost human. The head vanishes again.

"Back, Jewel," Cash shouts. "Back, Jewel." For another instant I see him leaning to the tilting wagon, his arm braced back against Addie and his tools; I see the bearded head of the rearing log strike up again, and beyond it Jewel holding the horse upreared, its head wrenched around, hammering its head with his fist. I jump from the wagon on the downstream side. Between two hills I see the mules once more. They roll up out of the water in succession, turning completely over, their legs stiffly extended as when they had lost contact with the earth.

Vardaman

■

Cash tried but she fell off and Darl jumped going under he went under and Cash hollering to catch her and I hollering running and hollering and Dewey Dell hollering at me Vardaman you vardaman you vardaman and Vernon passed me because he was seeing her come up and she jumped into the water again and Darl hadn't caught her yet

He came up to see and I hollering catch her Darl catch her and he didn't come back because she was too heavy he had to go on catching at her and I hollering catch her darl catch her darl because in the water she could go faster than a man and Darl had to grabble for her so I knew he could catch her because he is the best grabbler even with the mules in the way again they dived up rolling their feet stiff rolling down again and their backs up now and Darl had to again because in the water she could go faster than a man or a woman and I passed Vernon and he wouldn't get in the water and help Darl he wouldn't grabble for her with Darl he knew but he wouldn't help

The mules dived up again diving their legs stiff their stiff legs rolling slow and then Darl again and I hollering catch her darl catch her head her into the bank darl and Vernon wouldn't help and then Darl dodged past the mules where he could he had her under the water coming in to the bank coming in slow because in the water she fought to stay under the water but Darl is strong and he was coming in slow and so I knew he had her because he came slow and I ran down into the water to help and I couldn't stop hollering because Darl was strong and steady holding her under the water even if she did fight he would not let her go he was seeing me and he would hold her and it was all right now it was all right now it was all right

Then he comes up out of the water. He comes a long way up slow before his hands do but he's got to have her got to so I can bear it. Then his hands come up and all of him above the water. I cant stop. I have not got time to try. I will try to when I can but his hands came empty out of the water emptying the water emptying away

"Where is ma, Darl?" I said. "You never got her. You knew she is a fish but you let her get away. You never got her. Darl. Darl. Darl." I began to run along the bank, watching the mules dive up slow again and then down again.

Tull

■

When I told Cora how Darl jumped out of the wagon and left Cash sitting there trying to save it and the wagon turning over, and Jewel that was almost to the bank fighting that horse back where it had more sense than to go, she says "And you're one of the folks that says Darl is the queer one, the one that aint bright, and him the only one of them that had sense enough to get off that wagon. I notice Anse was too smart to been on it a-tall."

"He couldn't a done no good, if he'd been there," I said. "They was going about it right and they would have made it if it hadn't a been for that log."

"Log, fiddlesticks," Cora said. "It was the hand of God."

"Then how can you say it was foolish?" I said. "Nobody cant guard against the hand of God. It would be sacrilege to try to."

"Then why dare it?" Cora says. "Tell me that."

"Anse didn't," I said. "That's just what you faulted him for."

"His place was there," Cora said. "If he had been a man, he would a been there instead of making his sons do what he dursn't."

"I dont know what you want, then," I said. "One breath you say they was daring the hand of God to try it, and the next breath you jump on Anse because he wasn't with them." Then she begun to sing again, working at the washtub, with that singing look in her face like she had done give up folks and all their foolishness and had done went on ahead of them, marching up the sky, singing.

The wagon hung for a long time while the current built up under it, shoving it off the ford, and Cash leaning more and more, trying to keep the coffin braced so it wouldn't slip down and finish tilting the wagon over. Soon as the wagon got tilted good, to where the current could finish it, the log went on. It headed around the wagon and went on good as a swimming man could have done. It was like it had been sent there to do a job and done it and went on.

When the mules finally kicked loose, it looked for a minute like maybe Cash would get the wagon back. It looked like him and the wagon wasn't moving at all, and just Jewel fighting that horse back to the wagon. Then that boy passed me, running and hollering at Darl and the gal trying to catch him, and then I see the mules come rolling slow up out of the water, their legs spraddled stiff like they had balked upside down, and roll on into the water again.

Then the wagon tilted over and then it and Jewel and the horse was all mixed up together. Cash went outen sight, still holding the coffin braced, and then I couldn't tell anything for the horse lunging and splashing. I thought that Cash had give up then and was swimming for

it and I was yelling at Jewel to come on back and then all of a sudden
him and the horse went under too and I thought they was all going.
I knew that the horse had got dragged off the ford too, and with that
wild drowning horse and that wagon and that loose box, it was going
to be pretty bad, and there I was, standing knee deep in the water,
yelling at Anse behind me: "See what you done now? See what you
done now?"

The horse come up again. It was headed for the bank now, throwing its head up, and then I saw one of them holding to the saddle on
the downstream side, so I started running along the bank, trying to
catch sight of Cash because he couldn't swim, yelling at Jewel where
Cash was like a durn fool, bad as that boy that was on down the
bank still hollering at Darl.

So I went down into the water so I could still keep some kind of
a grip in the mud, when I saw Jewel. He was middle deep, so I knew
he was on the ford, anyway, leaning hard upstream, and then I see
the rope, and then I see the water building up where he was holding
the wagon snubbed just below the ford.

So it was Cash holding to the horse when it come splashing and
scrambling up the bank, moaning and groaning like a natural man.
When I come to it it was just kicking Cash loose from his holt on
the saddle. His face turned up a second when he was sliding back
into the water. It was gray, with his eyes closed and a long swipe of
mud across his face. Then he let go and turned over in the water. He
looked just like a old bundle of clothes kind of washing up and down
against the bank. He looked like he was laying there in the water on
his face, rocking up and down a little, looking at something on the
bottom.

We could watch the rope cutting down into the water, and we could
feel the weight of the wagon kind of blump and lunge lazy like, like it
just as soon as not, and that rope cutting down into the water hard as
a iron bar. We could hear the water hissing on it like it was red hot.
Like it was a straight iron bar stuck into the bottom and us holding
the end of it, and the wagon lazing up and down, kind of pushing and
prodding at us like it had come around and got behind us, lazy like,
like it just as soon as not when it made up its mind. There was a shoat
come by, blowed up like a balloon: one of them spotted shoats of Lon
Quick's. It bumped against the rope like it was a iron bar and bumped
off and went on, and us watching that rope slanting down into the
water. We watched it.

Darl

∎

Cash lies on his back on the earth, his head raised on a rolled garment. His eyes are closed, his face is gray, his hair plastered in a smooth smear across his forehead as though done with a paint brush. His face appears sunken a little, sagging from the bony ridges of eye sockets, nose, gums, as though the wetting had slacked the firmness which had held the skin full; his teeth, set in pale gums, are parted a little as if he had been laughing quietly. He lies pole-thin in his wet clothes, a little pool of vomit at his head and a thread of it running from the corner of his mouth and down his cheek where he couldn't turn his head quick or far enough, until Dewey Dell stoops and wipes it away with the hem of her dress.

Jewel approaches. He has the plane. "Vernon just found the square," he says. He looks down at Cash, dripping too. "Aint he talked none yet?"

"He had his saw and hammer and chalk-line and rule," I say. "I know that."

Jewel lays the square down. Pa watches him. "They cant be far away," pa says. "It all went together. Was there ere a such misfortunate man."

Jewel does not look at pa. "You better call Vardaman back here," he says. He looks at Cash. Then he turns and goes away. "Get him to talk soon as he can," he says, "so he can tell us what else there was."

We return to the river. The wagon is hauled clear, the wheels chocked (carefully: we all helped; it is as though upon the shabby, familiar, inert shape of the wagon there lingered somehow, latent yet still immediate, that violence which had slain the mules that drew it not an hour since) above the edge of the flood. In the wagon bed it lies profoundly, the long pale planks hushed a little with wetting yet still yellow, like gold seen through water, save for two long muddy smears. We pass it and go on to the bank.

One end of the rope is made fast to a tree. At the edge of the stream, knee-deep, Vardaman stands, bent forward a little, watching Vernon with rapt absorption. He has stopped yelling and he is wet to the armpits. Vernon is at the other end of the rope, shoulder-deep in the river, looking back at Vardaman. "Further back than that," he says. "You git back by the tree and hold the rope for me, so it cant slip."

Vardaman backs along the rope, to the tree, moving blindly, watching Vernon. When we come up he looks at us once, his eyes round and a little dazed. Then he looks at Vernon again in that posture of rapt alertness.

"I got the hammer too," Vernon says. "Looks like we ought to done already got that chalk-line. It ought to floated."

"Floated clean away," Jewel says. "We wont get it. We ought to find the saw, though."

"I reckon so," Vernon says. He looks at the water. "That chalk-line, too. What else did he have?"

"He aint talked yet," Jewel says, entering the water. He looks back at me. "You go back and get him roused up to talk," he says.

"Pa's there," I say. I follow Jewel into the water, along the rope. It feels alive in my hand, bellied faintly in a prolonged and resonant arc. Vernon is watching me.

"You better go," he says. "You better be there."

"Let's see what else we can get before it washes on down," I say.

We hold to the rope, the current curling and dimpling about our shoulders. But beneath that false blandness the true force of it leans against us lazily. I had not thought that water in July could be so cold. It is like hands molding and prodding at the very bones. Vernon is still looking back toward the bank.

"Reckon it'll hold us all?" he says. We too look back, following the rigid bar of the rope as it rises from the water to the tree and Vardaman crouched a little beside it, watching us. "Wish my mule wouldn't strike out for home," Vernon says.

"Come on," Jewel says. "Let's get outen here."

We submerge in turn, holding to the rope, being clutched by one another while the cold wall of the water sucks the slanting mud backward and upstream from beneath our feet and we are suspended so, groping along the cold bottom. Even the mud there is not still. It has a chill, scouring quality, as though the earth under us were in motion too. We touch and fumble at one another's extended arms, letting ourselves go cautiously against the rope; or, erect in turn, watch the water suck and boil where one of the other two gropes beneath the surface. Pa has come down to the shore, watching us.

Vernon comes up, streaming, his face sloped down into his pursed blowing mouth. His mouth is bluish, like a circle of weathered rubber. He has the rule.

"He'll be glad of that," I say. "It's right new. He bought it just last month out of the catalogue."

"If we just knowed for sho what else," Vernon says, looking over his shoulder and then turning to face where Jewel had disappeared. "Didn't he go down fore me?" Vernon says.

"I dont know," I say. "I think so. Yes. Yes, he did."

We watch the thick curling surface, streaming away from us in slow whorls.

"Give him a pull on the rope," Vernon says.

"He's on your end of it," I say.

"Aint nobody on my end of it," he says.

"Pull it in," I say. But he has already done that, holding the end above the water; and then we see Jewel. He is ten yards away; he comes up, blowing, and looks at us, tossing his long hair back with a jerk of his head, then he looks toward the bank; we can see him filling his lungs.

"Jewel," Vernon says, not loud, but his voice going full and clear along the water, peremptory yet tactful. "It'll be back here. Better come back."

Jewel dives again. We stand there, leaning back against the current, watching the water where he disappeared, holding the dead rope between us like two men holding the nozzle of a fire hose, waiting for the water. Suddenly Dewey Dell is behind us in the water. "You make him come back," she says. "Jewel!" she says. He comes up again, tossing his hair back from his eyes. He is swimming now, toward the bank, the current sweeping him downstream quartering. "You, Jewel!" Dewey Dell says. We stand holding the rope and see him gain the bank and climb out. As he rises from the water, he stoops and picks up something. He comes back along the bank. He has found the chalk-line. He comes opposite us and stands there, looking about as if he were seeking something. Pa goes on down the bank. He is going back to look at the mules again where their round bodies float and rub quietly together in the slack water within the bend.

"What did you do with the hammer, Vernon?" Jewel says.

"I give it to him," Vernon says, jerking his head at Vardaman. Vardaman is looking after pa. Then he looks at Jewel. "With the square." Vernon is watching Jewel. He moves toward the bank, passing Dewey Dell and me.

"You get on out of here," I say. She says nothing, looking at Jewel and Vernon.

"Where's the hammer?" Jewel says. Vardaman scuttles up the bank and fetches it.

"It's heavier than the saw," Vernon says. Jewel is tying the end of the chalk-line about the hammer shaft.

"Hammer's got the most wood in it," Jewel says. He and Vernon face one another, watching Jewel's hands.

"And flatter, too," Vernon says. "It'd float three to one, almost. Try the plane."

Jewel looks at Vernon. Vernon is tall, too; long and lean, eye to eye they stand in their close wet clothes. Lon Quick could look even at a cloudy sky and tell the time to ten minutes. Big Lon I mean, not little Lon.

"Why dont you get out of the water?" I say.

"It wont float like a saw," Jewel says.

"It'll float nigher to a saw than a hammer will," Vernon says.

"Bet you," Jewel says.

"I wont bet," Vernon says.

They stand there, watching Jewel's still hands.

"Hell," Jewel says. "Get the plane, then."

So they get the plane and tie it to the chalk-line and enter the water again. Pa comes back along the bank. He stops for a while and looks at us, hunched, mournful, like a failing steer or an old tall bird.

Vernon and Jewel return, leaning against the current. "Get out of the way," Jewel says to Dewey Dell. "Get out of the water."

She crowds against me a little so they can pass, Jewel holding the plane high as though it were perishable, the blue string trailing back over his shoulder. They pass us and stop; they fall to arguing quietly about just where the wagon went over.

"Darl ought to know," Vernon says. They look at me.

"I dont know," I says. "I wasn't there that long."

"Hell," Jewel says. They move on, gingerly, leaning against the current, reading the ford with their feet.

"Have you got a holt of the rope?" Vernon says. Jewel does not answer. He glances back at the shore, calculant, then at the water. He flings the plane outward, letting the string run through his fingers, his fingers turning blue where it runs over them. When the line stops, he hands it back to Vernon.

"Better let me go this time," Vernon says. Again Jewel does not answer; we watch him duck beneath the surface.

"Jewel," Dewey Dell whimpers.

"It aint so deep there," Vernon says. He does not look back. He is watching the water where Jewel went under.

When Jewel comes up he has the saw.

When we pass the wagon pa is standing beside it, scrubbing at the two mud smears with a handful of leaves. Against the jungle Jewel's horse looks like a patchwork quilt hung on a line.

Cash has not moved. We stand above him, holding the plane, the saw, the hammer, the square, the rule, the chalk-line, while Dewey Dell squats and lifts Cash's head. "Cash," she says; "Cash."

He opens his eyes, staring profoundly up at our inverted faces.

"If ever was such a misfortunate man," pa says.

"Look, Cash," we say, holding the tools up so he can see; "what else did you have?"

He tries to speak, rolling his head, shutting his eyes.

"Cash," we say; "Cash."

It is to vomit he is turning his head. Dewey Dell wipes his mouth on the wet hem of her dress; then he can speak.

"It's his saw-set," Jewel says. "The new one he bought when he bought the rule." He moves, turning away. Vernon looks up after him, still squatting. Then he rises and follows Jewel down to the water.

"If ever was such a misfortunate man," pa says. He looms tall above us as we squat; he looks like a figure carved clumsily from tough wood by a drunken caricaturist. "It's a trial," he says. "But I dont begrudge her it. No man can say I begrudge her it." Dewey Dell has laid Cash's head back on the folded coat, twisting his head a little to avoid the vomit. Beside him his tools lie. "A fellow might call it lucky it was the same leg he broke when he fell offen that church," pa says. "But I dont begrudge her it."

Jewel and Vernon are in the river again. From here they do not appear to violate the surface at all; it is as though it had severed them both at a single blow, the two torsos moving with infinitesimal and ludicrous care upon the surface. It looks peaceful, like machinery does after you have watched it and listened to it for a long time. As though the clotting which is you had dissolved into the myriad original motion, and seeing and hearing in themselves blind and deaf; fury in itself quiet with stagnation. Squatting, Dewey Dell's wet dress shapes for the dead eyes of three blind men those mammalian ludicrosities which are the horizons and the valleys of the earth.

Cash

■

It wasn't on a balance. I told them that if they wanted it to tote and ride on a balance, they would have to

Cora

■

One day we were talking. She had never been pure religious, not even after that summer at the camp meeting when Brother Whitfield wrestled with her spirit, singled her out and strove with the vanity in her mortal heart, and I said to her many a time, "God gave you children to comfort your hard human lot and for a token of His own suffering and love, for in love you conceived and bore them." I said that because she took God's love and her duty to Him too much as a matter of course, and such conduct is not pleasing to Him. I said, "He gave us the gift to raise our voices in His undying praise" because I said there is more rejoicing in heaven over one sinner than over a hundred that never sinned.[1] And she said "My daily life is an acknowledgment and expiation of my sin" and I said "Who are you, to say what is sin and what is not sin? It is the Lord's part to judge; ours to praise His mercy and His holy name in the hearing of our fellow mortals" because He alone can see into the heart, and just because a woman's life is right in the sight of man, she cant know if there is no sin in her heart without she opens her heart to the Lord and receives His grace. I said, "Just because you have been a faithful wife is no sign that there is no sin in your heart, and just because your life is hard is no sign that the Lord's grace is absolving you." And she said, "I know my own sin.[2] I know that I deserve my punishment. I do not begrudge it." And I said, "It is out of your vanity that you would judge sin and salvation in the Lord's place. It is our mortal lot to suffer and to raise our voices in praise of Him who judges the sin and offers the salvation through our trials and tribulations time out of mind amen. Not even after Brother Whitfield, a godly man if ever one breathed God's breath, prayed for you and strove as never a man could except him," I said.

Because it is not us that can judge our sins or know what is sin in the Lord's eyes. She has had a hard life, but so does every woman. But you'd think from the way she talked that she knew more about sin and salvation than the Lord God Himself, than them who have strove and labored with the sin in this human world. When the only sin she ever committed was being partial to Jewel that never loved her and was its own punishment, in preference to Darl that was touched by God Himself and considered queer by us mortals and that did love her. I said, "There is your sin. And your punishment too.

---

1. Cf. Psalm 66.8: "O bless our God, ye people, and make the voice of his praise to be heard." Cf. Luke 15.7: "I say unto you, that likewise joy shall be in heaven over one sinner that repenteth, more than over ninety and nine just persons, which need no repentance."
2. Cf. Psalms 51.3: "For I acknowledge my transgressions: and my sin is ever before me."

Jewel is your punishment. But where is your salvation? And life is short enough," I said, "to win eternal grace in. And God is a jealous God.[3] It is His to judge and to mete; not yours."[4]

"I know," she said. "I——" Then she stopped, and I said, "Know what?"

"Nothing," she said. "He is my cross and he will be my salvation. He will save me from the water and from the fire.[5] Even though I have laid down my life, he will save me."

"How do you know, without you open your heart to Him and lift your voice in His praise?" I said. Then I realised that she did not mean God. I realised that out of the vanity of her heart she had spoken sacrilege. And I went down on my knees right there. I begged her to kneel and open her heart and cast from it the devil of vanity and cast herself upon the mercy of the Lord. But she wouldn't. She just sat there, lost in her vanity and her pride, that had closed her heart to God and set that selfish mortal boy in His place. Kneeling there I prayed for her. I prayed for that poor blind woman as I had never prayed for me and mine.

3. Cf. Exodus 20.5: "Thou shalt not bow down thyself to them, nor serve them: for I the Lord thy God am a jealous God, visiting the iniquity of the fathers upon the children unto the third and fourth generation of them that hate me."
4. Cf. Matthew 7.1–2: "Judge not, that ye be not judged. For with what judgment ye judge, ye shall be judged: and with what measure ye mete, it shall be measured to you again."
5. Cf. Isaiah 43.2: "When thou passest through the waters, I will be with thee; and through the rivers, they shall not overflow thee: when thou walkest through the fire, thou shalt not be burned; neither shall the flame kindle upon thee."

Addie

■

In the afternoon when school was out and the last one had left with his little dirty snuffling nose, instead of going home I would go down the hill to the spring where I could be quiet and hate them. It would be quiet there then, with the water bubbling up and away and the sun slanting quiet in the trees and the quiet smelling of damp and rotting leaves and new earth; especially in the early spring, for it was worst then.

I could just remember how my father used to say that the reason for living was to get ready to stay dead a long time. And when I would have to look at them day after day, each with his and her secret and selfish thought, and blood strange to each other blood and strange to mine, and think that this seemed to be the only way I could get ready to stay dead, I would hate my father for having ever planted me. I would look forward to the times when they faulted, so I could whip them. When the switch fell I could feel it upon my flesh; when it welted and ridged it was my blood that ran, and I would think with each blow of the switch: Now you are aware of me! Now I am something in your secret and selfish life, who have marked your blood with my own for ever and ever.

And so I took Anse. I saw him pass the school house three or four times before I learned that he was driving four miles out of his way to do it. I noticed then how he was beginning to hump—a tall man and young—so that he looked already like a tall bird hunched in the cold weather, on the wagon seat. He would pass the school house, the wagon creaking slow, his head turning slow to watch the door of the school house as the wagon passed, until he went on around the curve and out of sight. One day I went to the door and stood there when he passed. When he saw me he looked quickly away and did not look back again.

In the early spring it was worst. Sometimes I thought that I could not bear it, lying in bed at night, with the wild geese going north and their honking coming faint and high and wild out of the wild darkness, and during the day it would seem as though I couldn't wait for the last one to go so I could go down to the spring. And so when I looked up that day and saw Anse standing there in his Sunday clothes, turning his hat round and round in his hands, I said:

"If you've got any womenfolks, why in the world dont they make you get your hair cut?"

"I aint got none," he said. Then he said suddenly, driving his eyes at me like two hounds in a strange yard: "That's what I come to see you about."

"And make you hold your shoulders up," I said. "You haven't got any? But you've got a house. They tell me you've got a house and a good farm. And you live there alone, doing for yourself, do you?" He just looked at me, turning the hat in his hands. "A new house," I said. "Are you going to get married?"

And he said again, holding his eyes to mine: "That's what I come to see you about."

Later he told me, "I aint got no people. So that wont be no worry to you. I dont reckon you can say the same."

"No. I have people. In Jefferson."

His face fell a little. "Well, I got a little property. I'm forehanded; I got a good honest name. I know how town folks are, but maybe when they talk to me. . . . . . ."

"They might listen," I said. "But they'll be hard to talk to." He was watching my face. "They're in the cemetery."

"But your living kin," he said. "They'll be different."

"Will they?" I said. "I dont know. I never had any other kind."

So I took Anse. And when I knew that I had Cash, I knew that living was terrible and that this was the answer to it. That was when I learned that words are no good; that words dont ever fit even what they are trying to say at. When he was born I knew that motherhood was invented by someone who had to have a word for it because the ones that had the children didn't care whether there was a word for it or not. I knew that fear was invented by someone that had never had the fear; pride, who never had the pride. I knew that it had been, not that they had dirty noses, but that we had had to use one another by words like spiders dangling by their mouths from a beam, swinging and twisting and never touching, and that only through the blows of the switch could my blood and their blood flow as one stream. I knew that it had been, not that my aloneness had to be violated over and over each day, but that it had never been violated until Cash came. Not even by Anse in the nights.

He had a word, too. Love, he called it. But I had been used to words for a long time. I knew that that word was like the others: just a shape to fill a lack; that when the right time came, you wouldn't need a word for that anymore than for pride or fear. Cash did not need to say it to me nor I to him, and I would say, Let Anse use it, if he wants to. So that it was Anse or love; love or Anse: it didn't matter.

I would think that even while I lay with him in the dark and Cash asleep in the cradle within the swing of my hand. I would think that if he were to wake and cry, I would suckle him, too. Anse or love: it didn't matter. My aloneness had been violated and then made whole again by the violation: time, Anse, love, what you will, outside the circle.

Then I found that I had Darl. At first I would not believe it. Then I believed that I would kill Anse. It was as though he had tricked me, hidden within a word like within a paper screen and struck me in the back through it. But then I realised that I had been tricked by words older than Anse or love, and that the same word had tricked Anse too, and that my revenge would be that he would never know I was taking revenge. And when Darl was born I asked Anse to promise to take me back to Jefferson when I died, because I knew that father had been right, even when he couldn't have known he was right anymore than I could have known I was wrong.

"Nonsense," Anse said; "you and me aint nigh done chapping yet, with just two."

He did not know that he was dead, then. Sometimes I would lie by him in the dark, hearing the land that was now of my blood and flesh, and I would think: Anse. Why Anse. Why are you Anse. I would think about his name until after a while I could see the word as a shape, a vessel, and I would watch him liquify and flow into it like cold molasses flowing out of the darkness into the vessel, until the jar stood full and motionless: a significant shape profoundly without life like an empty door frame; and then I would find that I had forgotten the name of the jar. I would think: The shape of my body where I used to be a virgin is in the shape of a   and I couldn't think *Anse*, couldn't remember *Anse*. It was not that I could think of myself as no longer unvirgin, because I was three now. And when I would think *Cash* and *Darl* that way until their names would die and solidify into a shape and then fade away, I would say, All right. It doesn't matter. It doesn't matter what they call them.

And so when Cora Tull would tell me I was not a true mother, I would think how words go straight up in a thin line, quick and harmless, and how terribly doing goes along the earth, clinging to it, so that after a while the two lines are too far apart for the same person to straddle from one to the other; and that sin and love and fear are just sounds that people who never sinned nor loved nor feared have for what they never had and cannot have until they forget the words. Like Cora, who could never even cook.

She would tell me what I owed to my children and to Anse and to God. I gave Anse the children. I did not ask for them. I did not even ask him for what he could have given me: not-Anse. That was my duty to him, to not ask that, and that duty I fulfilled. I would be I; I would let him be the shape and echo of his word. That was more than he asked, because he could not have asked for that and been Anse, using himself so with a word.

And then he died. He did not know he was dead. I would lie by him in the dark, hearing the dark land talking of God's love and His beauty and His sin; hearing the dark voicelessness in which the words are the deeds,[1] and the other words that are not deeds, that are just the gaps in people's lacks, coming down like the cries of the geese out of the wild darkness in the old terrible nights, fumbling at the deeds like orphans to whom are pointed out in a crowd two faces and told, That is your father, your mother.

I believed that I had found it. I believed that the reason was the duty to the alive, to the terrible blood, the red bitter flood boiling through the land. I would think of sin as I would think of the clothes we both wore in the world's face, of the circumspection necessary because he was he and I was I; the sin the more utter and terrible since he was the instrument ordained by God who created the sin, to sanctify that sin He had created. While I waited for him in the woods, waiting for him before he saw me, I would think of him as dressed in sin. I would think of him as thinking of me as dressed also in sin, he the more beautiful since the garment which he had exchanged for sin was sanctified. I would think of the sin as garments which we would remove in order to shape and coerce the terrible blood to the forlorn echo of the dead word high in the air. Then I would lay with Anse again—I did not lie to him: I just refused, just as I refused my breast to Cash and Darl after their time was up—hearing the dark land talking the voiceless speech.

I hid nothing. I tried to deceive no one. I would not have cared. I merely took the precautions that he thought necessary for his sake, not for my safety, but just as I wore clothes in the world's face. And I would think then when Cora talked to me, of how the high dead words in time seemed to lose even the significance of their dead sound.

Then it was over. Over in the sense that he was gone and I knew that, see him again though I would, I would never again see him coming swift and secret to me in the woods dressed in sin like a gallant garment already blowing aside with the speed of his secret coming.

But for me it was not over. I mean, over in the sense of beginning and ending, because to me there was no beginning nor ending to anything then. I even held Anse refraining still, not that I was holding him recessional, but as though nothing else had ever been. My children were of me alone, of the wild blood boiling along the earth, of me and of all that lived; of none and of all. Then I found that I had Jewel. When I waked to remember to discover it, he was two months gone.

My father said that the reason for living is getting ready to stay dead. I knew at last what he meant and that he could not have known

1. Cf. 1 John 3.18: "My little children, let us not love in word, neither in tongue; but in deed and in truth."

what he meant himself, because a man cannot know anything about cleaning up the house afterward. And so I have cleaned my house.[2] With Jewel—I lay by the lamp, holding up my own head, watching him cap and suture it before he breathed—the wild blood boiled away and the sound of it ceased. Then there was only the milk, warm and calm, and I lying calm in the slow silence, getting ready to clean my house.

I gave Anse Dewey Dell to negative Jewel. Then I gave him Vardaman to replace the child I had robbed him of. And now he has three children that are his and not mine. And then I could get ready to die.

One day I was talking to Cora. She prayed for me because she believed I was blind to sin, wanting me to kneel and pray too, because people to whom sin is just a matter of words, to them salvation is just words too.

---

2. Cf. Isaiah 38.1: "In those days was Hezekiah sick unto death. And Isaiah the prophet the son of Amoz came unto him, and said unto him, Thus saith the Lord, Set thine house in order: for thou shalt die, and not live."

Whitfield

■

When they told me she was dying, all that night I wrestled with Satan, and I emerged victorious. I woke to the enormity of my sin; I saw the true light at last, and I fell on my knees and confessed to God and asked His guidance and received it. "Rise," He said; "repair to that home in which you have put a living lie, among those people with whom you have outraged My Word; confess your sin aloud. It is for them, for that deceived husband, to forgive you: not I." So I went. I heard that Tull's bridge was gone; I said "Thanks, O Lord, O Mighty Ruler of all;" for by those dangers and difficulties which I should have to surmount I saw that He had not abandoned me; that my reception again into His holy peace and love would be the sweeter for it. "Just let me not perish before I have begged the forgiveness of the man whom I betrayed," I prayed; "let me not be too late; let not the tale of mine and her transgression come from her lips instead of mine. She had sworn then that she would never tell it, but eternity is a fearsome thing to face: have I not wrestled thigh to thigh with Satan myself? let me not have also the sin of her broken vow upon my soul. Let not the waters of Thy Mighty Wrath encompass me until I have cleansed my soul in the presence of them whom I injured."

It was His hand that bore me safely above the flood, that fended from me the dangers of the waters. My horse was frightened, and my own heart failed me as the logs and the uprooted trees bore down upon my littleness. But not my soul: time after time I saw them averted at destruction's final instant, and I lifted my voice above the noise of the flood: "Praise to Thee, O Mighty Lord and King. By this token shall I cleanse my soul and gain again into the fold of Thy undying love."

I knew then that forgiveness was mine. The flood, the danger, behind, and as I rode on across the firm earth again and the scene of my Gethsemane drew closer and closer, I framed the words which I should use.[1] I would enter the house; I would stop her before she had

---

1. The garden where Christ awaited his betrayal by Judas, praying that he might be spared his ordeal. Cf. Matthew 26.36–39: "Then cometh Jesus with them unto a place called Gethsemane, and saith unto the disciples, Sit ye here, while I go and pray yonder. And he took with him Peter and the two sons of Zebedee, and began to be sorrowful and very heavy. Then saith he unto them, My soul is exceeding sorrowful, even unto death: tarry ye here, and watch with me."

Cf. also Mark 14.32–36: "And they came to a place which was named Gethsemane: and he saith to his disciples, Sit ye here, while I shall pray. And he taketh with him Peter and James and John, and began to be sore amazed, and to be very heavy; And saith unto them, My soul is exceeding sorrowful unto death: tarry ye here, and watch. And he went forward a little, and fell on the ground, and prayed that, if it were possible, the hour might pass from him. And he said, Abba, Father, all things are possible unto thee; take away this cup from me: nevertheless not what I will, but what thou wilt."

spoken; I would say to her husband: "Anse, I have sinned.[2] Do with me as you will."

It was already as though it were done. My soul felt freer, quieter than it had in years; already I seemed to dwell in abiding peace again as I rode on. To either side I saw His hand; in my heart I could hear His voice: "Courage. I am with thee."

Then I reached Tull's house. His youngest girl came out and called to me as I was passing. She told me that she was already dead.

I have sinned, O Lord. Thou knowest the extent of my remorse and the will of my spirit. But He is merciful; He will accept the will for the deed, Who knew that when I framed the words of my confession it was to Anse I spoke them, even though he was not there. It was He in His infinite wisdom that restrained the tale from her dying lips as she lay surrounded by those who loved and trusted her; mine the travail by water which I sustained by the strength of His hand. Praise to Thee in Thy bounteous and omnipotent love; O praise.

I entered the house of bereavement, the lowly dwelling where another erring mortal lay while her soul faced the awful and irrevocable judgment, peace to her ashes.

"God's grace upon this house," I said.

---

2. Cf. Luke 15.18–19, from the parable of the Prodigal Son: "I will arise and go to my father, and will say unto him, Father, I have sinned against heaven, and before thee, And am no more worthy to be called thy son: make me as one of thy hired servants."

Darl

■

On the horse he rode up to Armstid's and *came back on the horse,* leading Armstid's team. We hitched up and laid Cash on top of Addie. When we laid him down he vomited again, but he got his head over the wagon bed in time.

"He taken a lick in the stomach, too," Vernon said.

"The horse may have kicked him in the stomach too," I said. "Did he kick you in the stomach, Cash?"

He tried to say something. Dewey Dell wiped his mouth again.

"What's he say?" Vernon said.

"What is it, Cash?" Dewey Dell said. She leaned down. "His tools," she said. Vernon got them and put them into the wagon. Dewey Dell lifted Cash's head so he could see. We drove on, Dewey Dell and I sitting beside Cash to steady him *and he riding on ahead on the horse.* Vernon stood watching us for a while. Then he turned and went back toward the bridge. He walked gingerly, beginning to flap the wet sleeves of his shirt as though he had just got wet.

He was sitting the horse before the gate. Armstid was waiting at the gate. We stopped *and he got down* and we lifted Cash down and carried him into the house, where Mrs Armstid had the bed ready. We left her and Dewey Dell undressing him.

We followed pa out to the wagon. He went back and got into the wagon and drove on, we following on foot, into the lot. The wetting had helped, because Armstid said, "You're welcome to the house. You can put it there." *He followed, leading the horse, and stood beside the wagon, the reins in his hand.*

"I thank you," pa said. "We'll use in the shed yonder. I know it's a imposition on you."

"You're welcome to the house," Armstid said. *He had that wooden look on his face again; that bold, surly, high-colored rigid look like his face and eyes were two colors of wood, the wrong one pale and the wrong one dark. His shirt was beginning to dry, but it still clung close upon him when he moved.*

"She would appreciate it," pa said.

We took the team out and rolled the wagon back under the shed. One side of the shed was open.

"It wont rain under," Armstid said. "But if you'd rather. . . . . ."

Back of the barn was some rusted sheets of tin roofing. We took two of them and propped them against the open side.

"You're welcome to the house," Armstid said.

"I thank you," pa said. "I'd take it right kind if you'd give them a little snack."

"Sho," Armstid said. "Lula'll have supper ready soon as she gets Cash comfortable." *He had gone back to the horse and he was taking the saddle off, his damp shirt lapping flat to him when he moved.*

Pa wouldn't come in the house.

"Come in and eat," Armstid said. "It's nigh ready."

"I wouldn't crave nothing," pa said. "I thank you."

"You come in and dry and eat," Armstid said. "It'll be all right here."

"It's for her," pa said. "It's for her sake I am taking the food. I got no team, no nothing. But she will be grateful to ere a one of you."

"Sho," Armstid said. "You folks come in and dry."

But after Armstid gave pa a drink, he felt better, and when we went in to see about Cash *he hadn't come in with us. When I looked back he was leading the horse into the barn* he was already talking about getting another team, and by supper time he had good as bought it. *He is down there in the barn, sliding fluidly past the gaudy lunging swirl, into the stall with it. He climbs onto the manger and drags the hay down and leaves the stall and seeks and finds the curry-comb. Then he returns and slips quickly past the single crashing thump and up against the horse, where it cannot overreach. He applies the curry-comb, holding himself within the horse's striking radius with the agility of an acrobat, cursing the horse in a whisper of obscene caress. Its head flashes back, tooth-cropped; its eyes roll in the dusk like marbles on a gaudy velvet cloth as he strikes it upon the face with the back of the curry-comb.*

Armstid

■

But time I give him another sup of whisky and supper was about ready, he had done already bought a team from somebody, on a credit. Picking and choosing he were by then, saying how he didn't like this span and wouldn't put his money in nothing so-and-so owned, not even a hen coop.

"You might try Snopes," I said. "He's got three-four span. Maybe one of them would suit you."

Then he begun to mumble his mouth, looking at me like it was me that owned the only span of mules in the county and wouldn't sell them to him, when I knew that like as not it would be my team that would ever get them out of the lot at all. Only I dont know what they would do with them, if they had a team. Littlejohn had told me that the levee through Haley bottom had done gone for two miles and that the only way to get to Jefferson would be to go around by Mottson. But that was Anse's business.

"He's a close man to trade with," he says, mumbling his mouth. But when I give him another sup after supper, he cheered up some. He was aiming to go back to the barn and set up with her. Maybe he thought that if he just stayed down there ready to take out, Santa Claus would maybe bring him a span of mules. "But I reckon I can talk him around," he says. "A man'll always help a fellow in a tight, if he's got ere a drop of Christian blood in him."

"Of course you're welcome to the use of mine," I said, me knowing how much he believed that was the reason.

"I thank you," he said. "She'll want to go in ourn," and him knowing how much I believed that was the reason.

After supper Jewel rode over to the Bend to get Peabody. I heard he was to be there today at Varner's. Jewel come back about midnight. Peabody had gone down below Inverness somewhere, but Uncle Billy come back with him, with his satchel of horse-physic. Like he says, a man aint so different from a horse or a mule, come long come short, except a mule or a horse has got a little more sense. "What you been into now, boy?" he says, looking at Cash. "Get me a mattress and a chair and a glass of whisky," he says.

He made Cash drink the whisky, then he run Anse out of the room. "Lucky it was the same leg he broke last summer," Anse says, mournful, mumbling and blinking. "That's something."

We folded the mattress across Cash's legs and set the chair on the mattress and me and Jewel set on the chair and the gal held the lamp and Uncle Billy taken a chew of tobacco and went to work. Cash fought pretty hard for a while, until he fainted. Then he laid still, with

big balls of sweat standing on his face like they had started to roll
down and then stopped to wait for him.

When he waked up, Uncle Billy had done packed up and left. He
kept on trying to say something until the gal leaned down and wiped
his mouth. "It's his tools," she said.

"I brought them in," Darl said. "I got them."

He tried to talk again; she leaned down. "He wants to see them,"
she said. So Darl brought them in where he could see them. They
shoved them under the side of the bed, where he could reach his hand
and touch them when he felt better. Next morning Anse taken that
horse and rode over to the Bend to see Snopes. Him and Jewel stood
in the lot talking a while, then Anse got on the horse and rode off. I
reckon that was the first time Jewel ever let anybody ride that horse,
and until Anse come back he hung around in that swole-up way,
watching the road like he was half a mind to take out after Anse and
get the horse back.

Along toward nine oclock it begun to get hot. That was when I see
the first buzzard. Because of the wetting, I reckon. Anyway it wasn't
until well into the day that I see them. Lucky the breeze was setting
away from the house, so it wasn't until well into the morning. But
soon as I see them it was like I could smell it in the field a mile away
from just watching them, and them circling and circling for everybody in the county to see what was in my barn.

I was still a good half a mile from the house when I heard that boy
yelling. I thought maybe he might have fell into the well or something, so I whipped up and come into the lot on the lope.

There must have been a dozen of them setting along the ridge-pole
of the barn, and that boy was chasing another one around the lot like
it was a turkey and it just lifting enough to dodge him and go flopping
back to the roof of the shed again where he had found it setting on
the coffin. It had got hot then, right, and the breeze had dropped or
changed or something, so I went and found Jewel, but Lula come out.

"You got to do something," she said. "It's a outrage."

"That's what I aim to do," I said.

"It's a outrage," she said. "He should be lawed for treating her so."

"He's getting her into the ground the best he can," I said. So I found
Jewel and asked him if he didn't want to take one of the mules and go
over to the Bend and see about Anse. He didn't say nothing. He just
looked at me with his jaws going bone-white and them bone-white
eyes of hisn, then he went and begun to call Darl.

"What you fixing to do?" I said.

He didn't answer. Darl come out. "Come on," Jewel said.

"What you aim to do?" Darl said.

"Going to move the wagon," Jewel said over his shoulder.

"Dont be a fool," I said. "I never meant nothing. You couldn't help it." And Darl hung back too, but nothing wouldn't suit Jewel.

"Shut your goddamn mouth," he says.

"It's got to be somewhere," Darl said. "We'll take out soon as pa gets back."

"You wont help me?" Jewel says, them white eyes of hisn kind of blaring and his face shaking like he had a aguer.[1]

"No," Darl said. "I wont. Wait till pa gets back."

So I stood in the door and watched him push and haul at that wagon. It was on a downhill, and once I thought he was fixing to beat out the back end of the shed. Then the dinner bell rung. I called him, but he didn't look around. "Come on to dinner," I said. "Tell that boy." But he didn't answer, so I went on to dinner. The gal went down to get that boy, but she come back without him. About half through dinner we heard him yelling again, running that buzzard out.

"It's a outrage," Lula said; "a outrage."

"He's doing the best he can," I said. "A fellow dont trade with Snopes in thirty minutes. They'll set in the shade all afternoon to dicker."

"Do?" she says. "Do? He's done too much, already."

And I reckon he had. Trouble is, his quitting was just about to start our doing. He couldn't buy no team from nobody, let alone Snopes, withouten he had something to mortgage he didn't know would mortgage yet. And so when I went back to the field I looked at my mules and same as told them goodbye for a spell. And when I come back that evening and the sun shining all day on that shed, I wasn't so sho I would regret it.

He come riding up just as I went out to the porch, where they all was. He looked kind of funny: kind of more hang-dog than common, and kind of proud too. Like he had done something he thought was cute but wasn't so sho now how other folks would take it.

"I got a team," he said.

"You bought a team from Snopes?" I said.

"I reckon Snopes aint the only man in this country that can drive a trade," he said.

"Sho," I said. He was looking at Jewel, with that funny look, but Jewel had done got down from the porch and was going toward the horse. To see what Anse had done to it, I reckon.

"Jewel," Anse says. Jewel looked back. "Come here," Anse says. Jewel come back a little and stopped again.

"What you want?" he said.

---

1. Ague or fever.

"So you got a team from Snopes," I said. "He'll send them over to-night, I reckon? You'll want a early start tomorrow, long as you'll have to go by Mottson."

Then he quit looking like he had been for a while. He got that badgered look like he used to have, mumbling his mouth.

"I do the best I can," he said. "Fore God, if there were ere a man in the living world suffered the trials and floutings I have suffered."

"A fellow that just beat Snopes in a trade ought to feel pretty good," I said. "What did you give him, Anse?"

He didn't look at me. "I give a chattel mortgage on my cultivator and seeder," he said.[2]

"But they aint worth forty dollars. How far do you aim to get with a forty dollar team?"

They were all watching him now, quiet and steady. Jewel was stopped, halfway back, waiting to go on to the horse. "I give other things," Anse said. He begun to mumble his mouth again, standing there like he was waiting for somebody to hit him and him with his mind already made up not to do nothing about it.

"What other things?" Darl said.

"Hell," I said. "You take my team. You can bring them back. I'll get along someway."

"So that's what you were doing in Cash's clothes last night," Darl said. He said it just like he was reading it outen the paper. Like he never give a durn himself one way or the other. Jewel had come back now, standing there, looking at Anse with them marble eyes of hisn. "Cash aimed to buy that talking machine from Suratt with that money," Darl said.

Anse stood there, mumbling his mouth. Jewel watched him. He aint never blinked yet.

"But that's just eight dollars more," Darl said, in that voice like he was just listening and never give a durn himself. "That still wont buy a team."

Anse looked at Jewel, quick, kind of sliding his eyes that way, then he looked down again. "God knows, if there were ere a man," he says. Still they didn't say nothing. They just watched him, waiting, and him sliding his eyes toward their feet and up their legs but no higher. "And the horse," he says.

"What horse?" Jewel said. Anse just stood there. I be durn, if a man cant keep the upper hand of his sons, he ought to run them away from home, no matter how big they are. And if he cant do that, I

---

2. Two types of primitive, mule-drawn plows. The former was used to cultivate—that is, to weed and aerate—the soil between rows of cotton plants; the latter was used for planting cotton seeds. In the 1920s, modern machinery began largely to replace these kinds of plows.

be durn if he oughtn't to leave himself. I be durn if I wouldn't. "You mean, you tried to swap my horse?" Jewel says.

Anse stands there, dangle-armed. "For fifteen years I aint had a tooth in my head," he says. "God knows it. He knows in fifteen years I aint et the victuals He aimed for man to eat to keep his strength up, and me saving a nickel here and a nickel there so my family wouldn't suffer it, to buy them teeth so I could eat God's appointed food. I give that money. I thought that if I could do without eating, my sons could do without riding. God knows I did."

Jewel stands with his hands on his hips, looking at Anse. Then he looks away. He looked out across the field, his face still as a rock, like it was somebody else talking about somebody else's horse and him not even listening. Then he spit, slow, and said "Hell" and he turned and went on to the gate and unhitched the horse and got on it. It was moving when he come into the saddle and by the time he was on it they was tearing down the road like the Law might have been behind them. They went out of sight that way, the two of them looking like some kind of a spotted cyclone.

"Well," I says. "You take my team," I said. But he wouldn't do it. And they wouldn't even stay, and that boy chasing them buzzards all day in the hot sun until he was nigh as crazy as the rest of them. "Leave Cash here, anyway," I said. But they wouldn't do that. They made a pallet for him with quilts on top of the coffin and laid him on it and set his tools by him, and we put my team in and hauled the wagon about a mile down the road.

"If we'll bother you here," Anse says, "just say so."

"Sho," I said. "It'll be fine here. Safe, too. Now let's go back and eat supper."

"I thank you," Anse said. "We got a little something in the basket. We can make out."

"Where'd you get it?" I said.

"We brought it from home."

"But it'll be stale now," I said. "Come and get some hot victuals."

But they wouldn't come. "I reckon we can make out," Anse said. So I went home and et and taken a basket back to them and tried again to make them come back to the house.

"I thank you," he said. "I reckon we can make out." So I left them there, squatting around a little fire, waiting; God knows what for.

I come on home. I kept thinking about them there, and about that fellow tearing away on that horse. And that would be the last they would see of him. And I be durn if I could blame him. Not for wanting to not give up his horse, but for getting shut of such a durn fool as Anse.

Or that's what I thought then. Because be durn if there aint something about a durn fellow like Anse that seems to make a man have to help him, even when he knows he'll be wanting to kick himself next minute. Because about a hour after breakfast next morning Eustace Grimm that works Snopes' place come up with a span of mules, hunting Anse.

"I thought him and Anse never traded," I said.

"Sho," Eustace said. "All they liked was the horse. Like I said to Mr Snopes, he was letting this team go for fifty dollars, because if his uncle Flem had a just kept them Texas horses when he owned them, Anse wouldn't a never——"

"The horse?" I said. "Anse's boy taken that horse and cleared out last night, probably half way to Texas by now, and Anse——"

"I didn't know who brung it," Eustace said. "I never see them. I just found the horse in the barn this morning when I went to feed, and I told Mr Snopes and he said to bring the team on over here."

Well, that'll be the last they'll ever see of him now, sho enough. Come Christmas time they'll maybe get a postal card from him in Texas, I reckon. And if it hadn't a been Jewel, I reckon it'd a been me; I owe him that much, myself. I be durn if Anse dont conjure a man, some way. I be durn if he aint a sight.

Vardaman

■

Now there are seven of them, in little tall black circles.

"Look, Darl," I say; "see?"

He looks up. We watch them in little tall black circles of not-moving.

"Yesterday there were just four," I say.

There were more than four on the barn.

"Do you know what I would do if he tries to light on the wagon again?" I say.

"What would you do?" Darl says.

"I wouldn't let him light on her," I say. "I wouldn't let him light on Cash, either."

Cash is sick. He is sick on the box. But my mother is a fish.

"We got to get some medicine in Mottson," pa says. "I reckon we'll just have to."

"How do you feel, Cash?" Darl says.

"It dont bother none," Cash says.

"Do you want it propped a little higher?" Darl says.

Cash has a broken leg. He has had two broken legs. He lies on the box with a quilt rolled under his head and a piece of wood under his knee.

"I reckon we ought to left him at Armstid's," pa says.

I haven't got a broken leg and pa hasn't and Darl hasn't and "It's just the bumps," Cash says. "It kind of grinds together a little on a bump. It dont bother none." Jewel *has gone away. He and his horse went away one supper time*

"It's because she wouldn't have us beholden," pa says. "Fore God, I do the best that ere a man" *Is it because Jewel's mother is a horse Darl? I said.*

"Maybe I can draw the ropes a little tighter," Darl says. *That's why Jewel and I were both in the shed and she was in the wagon because the horse lives in the barn and I had to keep on running the buzzard away from*

"If you just would," Cash says. And Dewey Dell hasn't got a broken leg and I haven't. Cash is my brother.

We stop. When Darl loosens the rope Cash begins to sweat again. His teeth look out.

"Hurt?" Darl says.

"I reckon you better put it back," Cash says.

Darl puts the rope back, pulling hard. Cash's teeth look out.

"Hurt?" Darl says.

"It dont bother none," Cash says.

"Do you want pa to drive slower?" Darl says.

"No," Cash says. "Aint no time to hang back. It dont bother none."

"We'll have to get some medicine at Mottson," pa says. "I reckon we'll have to."

"Tell him to go on," Cash says. We go on. Dewey Dell leans back and wipes Cash's face. Cash is my brother. *But Jewel's mother is a horse. My mother is a fish. Darl says that when we come to the water again I might see her and Dewey Dell said, She's in the box; how could she have got out? She got out through the holes I bored, into the water I said, and when we come to the water again I am going to see her. My mother is not in the box. My mother does not smell like that. My mother is a fish*

"Those cakes will be in fine shape by the time we get to Jefferson," Darl says.

Dewey Dell does not look around.

"You better try to sell them in Mottson," Darl says.

"When will we get to Mottson, Darl?" I say.

"Tomorrow," Darl says. "If this team dont rack to pieces. Snopes must have fed them on sawdust."

"Why did he feed them on sawdust, Darl?" I say.

"Look," Darl says. "See?"

Now there are nine of them, tall in little tall black circles.

When we come to the foot of the hill pa stops and Darl and Dewey Dell and I get out. Cash cant walk because he has a broken leg. "Come up, mules," pa says. The mules walk hard; the wagon creaks. Darl and Dewey Dell and I walk behind the wagon, up the hill. When we come to the top of the hill pa stops and we get back into the wagon.

Now there are ten of them, tall in little tall black circles on the sky.

Moseley

∎

I happened to look up, and saw her outside the window, looking in. Not close to the glass, and not looking at anything in particular; just standing there with her head turned this way and her eyes full on me and kind of blank too, like she was waiting for a sign. When I looked up again she was moving toward the door.

She kind of bumbled at the screen door a minute, like they do, and came in. She had on a stiff-brimmed straw hat setting on the top of her head and she was carrying a package wrapped in newspaper: I thought that she had a quarter or a dollar at the most, and that after she stood around a while she would maybe buy a cheap comb or a bottle of nigger toilet water, so I never disturbed her for a minute or so except to notice that she was pretty in a kind of sullen, awkward way, and that she looked a sight better in her gingham dress and her own complexion than she would after she bought whatever she would finally decide on. Or tell that she wanted. I knew that she had already decided before she came in. But you have to let them take their time. So I went on with what I was doing, figuring to let Albert wait on her when he caught up at the fountain, when he came back to me.

"That woman," he said. "You better see what she wants."

"What does she want?" I said.

"I dont know. I cant get anything out of her. You better wait on her."

So I went around the counter. I saw that she was barefooted, standing with her feet flat and easy on the floor, like she was used to it. She was looking at me, hard, holding the package; I saw she had about as black a pair of eyes as ever I saw, and she was a stranger. I never remembered seeing her in Mottson before. "What can I do for you?" I said.

Still she didn't say anything. She stared at me without winking. Then she looked back at the folks at the fountain. Then she looked past me, toward the back of the store.

"Do you want to look at some toilet things?" I said. "Or is it medicine you want?"

"That's it," she said. She looked quick back at the fountain again. So I thought maybe her ma or somebody had sent her in for some of this female dope and she was ashamed to ask for it. I knew she couldn't have a complexion like hers and use it herself, let alone not being much more than old enough to barely know what it was for. It's a shame, the way they poison themselves with it. But a man's got to stock it or go out of business in this country.

"Oh," I said. "What do you use? We have——" She looked at me again, almost like she had said hush, and looked toward the back of the store again.

"I'd liefer go back there," she said.

"All right," I said. You have to humor them. You save time by it. I followed her to the back. She put her hand on the gate. "There's nothing back there but the prescription case," I said. "What do you want?" She stopped and looked at me. It was like she had taken some kind of a lid off her face, her eyes. It was her eyes: kind of dumb and hopeful and sullenly willing to be disappointed all at the same time. But she was in trouble of some sort; I could see that. "What's your trouble?" I said. "Tell me what it is you want. I'm pretty busy." I wasn't meaning to hurry her, but a man just hasn't got the time they have out there.

"It's the female trouble," she said.

"Oh," I said. "Is that all?" I thought maybe she was younger than she looked, and her first one had scared her, or maybe one had been a little abnormal as it will in young women. "Where's your ma?" I said. "Haven't you got one?"

"She's out yonder in the wagon," she said.

"Why not talk to her about it before you take any medicine," I said. "Any woman would have told you about it." She looked at me, and I looked at her again and said, "How old are you?"

"Seventeen," she said.

"Oh," I said. "I thought maybe you were. . . . . . ." She was watching me. But then, in the eyes all of them look like they had no age and knew everything in the world, anyhow. "Are you too regular, or not regular enough?"

She quit looking at me but she didn't move. "Yes," she said. "I reckon so. Yes."

"Well, which?" I said. "Dont you know?" It's a crime and a shame; but after all, they'll buy it from somebody. She stood there, not looking at me. "You want something to stop it?" I said. "Is that it?"

"No," she said. "That's it. It's already stopped."

"Well, what——" Her face was lowered a little, still, like they do in all their dealings with a man so he dont ever know just where the lightning will strike next. "You are not married, are you?" I said.

"No."

"Oh," I said. "And how long has it been since it stopped? about five months maybe?"

"It aint been but two," she said.

"Well, I haven't got anything in my store you want to buy," I said, "unless it's a nipple. And I'd advise you to buy that and go back home and tell your pa, if you have one, and let him make somebody buy you a wedding license. Was that all you wanted?"

But she just stood there, not looking at me.

"I got the money to pay you," she said.

"Is it your own, or did he act enough of a man to give you the money?"

"He give it to me. Ten dollars. He said that would be enough."

"A thousand dollars wouldn't be enough in my store and ten cents wouldn't be enough," I said. "You take my advice and go home and tell your pa or your brothers if you have any or the first man you come to in the road."

But she didn't move. "Lafe said I could get it at the drugstore. He said to tell you me and him wouldn't never tell nobody you sold it to us."

"And I just wish your precious Lafe had come for it himself; that's what I wish. I dont know: I'd have had a little respect for him then. And you can go back and tell him I said so—if he aint halfway to Texas by now, which I dont doubt. Me, a respectable druggist, that's kept store and raised a family and been a church-member for fifty-six years in this town. I'm a good mind to tell your folks myself, if I can just find who they are."

She looked at me now, her eyes and face kind of blank again like when I first saw her through the window. "I didn't know," she said. "He told me I could get something at the drugstore. He said they might not want to sell it to me, but if I had ten dollars and told them I wouldn't never tell nobody. . . ."

"He never said this drug-store," I said. "If he did or mentioned my name, I defy him to prove it. I defy him to repeat it or I'll prosecute him to the full extent of the law, and you can tell him so."

"But maybe another drugstore would," she said.

"Then I dont want to know it. Me, that's——" Then I looked at her. But it's a hard life they have; sometimes a man. . . . . . if there can ever be any excuse for sin, which it cant be. And then, life wasn't made to be easy on folks: they wouldn't ever have any reason to be good and die. "Look here," I said. "You get that notion out of your head. The Lord gave you what you have, even if He did use the devil to do it; you let Him take it away from you if it's His will to do so. You go on back to Lafe and you and him take that ten dollars and get married with it."

"Lafe said I could get something at the drugstore," she said.

"Then go and get it," I said. "You wont get it here."

She went out, carrying the package, her feet making a little hissing on the floor. She bumbled again at the door and went out. I could see her through the glass going on down the street.

It was Albert told me about the rest of it. He said the wagon was stopped in front of Grummet's hardware store, with the ladies all scattering up and down the street with handkerchiefs to their noses, and a crowd of hard-nosed men and boys standing around the wagon, listening to the marshal arguing with the man. He was a kind of tall, gaunted man sitting on the wagon, saying it was a public street and he reckoned he had as much right there as anybody, and the marshal telling him he would have to move on; folks couldn't stand it. It had been dead eight days, Albert said. They came from some place out in Yoknapatawpha county,[1] trying to get to Jefferson with it. It must have been like a piece of rotten cheese coming into an ant-hill, in that ramshackle wagon that Albert said folks were scared would fall all to pieces before they could get it out of town, with that home-made box and another fellow with a broken leg lying on a quilt on top of it, and the father and a little boy sitting on the seat and the marshal trying to make them get out of town.

"It's a public street," the man says. "I reckon we can stop to buy something same as airy other man. We got the money to pay for hit, and hit aint airy law that says a man cant spend his money where he wants."

They had stopped to buy some cement. The other son was in Grummet's, trying to make Grummet break a sack and let him have ten cents' worth, and finally Grummet broke the sack to get him out. They wanted the cement to fix the fellow's broken leg, someway.

"Why, you'll kill him," the marshal said. "You'll cause him to lose his leg. You take him on to a doctor, and you get this thing buried soon as you can. Dont you know you're liable to jail for endangering the public health?"

"We're doing the best we can," the father said. Then he told a long tale about how they had to wait for the wagon to come back and how the bridge was washed away and how they went eight miles to another bridge and it was gone too so they came back and swum the ford and the mules got drowned and how they got another team and found that the road was washed out and they had to come clean around by Mottson, and then the one with the cement came back and told him to shut up.

"We'll be gone in a minute," he told the marshal.

"We never aimed to bother nobody," the father said.

"You take that fellow to a doctor," the marshal told the one with the cement.

"I reckon he's all right," he said.

"It aint that we're hard-hearted," the marshal said. "But I reckon you can tell yourself how it is."

"Sho," the other said. "We'll take out soon as Dewey Dell comes back. She went to deliver a package."

So they stood there with the folks backed off with handkerchiefs to their faces, until in a minute the girl came up with that newspaper package.

"Come on," the one with the cement said, "we've lost too much time." So they got in the wagon and went on. And when I went to

---

1. Faulkner's fictional county, based upon Lafayette County, Mississippi. Yoknapatawpha is the old name for the Yocona River, which runs a few miles south of Oxford, the county seat. This is Faulkner's first use of the name.

supper it still seemed like I could smell it. And the next day I met the marshal and I began to sniff and said,

"Smell anything?"

"I reckon they're in Jefferson by now," he said.

"Or in jail. Well, thank the Lord it's not our jail."

"That's a fact," he said.

Darl

■

"Here's a place," pa says. He pulls the team up and sits looking at the house. "We could get some water over yonder."

"All right," I say. "You'll have to borrow a bucket from them, Dewey Dell."

"God knows," pa says. "I wouldn't be beholden, God knows."

"If you see a good-sized can, you might bring it," I say. Dewey Dell gets down from the wagon, carrying the package. "You had more trouble than you expected, selling those cakes in Mottson," I say. How do our lives ravel out into the no-wind, no-sound, the weary gestures wearily recapitulant: echoes of old compulsions with no-hand on no-strings: in sunset we fall into furious attitudes, dead gestures of dolls. Cash broke his leg and now the sawdust is running out. He is bleeding to death is Cash.

"I wouldn't be beholden," pa says. "God knows."

"Then make some water yourself," I say. "We can use Cash's hat."

When Dewey Dell comes back the man comes with her. Then he stops and she comes on and he stands there and after a while he goes back to the house and stands on the porch, watching us.

"We better not try to lift him down," pa says. "We can fix it here."

"Do you want to be lifted down, Cash?" I say.

"Wont we get to Jefferson tomorrow?" he says. He is watching us, his eyes interrogatory, intent, and sad. "I can last it out."

"It'll be easier on you," pa says. "It'll keep it from rubbing together."

"I can last it," Cash says. "We'll lose time stopping."

"We done bought the cement, now," pa says.

"I could last it," Cash says. "It aint but one more day. It dont bother to speak of." He looks at us, his eyes wide in his thin gray face, questioning. "It sets up so," he says.

"We done bought it now," pa says.

I mix the cement in the can, stirring the slow water into the pale green thick coils. I bring the can to the wagon where Cash can see. He lies on his back, his thin profile in silhouette, ascetic and profound against the sky. "Does that look about right?" I say.

"You dont want too much water, or it wont work right," he says.

"Is this too much?"

"Maybe if you could get a little sand," he says. "It aint but one more day," he says. "It dont bother me none."

Vardaman goes back down the road to where we crossed the branch and returns with sand. He pours it slowly into the thick coiling in the can. I go to the wagon again.

"Does that look all right?"

"Yes," Cash says. "I could have lasted. It dont bother me none."

We loosen the splints and pour the cement over his leg slow.

"Watch out for it," Cash says. "Dont get none on it if you can help."

"Yes," I say. Dewey Dell tears a piece of paper from the package and wipes the cement from the top of it as it drips from Cash's leg.

"How does that feel?"

"It feels fine," he says. "It's cold. It feels fine."

"If it'll just help you," pa says. "I asks your forgiveness. I never foreseen it no more than you."

"It feels fine," Cash says.

If you could just ravel out into time. That would be nice. It would be nice if you could just ravel out into time.

We replace the splints, the cords, drawing them tight, the cement in thick pale green slow surges among the cords, Cash watching us quietly with that profound questioning look.

"That'll steady it," I say.

"Ay," Cash says. "I'm obliged."

Then we all turn on the wagon and watch him. He is coming up the road behind us, wooden-backed, wooden-faced, moving only from his hips down. He comes up without a word, with his pale rigid eyes in his high sullen face, and gets into the wagon.

"Here's a hill," pa says. "I reckon you'll have to get out and walk."

Vardaman

■

Darl and Jewel and Dewey Dell and I are walking up the hill, behind the wagon. Jewel came back. He came up the road and got into the wagon. He was walking. Jewel hasn't got a horse anymore. Jewel is my brother. Cash is my brother. Cash has a broken leg. We fixed Cash's leg so it doesn't hurt. Cash is my brother. Jewel is my brother too, but he hasn't got a broken leg.

Now there are five of them, tall in little tall black circles.

"Where do they stay at night, Darl?" I say. "When we stop at night in the barn, where do they stay?"

The hill goes off into the sky. Then the sun comes up from behind the hill and the mules and the wagon and pa walk on the sun. You cannot watch them, walking slow on the sun. In Jefferson it is red on the track behind the glass. The track goes shining round and round. Dewey Dell says so.

Tonight I am going to see where they stay while we are in the barn.

Darl

■

"Jewel," I say, "whose son are you?"

The breeze was setting up from the barn, so we put her under the apple tree, where the moonlight can dapple the apple tree upon the long slumbering flanks within which now and then she talks in little trickling bursts of secret and murmurous bubbling. I took Vardaman to listen. When we came up the cat leaped down from it and flicked away with silver claw and silver eye into the shadow.

"Your mother was a horse, but who was your father, Jewel?"

"You goddamn lying son of a bitch."

"Dont call me that," I say.

"You goddamn lying son of a bitch."

"Dont you call me that, Jewel." In the tall moonlight his eyes look like spots of white paper pasted on a high small football.

After supper Cash began to sweat a little. "It's getting a little hot," he said. "It was the sun shining on it all day, I reckon."

"You want some water poured on it?" we say. "Maybe that will ease it some."

"I'd be obliged," Cash said. "It was the sun shining on it, I reckon. I ought to thought and kept it covered."

"We ought to thought," we said. "You couldn't have suspicioned."

"I never noticed it getting hot," Cash said. "I ought to minded it."

So we poured the water over it. His leg and foot below the cement looked like they had been boiled. "Does that feel better?" we said.

"I'm obliged," Cash said. "It feels fine."

Dewey Dell wipes his face with the hem of her dress.

"See if you can get some sleep," we say.

"Sho," Cash says. "I'm right obliged. It feels fine now."

Jewel, I say, Who was your father, Jewel?

Goddamn you. Goddamn you.

Vardaman

■

She was under the apple tree and Darl and I go across the moon and the cat jumps down and runs and we can hear her inside the wood.

"Hear?" Darl says. "Put your ear close."

I put my ear close and I can hear her. Only I cant tell what she is saying.

"What is she saying, Darl?" I say. "Who is she talking to?"

"She's talking to God," Darl says. "She is calling on Him to help her."

"What does she want Him to do?" I say.

"She wants Him to hide her away from the sight of man," Darl says.

"Why does she want to hide her away from the sight of man, Darl?"

"So she can lay down her life," Darl says.

"Why does she want to lay down her life, Darl?"

"Listen," Darl says. We hear her. We hear her turn over on her side. "Listen," Darl says.

"She's turned over," I say. "She's looking at me through the wood."

"Yes," Darl says.

"How can she see through the wood, Darl?"

"Come," Darl says. "We must let her be quiet. Come."

"She cant see out there, because the holes are in the top," I say. "How can she see, Darl?"

"Let's go see about Cash," Darl says.

And I saw something Dewey Dell told me not to tell nobody

Cash is sick in his leg. We fixed his leg this afternoon, but he is sick in it again, lying on the bed. We pour water on his leg and then he feels fine.

"I feel fine," Cash says. "I'm obliged to you."

"Try to get some sleep," we say.

"I feel fine," Cash says. "I'm obliged to you."

And I saw something Dewey Dell told me not to tell nobody. It is not about pa and it is not about Cash and it is not about Jewel and it is not about Dewey Dell and it is not about me

Dewey Dell and I are going to sleep on the pallet. It is on the back porch, where we can see the barn, and the moon shines on half of the pallet and we will lie half in the white and half in the black, with the moonlight on our legs. And then I am going to see where they stay at night while we are in the barn. We are not in the barn tonight but I can see the barn and so I am going to find where they stay at night.

We lie on the pallet, with our legs in the moon.

"Look," I say, "my legs look black. Your legs look black, too."

"Go to sleep," Dewey Dell says.

Jefferson is a far piece.

"Dewey Dell."

"What."

"If it's not Christmas now, how will it be there?"

It goes round and round on the shining track. Then the track goes shining round and round.

"Will what be there?"

"That train. In the window."

"You go to sleep. You can see tomorrow if it's there."

Maybe Santa Claus wont know they are town boys.

"Dewey Dell."

"You go to sleep. He aint going to let none of them town boys have it."

It was behind the window, red on the track, the track shining round and round. It made my heart hurt. And then it was pa and Jewel and Darl and Mr. Gillespie's boy. Mr Gillespie's boy's legs come down under his nightshirt. When he goes into the moon, his legs fuzz. They go on around the house toward the apple tree.

"What are they going to do, Dewey Dell?"

They went around the house toward the apple tree.

"I can smell her," I say. "Can you smell her, too?"

"Hush," Dewey Dell says. "The wind's changed. Go to sleep."

And so I am going to know where they stay at night soon. They come around the house, going across the yard in the moon, carrying her on their shoulders. They carry her down to the barn, the moon shining flat and quiet on her. Then they come back and go into the house again. While they were in the moon, Mr Gillespie's boy's leg fuzzed. And then I waited and I said Dewey Dell? and then I waited and then I went to find where they stay at night and I saw something that Dewey Dell told me not to tell nobody.

Darl

■

Against the dark doorway he seems to materialise out of darkness, lean as a race horse in his underclothes in the beginning of the glare. He leaps to the ground with on his face an expression of furious unbelief. He has seen me without even turning his head or his eyes in which the glare swims like two small torches. "Come on," he says, leaping down the slope toward the barn.

For an instant longer he runs silver in the moonlight, then he springs out like a flat figure cut leanly from tin against an abrupt and soundless explosion as the whole loft of the barn takes fire at once, as though it had been stuffed with powder. The front, the conical façade with the square orifice of doorway broken only by the square squat shape of the coffin on the sawhorses like a cubistic bug, comes into relief. Behind me pa and Gillespie and Mack and Dewey Dell and Vardaman emerge from the house.

He pauses at the coffin, stooping, looking at me, his face furious. Overhead the flames sound like thunder; across us rushes a cool draft: there is no heat in it at all yet, and a handful of chaff lifts suddenly and sucks swiftly along the stalls where a horse is screaming. "Quick," I say; "the horses."

He glares a moment longer at me, then at the roof overhead, then he leaps toward the stall where the horse screams. It plunges and kicks, the sound of the crashing blows sucking up into the sound of the flames. They sound like an interminable train crossing an endless trestle. Gillespie and Mack pass me, in knee-length nightshirts, shouting, their voices thin and high and meaningless and at the same time profoundly wild and sad: ". . . . . . .cow. . . . . . .stall. . . . . . ." Gillespie's nightshirt rushes ahead of him on the draft, ballooning about his hairy thighs.

The stall door has swung shut. Jewel thrusts it back with his buttocks and he appears, his back arched, the muscles ridged through his garment as he drags the horse out by its head. In the glare its eyes roll with soft, fleet, wild opaline fire; its muscles bunch and run as it flings its head about, lifting Jewel clear of the ground. He drags it on, slowly, terrifically; again he gives me across his shoulder a single glare furious and brief. Even when they are clear of the barn the horse continues to fight and lash backward toward the doorway until Gillespie passes me, stark-naked, his nightshirt wrapped about the mule's head, and beats the maddened horse on out of the door.

Jewel returns, running; again he looks down at the coffin. But he comes on. "Where's cow?" he cries, passing me. I follow him. In the stall Mack is struggling with the other mule. When its head turns into the glare I can see the wild rolling of its eye too, but it makes no sound. It just stands there, watching Mack over its shoulder, swinging its hind quarters toward him whenever he approaches. He looks back at us, his eyes and mouth three round holes in his face on which the freckles look like english peas on a plate. His voice is thin, high, faraway.

"I cant do nothing. . . . . . ." It is as though the sound had been swept from his lips and up and away, speaking back to us from an immense distance of exhaustion. Jewel slides past us; the mule whirls and lashes out, but he has already gained its head. I lean to Mack's ear:

"Nightshirt. Around his head."

Mack stares at me. Then he rips the nightshirt off and flings it over the mule's head, and it becomes docile at once. Jewel is yelling at him: "Cow? Cow?"

"Back," Mack cries. "Last stall."

The cow watches us as we enter. She is backed into the corner, head lowered, still chewing though rapidly. But she makes no move. Jewel has paused, looking up, and suddenly we watch the entire floor to the loft dissolve. It just turns to fire; a faint litter of sparks rains down. He glances about. Back under the trough is a three legged milking stool. He catches it up and swings it into the planking of the rear wall. He splinters a plank, then another, a third; we tear the fragments away. While we are stooping to the opening something charges into us from behind. It is the cow; with a single whistling breath she rushes between us and through the gap and into the outer glare, her tail erect and rigid as a broom nailed upright to the end of her spine.

Jewel turns back into the barn. "Here," I say; "Jewel!" I grasp at him; he strikes my hand down. "You fool," I say, "dont you see you cant make it back yonder?" The hallway looks like a searchlight turned into rain. "Come on," I say, "around this way."

When we are through the gap he begins to run. "Jewel," I say, running. He darts around the corner. When I reach it he has almost reached the next one, running against the glare like that figure cut from tin. Pa and Gillespie and Mack are some distance away, watching the barn, pink against the darkness where for the time the moonlight has been vanquished. "Catch him!" I cry; "stop him!"

When I reach the front, he is struggling with Gillespie; the one lean in underclothes, the other stark naked. They are like two figures in a Greek frieze, isolated out of all reality by the red glare. Before I can reach them he has struck Gillespie to the ground and turned and run back into the barn.

The sound of it has become quite peaceful now, like the sound of the river did. We watch through the dissolving proscenium of the doorway as Jewel runs crouching to the far end of the coffin and stoops to it. For an instant he looks up and out at us through the rain of burning hay like a portière of flaming beads, and I can see his mouth shape as he calls my name.

"Jewel!" Dewey Dell cries; "Jewel!" It seems to me that I now hear the accumulation of her voice through the last five minutes, and I hear her scuffling and struggling as pa and Mack hold her, screaming "Jewel! Jewel!" But he is no longer looking at us. We see his shoulders strain as he upends the coffin and slides it single-handed from the saw-horses. It looms unbelievably tall, hiding him: I would not have believed that Addie Bundren would have needed that much room to lie comfortable in; for another instant it stands upright while the sparks rain on it in scattering bursts as though they engendered other sparks from the contact. Then it topples forward, gaining momentum, revealing Jewel and the sparks raining on him too in engendering gusts, so that he appears to be enclosed in a thin nimbus of fire. Without stopping it overends and rears again, pauses, then crashes slowly forward and through the curtain. This time Jewel is riding upon it, clinging to it, until it crashes down and flings him forward and clear and Mack leaps forward into a thin smell of scorching meat and slaps at the widening crimson-edged holes that bloom like flowers in his undershirt.

Vardaman

∎

When I went to find where they stay at night, I saw something They said, "Where is Darl? Where did Darl go?"

They carried her back under the apple tree.

The barn was still red, but it wasn't a barn now. It was sunk down, and the red went swirling up. The barn went swirling up in little red pieces, against the sky and the stars so that the stars moved backward.

And then Cash was still awake. He turned his head from side to side, with sweat on his face.

"Do you want some more water on it, Cash?" Dewey Dell said.

Cash's leg and foot turned black. We held the lamp and looked at Cash's foot and leg where it was black.

"Your foot looks like a nigger's foot, Cash," I said.

"I reckon we'll have to bust it off," pa said.

"What in the tarnation you put it on there for," Mr Gillespie said.

"I thought it would steady it some," pa said. "I just aimed to help him."

They got the flat iron and the hammer. Dewey Dell held the lamp. They had to hit it hard. And then Cash went to sleep.

"He's asleep now," I said. "It cant hurt him while he's asleep."

It just cracked. It wouldn't come off.

"It'll take the hide, too," Mr Gillespie said. "Why in the tarnation you put it on there. Didn't none of you think to grease his leg first?"

"I just aimed to help him," pa said. "It was Darl put it on."

"Where is Darl?" they said.

"Didn't none of you have more sense than that?" Mr Gillespie said. "I'd a thought he would, anyway."

Jewel was lying on his face. His back was red. Dewey Dell put the medicine on it. The medicine was made out of butter and soot, to draw out the fire. Then his back was black.

"Does it hurt, Jewel?" I said. "Your back looks like a nigger's, Jewel," I said. Cash's foot and leg looked like a nigger's. Then they broke it off. Cash's leg bled.

"You go on back and lay down," Dewey Dell said. "You ought to be asleep."

"Where is Darl?" they said.

He is out there under the apple tree with her, lying on her. He is there so the cat wont come back. I said, "Are you going to keep the cat away, Darl?"

The moonlight dappled on him too. On her it was still, but on Darl it dappled up and down.

"You needn't to cry," I said. "Jewel got her out. You needn't to cry, Darl."

The barn is still red. It used to be redder than this. Then it went swirling, making the stars run backward without falling. It hurt my heart like the train did.

When I went to find where they stay at night, I saw something that Dewey Dell says I mustn't tell nobody

Darl

■

We have been passing the signs for sometime now: the drug stores, the clothing stores, the patent medicine and the garages and cafés, and the mile-boards diminishing, becoming more starkly reaccruent: 3 mi. 2 mi. From the crest of a hill, as we get into the wagon again, we can see the smoke low and flat, seemingly unmoving in the unwinded afternoon.

"Is that it, Darl?" Vardaman says. "Is that Jefferson?" He too has lost flesh; like ours, his face has an expression strained, dreamy, and gaunt.

"Yes," I say. He lifts his head and looks at the sky. High against it they hang in narrowing circles, like the smoke, with an outward semblance of form and purpose, but with no inference of motion, progress or retrograde. We mount the wagon again where Cash lies on the box, the jagged shards of cement cracked about his leg. The shabby mules droop rattling and clanking down the hill.

"We'll have to take him to the doctor," pa says. "I reckon it aint no way around it." The back of Jewel's shirt, where it touches him, stains slow and black with grease. Life was created in the valleys. It blew up onto the hills on the old terrors, the old lusts, the old despairs. That's why you must walk up the hills so you can ride down.

Dewey Dell sits on the seat, the newspaper package on her lap. When we reach the foot of the hill where the road flattens between close walls of trees, she begins to look about quietly from one side of the road to the other. At last she says,

"I got to stop."

Pa looks at her, his shabby profile that of anticipant and disgruntled annoyance. He does not check the team. "What for?"

"I got to go to the bushes," Dewey Dell says.

Pa does not check the team. "Cant you wait till we get to town? It aint over a mile now."

"Stop," Dewey Dell says. "I got to go to the bushes."

Pa stops in the middle of the road and we watch Dewey Dell descend, carrying the package. She does not look back.

"Why not leave your cakes here?" I say. "We'll watch them."

She descends steadily, not looking at us.

"How would she know where to go if she waited till we get to town?" Vardaman says. "Where would you go to do it in town, Dewey Dell?"

She lifts the package down and turns and disappears among the trees and undergrowth.

"Dont be no longer than you can help," pa says. "We aint got no time to waste." She does not answer. After a while we cannot hear her even. "We ought to done like Armstid and Gillespie said and sent word to town and had it dug and ready," he says.

"Why didn't you?" I say. "You could have telephoned."

"What for?" Jewel says. "Who the hell cant dig a hole in the ground?"

A car comes over the hill. It begins to sound the horn, slowing. It runs along the roadside in low gear, the outside wheels in the ditch, and passes us and goes on. Vardaman watches it until it is out of sight.

"How far is it now, Darl?" he says.

"Not far," I say.

"We ought to done it," pa says. "I just never wanted to be beholden to none except her flesh and blood."

"Who the hell cant dig a damn hole in the ground?" Jewel says.

"It aint respectful, talking that way about her grave," pa says. "You all dont know what it is. You never pure loved her, none of you." Jewel does not answer. He sits a little stiffly erect, his body arched away from his shirt. His high-colored jaw juts.

Dewey Dell returns. We watch her emerge from the bushes, carrying the package, and climb into the wagon. She now wears her Sunday dress, her beads, her shoes and stockings.

"I thought I told you to leave them clothes to home," pa says. She does not answer, does not look at us. She sets the package in the wagon and gets in. The wagon moves on.

"How many more hills now, Darl?" Vardaman says.

"Just one," I say. "The next one goes right up into town."

This hill is red sand, bordered on either hand by negro cabins; against the sky ahead the massed telephone lines run, and the clock on the courthouse lifts among the trees. In the sand the wheels whisper, as though the very earth would hush our entry. We descend as the hill commences to rise.

We follow the wagon, the whispering wheels, passing the cabins where faces come suddenly to the doors, white-eyed. We hear sudden voices, ejaculant. Jewel has been looking from side to side; now his head turns forward and I can see his ears taking on a still deeper tone of furious red. Three negroes walk beside the road ahead of us; ten feet ahead of them a white man walks. When we pass the negroes their heads turn suddenly with that expression of shock and instinctive outrage. "Great God," one says; "what they got in that wagon?"

Jewel whirls. "Son of a bitches," he says. As he does so he is abreast of the white man, who has paused. It is as though Jewel had gone blind for the moment, for it is the white man toward whom he whirls.

"Darl!" Cash says from the wagon. I grasp at Jewel. The white man has fallen back a pace, his face still slack-jawed; then his jaw tightens, claps to. Jewel leans above him, his jaw muscles gone white.

"What did you say?" he says.

"Here," I say. "He dont mean anything, mister. Jewel," I say. When I touch him he swings at the man. I grasp his arm; we struggle. Jewel has never looked at me. He is trying to free his arm. When I see the man again he has an open knife in his hand.

"Hold up, mister," I say; "I've got him. Jewel," I say.

"Thinks because he's a goddamn town fellow," Jewel says, panting, wrenching at me. "Son of a bitch," he says.

The man moves. He begins to edge around me, watching Jewel, the knife low against his flank. "Cant no man call me that," he says. Pa has got down, and Dewey Dell is holding Jewel, pushing at him. I release him and face the man.

"Wait," I say. "He dont mean nothing. He's sick; got burned in a fire last night, and he aint himself."

"Fire or no fire," the man says, "cant no man call me that."

"He thought you said something to him," I say.

"I never said nothing to him. I never see him before."

"Fore God," pa says; "fore God."

"I know," I say. "He never meant anything. He'll take it back."

"Let him take it back then."

"Put up your knife, and he will."

The man looks at me. He looks at Jewel. Jewel is quiet now.

"Put up your knife." I say.

The man shuts the knife.

"Fore God," pa says. "Fore God."

"Tell him you didn't mean anything, Jewel," I say.

"I thought he said something," Jewel says. "Just because he's——"

"Hush," I say. "Tell him you didn't mean it."

"I didn't mean it," Jewel says.

"He better not," the man says. "Calling me a——"

"Do you think he's afraid to call you that?" I say.

The man looks at me. "I never said that," he said.

"Dont think it, neither," Jewel says.

"Shut up," I say. "Come on. Drive on, pa."

The wagon moves. The man stands watching us. Jewel does not look back. "Jewel would a whipped him," Vardaman says.

We approach the crest, where the street runs, where cars go back and forth; the mules haul the wagon up and onto the crest and the street. Pa stops them. The street runs on ahead, where the square opens and the monument stands before the courthouse. We mount again while the heads turn with that expression which we know; save Jewel. He does not get on, even though the wagon has started again. "Get in, Jewel," I say. "Come on. Let's get away from here." But he does not get in. Instead he sets his foot on the turning hub of the rear wheel, one hand grasping the stanchion, and with the hub turning smoothly under his sole he lifts the other foot and squats there, staring straight ahead, motionless, lean, wooden-backed, as though carved squatting out of the lean wood.

Cash

■

It wasn't nothing else to do. It was either send him to Jackson, or have Gillespie sue us, because he knowed some way that Darl set fire to it.[1] I dont know how he knowed, but he did. Vardaman seen him do it, but he swore he never told nobody but Dewey Dell and that she told him not to tell nobody. But Gillespie knowed it. But he would a suspicioned it sooner or later. He could have done it that night just watching the way Darl acted.

And so pa said, "I reckon there aint nothing else to do," and Jewel said,

"You want to fix him now?"

"Fix him?" pa said.

"Catch him and tie him up," Jewel said. "Goddamn it, do you want to wait until he sets fire to the goddamn team and wagon?"

But there wasn't no use in that. "There aint no use in that," I said. "We can wait till she is underground." A fellow that's going to spend the rest of his life locked up, he ought to be let to have what pleasure he can have before he goes.

"I reckon he ought to be there," pa says. "God knows, it's a trial on me. Seems like it aint no end to bad luck when once it starts."

Sometimes I aint so sho who's got ere a right to say when a man is crazy and when he aint. Sometimes I think it aint none of us pure crazy and aint none of us pure sane until the balance of us talks him that-a-way. It's like it aint so much what a fellow does, but it's the way the majority of folks is looking at him when he does it.

Because Jewel is too hard on him. Of course it was Jewel's horse was traded to get her that nigh to town, and in a sense it was the value of the horse Darl tried to burn up. But I thought more than once before we crossed the river and after, how it would be God's blessing if He did take her outen our hands and get shut of her in some clean way, and it seemed to me that when Jewel worked so to get her outen the river, he was going against God in a way, and then when Darl seen that it looked like one of us would have to do something, I can almost

<hr />

1. In *The Hamlet* (1940), Faulkner presents the burning of farm buildings as frequent enough to be recognizable as its own form of crime. Such arson has a long history—in nineteenth-century England hayricks were the usual target—and in Faulkner's world it is usually carried out by a sharecropper or tenant farmer against the property of a landlord perceived as unjust. In *Faulkner and the Great Depression* (Athens, Georgia: University of Georgia Press, 2006) Ted Atkinson offers a political reading of such fires, seeing them as an act of protest by those otherwise without power. Darl has no quarrel with Gillespie, but his attempt to burn his mother's coffin can be understood as a cry against the continued if self-imposed oppression of the Bundrens's journey. See also Faulkner's 1939 story "Barn-Burning." *Jackson*: Here not the state capital *per se* but the Mississippi State Insane Hospital, which was located there. In 1927 it held about 2,250 patients in a facility built for 1,600. See pp. 227–31 of this Norton Critical Edition.

believe he done right in a way. But I dont reckon nothing excuses setting fire to a man's barn and endangering his stock and destroying his property. That's how I reckon a man is crazy. That's how he cant see eye to eye with other folks. And I reckon they aint nothing else to do with him but what the most folks say is right.

But it's a shame, in a way. Folks seem to get away from the olden right teaching that says to drive the nails down and trim the edges well always like it was for your own use and comfort you were making it. It's like some folks has the smooth, pretty boards to build a courthouse with and others dont have no more than rough lumber fitten to build a chicken coop. But it's better to build a tight chicken coop than a shoddy courthouse, and when they both build shoddy or build well, neither because it's one or tother is going to make a man feel the better nor the worse.

So we went up the street, toward the square, and he said, "We better take Cash to the doctor first. We can leave him there and come back for him." That's it. It's because me and him was born close together, and it nigh ten years before Jewel and Dewey Dell and Vardaman begun to come along. I feel kin to them, all right, but I dont know. And me being the oldest, and thinking already the very thing that he done: I dont know.

Pa was looking at me, then at him, mumbling his mouth.

"Go on," I said. "We'll get it done first."

"She would want us all there," pa says.

"Let's take Cash to the doctor first," Darl said. "She'll wait. She's already waited nine days."

"You all dont know," pa says. "The somebody you was young with and you growed old in her and she growed old in you, seeing the old coming on and it was the one somebody you could hear say it dont matter and know it was the truth outen the hard world and all a man's grief and trials. You all dont know."

"We got the digging to do, too," I said.

"Armstid and Gillespie both told you to send word ahead," Darl said. "Dont you want to go to Peabody's now, Cash?"

"Go on," I said. "It feels right easy now. It's best to get things done in the right place."

"If it was just dug," pa says. "We forgot our spade, too."

"Yes," Darl said. "I'll go to the hardware store. We'll have to buy one."

"It'll cost money," pa says.

"Do you begrudge her it?" Darl says.

"Go on and get a spade," Jewel said. "Here. Give me the money."

But pa didn't stop. "I reckon we can get a spade," he said. "I reckon there are Christians here." So Darl set still and we went on, with Jewel squatting on the tail-gate, watching the back of Darl's head. He

looked like one of these bull dogs, one of these dogs that dont bark
none, squatting against the rope, watching the thing he was waiting
to jump at.

He set that way all the time we was in front of Mrs Bundren's
house, hearing the music, watching the back of Darl's head with them
hard white eyes of hisn.

The music was playing in the house. It was one of them graphophones. It was natural as a music-band.

"Do you want to go to Peabody's?" Darl said. "They can wait here
and tell pa, and I'll drive you to Peabody's and come back for them."

"No," I said. It was better to get her underground, now we was
this close, just waiting until pa borrowed the shovel. He drove along
the street until we could hear the music.

"Maybe they got one here," he said. He pulled up at Mrs Bundren's. It was like he knowed. Sometimes I think that if a working
man could see work as far ahead as a lazy man can see laziness. So
he stopped there like he knowed, before that little new house, where
the music was. We waited there, hearing it. I believe I could have
dickered Suratt down to five dollars on that one of his. It's a comfortable thing, music is. "Maybe they got one here," pa says.

"You want Jewel to go," Darl says, "or do you reckon I better?"

"I reckon I better," pa says. He got down and went up the path
and around the house to the back. The music stopped, then it started
again.

"He'll get it, too," Darl said.

"Ay," I said. It was just like he knowed, like he could see through
the walls and into the next ten minutes.

Only it was more than ten minutes. The music stopped and never
commenced again for a good spell, where her and pa was talking at
the back. We waited in the wagon.

"You let me take you back to Peabody's," Darl said.

"No," I said. "We'll get her underground."

"If he ever gets back," Jewel said. He begun to cuss. He started to
get down from the wagon. "I'm going," he said.

Then we saw pa coming back. He had two spades, coming around
the house. He laid them in the wagon and got in and we went on.
The music never started again. Pa was looking back at the house. He
kind of lifted his hand a little and I saw the shade pulled back a little
at the window and her face in it.

But the curiousest thing was Dewey Dell. It surprised me. I see all
the while how folks could say he was queer, but that was the very
reason couldn't nobody hold it personal. It was like he was outside of
it too, same as you, and getting mad at it would be kind of like getting mad at a mud-puddle that splashed you when you stepped in it.
And then I always kind of had a idea that him and Dewey Dell kind

of knowed things betwixt them. If I'd a said it was ere a one of us she liked better than ere a other, I'd a said it was Darl. But when we got it filled and covered and drove out the gate and turned into the lane where them fellows was waiting, when they come out and come on him and he jerked back, it was Dewey Dell that was on him before even Jewel could get at him. And then I believed I knowed how Gillespie knowed about how his barn taken fire.

She hadn't said a word, hadn't even looked at him, but when them fellows told him what they wanted and that they had come to get him and he throwed back, she jumped on him like a wild cat so that one of the fellows had to quit and hold her and her scratching and clawing at him like a wild cat, while the other one and pa and Jewel throwed Darl down and held him lying on his back, looking up at me.

"I thought you would have told me," he said. "I never thought you wouldn't have."

"Darl," I said. But he fought again, him and Jewel and the fellow, and the other one holding Dewey Dell and Vardaman yelling and Jewel saying,

"Kill him. Kill the son of a bitch."

It was bad so. It was bad. A fellow cant get away from a shoddy job. He cant do it. I tried to tell him, but he just said, "I thought you'd a told me. It's not that I," he said, then he begun to laugh. The other fellow pulled Jewel off of him and he sat there on the ground, laughing.

I tried to tell him. If I could have just moved, even set up. But I tried to tell him and he quit laughing, looking up at me.

"Do you want me to go?" he said.

"It'll be better for you," I said. "Down there it'll be quiet, with none of the bothering and such. It'll be better for you, Darl," I said.

"Better," he said. He begun to laugh again. "Better," he said. He couldn't hardly say it for laughing. He sat on the ground and us watching him, laughing and laughing. It was bad. It was bad so. I be durn if I could see anything to laugh at. Because there just aint nothing justifies the deliberate destruction of what a man has built with his own sweat and stored the fruit of his sweat into.

But I aint so sho that ere a man has the right to say what is crazy and what aint. It's like there was a fellow in every man that's done a-past the sanity or the insanity, that watches the sane and the insane doings of that man with the same horror and the same astonishment.

Peabody

■

I said, "I reckon a man in a tight might let Bill Varner patch him up like a damn mule, but I be damned if the man that'd let Anse Bundren treat him with raw cement aint got more spare legs than I have."

"They just aimed to ease hit some," he said.

"Aimed, hell," I said. "What in hell did Armstid mean by even letting them put you on that wagon again?"

"Hit was gittin right noticeable," he said. "We never had time to wait." I just looked at him. "Hit never bothered me none," he said.

"Dont you lie there and try to tell me you rode six days on a wagon without springs, with a broken leg and it never bothered you."

"It never bothered me much," he said.

"You mean, it never bothered Anse much," I said. "No more than it bothered him to throw that poor devil down in the public street and handcuff him like a damn murderer. Dont tell me. And dont tell me it aint going to bother you to lose sixty-odd square inches of skin to get that concrete off. And dont tell me it aint going to bother you to have to limp around on one short leg for the balance of your life—if you walk at all again. Concrete," I said. "God Almighty, why didn't Anse carry you to the nearest sawmill and stick your leg in the saw? That would have cured it. Then you all could have stuck his head into the saw and cured a whole family. . . . . . . Where is Anse, anyway? What's he up to now?"

"He's taking back them spades he borrowed," he said.

"That's right," I said. "Of course he'd have to borrow a spade to bury his wife with. Unless he could borrow a hole in the ground. Too bad you all didn't put him in it too. . . . . . . Does that hurt?"

"Not to speak of," he said, and the sweat big as marbles running down his face and his face about the color of blotting paper.

"Course not," I said. "About next summer you can hobble around fine on this leg. Then it wont bother you, not to speak of. . . . . . . If you had anything you could call luck, you might say it was lucky this is the same leg you broke before," I said.

"Hit's what paw says," he said.

MacGowan

■

It happened I am back of the prescription case, pouring up some chocolate sauce, when Jody comes back and says, "Say, Skeet, there's a woman up front that wants to see the doctor and when I said What doctor you want to see, she said she wants to see the doctor that works here and when I said There aint any doctor works here, she just stood there, looking back this way."

"What kind of a woman is it?" I says. "Tell her to go upstairs to Alford's office."

"Country woman," he says.

"Send her to the courthouse," I says. "Tell her all the doctors have gone to Memphis to a Barbers' Convention."

"All right," he says, going away. "She looks pretty good for a country girl," he says.

"Wait," I says. He waited and I went and peeped through the crack. But I couldn't tell nothing except she had a good leg against the light. "Is she young, you say?" I says.

"She looks like a pretty hot mamma, for a country girl," he says.

"Take this," I says, giving him the chocolate. I took off my apron and went up there. She looked pretty good. One of them black eyed ones that look like she'd as soon put a knife in you as not if you two-timed her. She looked pretty good. There wasn't nobody else in the store; it was dinner time.

"What can I do for you?" I says.

"Are you the doctor?" she says.

"Sure," I says. She quit looking at me and was kind of looking around.

"Can we go back yonder?" she says.

It was just a quarter past twelve, but I went and told Jody to kind of watch out and whistle if the old man come in sight, because he never got back before one.

"You better lay off of that," Jody says. "He'll fire your stern out of here so quick you cant wink."

"He dont never get back before one," I says. "You can see him go into the postoffice. You keep your eye peeled, now, and give me a whistle."

"What you going to do?" he says.

"You keep your eye out. I'll tell you later."

"Aint you going to give me no seconds on it?" he says.

"What the hell do you think this is?" I says; "a stud-farm? You watch out for him. I'm going into conference."

So I go on to the back. I stopped at the glass and smoothed my hair, then I went behind the prescription case, where she was waiting. She is looking at the medicine cabinet, then she looks at me.

"Now, madam," I says; "what is your trouble?"

"It's the female trouble," she says, watching me. "I got the money," she says.

"Ah," I says. "Have you got female troubles or do you want female troubles? If so, you come to the right doctor." Them country people. Half the time they dont know what they want, and the balance of the time they cant tell it to you. The clock said twenty past twelve.

"No," she says.

"No which?" I says.

"I aint had it," she says. "That's it." She looked at me. "I got the money," she says.

So I knew what she was talking about.

"Oh," I says. "You got something in your belly you wish you didn't have." She looks at me. "You wish you had a little more or a little less, huh?"

"I got the money," she says. "He said I could git something at the drugstore for hit."

"Who said so?" I says.

"He did," she says, looking at me.

"You dont want to call no names," I says. "The one that put the acorn in your belly? He the one that told you?" She dont say nothing. "You aint married, are you?" I says. I never saw no ring. But like as not, they aint heard yet out there that they use rings.

"I got the money," she says. She showed it to me, tied up in her handkerchief: a ten spot.

"I'll swear you have," I says. "He give it to you?"

"Yes," she says.

"Which one?" I says. She looks at me. "Which one of them give it to you?"

"It aint but one," she says. She looks at me.

"Go on," I says. She dont say nothing. The trouble about the cellar is, it aint but one way out and that's back up the inside stairs. The clock says twenty-five to one. "A pretty girl like you," I says.

She looks at me. She begins to tie the money back up in the handkerchief. "Excuse me a minute," I says. I go around the prescription case. "Did you hear about that fellow sprained his ear?" I says. "After that he couldn't even hear a belch."

"You better get her out from back there before the old man comes," Jody says.

"If you'll stay up there in front where he pays you to stay, he wont catch nobody but me," I says.

He goes on, slow, toward the front. "What you doing to her, Skeet?" he says.

"I cant tell you," I says. "It wouldn't be ethical. You go on up there and watch."

"Say, Skeet," he says.

"Ah, go on," I says. "I aint doing nothing but filling a prescription."

"He may not do nothing about that woman back there, but if he finds you monkeying with that prescription case, he'll kick your stern clean down them cellar stairs."

"My stern has been kicked by bigger bastards than him," I says. "Go back and watch out for him, now."

So I come back. The clock said fifteen to one. She is tying the money in the handkerchief. "You aint the doctor," she says.

"Sure I am," I says. She watches me. "Is it because I look too young, or am I too handsome?" I says. "We used to have a bunch of old water-jointed doctors here," I says; "Jefferson used to be a kind of Old Doctors' Home for them. But business started falling off and folks stayed so well until one day they found out that the women wouldn't never get sick at all. So they run all the old doctors out and got us young good-looking ones that the women would like and then the women begun to get sick again and so business picked up. They're doing that all over the country. Hadn't you heard about it? Maybe it's because you aint never needed a doctor."

"I need one now," she says.

"And you come to the right one," I says. "I already told you that."

"Have you got something for it?" she says. "I got the money."

"Well," I says, "of course a doctor has to learn all sorts of things while he's learning to roll calomel,[1] he cant help himself. But I dont know about your trouble."

"He told me I could get something. He told me I could get it at the drugstore."

"Did he tell you the name of it?" I says. "You better go back and ask him."

She quit looking at me, kind of turning the handkerchief in her hands. "I got to do something," she says.

"How bad do you want to do something?" I says. She looks at me. "Of course, a doctor learns all sorts of things folks dont think he knows. But he aint supposed to tell all he knows. It's against the law."

---

1. Mercurous chloride. Once used, in pill form, as an all-purpose purgative and disinfectant, and in the treatment of syphilis. Frequent cause of mercury poisoning. Fading from medical practice at the time this novel is set, and used here as a synonym for rolling pills of all kinds.

Up front Jody says, "Skeet."

"Excuse me a minute," I says. I went up front. "Do you see him?" I says.

"Aint you done yet?" he says. "Maybe you better come up here and watch and let me do that consulting."

"Maybe you'll lay a egg," I says. I come back. She is looking at me. "Of course you realise that I could be put in the penitentiary for doing what you want," I says. "I would lose my license and then I'd have to go to work. You realise that?"

"I aint got but ten dollars," she says. "I could bring the rest next month, maybe."

"Pooh," I says, "ten dollars? You see, I cant put no price on my knowledge and skill. Certainly not for no little paltry sawbuck."

She looks at me. She dont even blink. "What you want, then?"

The clock said four to one. So I decided I better get her out. "You guess three times and then I'll show you," I says.

She dont even blink her eyes. "I got to do something," she says. She looks behind her and around, then she looks toward the front. "Gimme the medicine first," she says.

"You mean, you're ready to right now?" I says. "Here?"

"Gimme the medicine first," she says.

So I took a graduated glass and kind of turned my back to her and picked out a bottle that looked all right, because a man that would keep poison setting around in a unlabelled bottle ought to be in jail, anyway. It smelled like turpentine. I poured some into the glass and give it to her. She smelled it, looking at me across the glass.

"Hit smells like turpentine," she says.

"Sure," I says. "That's just the beginning of the treatment. You come back at ten o'clock tonight and I'll give you the rest of it and perform the operation."

"Operation?" she says.

"It wont hurt you. You've had the same operation before. Ever hear about the hair of the dog?"

She looks at me. "Will it work?" she says.

"Sure it'll work. If you come back and get it."

So she drunk whatever it was without batting a eye, and went out. I went up front.

"Didn't you get it?" Jody says.

"Get what?" I says.

"Ah, come on," he says. "I aint going to try to beat your time."

"Oh, her," I says. "She just wanted a little medicine. She's got a bad case of dysentery and she's a little ashamed about mentioning it with a stranger there."

It was my night, anyway, so I helped the old bastard check up and I got his hat on him and got him out of the store by eight-thirty. I went as far as the corner with him and watched him until he passed under two street lamps and went on out of sight. Then I came back to the store and waited until nine-thirty and turned out the front lights and locked the door and left just one light burning at the back, and I went back and put some talcum powder into six capsules and kind of cleared up the cellar and then I was all ready.

She come in just at ten, before the clock had done striking. I let her in and she come in, walking fast. I looked out the door, but there wasn't nobody but a boy in overalls sitting on the curb. "You want something?" I says. He never said nothing, just looking at me. I locked the door and turned off the light and went on back. She was waiting. She didn't look at me now.

"Where is it?" she said.

I gave her the box of capsules. She held the box in her hand, looking at the capsules.

"Are you sure it'll work?" she says.

"Sure," I says. "When you take the rest of the treatment."

"Where do I take it?" she says.

"Down in the cellar," I says.

Vardaman

∎

Now it is wider and lighter, but the stores are dark because they have all gone home. The stores are dark, but the lights pass on the windows when we pass. The lights are in the trees around the courthouse. They roost in the trees, but the courthouse is dark. The clock on it looks four ways, because it is not dark. The moon is not dark too. Not very dark. *Darl he went to Jackson is my brother Darl is my brother* Only it was over that way, shining on the track.

"Let's go that way, Dewey Dell," I say.

"What for?" Dewey Dell says. The track went shining around the window, it red on the track. But she said he would not sell it to the town boys. "But it will be there Christmas," Dewey Dell says. "You'll have to wait till then, when he brings it back."

Darl went to Jackson. Lots of people didn't go to Jackson. Darl is my brother. My brother is going to Jackson

While we walk the lights go around, roosting in the trees. On all sides it is the same. They go around the courthouse and then you cannot see them. But you can see them in the black windows beyond. They have all gone home to bed except me and Dewey Dell.

Going on the train to Jackson. My brother

There is a light in the store, far back. In the window are two big glasses of soda water, red and green. Two men could not drink them. Two mules could not. Two cows could not. *Darl*

A man comes to the door. He looks at Dewey Dell.

"You wait out here," Dewey Dell says.

"Why cant I come in?" I say. "I want to come in, too."

"You wait out here," she says.

"All right," I say.

Dewey Dell goes in.

Darl is my brother. Darl went crazy

The walk is harder than sitting on the ground. He is in the open door. He looks at me. "You want something?" he says. His head is slick. Jewel's head is slick sometimes. Cash's head is not slick. *Darl he went to Jackson my brother Darl* In the street he ate a banana. *Wouldn't you rather have bananas? Dewey Dell said. You wait till Christmas. It'll be there then. Then you can see it. So we are going to have some bananas. We are going to have a bag full, me and Dewey Dell.* He locks the door. Dewey Dell is inside. Then the light winks out.

He went to Jackson. He went crazy and went to Jackson both. Lots of people didn't go crazy. Pa and Cash and Jewel and Dewey Dell and me didn't go crazy. We never did go crazy. We didn't go to Jackson either. Darl

I hear the cow a long time, clopping   on the street. Then she comes into the square. She goes across the square, her head down   clopping   . She lows. There was nothing in the square before she lowed, but it wasn't empty. Now it is empty after she lowed. She goes on,   clopping   . She lows. *My brother is Darl. He went to Jackson on the train. He didn't go on the train to go crazy. He went crazy in our wagon. Darl* She has been in there a long time. And the cow is gone too. A long time. She has been in there longer than the cow was. But not as long as empty. *Darl is my brother. My brother Darl*

Dewey Dell comes out. She looks at me.

"Let's go around that way now," I say.

She looks at me. "It aint going to work," she says. "That son of a bitch."

"What aint going to work, Dewey Dell?"

"I just know it wont," she says. She is not looking at anything. "I just know it."

"Let's go that way," I say.

"We got to go back to the hotel. It's late. We got to slip back in."

"Cant we go by and see, anyway?"

"Hadn't you rather have bananas? Hadn't you rather?"

"All right." *My brother he went crazy and he went to Jackson too. Jackson is further away than crazy*

"It wont work," Dewey Dell says. "I just know it wont."

"What wont work?" I say. *He had to get on the train to go to Jackson. I have not been on the train, but Darl has been on the train. Darl. Darl is my brother. Darl. Darl*

146

Darl

■

Darl has gone to Jackson. They put him on the train, laughing, down the long car laughing, the heads turning like the heads of owls when he passed. "What are you laughing at?" I said.

"Yes yes yes yes yes."

Two men put him on the train. They wore mismatched coats, bulging behind over their right hip pockets. Their necks were shaved to a hairline, as though the recent and simultaneous barbers had had a chalk-line like Cash's. "Is it the pistols you're laughing at?" I said. "Why do you laugh?" I said. "Is it because you hate the sound of laughing?"

They pulled two seats together so Darl could sit by the window to laugh. One of them sat beside him, the other sat on the seat facing him, riding backward. One of them had to ride backward because the state's money has a face to each backside and a backside to each face, and they are riding on the state's money which is incest. A nickel has a woman on one side and a buffalo on the other; two faces and no back. I dont know what that is. Darl had a little spy-glass he got in France at the war.[1] In it it had a woman and a pig with two backs and no face.[2] I know what that is. "Is that why you are laughing, Darl?"

"Yes yes yes yes yes."

The wagon stands on the square, hitched, the mules motionless, the reins wrapped about the seat-spring, the back of the wagon toward the courthouse. It looks no different from a hundred other wagons there; Jewel standing beside it and looking up the street like any other man in town that day, yet there is something different, distinctive. There is about it that unmistakable air of definite and imminent departure that trains have, perhaps due to the fact that Dewey Dell and Vardaman on the seat and Cash on a pallet in the wagon bed are eating bananas from a paper bag. "Is that why you are laughing, Darl?"

Darl is our brother, our brother Darl. Our brother Darl in a cage in Jackson where, his grimed hands lying light in the quiet interstices, looking out he foams.

"Yes yes yes yes yes yes yes yes."

1. I.e., during World War I.
2. *Othello* 1.1.112–13, Iago to Brabantio: "I am one, sir, that comes to tell you your daughter and the Moor are now making the beast with two backs."

Dewey Dell

■

When he saw the money I said, "It's not my money, it doesn't belong to me."

"Whose is it, then?"

"It's Cora Tull's money. It's Mrs Tull's. I sold the cakes for it."

"Ten dollars for two cakes?"

"Dont you touch it. It's not mine."

"You never had them cakes. It's a lie. It was them Sunday clothes you had in that package."

"Dont you touch it! If you take it you are a thief."

"My own daughter accuses me of being a thief. My own daughter."

"Pa. Pa."

"I have fed you and sheltered you. I give you love and care, yet my own daughter, the daughter of my dead wife, calls me a thief over her mother's grave."

"It's not mine, I tell you. If it was, God knows you could have it."

"Where did you get ten dollars?"

"Pa. Pa."

"You wont tell me. Did you come by it so shameful you dare not?"

"It's not mine, I tell you. Cant you understand it's not mine?"

"It's not like I wouldn't pay it back. But she calls her own father a thief."

"I cant, I tell you. I tell you it's not my money. God knows you could have it."

"I wouldn't take it. My own born daughter that has et my food for seventeen years, begrudges me the loan of ten dollars."

"It's not mine, I cant."

"Whose is it, then?"

"It was give to me. To buy something with."

"To buy what with?"

"Pa. Pa."

"It's just a loan. God knows, I hate for my blooden children to reproach me. But I give them what was mine without stint. Cheerful I give them, without stint. And now they deny me. Addie. It was lucky for you you died, Addie."

"Pa. Pa."

"God knows it is."

He took the money and went out.

Cash

■

So when we stopped there to borrow the shovels we heard the graphophone playing in the house, and so when we got done with the shovels pa says, "I reckon I better take them back."

So we went back to the house. "We better take Cash on to Peabody's," Jewel said.

"It wont take but a minute," pa said. He got down from the wagon. The music was not playing now.

"Let Vardaman do it," Jewel said. "He can do it in half the time you can. Or here, you let me——"

"I reckon I better do it," pa says. "Long as it was me that borrowed them."

So we set in the wagon, but the music wasn't playing now. I reckon it's a good thing we aint got ere a one of them. I reckon I wouldn't never get no work done a-tall for listening to it. I dont know if a little music aint about the nicest thing a fellow can have. Seems like when he comes in tired of a night, it aint nothing could rest him like having a little music played and him resting. I have seen them that shuts up like a hand-grip, with a handle and all, so a fellow can carry it with him wherever he wants.

"What you reckon he's doing?" Jewel says. "I could a toted them shovels back and forth ten times by now."

"Let him take his time," I said. "He aint as spry as you, remember."

"Why didn't he let me take them back, then? We got to get your leg fixed up so we can start home tomorrow."

"We got plenty of time," I said. "I wonder what them machines costs on the installment."

"Installment of what?" Jewel said. "What you got to buy it with?"

"A fellow cant tell," I said. "I could a bought that one from Suratt for five dollars, I believe."

And so pa come back and we went to Peabody's. While we was there pa said he was going to the barbershop and get a shave. And so that night he said he had some business to tend to, kind of looking away from us while he said it, with his hair combed wet and slick and smelling sweet with perfume, but I said leave him be; I wouldn't mind hearing a little more of that music myself.

And so next morning he was gone again, then he come back and told us to get hitched up and ready to take out and he would meet us and when they was gone he said,

"I dont reckon you got no more money."

"Peabody just give me enough to pay the hotel with," I said. "We dont need nothing else, do we?"

"No," pa said; "no. We dont need nothing." He stood there, not looking at me.

"If it is something we got to have, I reckon maybe Peabody," I said.

"No," he said; "it aint nothing else. You all wait for me at the corner."

So Jewel got the team and come for me and they fixed me a pallet in the wagon and we drove across the square to the corner where pa said, and we was waiting there in the wagon, with Dewey Dell and Vardaman eating bananas, when we see them coming up the street. Pa was coming along with that kind of daresome and hangdog look all at once like when he has been up to something he knows ma aint going to like, carrying a grip in his hand, and Jewel says,

"Who's that?"

Then we see it wasn't the grip that made him look different; it was his face, and Jewel says, "He got them teeth."

It was a fact. It made him look a foot taller, kind of holding his head up, hangdog and proud too, and then we see her behind him, carrying the other grip—a kind of duck-shaped woman all dressed up, with them kind of hardlooking pop eyes like she was daring ere a man to say nothing. And there we set watching them, with Dewey Dell's and Vardaman's mouth half open and half-et bananas in their hands and her coming around from behind pa, looking at us like she dared ere a man. And then I see that the grip she was carrying was one of them little graphophones. It was for a fact, all shut up as pretty as a picture, and everytime a new record would come from the mail order and us setting in the house in the winter, listening to it, I would think what a shame Darl couldn't be to enjoy it too. But it is better so for him. This world is not his world; this life his life.

"It's Cash and Jewel and Vardaman and Dewey Dell," pa says, kind of hangdog and proud too, with his teeth and all, even if he wouldn't look at us. "Meet Mrs Bundren," he says.

BACKGROUNDS AND CONTEXTS

Contemporary Reception

The myth about Faulkner's reception holds that in America his best work was either unnoticed or attacked on its initial appearance; and like most myths that tale does contain a fragment of the truth. Faulkner liked titles with a pedigree. *As I Lay Dying* came out of Homer, and he got *The Sound and the Fury* from *Macbeth*'s most famous soliloquy. That, however, was an invitation to trouble, and one reviewer ended his account of that novel by lifting a few words from the same speech: "signifying nothing."[1] Faulkner's prose was difficult and his matter obscure—and a good thing too, some might have said, given the freight of rape, incest, and miscegenation that his books so often seemed to carry. So much for the myth. The full story is more complicated, and more interesting. The reviews of *As I Lay Dying* were strong, and even those critics who didn't like it recognized the individuality of both this novel and Faulkner's quickly growing body of work as a whole. Some readers connected his books to the varied forms of modernist experimentation, and others linked it to different strands in the fiction of the American South. Yet they all saw his work as utterly distinctive. It is worth noting, too, that they were not baffled by the novel's formal complications. Academic criticism would later worry over the book's difficulties—its fifteen narrators, its voice from beyond the grave, and above all its characters' use of a diction they could not realistically command. Its reviewers accepted all that; they knew what they were reading.

Not that those reviews meant sales—certainly not on the scale of Hemingway or Fitzgerald. *As I Lay Dying* had a print run of around 2,500 copies, and it went back to press only once, in 1933. Faulkner never again had to take a job remotely like his position in the power plant, but as the 1930s wore on he did need to find something more lucrative than his novels; not least because he had assumed responsibility for much of his extended family, including a widowed sister-in-law and her child. Some of the money came from Hollywood; he got little in the way of screen credit but was a fast and skillful doctor to other writers' scripts. And some of it came from magazine stories, where his name carried prestige even if he often had to simplify his narratives. Three of his novels at least are made up of linked stories, stories revised into grandeur from what he himself called potboilers: *The Unvanquished*, *The Hamlet*, and *Go Down, Moses*.

---

1. Winfield Townley Scott, *Providence Journal*, 20 October 1929.

One mark of that prestige—indeed of fame—is the fact that the 1939 *Wild Palms* put him on the cover of *Time*. Still, by the mid-1940s, Faulkner had entered a difficult period, and one which now looks responsible for that myth. He had set a frantic pace throughout the first fifteen years of his career, but after *Go Down, Moses* he seemed to fall silent. Some of that silence was related to alchohol. Some grew out of his need for a Hollywood paycheck, and in 1946 his name did appear on the great Howard Hawks film of Raymond Chandler's *The Big Sleep*. But no new book put him before the public, and the paperback industry had not yet developed to the point of keeping a writer's backlist on bookstore shelves. By 1946 all of Faulkner's work, with the exception of the Modern Library edition of *Sanctuary*, had fallen out of print. Then things changed. In that year Malcolm Cowley's *Portable Faulkner* gave readers a way to start upon what seemed a forbidding *oeuvre*, tracing a consistent set of themes and concerns through the Yoknapatawpha country as a whole. At the same time the Modern Library republished *The Sound and the Fury* and *As I Lay Dying* in a single volume. Faulkner's years in the wilderness were over. He finished a new book, *Intruder in the Dust*. A novel about race relations cast in the form of a mystery, it appeared in 1948 and was immediately filmed. And in 1950 the publication of his *Collected Stories* coincided with his receipt of the Nobel Prize.

A second part of the myth about Faulkner's reception holds that his reputation in France was responsible for that prize. Certainly it helped, and Jean-Paul Sartre, whose 1939 essay on *The Sound and the Fury* remains essential, was only one of the important French writers to support him.[2] What seems more significant today, however, is the fact that French critics were quick to find the proper terms of comparison. The American reviews of *As I Lay Dying* linked Faulkner to such contemporaries as Theodore Dreiser, Sherwood Anderson, Thomas Wolfe, and, inevitably, to Hemingway. Southern newspapers also drew connections between Faulkner's work and that of other writers from the region, like the best-selling Erskine Caldwell or the now-forgotten T. S. Stribling. Some accounts compared his frenzied lyricism to that of the Elizabethans, a comparison represented in this Norton Critical Edition by the reviews of Henry Nash Smith and Edwin Muir. What French critics supplied was a sense of the world stage. So in 1938 Edmond Jaloux suggested that Faulkner belonged in the company of Franz Kafka and Virginia Woolf,[3] and in his 1934 introduction to the French translation of *As I Lay Dying*, appearing here in English for the first time, the poet Valery Larbaud defined what has since become a critical commonplace. He saw the novel as a piece of exotica and yet nevertheless found something Homeric in the Bundrens' journey.

2. Sartre's essay first appeared in *La Nouvelle revue francaise*, LII (June 1939), and in English can most readily be found as "On *The Sound and the Fury*: Time in the Work of Faulkner" in the Norton Critical Edition of that novel, ed. David Minter, 2nd ed. (New York: Norton and Company, 1994), pp. 265–71.
3. Edmond Jaloux, *Les Nouvelles litteraires*, 17 September 1938.

MARGARET CHENEY DAWSON

Beside Addie's Coffin†

Given the names: Darl, Jewel, Vardaman, Cash, Dewey Dell and
Anse, you might think you were confronted with a comedy of the
Herman-Sherman-and-Vermin type. On the contrary, these are the
four sons, daughter and husband of a dying woman, Addie Bundren.
Outside her window, Cash fashions her coffin. The neighbors come
to see her, they sit like buzzards about her and talk. Presently Addie
dies. Cash works all night in the pouring rain to finish her coffin.
Then they load her onto the wagon and start for Jefferson to bury
her with her folks. The rains have washed away the bridges, so they
must try the ford. The wagon overturns, the mules are drowned, Cash
breaks a leg. But Jewel rescues the coffin. They stop off a night and
buy another team. All this takes time. Addie begins to smell. Buzzards
sit on the coffin, when they can get at it, but most of the time they
cannot because Cash—his leg set in cement—is lying on it. Little
Vardaman is half crazy, Darl also. Darl, in fact, sets fire to a barn
where the coffin is left one night. Jewel drags it out. Whenever possible Dewey Dell sneaks off to drug stores asking for something to
cure her "woman's trouble," by which she means that she is going to
have a child and is not married. But at last they reach Jefferson, bury
the rotting corpse, send Darl off to an asylum.

This meaty tale comes to us through the consciousness of first one
and then another of the characters. The method Mr. Faulkner used
in his last novel, *The Sound and the Fury*, is here greatly modified,
so that though something of that extraordinary madness hangs like a
red mist over it, the lines of demarcation are mercifully clear. This is
a great concession and a boon to people who are ready to weep with
exhaustion from the effort to interpret and absorb what might be
called a sort of photographic mysticism. But even so it cannot be
said that for such readers *As I Lay Dying* will prove much of a picnic.
Parts of it are written with that tense, defiant obscureness, the self-
sufficient dislocation of thought which withdraws itself from facile
understanding; and other passages, clear in themselves, are absolutely
unhinged from the point of view of the character whose mind they
expose and whose impressionistic portrait they seem to contradict.
For instance, what are we to think of a small boy, farm-bred, whose
reflections come to light as follows: "It is as though the dark were
resolving him [the horse] out of his integrity into an unrelated scattering of components—snuffings and stampings; smells of cooling

† From *New York Herald Tribune Books* (Oct. 5, 1930): 6.

flesh and ammoniac hair; an illusion of a co-ordinated whole of splotched hide and strong bones within which, detached and secret and familiar, an *is* different from my *is*."

By perfecting and giving literary beauty to the half-formed images that floated through young Vardaman's brain, the author alters a whole contour. How shall we fasten this onto the child whose mind in the next chapter runs on bananas and toy trains and city boys? In such instances the method seems to miscarry and the reader's main reaction is likely to be exasperation. But in other cases, such as the chapter wherein the dead woman speaks, it builds the terrifying, mysterious and intimate picture of a soul as nothing else could. And the same hot, subterranean power carries over into his objective descriptions of Jewel catching the horse "enclosed by a glittering maze of hooves as by an illusion of wings," of the wagon overturning in midstream and the drowned mules whose "round bodies float and rub quietly together in the black water within the bend," of the Bundren family squatting in a wayside barn around the foul-smelling coffin, of Anse, "hangdog and proud too" with his new false teeth. The fecundity of an imagination like this is amazing, and the ingenuity, too, with which it skips from one sphere of action to another. One wonders what would happen if it were compressed into an even sterner form if Mr. Faulkner were to experiment with tradition? Something in the way his strength mounts when he externalizes his subject matter suggests that it would be very exciting. But surely, whatever the next move is, he will not lack for audience any one who had followed his work thus far.

JULIA K. W. BAKER

Literature and Less†

Most of the men and women of promise who have contributed to the brilliance of recent American literature have shown an unfortunate tendency, after a splendid beginning, to go backwards or to stand still. Their promissory notes have not matured. Ernest Hemingway[1] has not advanced from the powerful sketches of *In Our Time*, though *A Farewell to Arms* was an admirable novel. What is true of Mr. Hemingway is true of most of his contemporary and of their immediate elders in American literature. Few of them have shown any true development. William Faulkner is a noteworthy exception. He

---

† From New Orleans *Times-Picayune* (Oct. 26, 1930): 33.
1. Ernest Hemingway (1899–1961), author of *In Our Time* (1925) and *A Farewell to Arms* (1929). Recipient of the Nobel Prize in 1954.

has developed steadily and impressively and has become in a very few years an important figure in contemporary fiction. On the face of the papers, he may become the most important.

* * *

Mr. Faulkner's new novel, *As I Lay Dying*, is a worthy companion piece to *The Sound and the Fury.* It lacks the intensity and driving power that make the latter one of the most remarkable of American novels, but it has an integrity of conception and firmness of handling that make it a distinctive and noteworthy work. It fulfills the promise of *Soldiers' Pay.*[2] It represents, in construction and technique, an advance beyond *The Sound and the Fury.* Mr. Faulkner continues to develop toward simplicity and power.

The Sound and the Fury dealt with the tragedy of the disintegration of an aristocratic family. *As I Lay Dying* deals with the tragedy of death among white trash. The tragedy of character is deeper than the tragedy of death, for death is a commonplace, whether among white trash or cavaliers. It stands to reason that *The Sound and the Fury* with its strange reverberations of madness should be a more striking novel than *As I Lay Dying* in which the action is sordidly matter-of-fact.

As I Lay Dying is a horrible book. It will scandalize the squeamish. But it is an admirable book, one to delight those who respect life well interpreted in fine fiction without attempting to dictate what subjects an author shall choose.

Addie Bundren lies dying. Outside the window her son Cash, an excellent carpenter, is making her coffin. She passes on every board with an appraising eye. Addie Bundren does not care to be buried with the Bundrens. She has made Anse, her husband, promise to bury her among her own folks in Jefferson community 40 miles away. When she is dead, they must wait three days for the wagon, which two of the sons have driven to town and wrecked. It begins raining. When finally they can start the trip to Jefferson the roads are quagmires, but they go, a bedraggled funeral cart on a dismal errand: Addie in the box, and accompanying her behind the two doomed mules, Anse and the children, Cash, the eldest; Darl, who cracks under the strain; Jewel, the highstrung son gotten in adultery, riding his blooded horse; Dewey Dell, the daughter who has been seduced and is in a desperate way, and Vardaman, the smallest boy in whose mind death has become a confused material symbol. The story is unrolled through the eyes of these actors and a few observers. The narrative, always in the first person, switches back and forth from one to another. It unrolls with sordid horror. The rivers are up and the bridges out. Again and again they retrace their course. The mules are drowned, Cash's leg broken

2. Faulkner's first novel (1926).

and the coffin barely saved in a disaster in midstream. Jewel trades his fine saddle horse for a new team. Cash's leg is mended with a dime's worth of cement. Buzzards circle over the wagon. Passersby shield their noses, for the body was not embalmed. After eight days of this gruesome pilgrimage (which is never gruesome to the Bundrens, who are merely doing what Anse promised to do) they arrive at Jefferson, and Addie Bundren is buried. There is a surprise at the end, just enough to relieve the burden of horror as you close the book. The burden, however, is never insupportable for throughout you perceive the situation through the eyes of the Bundrens. These primitive souls are not sensitive enough to perceive the indecency, the enormity of their conduct. It is matter-of-fact to them. And the fact of death is offset throughout by a fine zest for life which Mr. Faulkner shares with the primitive types he so successfully interprets.

The hard, toilsome trip to Jefferson is a sore trial to Anse Bundren, but over and over he says "I don't begrudge her it." And the children, except for Darl who goes mad, are doggedly loyal.

The style, save in the passages of conversation, which are excellent, is not strictly in dialect. Mr. Faulkner repeatedly uses rhetorical devices of his own, and a vocabulary such as a Bundren never dreamed of, to render the thought in the mind. He does this particularly when the thought is so vague that a Bundren would be inarticulate, merely sensible of his feelings.

The Bundrens are touchy, with the fierce pride of white trash. They wish "to be beholden to no man." . . .

Mr. Faulkner has in a few instances exaggerated to attain the horror he desired, but the story as a whole is convincing. As I Lay Dying is a distinguished novel. With The Sound and the Fury it entitles William Faulkner to rank with any living writer of fiction in America. All but a scant half dozen—Dreiser, Anderson,[3] Hemingway among them—he far surpasses.

CLIFTON P. FADIMAN

Morbidity in Fiction[†]

In his fourth novel Mr. Faulkner has to an extent departed from the irritating obscurity which marked "The Sound and the Fury." It still

3. Theodore Dreiser, (1871–1945), author of Sister Carrie (1900) and An American Tragedy (1925). Sherwood Anderson (1876–1941), author of Winesburg, Ohio (1919). Anderson was an early mentor of Faulkner's, and encouraged him to concentrate on Mississippi settings and concerns.
† From the Nation 131 (Nov. 5, 1930): 500–501.

seems that his is a far more involved technique than his material actually requires: impudent analysis might reduce this story to the dimensions of simple melodrama. But as people are always triumphantly reminding us, the same thing can be done with "Hamlet."

Mr. Faulkner has a set of romantic obsessions which he treats in a highly intellectual manner. He is fascinated by characters who border on idiocy; by brother-and-sister incest; by lurid religious mania; by physical and mental decay; by peasants with weird streaks of poetry; by bodily suffering; by the more horrifying aspects of sex. Though his approach is always objective, he specializes in emotional extremes—is a sort of prose Robinson Jeffers.

"As I Lay Dying" deals with the Bundren family who are transporting their coffined mother to her burial place in Jefferson, thirty miles away from the Bundren farm. During the course of this nightmare journey, which occupies nine days, we are taken inside the minds of the family and their neighbors. We learn that Dewey Dell is expecting an illegitimate child; that little Vardaman is a gibbering half-wit who believes his mother a fish; that Cash's mind is obsessed by his carpenter work on his mother's coffin. The strange tragedy of the dead Addie Bundren becomes clear as we listen to the weak-minded mutterings of old Anse, to the fanatic utterances of Cora Tull, a neighbor, and to the poetic, half-mad fantasies of Darl, another son. The whole affair is a psychological jig-saw puzzle, the pieces of which are represented by the distorted mentalities of half a dozen characters. The fascination of the story lies in the manner in which the phosphorescent rottenness of the family gradually reveals itself to the reader.

Despite the enthusiasm which has greeted Mr. Faulkner's work, it is difficult to believe him an important writer. His morbidity is interesting but tends to repeat itself. He seems very acute in his portrayal of defective mentalities—but how, really, can one check up on this portrayal? The minds of idiots are more or less a closed book to us. We may be thrilled by the terrors of Vardaman and the mad vagaries of Darl, and nevertheless long for a few characters whose experience occasionally identifies itself, if only vaguely, with our own. If we are to judge from his first novel, "Soldiers' Pay," Mr. Faulkner is quite capable of handling the more normal aspects of humanity; but out of an undoubtedly honest perversity he remains disturbingly faithful to his old lechers, his brutal drug-store clerks, his sexual inverts, and his insane dreamers. Mentally disintegrated types (unless the disintegration is of a subtle and complicated character) are not a very rich mine for investigation, as, for example, T. F. Powys[1] has discovered; and one hopes Mr. Faulkner before long will come to the same conclusion.

1. T. F. Powys (1875–1953), English novelist and short story writer. Author of *Mr. Weston's Good Wine* (1927).

But no one can doubt that the author of "As I Lay Dying" has a really interesting mind, apparently untouched by the major intellectual platitudes of our day. His cosmos is awry; but it is his own, self-created. Genuine idiosyncrasy is rare among our younger novelists. For the most part they explain themselves too easily; they are conveniently ticketed. Mr. Faulkner cannot be so ticketed; that is one reason why he deserves attentive consideration.

HENRY NASH SMITH

A Troubled Vision[†]

Someone has remarked before, I think, William Faulkner's kinship to the Elizabethans. In *As I Lay Dying*, it is still evident. There is for instance his preoccupation with unusual mental states—if not with actual imbecility, as in *The Sound and the Fury*, then with the insanity of Darl Bundren, with the morbid compulsion of Addie Bundren's family to bury her in the burying-ground back in Jefferson where she was reared, and with the boy Vardaman's conviction that his mother's soul has somehow got into the catfish he caught the afternoon she died. And even when it is seen through the eyes of the ostensibly normal characters, it is a morbid world, this rural Mississippi of William Faulkner's book: a Gothic world, productive only of hatred, passion, and frustration.

Faulkner is also like the Elizabethans in his touching of this violent matter with flashes of the poetry of rhetoric, a poetry which dwells lovingly on vivid colors and brave words, and seems almost to yearn for the blank verse which the modern democratic literary tradition has made impossible. When the men carry the homemade coffin into the room where Addie lies dead, "it is light, yet they move slowly; empty, yet they carry it carefully; lifeless, yet they move with hushed precautionary words to one another, speaking of it as though, complete, it now slumbered lightly alive, waiting to come awake." A woman's "wet dress shapes for the dead eyes of three blind men those mammalian ludicrosities which are the horizons and the valleys of the earth."

*   *   *

Readers are now inured to unpleasant incident; but Faulkner is unusual in the lurid intensity of his outlook. His work is the sort that you either detest or like passionately. I like it. However atrocious and

† Originally appeared in *Southwest Review* 16:2 (Winter 1931). Reprinted by permission.

distorted his outlook may seem when it is judged according to conventional standards of sweetness and light, he has one of the most genuinely artistic imaginations in America. He also has eloquence and courage. It may be that he is lacking cheerfulness and restraint: but I began by saying that he was like the Elizabethans.

HENRY SEIDEL CANBY

The School of Cruelty[†]

* * * The plodding naturalism of Dreiser was merely evidence that the world was dingy, which the imaginative could disregard, the harsh staccato of Hemingway had sentiment as an undertone, Lewis's[1] satire was at least based upon idealism. But this Mississippi writer (land of white columns draped in roses!) gives no quarter and leaves no field of the emotions unblighted. * * * Mr. Faulkner has come out at the further end of both Puritanism and anti-Puritanism, and in the dry light of complete objectivity weighs his subjects for their pound or ounce of life with no predilection for "ought," no interest in "why," and no concern for significance. He is cruel with a cool and interested cruelty, he hates his Mississippi and his Memphis and all their works, with a hatred that is neither passionate nor the result of thwarting, but calm, reasoned, and complete.

Unlike his fellow workers in the sadistic school, Mr. Faulkner can make character. * * * And better than any of them, better, I should say than Hemingway, Mr. Faulkner can write a still and deadly narrative that carries with it an unrolling series of events as vivid as modern caricature and as accurate as Dutch painting. I say *can,* for in the attempt to tell a story by its points of emphasis; omitting explanation and connectives, he is frequently elliptical and sometimes so incoherent that the reader loses his way and must go back after later enlightenment to see who was who in an earlier scene. Mr. Faulkner seems then to be trying to write a "talky," where the dialogue gives the situation while the continuity is left to the pictures, which, verbally presented, are not enough to clarify the reader's imagination. Yet narrative skill of a high order he undoubtedly possesses.

---

† From *Saturday Review of Literature* (Mar. 21, 1931): 673–74. This essay considers both *As I Lay Dying* and *Sanctuary* (1931), which appeared just a few months later, in order to make a general point not only about Faulkner but also about his literary generation as a whole. The material dealing with *Sanctuary* in particular—much of it plot summary—has been excised.

1. Sinclair Lewis (1885–1951), author of *Main Street* (1920) and *Babbitt* (1922). He was awarded the Nobel Prize in 1930.

*   *   *

Mr. Faulkner's Mississippi is, we trust, a partial portrait, but his vivid narrative style makes it convincing; nor can anyone doubt the force and truth of his characterizations.* * *

*   *   *

* * *[H]is imaginative and poetic *As I Lay Dying* [is] a book in which the intolerable strain of cruelty breaks down into one of those poetic escapes into beauty by which the real artist has always saved himself from too much logic. In *As I Lay Dying* there is again a cruel mob, but it is withdrawn, watching the spectacle of a half-mad family who tell their stories by monologue in which one finds how far less intolerable is misery and violence if one sees into the hearts of the characters. It is almost as if Mr. Faulkner had said: I am not God. I am not responsible for these people. If I look at the outward aspects of life in the Mississippi I know, they are so terrible that I respond by impulses of cruelty which lead me to describe coldly events which when read can only arouse wrath or disgust. Let me start again with simpler people, naïfs and crazy folk, uncorrupted if also unmoralized, and tell my story as they must have seen it, thus forgetting my own scorns and cruelties, and so get closer to ultimate truth.

*   *   *

The hard-boiled era is headed toward the dust heap where the soft-boiled era of the early 1900s has long preceded it. The post-war bitterness of wounded psyches has already subsided in England. Here it seems to be like an induced electricity where the pressure is higher but the substance less. The war-hurt generation is already too old for poetry, but just ripening for fiction. The candor behind their cruelties when they escape from the hard-boiled convention and grow wiser in life will give their work a substance and an edge which American fiction has too often lacked. They are not drugged, like Poe, nor have they his abnormal sensitivity which only the rightest of all possible worlds could have kept in bounds and only the most ethereal beauty could lift into the escape of real literature. They are—and I speak particularly of Faulkner and Hemingway—men of unusual ability who are working at their craft with a conscientiousness almost unknown to the easy going journalists who constitute so many of their contemporaries, and they have developed styles and methods, not better than, but different from, the practice of their established elders, such as Willa Cather[2] or Sinclair Lewis, and perhaps better

2. Willa Cather (1873–1947), author of *My Ántonia* (1918), *The Professor's House* (1925), and *Death Comes for the Archbishop* (1927).

adapted to the new decades as they and theirs will see them. Yet, hurt themselves, they have so far vented their irritation upon, and transferred, as the psychologists say, their inferiorities to, a country and a personnel which can be hated, as they hate it, only when the imagination is still fevered. That fever, as it subsides, leaves the problem of rediscovering America, for America has to be rediscovered by every generation, the problem of discovering not just the drunkards, gunmen, politicians, near virgins, and futile, will-less youths which have so deeply engaged them, but the American scene in all its complexity. They will never do it while one ounce of sadism, one trace of hysteria remains.

MAURICE-EDGAR COINDREAU

William Faulkner[†]

In 1929 he was still unknown. A long poem, *The Marble Faun* (1924), and two novels, *Soldier's Pay* (1926) and *Mosquitoes* (1927), had brought him neither fame nor gain. Only a few friends, among them Sherwood Anderson, had been able to see anything more than promise in his early works.

In 1929 *The Sound and the Fury* was a revelation. Soon, with snobbery playing its part, everyone at literary gatherings talked only of this strange book in which horror was mingled with obscenity. In 1930 *As I Lay Dying* aroused a more genuine kind of interest. The snobs were already seeking new enthusiasms. On the other hand, the serious admirers of William Faulkner, those whom *The Sound and the Fury* had interested because of its good qualities rather than its defects, were conscious that the United States had been enriched by the appearance of a powerfully original novelist with extraordinary vitality. The recent publication of *Sanctuary* allows no more doubt. William Faulkner is actually one of the most interesting figures in the young literature of America. *The Sound and the Fury,* an excruciating story of a cursed family, was a deformed, monstrous production, an

---

† From *La Nouvelle revue française* 236 (June 1931): 926–30. Trans. George McMillan Reeves in Coindreau and Reeves, *The Time of William Faulkner* (Columbia: University of South Carolina Press, 1971), pp. 25–30. Reprinted by permission.
　　French readers and critics were among the first to reach a proper valuation of Faulkner's work, in part because of the work of Maurice-Edgar Coindreau (1892–1990). This was the first article on Faulkner to come out in French, and the next year Coindreau began his long series of Faulkner translations with "Dry September" and "A Rose for Emily." His translation of *As I Lay Dying* appeared in 1934 as *Tandis que j'agonise.* Coindreau taught at Princeton for many years and in addition to Faulkner translated Hemingway, Nabokov, and Flannery O'Connor, among others. The essay's second half, a catalogue of moments, characters, and themes drawn from the body of Faulkner's work up through *Sanctuary,* has been cut.

accumulation of a very rich raw material which lacked only the work of a skilled and rigorous hand. This kind of work William Faulkner has accomplished in *As I Lay Dying* (1930) and *Sanctuary* (1931).

Addie Bundren has demanded that after her death her body be transported to Jefferson, the town of her birth. The coffin is loaded on a wagon and the whole family, Anse, the father, and the children, Cash, Darl, Vardaman, Jewel, and Dewey Dell accompany the body. A storm has washed away the bridges, and it is impossible to use the fords. A long detour is necessary. Nine days go by. The cadaver is decomposing. Vultures hover over the funeral carriage. Some incidents add complications to the difficulties of the road. The wagon turns over in a ford, and in attempting to right it Cash breaks his leg. He concludes the trip lying on his mother's coffin. His brothers have improvised a plaster cast for him, but gangrene develops quickly in the limb, which is too tightly compressed. One night Darl starts a fire that burns down the barn sheltering the wagon. Saved by Jewel, the coffin finally reaches Jefferson, where it is buried according to the wishes of the deceased.

Such is the subject of *As I Lay Dying*. One must not look for an exact chronology in that macabre odyssey. The fifteen characters whose interior monologues are divided into fifty-nine sections sometimes forget to light their lanterns. Nevertheless, there is no serious obscurity. The game of patience to which the author invited his reader has nothing in common with a Chinese puzzle. The well-cut pieces fit together easily and the design appears without effort in all its morbidity.

*   *   *

* * *[I]n the works of William Faulkner the subject is only a pretext for the display of a technique which, in this instance, approaches perfection. To be fair to Faulkner one must forget his themes and consider only the way he deals with them. Then he ceases to be the satanic creator of nightmares and becomes the virtuoso, the master of a new technique based on the power of the unexpressed.

"That was when I learned that words are no good; that words dont ever fit even what they are trying to say at," Addie thinks in *As I Lay Dying*. By virtue of this principle, every time that William Faulkner wishes to achieve a powerful effect he replaces words with images and facts with symbols. He no longer narrates, he suggests. The enticing scenes vanish into unfinished sentences which, while keeping one's curiosity aroused, inspire at once the desire and the fear of knowing. Because of the mystery that results from this enigmatic writing, the tragic scenes escape from the banality of melodrama and acquire the hallucinating quality which makes a book by Faulkner difficult to forget.

One cannot separate the Faulknerian technique from the characters which provide its reason for existing. In fact there is absolute accord between the characters and the manner in which they are presented. Faulkner deals only with exceptional individuals, and in this respect his work will never have a documentary value equal to that of the books, say, of Sinclair Lewis. The world he creates is his own world, full of strangeness and baseness. He has built it on precise data (sometimes autobiographical) but the historian of the American spirit would not be able to derive much benefit from it. On the other hand the psychiatrist will find in it ample matter for study. Degenerates, madmen, and idiots are William Faulkner's favorite characters. Using his technique of the unexpressed, he makes them into figures of astonishing power. Thus, as Mr. James Burnham has very accurately said, it is through what they cannot say that his heroes achieve greatness.[1] * * *

* * *

VALERY LARBAUD

"Preface" to *Tandis que j'agonise*[†]

This is a novel of rural manners that comes to us, well translated, from the State of Mississippi where the author, Mr. William Faulkner, was born in 1897 and still lives. *As I Lay Dying* is certainly more interesting and has a much higher esthetic value than the great majority of books that bear the label the trade will give it, for our convenience: "farm novels" [*romans paysans*].

First of all, it gives us a clear, powerful description of the landscapes and living conditions of groups of people in a region of the United States that Literature has rarely explored up to now: the part of a southern state roughly equidistant from the Atlantic and the Gulf of Mexico, whose principal products are cotton and corn. The climate is southern and continental; it certainly is the South, but a South that is fairly far from the Caribbean or the Mississippi delta that Paul Morand lets us glimpse at the end of his story "Baton Rouge."[1] The reader cannot fail to be struck by the purely agricultural character of the vast countryside, the absence of big cities, the lack of organized transportation and communication, and the low

---

1. "Trying to Say," *The Symposium: A Critical Review*, II (January 1931), pp. 51–59.
† From *Tandis que j'agonise* de William Faulkner. Trans. Maurice-Edgar Coindreau. (Paris: Gallimard, 1934). Reprinted by permission. Valery Larbaud (1881–1957) was a French poet, novelist, and translator. His preface has been translated by David Ball.
1. Paul Morand (1888–1976), French man of letters.

density of this population of farm owners. Their life seems much harder than the life of most rural people in central and Western Europe, farmers and sharecroppers alike. There is a great contrast between this United States and novels that take place in New England, Virginia, the Midwest and the West.

But the great value of this work does not lie in that portrayal. Mr. Faulkner's characters have a quality and a trueness to life that touch us more deeply than the exoticism of their milieu. Wretched and degraded as they may seem at first view, Anse Bundren and his neighbor Vernon Tull are men whose feelings cannot be indifferent or foreign to us. They are heads of the household in the "Aryan" way: as they are descendents of European émigrés, it is easy for us to put ourselves in their place as soon as we get to know them. In our imagination we share their lives, their sorrows, their meager joys, their problems and concerns. What is more—without wishing in any way to parody the subject of this novel—we can transpose it into an episode that has an epic character: the (Homeric) episode of the Funeral of the queen, Addie Bundren, performed according to her last wishes by her husband Anse and the princes, her children. Cash, the elder, a very skillful carpenter who limps like Hephaestus: Darl, possessed by a mad and prophetic spirit; Jewel, thought to be Anse's son but in reality a "living lie," the son born of her adulterous relationship with the minister, Reverend Whitfield; and the last-born, Vardaman, a child; and princess Dewey Dell, seventeen, who bears in her womb the fruit of her clandestine affair with a handsome "stranger"—Lafe, a farmhand who came from town to help with the cotton harvest. (His first name seems to indicate a Scandinavian origin: Leif?)

Queen Addie Bundren, the Mother, wanted Cash to make her coffin under her very eyes, and her remains to be driven on their wagon, surrounded by the family, to Jefferson, the "town" where her family is buried. And the weak, lazy, stubborn King Anse—a peasant Ulysses whose guile consists entirely of exploiting the pity that his very weakness and faults inspire in his neighbors, his children and everyone who comes near him—Anse has given his word that it would be done in this way. And the whole episode, from the moment Addie breathes her last, is nothing more than the story of this strange, interminable funeral, of the slow trip of that coffin with a hole in it (we will see who put it there and why) along bad roads ravaged by a recent storm, rivers with rotten bridges that have just been swept away by the waters, with stopovers in barns and farmhouses, under a hard July sky and the aerial escort of birds of prey attracted by the smell of the corpse . . . Until they arrive in town where the remains of the queen are laid in her grave, and King Anse, who has divested his family of Prince Darl (sent away to the insane asylum in the Capital) and acquired the set of false teeth that will enable him to fulfill

the dream he has had for years—to eat "God's appointed victuals"—
immediately finds a replacement for his departed queen: a new Mrs.
Bundren.

This central episode is quite naturally surrounded by anecdotal
situations, some present, some retrospective and biographical: the
construction of the coffin, the deathbed visit of the doctor, Addie's
adultery and her penitence, how Addie and Anse met and became
engaged, how the penniless Jewel was able to buy a horse, the abortive
confession of Reverend Whitfield, and the "virtuous" pharmacist of
Mottson; and the progression of Darl's madness, and the adventure
of Dewey Dell and the student in pharmacy (a subject worthy of Boccaccio or La Fontaine) . . . [2]

And along with the transposition to the Epic, the reader's imagination is sufficiently called upon to invent a transposition to the
Dramatic: around the king and princes, we find the Chorus and its
leaders. Vernon Tull on the men's side and the pious Cora Tull on
the women's, the male and female neighbors, the families who take
in the funeral procession, the people they meet on the road, and as
they approach the "town," a few Negroes.

From these brief notes you can imagine how intensely and minutely
the complexity of life is represented in this book, and how precisely the
characters are delineated. And this leads us to examine the form that
Mr. Faulkner has given to this novel.

It is the kind of form that makes one say he has staked everything
on it: it demands two very attentive readings, even from a reader
who is familiar with Robert Browning's dramatic monologues and
the interior monologue of Edouard Dujardin, Arthur Schnitzler and
James Joyce.[3] This necessary effort may discourage the mere literary
bystander, the reader who wants nothing more than entertainment
from works of the imagination. *As I Lay Dying* asks to be *looked at*,
considered in detail, examined closely, and studied. And if he really
appreciates it, savors it, the reader who has read up to Darl's arrest,
for example, will immediately think of Eula Tull's unhappiness when
the news will reach her: "He won't marry Eula Tull."

The use of stream of consciousness [*monologue intérieur*] in American novels is certainly a result of the publication of James Joyce's
Ulysses; but its appearance here, as in British prose, had been prepared by dramatic monologues. Like Robert Browning's monologues,

---

2. Giovanni Boccaccio (1313–1375), Italian author of *The Decameron*, a collection of 100
   short tales. Jean de La Fontaine (1621–1695), French poet best known for his collections
   of fables.
3. Robert Browning (1812–1889), English poet. Edouard Dujardin (1861–1949), French
   writer and early pioneer of the stream of consciousness. Arthur Schnitzler (1862–1931),
   Viennese doctor, playwright, and fiction writer. James Joyce (1882–1941), Irish author of
   Ulysses (1922).

the two poems called "The Quaker Widow" and "The Old Pennsylvania Farmer" in Bayard Taylor's *Home Ballads* show by what extension the interior monologue in prose—that new way of "putting something in front of our eyes"—came out of the dramatic monologue. (Compare the chapters called "Addie" and "Whitfield" to these two pieces by Bayard Taylor from this point of view.)[4]

Moreover, Mr. William Faulkner's treatment of this form is quite personal: it suggests the image of a machine to read and project thought—a kind of reflector—that the novelist trains on each of his characters in turn. We should also point out that the author does not systematically use this technique: *Sanctuary*, one of his most recent novels, is written in narrative form.

M. Maurice Coindreau, who is to be congratulated for having successfully performed a tricky task, has wisely not tried to render the characteristics of the patois spoken by the characters in *As I Lay Dying*. This patois may be interesting for the English-speaking reader ("to aim" is used as an auxiliary verb, for instance); but it is hardly more than a degraded English, marred by carelessness and bad habits. To us, it seemed more difficult than colorful or savory, although it does reflect the living conditions of those who speak it and certainly fits the atmosphere of the book. On the other hand, one may perhaps feel that the passages of the interior monologues are written in elevated language, often of great beauty, and thus out of keeping with the simple, intentionally clumsy manner that is the essence of the language in which most of the characters think. But we must point out that these country people possess a literary culture of high origin, rudimentary though it may be. Shaped by scraps and pieces from both Testaments, by hymns based on the Psalms and the clerical commentary of the Protestant sect to which the Bundrens and their neighbors belong, it is not surprising that this culture sometimes enables them to find—quite spontaneously—the tone of epic and prophecy.

EDWIN MUIR

From New Novels[†]

The note on the dust-cover of *As I Lay Dying* says that it 'has been long recognised in America as one of Mr Faulkner's most powerful and remarkable works'. We may probably assume, therefore, that it is one of his earliest novels; and indeed it shows many signs of

---

4. Bayard Taylor (1825–1878), American travel writer, poet, and translator.
† From *The Listener* (16 October 1935): 681. Edwin Muir (1887–1959) was a Scottish poet and translator of works by Franz Kafka.

immaturity, as well as a simplicity, not achieved but unconscious, which tells us a great deal more about the fundamental elements of his work than his later novels do, with their smothering complication. The real subject of this story, simple to the point of desperation, is the corpse of a woman in late middle age. A truer title would have been 'As I Lay Dead', but even that would give the story credit for more complexity than it has, for it is concerned not with death, but merely with the chemical changes which happen in a body after life has forsaken it. The 'dying' is very quickly and perfunctorily got over, for what Mr Faulkner—like the detective story-writer—is really after is the body, and the history he relates is the history of this body before it is finally shovelled underground and got out of the way. To have chosen such a curious theme, to have lingered over it with such professional solicitude, conscientiously and lovingly, must show the presence of a very deep-seated obsession. It may be objected that 'Webster was much possessed by death' and that Donne was such another; but death is a normal and indeed unavoidable subject of human thought, and, as Webster and Donne[1] conceived it, was inseparable from life. To Mr Faulkner, on the other hand, it is a sort of death absolute, or rather a sort of post-mortem life, that has no connection with human life at all. We are told far more about Addie Bundren's corpse, for instance, than about herself. A vision of the horror of death such as Webster's depends for its power on his sense of life. But it may be said of this story of Mr Faulkner that the most interesting character, or at least the character in which he shows most interest, is the corpse, not in its former incarnation as a human being with feelings, affections and a soul, but simply in its dead, or rather gruesomely alive, state. What we are to deduce from such an obsession it is hard to say; for it is not a comprehensible obsession, like Webster's, but a blind one. The effect that this story produces is, in any case, one of self-indulgence, self-indulgence pushed to the point of keeping a corpse for nine days above ground on its journey to a distant town, saving it from a flood and then from a fire, and reducing the family it left behind it to such a state that they end by confusing it with fishes and horses. Yet the effect is not horror but merely disgust, a much more cold and impotent emotion.

The story is interesting, nevertheless, as showing one of the probable reasons why Mr Faulkner complicates his method of presentation so elaborately, and why his short stories are so much better than his novels. His technique is so complicated because there is something blind, something unaccounted for by his intellect, in his vision of the

1. John Webster (c.1580–c.1634), English playwright known for his dark and sour tragedies; author of *The Duchess of Malfi* (c. 1614). John Donne (1572–1631), English poet and preacher.

world, so that it can only take the form of a series of circular wanderings making towards a circumference which it can never reach. This probably accounts also for the sulphurous and overcharged atmosphere in his novels, and the brilliance of the occasional flashes, for they always appear against this background of impenetrable darkness. There are such flashes in this book, for instance in the scene describing the fire:

> The stall door has swung shut. Jewel thrusts it back with his buttocks and he appears, his back arched, the muscles ridged through his garment as he drags the horse out by its head. In the glare its eyes roll with soft, fleet, wild opaline fire; its muscles bunch and run as it flings its head about, lifting Jewel clear of the ground. He drags it on, slowly, terrifically; again he gives me across his shoulders a single glare furious and brief.

The flash is produced in the most wasteful and amateurish way possible, amid a terrific hubbub of adjectives and adverbs, but in descriptions such as this of physical events Mr Faulkner has shown himself to be a remarkable writer. Little can be said for this story, however, except for a few isolated accounts of violent action. * * *

The Writer and His Work

Faulkner wrote little apart from his fiction. His letters are terse and unrevealing, he did almost no reviewing, and though he spent several years as a well-paid Hollywood script doctor, he never sought the kind of lucrative reporting assignments to which writers like Hemingway often turned. In the 1950s he did produce a dozen-odd essays, some of them travel sketches and others touching on the developing movement for civil rights, but his one volume of *Essays, Speeches, and Public Letters* appeared posthumously and covers just 230 generously spaced pages. More useful are the interviews collected as *Lion in the Garden* and the transcripts of the seminars he gave on his work at the University of Virginia in 1957–58. In this section I have assembled Faulkner's most interesting and substantive comments on *As I Lay Dying*, a sample chapter from its manuscript, some examples of his earliest fiction, and two documents without which no account of his work can now seem complete—his Nobel Prize address and the map he drew of Yoknapatawpha County. For a reader of this novel, however, that map cannot help but appear misleading. Faulkner first made it for the publication of *Absalom, Absalom* in 1936, and it locates the Bundren and the Tull farmsteads on opposite sides of Yoknapatawpha River, a topography that makes nonsense of the river crossing at the center of *As I Lay Dying*. Faulkner's imaginary landscape was not all created at once. It went on developing in his head, as did his understanding of his recurring characters, and for this novel we can trust that map only as a general indication of direction and distance.[1]

The earliest documents here show a writer in the process of self-discovery. In the opening paragraphs of "Adolescence" Faulkner sketches a marriage and gives us a name that seems a proleptic version of the Bundrens' own, although the remaining pages of this apprentice tale develop along a different line. More interesting is the existence of a story actually called "As I Lay Dying"—interesting even if, or perhaps because, it has virtually nothing to do with the novel. In 1926 Faulkner began a book called *Father Abraham*. He soon laid it aside, but it contained the germ of his Snopes stories, and its central episode involved the sale of some spotted horses. He tried several times over the next few years to write that story; two of its versions bore the name "As I Lay Dying," and the best of them is reprinted here. (Eventually he finished

---

1. See Dianne C. Luce, *Annotations to* As I Lay Dying (New York and London: Garland, 1990), pp. 77–78.

and sold a story called "Spotted Horses"; it appeared in the June 1931 issue of *Scribner's* and was again rewritten, and greatly expanded, for *The Hamlet*.) Faulkner alludes to that sale in this novel—Jewel's horse is descended from those original Texas ponies—but there are no Bundrens in this early story. The piece shares with the novel only some of its minor characters and a setting in the region of poor whites that Faulkner calls Frenchmen's Bend. I include it here for three reasons: first, its title suggests how much Faulkner liked the sound of those words, quite aside from their application to any particular work. Second, the fact that he alludes in the novel to the spotted horses incident, to a story he had not yet finished, let alone published, indicates the degree to which Yoknapatawpha County existed for him independent of and perhaps anterior to any particular story or novel, any of its individual articulations. Third, Faulkner conceived of the tale, however unpolished, as a comic oral performance. That mode of writing would dominate his later work, but it is also one of the ways in which he began; a style that developed simultaneously with the daemonic force of his greatest books.

Faulkner offered interesting if myth-making accounts of the writing of *As I Lay Dying* in his preface to the 1932 Modern Library edition of *Sanctuary*, and in a 1933 introduction to *The Sound and the Fury* that went unpublished at the time. He spoke about it in his *Paris Review* interview, and above all at the University of Virginia. That school's library now holds this novel's manuscript. A comparison of the finished book with the facsimiles reprinted here from both its holograph and its carbon typescript will allow one to judge the truth of his claim that he wrote the novel without changing a word. The chapter I have reproduced is typical in the scale of its revisions, and its finished version can be found on p. 62.

WILLIAM FAULKNER

Adolescence[†]

I

She was not indigenous to this section. Having been foisted upon it by the blind machinations of fate and of a still blinder county School Board, she would remain, to the end of her days, a stranger to this land of pine and rain gullied hills and fecund river bottoms. Hers should have been a background of faintly sentimental decadence, of formal ease among rites of tea and graceful pointless activities.

A smallish woman with enormous dark eyes, who found in the physically crude courtship of Joe Bunden the false romance with

† From *Uncollected Stories*, ed. Joseph Blotner (New York: Random House, 1979), pp. 459–73. Used by permission. According to Blotner, this story was likely written in the early 1920s.

which she had banked the fires of her presbyterian inhibitions. The first ten months of her married life—a time of unprecedented manual labor—failed to destroy her illusions; her mental life, projected forward about her expected child, supported her. She had hoped for twins, to be called Romeo and Juliet, but she was forced to lavish her starved affections on Juliet alone. Her husband condoned this choice of name with a tolerant guffaw. Paternity rested but lightly upon him: like the male of his kind, he regarded the inevitable arrival of children as one of the unavoidable inconveniences of marriage, like the risk of wetting the feet while fishing.

In regular succession thereafter appeared Cyril, one day to be sent to the State Legislature, Jeff Davis, who was finally hung in Texas for stealing a horse; then another boy whom, her spirit broken, she was too apathetic to name at all and who, as a matter of convenience, answered to Bud, and became a professor of latin with a penchant for Catullus at a small mid-western university. The fifth and last was born four years and seven months after her marriage; but from this event she fortunately failed to recover, whereupon Joe Bunden in an unusual access of sentimental remorse named his youngest son for himself, and married again. The second Mrs Bunden was a tall angular shrew who, serving as an instrument of retribution, was known to beat him soundly on occasion with stove wood.

* * *

WILLIAM FAULKNER

As I Lay Dying[†]

We were still two miles from Varner's store, driving peacefully along the shady river bottom road when, preceded by a sudden crashing of undergrowth, the animal appeared to materialise out of thin air directly above the center of the road. It looked like a goblin, like something unbelievable out of a nightmare; between the rearing lunge of our team I had a flying picture of something resembling a patchwork quilt in a cyclone or a Fourth of July pinwheel seen by daylight and magnified out of all reason and outraging very credibility. Then it was gone, leaving only the dwindling crash of its passage through the undergrowth on the other side of the road and our horses trembling and backing, one pair of forelegs astride the tongue.

"What in the——" I began.

† *Mississippi Quarterly* (Summer 1986): 369–85. Ed. and intro. James Meriwether, who dates the story to fall 1928. Copyright 1986 by W. W. Norton and Company. Used by permission.

My uncle was quieting the team. "Get out and take their heads," he said. I did so and stilled them and freed the breast yoke and lowered the tongue for Dan to step over it. The beast, whatever it was, had gone; Dan rippled his coat violently and snorted and stood while I slipped the tongue into the yoke again.

"What——" I began again. My uncle was laughing.

"It was one of those mustangs," he said. He sat in the buggy, laughing. "No wonder it took a whole day to auction off twenty-five of them. What surprises me is that these people here, close and canny as they are, bought them at any price—even at five dollars a piece."

"Oh," I said. The man at whose house we had stayed last night had told us about them, how Flem Snopes had returned from Texas four days ago, accompanied by a stranger and twenty-five unbroken range ponies shackled one to another with barbed wire, and about the auction; how the stranger had sold them for prices ranging from a dollar and fifty cents to eight dollars, stipulating first that none should claim his beast until all were sold, and of what happened when they entered the lot and tried to catch them and lead them home.

"And wont anybody ever know how much they made off of them things, neither," he said.

"They wont find out from Flem Snopes, anyway," my uncle said. "Specially if there's any trouble about catching them."

"Catching them?" the farmer said. "I heard fellers runnin one of them things across the bottom at twelve oclock last night. No, sir," he said, "not only wont anybody ever know how much Flem and that Texas feller made off of them things, wont anybody ever know for certain if Flem had anything to do with them at all."

"Flem's pretty close-mouthed," my uncle said.

"Close-mouthed," the farmer said. "Flem knows things he aint ever told himself, even."

He didn't tell us about Henry Armstid. We didn't learn about that until we reached Varner's store, which was a point in our quadriennial vote-garnering itinerary. Tethered to a veranda post was another rig: a sturdy mismatched team and a buckboard, to the rear of which was attached a thing like a sheet-iron dog-kennel.

"There's Suratt," my uncle said, "with his sewing machine." The sewing machine was his demonstrator. It fitted neatly into the dog-kennel, which was painted to resemble a house with two windows in each side, in each of which a woman's painted head simpered above a painted sewing machine. "Something can happen forty miles away, but he'll be there by the next morning."

As it happened he was departing and not arriving, for as we drove up and stopped he was saying: "Yes, sir, when I looked around and seen that thing in the door, a-blarin its eyes at me, I made sho Flem

Snopes had brung a tiger back from Texas by mistake." His listeners—
four of them—guffawed with sober appreciation. They squatted in
overalls against the wall, collarless, spitting across the porch into the
dust. The fifth man sat in the single chair tilted in the broad doorway.
He had a face like a nutcracker; a scrawny man of no particular age,
with merry secretive eyes. One of the squatting men held between his
teeth a sprig of peach bearing three blooms like miniature ballet skirts
of pink tulle. They saw my uncle and greeted him in their slow voices,
and Suratt, turning, said:

"Is this hyer votin year again? I be dawg if I can keep up with it,
till first thing I know, the country's full of politicians ever which way
I turn. Good mawnin, Judge. You're too late. Vernon Turpin's done
already taken Squire Whittington for his lawyer to sue Flem."

"Good morning, gentlemen," my uncle said. "What's Flem done
to Vernon Turpin?" A tall, loose man in careless clothes, with tem-
ples of silver distinction. I have heard him on two successive days
converse with a Harvard professor and a cane bottom farmer in
their respective idiom. "What's this I hear you boys have been
up to?"

The man in the chair slapped his thighs, cackling. "I reckon Flem'd
a brung some tigers back if he'd a knowed how you fellers was goin
to snap up them hosses," he said. "Him and Buck'd a brung monkeys
too, I reckon."

We mounted the steps and among them where they squatted with
their grave unceasing hands, whetting knife-blades on their shoes,
trimming minutely at splinters—hands so inured to toil that idleness
was no rest.

"And I reckon we'd a bought em," Suratt agreed sourly. He looked
at the man in the chair. "Say, I. O., how much did Flem make offen
them hosses?"

"He made a plenty, I reckon." The man in the chair cackled again;
his features clotted in the middle of his face like the plucking gesture of a hand. He too was a Snopes, Varner's clerk; successor to
Flem in that capacity. "Flem's pretty cute, he is."

From his overalls the man with the peach sprig took a small tin
cylinder. He uncapped it and filled the cap with snuff from the tin
and drew his lower lip away with his thumb and finger and tilted the
snuff into his lip. A second said:

"Flem claims he never had no inter-est in them hosses."

Suratt made a crude disparaging sound. "Does anybody here
believe that?"

"Will anybody ever know any better?" my uncle said.

The man in the chair cackled again, with a kind of secretive glee.
"Aint he a beatin feller, now? Yes, sir, you fellers needn't to think
Flem's goin to tell how much he made offen them hosses."

"And you needn't to act like you knowed, neither," Suratt told him. "Flem aint goin to tell you no more than anybody else, even if you are kin to him."

"I. O. seems to have had better sense than to buy one of them, anyway," my uncle said.

The man in the chair watched my uncle with bright, intent little eyes. He rubbed his hands slowly on his thighs.

"Then I. O.'s the only one of his kinfolks Flem never skun," Suratt said. "That's because Flem knowed that I. O. couldn't even buy a fo dollar hoss, I reckon."

I. O. cackled again. He rubbed his hands slowly on his thighs.

"What's this about Vernon Turpin?" my uncle said.

"He warn't hurt much," Suratt said. "Just skun him up some, where the team drug him outen the wagon when the traces broke. Miz Turpin says they was all settin in the wagon about half asleep, mules and all, when that ere varmint of Eck's come hellin onto the bridge. She says it run right slap betwixt the mules and clumb onto the wagon tongue like a cat and run right up across the dashboa'd and jumped out behind without ever stoppin. And then hyer come Eck Snopes and that boy of his'n with a rope, askin which-a-way it went, and Vernon layin on the bridge with the reins still wropped around his hands and the womenfolks pickin splinters outen him. She says they never caught their mules till after dinner next day. Lon Quick run into em just this side of Banner and sent em back. Lon left out with his wagon to catch his'n and aint got back yet—— Here comes Eck now."

A man and a small boy, both in overalls, came up the road and mounted to the veranda. "Hi, boys," Eck said. They went on and entered the store. I. O. Snopes rose from the chair and followed.

"Has Flem been back since?" my uncle said.

"Naw," Suratt said, "and what's more——"

"I seen him this mawnin," another said.

"You did?" Suratt said. "I heard Miz Littlejohn say he was back, but I never thought . . . . If I was him, I believe I'd——"

"You'd what?" the man with the peach sprig said. "Only man can prove anything on him is that Texas feller."

"I reckon so," Suratt agreed. "But a man that'll skin his own kinfolks—— Yes, sir, even Eck got trimmed. Not as bad as some, though. He was just reskin two for one."

"How was that?" my uncle asked.

"They give Eck one hoss to start the arction off," Suratt said. Eck emerged, with a paper sack. He squatted against the wall. The boy squatted beside him in diminutive replica. He had a round, innocent yellow head and eyes like periwinkles. Eck set the sack at his feet and opened his knife and drew the blade once across his thigh. He took from the sack a segment of cheese and shaved off a piece and handed it to the boy between knife blade and thumb.

"Aint you been home yet, Eck?" the man with the peach spray said.

"Naw," Eck said. He shaved off a bite of cheese, speared it into his mouth on the point of the knife. He took a handful of crackers from the bag and gave them to the boy.

"Yes, sir," Suratt said, "I got my opinion of a man that'll bring a herd of wild cattymounts into a town and sell em to his neighbors and kinfolks, and if I was——" he ceased. We watched Flem Snopes quietly as he crossed the road, whittling at a piece of soft pine, and mounted the steps. He was a tubby man, with eyes the color of pond water and a tight seam of a mouth like a patent tobacco pouch set into a hairless face going a little flabby at the jowls. He wore a black felt hat and—unique among them—a white shirt, but without collar or tie. Without looking at us he greeted us generally. The man in the chair rose with a sort of swaggering servility and went and leaned in the opposite side of the door.

"Good morning, Flem," my uncle said. Flem looked at him, then at me with his opaque expressionless eyes. He turned his head and spat backward into the road.

"Mawnin, Judge," he said. He took the chair. By right of Uncle Billy Varner's son-in-law, it was.

"I was just tellin Suratt," I. O. Snopes, leaning in the door, said, "that if you'd a knowed how them fellers was going to snap up them hosses, you'd a brung some monkeys and tigers back from Texas, too." Flem hooked his heels onto a rung of the chair. He trimmed a long sliver from the stick. Beneath the tilted brim of his hat I could see the slow thrust of his chewing. I. O. Snopes cackled. "Yes, sir, you boys cant git ahead of Flem."

"Vernon Turpin aims to," Suratt said. "Vernon says he's fixin to law you, Flem."

Flem trimmed a sliver from the stick. Falling, it clung to his trouser leg. He made no effort to remove it. He trimmed another. The others squatted covertly and motionless. Except Suratt. He was watching Flem with curiosity and a sort of grudging respect. "Say, Flem," he said. The others squatted with covert unostentation. "How much did you and that Texas feller make offen them hosses?"

Flem trimmed a slow intact sliver. He raised his head and spat across the porch. " 'Twarn't none of my hosses," he said.

I. O. Snopes guffawed. Suratt joined him, but more temperately. "Dont he beat all?" I. O. said. "You might just as well quit tryin to git around Flem."

"That's right," Suratt said. "We all takes a back seat for Flem. Well, he sho livened things up for us, even if him and that Texas feller did skin us outen sixty or seventy dollars. I heard——"

"How many did you buy, V. K.?" the man with the peach spray said, and the others laughed with sober appreciation. Except Flem and I. O. Flem trimmed deliberately at his stick. I. O. watched Suratt with his bright little eyes. Eck trimmed off another piece of cheese and gave it to the boy.

"I bought one less'n a lot of folks I know," Suratt said. "Two less'n Eck yonder. I heard folks chasin them things at ten oclock last night, but Eck aint been home a-tall."

"If he'd a just waited for the balance of us, we'd a caught them hosses," Eck said. The man with the peach sprig removed it and spat.

"Say, Eck, how many of them things was they in Miz Littlejohn's house that night? Suratt says there was one in ever' room and that you and her was chasin two more up and down the hall with washboa'ds."

" 'Twarn't but one," Eck said, chewing. "Just Ad's and mine."

"Well, it was the biggest drove of just one hoss I ever seen in my life," Suratt said. "I'd a swore they was a dozen, at least. For ten minutes ever' time I looked behind or in front of me, there was that blare-eyed, pink-faced, spotted varmint just runnin over me or just swirlin to run over Eck again. And that boy there, he stayed right under it for five minutes, I reckon."

They laughed again; I a little overloud above their sober mirth, and I found them watching me with that slow contemplation of country people for one in urban clothes. Eck speared another bit of cheese on his knife. The boy, a bitten cracker in his small dirty hand, watched Suratt roundly with his grave ineffable eyes, chewing. "But time Vernon Turpin gits done with Flem," Suratt said, "and Henery Armstid too——"

"Henry Armstid?" my uncle said. "Did Flem make Henry's team run away too?"

"Aint you heard?" Suratt said. Then they told us, in unhurried strophe and antistrophe, of the horse Henry had bought, his wife trying to stop him, to get him away, of how the Texas auctioneer tried to refuse to sell him the horse; of how he had struck his wife finally and driven her back to their wagon; of how in his rage he had entered the lot alone while the other purchasers were getting their ropes ready, and of his broken leg and the woman sitting motionless in her gray wrapper in the gray wagon in the fading dusk, like a timeless and patient figure of tragedy and despair.

I had seen her almost every Saturday in Jefferson, in her gray, faded, shapeless garment and canvas tennis shoes and a cloth sunbonnet and, in the winter, a man's wornout overcoat, going from house to house with a market basket on her arm, selling the objects she had knitted or woven, swapping them for old garments and rags to make yet other objects of. In our house at the time was a centerpiece she had crocheted of pieces of colored cotton string hoarded from parcels from the stores, and I have seen her with her gaunt face and her dead eyes and her gnarled hands that, motionless on her knees or moving slowly upon some outgrown garment of my own—she had five children—shaped even then the handle of a plow or the helve of an axe or a hoe, sitting in the library with my mother. She did the knitting and weaving at night. She did it by firelight until mother gave her a lamp.

"Miz Armstid can run a furrer straight as I can," the man with the peach sprig said.

"Well, she'll have plenty of chance to run em now," Suratt said. "That must be a power of satisfaction to Flem."

"Never nobody tricked Henery into buyin that hoss," I. O. Snopes said.

"That's right," another said. "Folks tried to keep him from it. That Texas feller said he wouldn't sell Henery no hoss. He wouldn't take that five dollars."

"Who did take it, then?" my uncle said.

They said nothing, squatting above their slow tobacco and their grave unceasing hands.

"Just because Henery happened to hand it to Flem dont prove nothin," I. O. Snopes said. "He might have handed it to me, or to Suratt, or anybody. But would that prove we owned them hosses?"

"Sho," Suratt said, "I know they never taken Henery's money. I know that. I reckon Miz Armstid's got that ere five dollars put away good right now. I reckon Flem and that Texas feller give ever' body his money back when they couldn't ketch them things. I reckon he give you yo'n back, didn't he, Eck?"

"Henery walked right into the middle of em and made em run over him," Eck said. "If he'd a just waited for the balance of us, we'd a caught em all."

"Henery Armstid's a bawn fool," I. O. said. "I haint no patience with a fool."

"Well," Suratt said, "if a man gits trimmed in a swap or a buy, it's his own fault. But a feller that'd take that woman's money is a pretty pore kind of a feller. I reckon that was ever' cent they had, that five dollars."

"What'd she let Henery do it for, then?" I. O. said. "Warn't no law makin him."

"That's right," Suratt said, "I nigh forgot. He wouldn't sell Henery no hoss. I 'member now. He told Miz Armstid she could git that five dollars from Flem next day. I reckon Flem done already taken it by Miz Littlejohn's and give it to her. Aint you, Flem?"

Flem trimmed a long sliver from the stick. He raised his head and spat neatly across the porch, into the dust. Across the road, above the rusted metal roof of the blacksmith shop, a peach tree stood pink against a tilted field bright with sprouting oats. A horse stood on three legs before the shop. Within the shop a measured hammer clanged.

"Flem aint never said them hosses was his'n yet," I. O. said. "Dont forget that."

"Well," Suratt said, "I reckon he ought to know whose they was. He come all the way from Texas with em. Or maybe he was just showin that Texas feller the road. But I be dawg if I didn't think Henery was dead, when they brung him in. Last time I seen him he was leanin on the gate and Miz Armstid was settin in the wagon, waitin; and the next thing I knowed, time that hoss quit runnin back and forth over me and Eck, they was fetchin Henery into the house. He looked more like a dead man than ever I see in my life; with his head hangin and a little moon of white showin under his eyeleds and her standin there at the foot of the bed with her hands rolled into her apron and them eyes of her'n that looked like she was already dead and somebody done already laid silver quarters on em."

"It beats all how a woman'll stick to a no-'count man," the man with the peach spray said. "I heard she sets up ever' night with Henery and helps Miz Littlejohn in the kitchen all day for her'n and Henery's keep."

"She drives out to their place ever' evenin to look after the stock and the chaps," another said.

"How many have they got?" my uncle said.

"Three or four," Suratt said. "I dont know exactly. Oldest must be about ten."

"They've got five," I said. "Mrs Armstid told Mother."

They looked at me, then away again. "That's right," the man with the peach spray said. "One of em aint hardly walkin yet."

"They livin out there alone now?" Suratt said.

"The oldest one's about twelve," the man with the peach sprig said. "I reckon she can take care of the little fellers."

"Well, a twelve year old gal ought to have that much sense," Suratt said.

"Got more sense than Henery, anyway," the second speaker said.

"Henery Armstid's a bawn fool," I. O. said. "Always was and always will be. I haint no patience with a fool."

"I reckon you wouldn't set up at night with no hurt feller, I. O.," Suratt said.

"Not if he hurt hisself bein a fool," I. O. said. "Henery can affo'd to spend five dollars for a hoss as well as Eck can. What you fellers keep on talkin like never nobody ever bought a hoss before Henery Armstid?"

"If he'd just waited for the balance of us, we'd a caught them hosses," Eck said.

"That warn't Henery's money," the man with the peach spray said. "Henery Armstid never had five dollars in his life."

"She kept tellin that Texas feller it was her'n," another said. "She said she earned it a-weavin after dark. She said if he taken it, it'd be a curse on him. 'Mister,' she says, 'if you take that five dollars I earned my chaps a-weavin, it'll be a curse on you all the time of man,' she says."

"I've seen her in town, totin them things from house to house," a third said. "That's wher their clothes come from, her'n and the chaps'. They aint never made more'n a bare livin off that place, and never will. Henery cant even affo'd tobacker. Ernest there lends em tools. You give em two whole days last month, didn't you, Ernest?"

"She can run a furrer straight as I can," the man with the peach spray said.

"I heard her and Miz Littlejohn talkin in the kitchen this mawnin," Suratt said. "I was eatin breakfast and they was in the kitchen and Miz Littlejohn says she seen Flem goin past and she asked Miz Armstid if she asked Flem for that money yet like that Texas feller tole her to and Miz Armstid says she aint and Miz Littlejohn says, Well, you goin to? and Miz Armstid says, You reckon it'll do any good? and Miz Littlejohn says she dont reckon Flem would give it back to her but askin wouldn't hurt and Miz Armstid——"

"What was you doin when you heard all that?" I. O. said.

"Listenin," Suratt said. "And Miz Armstid says if Flem aint goin to give it back, it wont do no good to ask and Miz Littlejohn says if it was her'n she'd do it and Miz Armstid says he wont give it back, and they worked for a while, clatterin dishes and things and Miz Armstid says, He might give it back and Miz Littlejohn didn't say anything. After a while Miz Armstid says they was folks seen Flem take the money and heard the Texas feller say she could git it from him next day and Miz Littlejohn says, Well, why dont you go and git it, then. Flem'll be settin up yonder in that chair all day and Miz Armstid says, You reckon I ought to? and Miz Littlejohn didn't say anything, and they clattered some more. Then Miz Armstid says, Maybe I better talk it over with Henery and Miz Littlejohn says, I would, so Henery can fix up to buy another spotted hoss with it and Miz Armstid says, I reckon I better talk it over with Henery. Then it sounded like somebody throwed the woodbox at the stove, and I come away." He let himself go restfully against a post. Eck and the boy ate slowly from the paper bag. Across the road the blacksmith's hammer clanged. "I reckon we wont never know how much money was made on that arction[1], but if they was any made, Flem Snopes got some of it. But I wouldn't want that woman's money on my conscience."

"Who has?" I. O. said. "Can you prove Flem had anything to do with them hosses?"

From a half mile away, borne on the soft April air, I heard a wagon on the wooden bridge across the creek. In that direction, against the

1. Auction [*Editor*].

rich wall of the river bottom, dogwood and judas-trees were white and crimson splotches.

"Who can stand between a fool and his folly?" my uncle said.

"That's right," one said. He spat into the dust. "Trouble is, 'taint never the fool hisself that the folly hurts."

"Well," Suratt said, "a bruck leg would satisfy me for a while."

"Bruck leg?" the second speaker said. "That aint no more than a holiday for Henery. Layin there, eatin and sleepin, liftin no hand day in and day out. I reckon Miz Armstid'd swap places with him any day, if she didn't know he'd have em all in the pore-house time she was able to walk there."

"I be dawg," Suratt said, "if Vernon dont sue Flem, Henery ought. And if they dont, I be dawg if I dont sue him myself. Skeering me like that. When the supper bell rung Henery was leanin on the gate and Miz Armstid settin in the wagon while the rest of em was gittin ropes. So I come in and et and went to my room and was undressin when the commotion busted. So there I was, in my underclo'se, with one sock on and the other in my hand, leanin out the winder when that thing come bustin in the door. It was in my room and Miz Littlejohn was cussin it on the back porch and beatin it over the head with a washboa'd and it was runnin over Eck and that boy in the hall, all at the same time. And time I could jump out the winder and run around to the door again, hyer it come, soarin over that boy's head like a hawk, with its eyes lookin like two of these hyer colored electric lights and its mane like a grass fire. . . ."

Then he ceased and we watched the gray woman come up the road in the mild dust. She wore the sunbonnet, her hands were folded across her middle, and the garment appeared to progress without visible motion, like something on a float in a parade.

"You still got time to run, Flem," Suratt said. "You can go out the back. She aint seen you yet."

"Go out the back and wait," I. O. said. "I'll tell her you went home."

Flem was whittling at the stick in small, neat jabs of the blade. Beneath the rim of his hat his jaw moved with slow, rythmic thrust.

"You aint goin to run, are you?" Suratt said. "Well, if a man does devil-ment—— Good mawnin, Miz Armstid."

"Good morning, Mrs Armstid," my uncle said. She mounted the steps, gaunt in her shapeless garment, her stained tennis shoes hissing faintly on the bare boards. Her eyes were dog's eyes and she stood among the grave, squatting men with her hands folded across her middle, not looking at anyone or anything.

"He said that day that he wouldn't sell Henery no hoss," she said in a flat voice, in the toneless voice of one who has had no occasion for speech in a long time. "He said you was keepin Henery's money for him."

Flem trimmed a lean sliver from the stick. He raised his head without ceasing the stroke of the knife and spat neatly past the woman, into the red dust.

"He taken that money off with him when he left," he said.

The woman's eyes looked at nothing: the ghost of vision turned inward, contemplating nothing there, even. Motionless, the gray garment drooped in rigid, formal folds, like drapery in bronze. The man with the peach spray removed it and spat carefully and put the sprig in his mouth again.

"He said Henery hadn't bought no hoss," she said. "He said for me to get the money from you."

"I reckon he forgot it," Flem said. "He taken that money away with him when he left." He trimmed steadily at the stick. I. O. leaned in the door, rubbing his back slowly against the jamb. The wagon came up the hill and creaked past. Its occupants saluted us with sober raised hands. It went on in the dust and stopped at the blacksmith's and the smith came to the door and rested his hand on the rump of the horse tethered there. The woman looked after the wagon. The road went on in grave red curves ascending, passing the cemetery with its sparse marble among sombre cedars through the long summer afternoons loved of doves. The woman moved on her hissing rubber.

"I reckon it's about time to get dinner started," she said.

"How's Henry this morning, Mrs Armstid?" my uncle said.

She looked at him; her desolate eyes waked for an instant. "He's restin, I thank you kindly." Then her eyes died again. Flem closed his knife with his thumb and rose, shedding a litter of minute shavings, some of which still clung to his legs.

"Wait a minute, Miz Armstid," he said. The woman became motionless again. Flem entered the store. I. O. ceased rubbing his back against the jamb and craned his turkey neck after him. The boy found a final cracker in the bag and ate it slowly.

Flem returned, with a small paper sack. He put it into the woman's hand. Her hand turned just enough to receive it. "A little sweetenin fer the chaps," he said. He sat down and spat neatly past her, into the road.

"You're right kind," she said. She folded the sack into her apron, against her stomach, the boy watching her hands with his unwinking periwinkles. "I reckon I better get on and help with dinner," she said. She descended the steps and went on down the road: a figure that progressed without motion, like a blasted tree trunk moving, somehow upright, upon a flood. The wagon had moved again, creaking on in the dust; the blacksmith's hammer clanged upon the soft air. I. O. cackled drily.

"Aint he a beatin feller, now?"

WILLIAM FAULKNER

Introduction to the Modern Library
Edition of *Sanctuary*†

This book was written three years ago. To me it is a cheap idea, because it was deliberately conceived to make money. I had been writing books for about five years, which got published and not bought. But that was all right. I was young then and hard-bellied. I had never lived among nor known people who wrote novels and stories and I suppose I did not know that people got money for them. I was not very much annoyed when publishers refused the mss. now and then. Because I was hard-gutted then. I could do a lot of things that could earn what little money I needed, thanks to my father's unfailing kindness which supplied me with bread at need despite the outrage to his principles at having been of a bum progenitive.

Then I began to get a little soft. I could still paint houses and do carpenter work, but I got soft. I began to think about making money by writing. I began to be concerned when magazine editors turned down short stories, concerned enough to tell them that they would buy these stories later anyway, and hence why not now. Meanwhile, with one novel completed and consistently refused for two years, I had just written my guts into *The Sound and the Fury* though I was not aware until the book was published that I had done so, because I had done it for pleasure. I believed then that I would never be published again. I had stopped thinking of myself in publishing terms.

But when the third mss., *Sartoris*, was taken by a publisher and (he having refused *The Sound and the Fury*) it was taken by still another publisher, who warned me at the time that it would not sell, I began to think of myself again as a printed object. I began to think of books in terms of possible money. I decided I might just as well make some of it myself. I took a little time out, and speculated what a person in Mississippi would believe to be current trends, chose what I thought was the right answer and invented the most horrific tale I could imagine and wrote it in about three weeks and sent it to Smith, who had done *The Sound and the Fury* and who wrote me immediately, "Good God, I can't publish this. We'd both be in jail." So I told Faulkner, "You're damned. You'll have to work now and then for the rest of your life." That was in the summer of 1929. I got a job in the power plant, on the night shift, from 6 P.M. to 6 A.M., as a coal passer. I shoveled coal from the bunker into a wheelbarrow

---

† From *Sanctuary* (New York: Random House, 1932). Drawn from William Faulkner, *Essays, Speeches, and Public Letters*, ed. James B. Meriwether (New York: Random House, 1965), pp. 176–78. Used by permission.

and wheeled it in and dumped it where the fireman could put it into the boiler. About 11 o'clock the people would be going to bed, and so it did not take so much steam. Then we could rest, the fireman and I. He would sit in a chair and doze. I had invented a table out of a wheelbarrow in the coal bunker, just beyond a wall from where a dynamo ran. It made a deep, constant humming noise. There was no more work to do until about 4 A.M., when we would have to clean the fires and get up steam again. On these nights, between 12 and 4, I wrote *As I Lay Dying* in six weeks, without changing a word. I sent it to Smith and wrote him that by it I would stand or fall.[1]

I think I had forgotten about *Sanctuary*, just as you might forget about anything made for an immediate purpose, which did not come off. *As I Lay Dying* was published and I didn't remember the mss. of *Sanctuary* until Smith sent me the galleys. Then I saw that it was so terrible that there were but two things to do: tear it up or rewrite it. I thought again, "It might sell; maybe 10,000 of them will buy it." So I tore the galleys down and rewrote the book. It had been already set up once, so I had to pay for the privilege of rewriting it, trying to make out of it something which would not shame *The Sound and the Fury* and *As I Lay Dying* too much and I made a fair job and I hope you will buy it and tell your friends and I hope they will buy it too.

WILLIAM FAULKNER

An Introduction for *The Sound and the Fury*†

* * *

* * * While writing Sanctuary, the next novel to The Sound and the Fury, that part of me which learned as I wrote, which perhaps is the very force which drives a writer to the travail of invention and the drudgery of putting seventy-five or a hundred thousand words on paper, was absent. * * * I learned only from the writing of Sanctuary that there was something missing; something which The Sound and the Fury gave me and Sanctuary did not. When I began As I Lay Dying I had discovered what it was and knew that it would be also missing in this case because this would be a deliberate book. I set

---

1. Cf. Joseph Conrad's 1914 "To My Readers in America" in which he identifies his early *Nigger of the Narcissus* (1897) as "the book by which, not as a novelist perhaps, but as an artist striving for the utmost sincerity of expression, I am willing to stand or fall."
† From "An Introduction for *The Sound and the Fury*." Written 1933, but unpublished during Faulkner's lifetime. First appeared in *The Southern Review* 8 (N.S., 1972): 705–10, ed. James B. Meriwether. Text drawn from the Norton Critical Edition of *The Sound and the Fury*, ed. David Minter (New York: Norton, 1994). Used by permission.

out deliberately to write a tour-de-force. Before I ever put pen to paper and set down the first word, I knew what the last word would be and almost where the last period would fall. Before I began I said, I am going to write a book by which, at a pinch, I can stand or fall if I never touch ink again. So when I finished it the cold satisfaction was there, as I had expected, but as I had also expected the other quality which The Sound and the Fury had given me was absent: that emotion definite and physical and yet nebulous to describe: that ecstasy, that eager and joyous faith and anticipation of surprise which the yet unmarred sheet beneath my hand held inviolate and unfailing, waiting for release. It was not there in As I Lay Dying. I said, It is because I knew too much about this book before I began to write it. I said, More than likely I shall never again have to know this much about a book before I begin to write it. * * *

* * *

WILLIAM FAULKNER

Address upon Receiving the Nobel Prize
for Literature†

STOCKHOLM, DECEMBER 10, 1950

I feel that this award was not made to me as a man, but to my work—a life's work in the agony and sweat of the human spirit, not for glory and least of all for profit, but to create out of the materials of the human spirit something which did not exist before. So this award is only mine in trust. It will not be difficult to find a dedication for the money part of it commensurate with the purpose and significance of its origin. But I would like to do the same with the acclaim too, by using this moment as a pinnacle from which I might be listened to by the young men and women already dedicated to the same anguish and travail, among whom is already that one who will some day stand here where I am standing.

Our tragedy today is a general and universal physical fear so long sustained by now that we can even bear it. There are no longer problems of the spirit. There is only the question: When will I be blown up? Because of this, the young man or woman writing today has forgotten the problems of the human heart in conflict with itself which

† From Essays, Speeches, and Public Letters, pp. 119–21. First published in New York Herald Tribune Book Review, 14 January 1951.

alone can make good writing because only that is worth writing about, worth the agony and the sweat.

He must learn them again. He must teach himself that the basest of all things is to be afraid; and, teaching himself that, forget it forever, leaving no room in his workshop for anything but the old verities and truths of the heart, the old universal truths lacking which any story is ephemeral and doomed—love and honor and pity and pride and compassion and sacrifice. Until he does so, he labors under a curse. He writes not of love but of lust, of defeats in which nobody loses anything of value, of victories without hope and, worst of all, without pity or compassion. His griefs grieve on no universal bones, leaving no scars. He writes not of the heart but of the glands.

Until he relearns these things, he will write as though he stood among and watched the end of man. I decline to accept the end of man. It is easy enough to say that man is immortal simply because he will endure: that when the last ding-dong of doom has clanged and faded from the last worthless rock hanging tideless in the last red and dying evening, that even then there will still be one more sound: that of his puny inexhaustible voice, still talking. I refuse to accept this. I believe that man will not merely endure: he will prevail. He is immortal, not because he alone among creatures has an inexhaustible voice, but because he has a soul, a spirit capable of compassion and sacrifice and endurance. The poet's, the writer's, duty is to write about these things. It is his privilege to help man endure by lifting his heart, by reminding him of the courage and honor and hope and pride and compassion and pity and sacrifice which have been the glory of his past. The poet's voice need not merely be the record of man, it can be one of the props, the pillars to help him endure and prevail.

WILLIAM FAULKNER

The *Paris Review* Interview†

Q: Mr. Faulkner, you were saying a while ago that you don't like interviews.

FAULKNER: The reason I don't like interviews is that I seem to react violently to personal questions. If the questions are about the work, I try to answer them. When they are about me, I may answer or

† From the *Paris Review*, Spring 1956. Interview by Jean Stein. Text drawn from *Lion in the Garden: Interviews with William Faulkner, 1926–1962*, ed. James B. Meriwether and Michael Millgate (New York: Random House, 1968). Excerpts from pp. 237, 243–44, 253, 254. Reprinted by permission of Jean Stein.

I may not, but even if I do, if the same question is asked tomorrow, the answer may be different.

* * *

Q: You say that the writer must compromise in working for the motion pictures. How about his writing? Is he under any obligation to his reader?

FAULKNER: His obligation is to get the work done the best he can do it; whatever obligation he has left over after that he can spend any way he likes. I myself am too busy to care about the public. I have no time to wonder who is reading me. I don't care about John Doe's opinion on mine or anyone else's work. Mine is the standard which has to be met, which is when the work makes me feel the way I do when I read *La Tentation de Saint Antoine*,[1] or the Old Testament. They make me feel good. So does watching a bird make me feel good . . . you know that if I were reincarnated, I'd want to come back a buzzard. Nothing hates him or envies him or wants him or needs him. He is never bothered or in danger, and he can eat anything.

Q: What technique do you use to arrive at your standard?

FAULKNER: Let the writer take up surgery or bricklaying if he is interested in technique. There is no mechanical way to get the writing done, no short cut. The young writer would be a fool to follow a theory. Teach yourself by your own mistakes; people learn only by error. The good artist believes that nobody is good enough to give him advice. He has supreme vanity. No matter how much he admires the old writer, he wants to beat him.

Q: Then would you deny the validity of technique?

FAULKNER: By no means. Sometimes technique charges in and takes command of the dream before the writer himself can get his hands on it. That is *tour de force* and the finished work is simply a matter of fitting bricks neatly together, since the writer knows probably every single word right to the end before he puts the first one down. This happened with *As I Lay Dying*. It was not easy. No honest work is. It was simple in that all the material was already at hand. It took me just about six weeks in the spare time from a 12 hour a day job at manual labor. I simply imagined a group of people and subjected them to the simple universal natural catastrophes which are flood and fire with a simple natural motive to give direction to their progress. But then, when technique does not intervene, in another sense writing is easier too. Because with me there is always a point in the book where the characters themselves rise up and take charge and finish the job—say somewhere about page 275. Of

---

1. *La Tentation de Saint Antoine* (1874), by Gustave Flaubert (1821–1880).

course, I don't know what would happen if I finished the book on page 274. * * *

* * *

Q: It has been said by Malcolm Cowley that your characters carry a sense of submission to their fate.

FAULKNER: That is his opinion. I would say that some of them do and some of them don't, like everybody else's characters. * * *

The Bundren family in As I Lay Dying pretty well coped with theirs. The Father having lost his wife would naturally need another one, so he got one. At one blow he not only replaced the family cook, he acquired a gramophone to give them all pleasure while they were resting. The pregnant daughter failed this time to undo her condition, but she was not discouraged. She intended to try again and even if they all failed right up to the last, it wasn't anything but just another baby.

* * *

WILLIAM FAULKNER

Class Conferences at the University of Virginia[†]

Session Eight[1]

March 13, 1957[2]

UNIVERSITY RADIO

ENGISH DEPARTMENT LANGUAGE PROGRAM

* * *

Q. Sir, do you have any solution for a man to find peace if he cannot write, as you?

A. Well, I don't think the writer finds peace. If he did, he would quit writing. Maybe man is incapable of peace. Maybe that is what differentiates man from a vegetable. Though maybe the vegetable don't even find peace. Maybe there's no such thing as peace, that it is a negative quality.

---

† From *Faulkner in the University: Class Conferences at the University of Virginia, 1957–58,* ed. Frederick L Gwynn and Joseph Blotner (New York; Charlottesville: The University of Virginia Press, 1959).
1. Pp. 66–67.
2. The Virginia volume lists this as 1958, a date clearly wrong and out of sequence.

Q. I am speaking of peace in his own heart.

A. Yes, well, I'm inclined to think that the only peace man knows is—he says, Why good gracious, yesterday I was happy. That at the moment he's too busy. That maybe peace is only a condition in retrospect, when the subconscious has got rid of the gnats and the tacks and the broken glass in experience and has left only the peaceful pleasant things—that was peace. Maybe peace is not is, but was.

* * *

Session Fourteen[3]

May 6, 1957

GRADUATE COURSE IN AMERICAN FICTION

UNDERGRADUATE COURSE IN AMERICAN LITERATURE

* * *

Q. Mr. Faulkner, in *As I Lay Dying*, did Jewel purchase the horse as a substitute for his mother?

A. Well, now that's something for the psychologist. He bought that horse because he wanted that horse. Now there was the need to use symbolism which I dug around, scratched around in my lumber room, and dragged out. That was an indication, a simple quick way to show that he did not belong to that family. That he was the alien there. Now just exactly what the connection is between the desire to buy a dangerous untamed horse and to be a country preacher I don't know, but that was the reason for the horse—to show quickly that he did not belong to the rest of the family.

Q. Can we attach any significance to his letting his father sell the horse later on in the story?

A. Only that people want to do better than they can do. That this man who loved nothing but that horse would never have believed that he would have sacrificed that horse for anything, yet when the crisis came he did behave better than he thought he would behave. He sacrificed the only thing he loved for someone else's good.

Q. Mr. Faulkner, does Jewel actually know or did he just sense that he is illegitimate?

A. He don't know and he probably don't care, but his mother knew, and whether she ever—no, she probably never told him. To him it made no difference.

Q. In the same book, was Darl out of his mind all through the book? Or did that come as a result of things happening during the book?

A. Darl was mad from the first. He got progressively madder because he didn't have the capacity—not so much of sanity but of inertness

3. Pp. 109–11, 111–15, 121–22.

to resist all the catastrophes that happened to the family. Jewel resisted because he was sane and he was the toughest. The others resisted through probably simple inertia, but Darl couldn't resist it and so he went completely off his rocker. But he was mad all the time.

Q. Is that why he speaks more beautifully than anybody else?

A. Yes.

Q. Mr. Faulkner, was Darl's motive in burning the barn—is that simply an indication of his madness or was he motivated by his desire to make of no consequence Jewel's sacrifice of his horse in order to get his mother's body to Jefferson?

A. Probably in Darl's mind that was a violation of some concept, some shape of beauty, to drag that dead putrefying body around any further, and he did the only thing his mad brain could conceive to rid the earth of something which should have been under ground days ago.

Q. Mr. Faulkner, why did Vardaman say "My mother is a fish"?

A. That was the child, nobody had paid any attention to him. He saw things that baffled and puzzled him, and nobody—none of the adults would stop long enough to show him any tenderness, any affection, and he was groping and that occurred to him that because of the—now, that's another book I should have read, I don't remember exactly what happened, except when he brought the fish home, something that happened from the outside got the fish confused with the fact that he knew his mother's body was in a room and that she was no longer his mother. She couldn't talk or—anyway, suddenly her position in the mosaic of the household was vacant.

Q. Then Vardaman was really—well, he was sane too, it was really just his inability to distinguish illusion and reality that—

A. That's right. He was a child trying to cope with this adult's world which to him was, and to any sane person, completely mad. That these people would want to drag that body over the country and go to all that trouble, and he was baffled and puzzled. He didn't know what to do about it.

Q. Would you say that Vardaman's love for his mother was the most sincere?

A. Well, it was because of the child's dependence on his mother, and probably to that child nobody else except the mother paid any attention to him. She was something stable, and his love for her was clinging to something that was stable in his world.

Q. In the end of the story, sir, Anse marries a woman whose name is already Bundren. Could you explain this?

A. No no, her name wasn't Bundren, but he heard the gramophone and as soon as he got his first wife buried he got a wedding license and two dollars and went back and married the one with the gramophone. Her name was Bundren when his family saw her, but it hadn't been until then. They were married then.

* * *

Q. In your novel *As I Lay Dying*, Mr. Faulkner, if there has to be a villain in the story could I be wrong in saying that he was Anse?

A. I'm not too sure there has to be a villain in the story. If there is a villain in that story it's the convention in which people have to live, in which in that case insisted that because this woman had said, I want to be buried twenty miles away, that people would go to any trouble and anguish to get her there. The simplest thing would have been to bury her where she was in any pleasant place. If they wanted to be sentimental about it they could have buried her in some place that she would like to go and sit by herself for a while. Or if they wanted to be practical they could have taken her out to the back yard and burned her. So if there was a villain it was the convention which gave them no out except to carry her through fire and flood twenty miles in order to follow the dying wish, which by that time to her meant nothing.

* * *

Q. What is the feeling that Dewey Dell in *As I Lay Dying*—what is the feeling that Dewey Dell has towards her brother Darl?

A. She knows without being able to phrase it that he is different somehow from the others through his madness. That maybe he is more perceptive. That he could be more tolerant of her—that is, she knows by instinct that if he found out that she was pregnant it wouldn't make a great deal of difference, but if Jewel found out she was pregnant he would go out and find somebody to kill, and for that reason she knows that Darl is capable of a sympathy, a sensitivity, that won't react in violence to serve an empty and to a woman fool-ish and silly code, and he is the only one in the family that she could say, I'm pregnant, I'm in trouble, and would get—well, maybe not too much sympathy, but no violent reaction that would merely add more trouble to what she already had.

Q. Mr. Faulkner, as long as we are on Darl, how is it that he could give such detailed description to his mother's death while he is out cutting wood some place else?

A. Who can say how much of the good poetry in the world has come out of madness, and who can say just how much of super-perceptivity the—a mad person might not have? It may not be so, but it's nice to think that there is some compensation for madness. That maybe the madman does see more than the sane man. That the world is more moving to him. That he is more perceptive. He has something of clair-voyance, maybe, a capacity for telepathy. Anyway, nobody can dispute it and that was a very, good way, I thought, a very effective way to tell what was happening back there at home—well, call it a change of pace. A trick, but since the whole book was a *tour de force,* I think that is a permissible trick.

Q. Sir, Dr. Peabody—I think his name is—is he put in just to afford a sort of comic relief or a definite purpose, because of his size and difficulty in getting up the mountain and so forth?

A. Mainly it was to give for the moment what may be called a nudge of credibility to a condition which was getting close to the realm of unbelief. That is, he is brought in from comparatively the metropolitan outland for a moment which says, Well, if he comes out there and sees these people, well then maybe they do exist. Up to that time they were functioning in this bizarre fashion almost inside a vacuum, and pretty soon you wouldn't have believed it until some stranger came in as a witness. Another trick.

Q. Mr. Faulkner, Whitfield appears to be a pretty hypocritical man in *As I Lay Dying*? By the time we see him as an older man in "Barn Burning" he seems to be a pretty delightful person. Has anything that we don't know about happened to him in between?

A. No, I wouldn't say he was a hypocritical man. He had to live a hypocritical life. That is, he had to live in public the life which the ignorant fanatic people of the isolated and rural South demand of a man of God, when actually he was just a man like any of them. I don't mean that all rural preachers are capable of behaving in private like he did, but they themselves are doing the best they can for a reason. They believe that man is doomed to sin, that he must struggle always against the Devil, and if he sins then he confesses and tries to do better, and tries to earn salvation still even if he does sin. That he was the victim of his environment also, of land in which there wasn't much relief from the arduous hard work for very little of the time, there was nothing to please the spirit—no music, no pictures, most of them couldn't read and when they could, the books were not available, and so they took what relief they could, knowing that they were committing sin but they would try to do better tomorrow.

Q. Mr. Faulkner, . . . [in] *As I Lay Dying*, Addie says, when she finds she is going to have Cash, "that living was terrible, and that this was the answer to it." Does this mean that this is the confirmation to the fact that living is terrible, or does this mean that she is wrong, that it isn't terrible?

A. She had probably married Anse because of pressure from her people,[1] but she probably saw through him that he was no good. She was ambitious probably and she married him against her inclination and she saw nothing ahead of her but a dull and dreary life as a slave without—just a slave, no pay, no compensation—then suddenly she found that there was something in motherhood that didn't, maybe

---

1. Faulkner forgets here that all "her people" are already in the cemetery at Jefferson [*Editor*].

didn't compensate for it but alleviated it. That there was some reason for the suffering and the anguish that people, all people, seem to have to go through with. Cash was the first child, and she said to herself, For the sake of this helpless child I can endure. That's what is meant by that, I think.

Q. Did you consciously or unconsciously parallel *As I Lay Dying* with *The Scarlet Letter*?

A. No, a writer don't have to consciously parallel because he robs and steals from everything he ever wrote or read or saw. I was simply writing a *tour de force* and as every writer does, I took whatever I needed wherever I could find it, without any compunction and with no sense of violating any ethics or hurting anyone's feelings because any writer feels that anyone after him is perfectly welcome to take any trick he has learned or any plot that he has used. Of course we don't know just who Hawthorne took his from. Which he probably did because there are so few plots to write about.

Q. Mr. Faulkner, I think that the *Times* said that you take some of your names of caricatures of Southern politicians and so forth, such as Vardaman, and I just wondered where you got, if that was true, and if so, where did you get the rest of your names like Darl? They seem sort of unusual.

A. Darl was of course the rural Mississippi pronunciation of Darrell. They would call it Darl. Vardaman, Bilbo—they are very popular with country people in Mississippi to name their children after governors and senators and the politicians that come out and shake their hands and say, I'm one of you all, even if I do have a white shirt every day. I'm just—you're just as good as I am and I'm one of you, and so they name their children after the successful politicians.

*   *   *

Q. According to your answer to my earlier question, I suppose you connect no—make no connection at all between the family relationships in *The Sound and the Fury* and those of *As I Lay Dying*.

A. Well, there would be certain similarities because of simple geography. That is, there are certain similarities in family relationships between a family of planters and a family of tenant farmers. The superficial differences could be vast and varied, but basically the same relationship is there because it's based on the need for solidarity in a country which not too long ago was still frontier. It's all because of the influence of a violent form of the Protestant religion, on politics, something on the economy of the country. So the relationships would be in that sense basically similar.

Q. Then you couldn't go so far as to say, for example, that Darl is the Quentin of the Bundrens and that Cash is the Jason of the Bundrens.

A. Well, you could if that is any pleasure to you. I mean by that that some people get a certain amount of pleasure in hunting around in a writer's work for reasons, for symbols, for similarities, and of course they are very likely all there, but the writer himself is too busy simply writing about people in conflict with themselves and one another and their background to wonder or even care whether he repeats himself or whether he uses symbols or not. He would use a symbol at the drop of a hat if that was the simplest way to throw the light on the particular incident he's telling about, and it's perfectly valid, I think, for anyone to seek for those symbols. That there's a pleasure in doing that just like the reason for reading a book is—it's a pleasure.

* * *

Session Fifteen[4]

May 7, 1957

UNIVERSITY RADIO

ENGLISH DEPARTMENT LANGUAGE PROGRAM

* * *

Q. Mr. Faulkner, I had—have down here on a list several words that I would like to ask you about. One is the word *pussel-gutted*. You spoke about Jewel calling his horse *pussel-gutted* and that was in mock affection. And then in another place Peabody—this is by the way in *As I Lay Dying*—Peabody has *pussel-gutted* himself eating cold greens. I suppose that means make yourself flabby.

A. Bloated. Yes.

Q. That's a Georgia term. I know that term.

Q. Is there a plant that you're—that is behind that figure of speech, *pussel*?

A. No.

Q. There's a plant in Virginia called pursley and I thought maybe it was the same thing. It's a hideous plant, an ugly plant, it gets full of water.

A. It could derive from that. I don't know. I've heard it all my life. It means someone that is bloated, that has a tremendous belly that he shouldn't have.

* * *

4. Pp. 125–26. Transcript continued on p. 202 of this Norton Critical Edition.

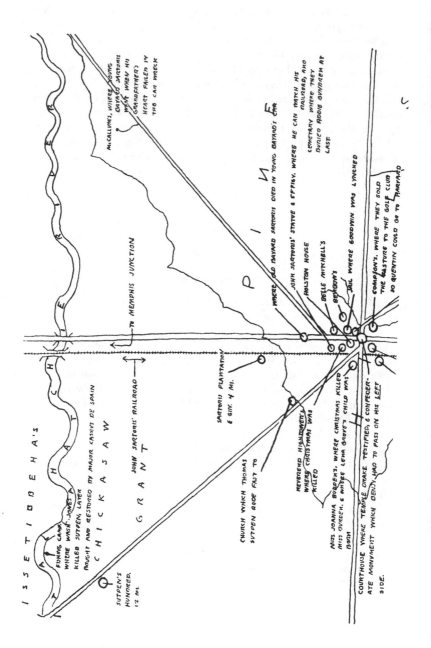

ISSETIBBEHA'S

FISHING CAMP, WHERE WASH JONES KILLED SUTPEN, LATER BOUGHT AND RESTORED BY MAJOR CASSIUS DE SPAIN

CHICKASAW

CHITTAHATCHIE RIVER

GRANT

JOHN SARTORIS' RAILROAD

SUTPEN'S HUNDRED, 12 MI.

CHURCH WHICH THOMAS SUTPEN RODE FAST TO

REVEREND HIGHTOWER'S, WHERE CHRISTMAS WAS KILLED

MISS JOANNA BURDEN'S, WHERE CHRISTMAS KILLED MISS BURDEN, & WHERE LENA GROVE'S CHILD WAS BORN

COURTHOUSE WHERE TEMPLE DRAKE TESTIFIED, & CONFEDERATE MONUMENT WHICH BENJY HAD TO PASS ON HIS LEFT SIDE.

—TO MEMPHIS JUNCTION

SARTORIS PLANTATION & GIN, 4 MI.

McCALLUM'S, WHERE YOUNG BAYARD SARTORIS WENT WHEN HIS GRANDFATHER'S HEART FAILED IN THE CAR WRECK

WHERE OLD BAYARD SARTORIS DIED IN YOUNG BAYARD'S CAR

JOHN SARTORIS' STATUE & EFFIGY, WHERE HE CAN WATCH HIS RAILROAD, AND CEMETERY WHERE THEY BURIED ADDIE BUNDREN AT LAST

HOLSTON HOUSE

BELLE MITCHELL'S

BENBOW'S

JAIL, WHERE GOODWIN WAS LYNCHED

COMPSON'S, WHERE THEY SOLD THE PASTURE TO THE GOLF CLUB TO QUENTIN COULD GO TO HARVARD

PINE

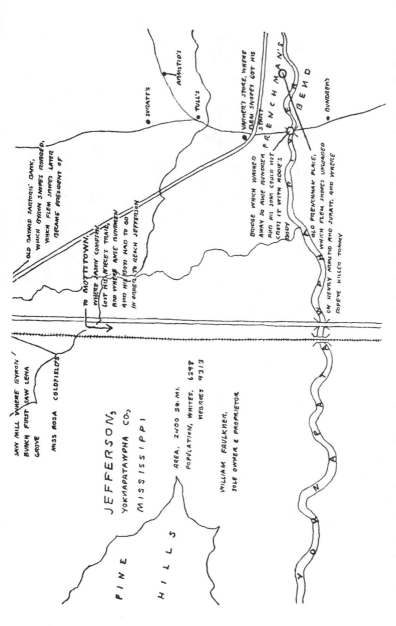

From *Absalom, Absalom* (1936). Note the confusing placement of the Tull and Bundren farms in relation to the Yoknapatawpha River, as well as the spelling of the town that in this novel is called "Mottson."

From *William Faulkner Manuscripts 7: As I Lay Dying*, ed. Thomas L. McHaney. Used by permission of W. W. Norton & Company, Inc. This is p. 43 of the manuscript's 107 sheets. Note Faulkner's second thoughts about his dialogue.

DARL

He comes up the lane fast, yet we are three hundred
yards beyond the mouth of it when he turns into the road, the
mud flying beneath the flicking drive of the hooves. Then he
slows a little, light and erect in the saddle, the horse mincing through the mud.

Tull is in his lot. He looks at us, lifts his hand.
We go on, the wagon creaking, the mud whispering on the wheels.
Vernon still stands there. He watches Jewel as he passes, the
horse moving with a light, high-kneed driving gait, three hundred yards back. We go on, with a motion so soporific, so
dreamlike as to be uninferant of progress, as though time and
not space were decreasing between us and it.

It turns off at right angles, the wheel-marks of
last Sunday healed away now: a smooth, red scoriation curving
away into the pines; a white signboard with faded lettering:
New Hope Church. 3 mi. It wheels up like a motionless hand
lifted above the profound desolation of the ocean; beyond it
the red road lies like a spoke of which Addie Bundren is the
rim. It wheels past, empty, unscarred, the white signboard
turns away its fading and tranquil assertion. Cash looks up

102.

From *William Faulkner Manuscripts 7: As I Lay Dying*, ed. Thomas L.
McHaney. (New York and London: Garland, 1987), pp. 322–23. Virtually
identical with the printed version, which appears on pp. 62 of this Norton
Critical Edition. But see the second paragraph—only its first sentence appears
in the manuscript, and that as an interpolation.

the road quietly, his head turning as we pass it like an owl's
head, his face composed. Pa looks straight ahead, humped. Dewey Dell looks at the road too, then she looks back at me, her
eyes watchful and repudiant, not like that question in those
of Cash, for a smoldering while. The signboard passes; the unscarred road wheels on. Then Dewey Dell turns her head. The
wagon creaks on.

Cash spits over the wheel. "In a couple of days now
it'll be smelling," he says.

"You might tell Jewel that," I say.

He is motionless now, sitting the horse at the junction, upright, watching us, no less still than the signboard
that lifts its fading capitualation opposite him.

"It aint balanced right for no long ride," Cash says.

"Tell him that, too," I say. The wagon creaks on.

A mile further along he passes us, the horse, archnecked, reined back to a swift singlefoot. He sits lightly,
poised, upright, wooden-faced in the saddle, the broken hat
raked at a swaggering angle. He passes us swiftly, without looking at us, the horse driving, its hooves hissing in the mud.
A gout of mud, backflung, plops onto the box. Cash leans forward
and takes a tool from his box and removes it carefully. Then
the road crosses Whiteleaf, the willows leaning near enough, he
breaks off a branch and scours at the stain with the wet leaves.

Q. Mr. Faulkner, I noticed that Vernon and Uncle Billy, in *As I Lay Dying*, often say *aye* for *yes*. I wondered if that was common or whether it was just characteristic of the older generation.

A. That is common among the older people whose ancestry was Scottish. They came to the mountains of North Carolina, then they came to the mountains of Virginia, then they came to the hills of Mississippi and they kept their old ways. They would say *to red up a room*, just as you hear in Scotland—means to clean a room, to make the beds, sweep.

* * *

Session Thirty[5]

May 2, 1958

UNDERGRADUATE COURSE IN CONTEMPORARY
AMERICAN LITERATURE

UNDERGRADUATE COURSE IN WRITING

GRADUATE COURSE IN AMERICAN FICTION

* * *

Q. Sir, in *As I Lay Dying*, what was the significance of Darl's lying in front of his mother's coffin after it was saved from the fire?

A. Darl was mad. He did things which it seemed to me he had to do or he insisted on doing. His reasons I could try to rationalize to suit myself, even if I couldn't rationalize his reasons to please me I had to accept the act because Darl insisted on doing that. I mean that any character that you write takes charge of his own behavior. You can't make him do things once he comes alive and stands up and casts his own shadow. Darl did things which I am sure were for his own mad reasons quite logical. I couldn't always understand why he did things, but he did insist on doing things, and when we would quarrel about it, he always won, because at that time he was alive, he was under his own power.

---

5. Pp. 263–64.

Cultural Context

Faulkner's work needs to be seen in two contexts at once. The first is that of international modernism. The second is that of the American South, and in part of what was called the Southern Renaissance. This Norton Critical Edition allows the question of modernism to percolate through its selection of reviews and criticism. I have not, for example, included material on the "stream of consciousness" as such, for that seems to me best handled in terms of its place within the text itself. The selections here serve instead to locate Faulkner's novel within its particular moment in the history of his native region. That is harder to do with *As I Lay Dying* than with the rest of his work, for the novel avoids the intertwined pillars of race and remembrance on which his other important books rest. This story about a family of poor whites does not mention the Civil War or the Lost Cause. It offers no trace of plantation myth, and is almost entirely without the presence of black characters; absences that are themselves signficant. Still, Faulkner's portrait of the Bundrens does find its echo in the culture of his period.

In 1935 the Richmond-based novelist Ellen Glasgow, whose long career had given her an unofficial position as the doyenne of Southern fiction, wrote of her distaste for what she called the school of "Raw-Head-and-Bloody-Bones." She included Faulkner among the writers in that school, and gave it a name that summed up what she saw as its fascination with the macabre and the grotesque: "Southern Gothic."[1] The term has had legs, and has been used to describe several generations of Faulkner's successors, including such now-canonical figures as Flannery O'Connor. Both Carson McCullers' "The Russian Realists and Southern Literature" and Fred Hobson's "Benighted South" serve to complicate our notions of the Southern grotesque. Some of McCullers's own fiction can stand as an example of that home-grown Gothic. But a more interesting comparison, she suggests, is that between Southern fiction and the nineteenth-century Russian novel, and she links Faulkner's world to the mix of "anguish and farce" that one finds in Gogol and Dostoyevsky. Hobson's entry from the *Encylopaedia of Southern Culture* historicizes the popular image of the South as "savage or barbarian . . . uncivilized, unsanitary, and violent," and suggests some of the reasons for what has proved an enduring caricature.

---

1. Ellen Glasgow, "Heroes and Monsters," *Saturday Review of Literature* 12 (4 May 1935): 3–4.

As I Lay Dying appeared in the same year as a book called I'll Take My Stand: The South and the Agrarian Tradition. This collection of essays by "Twelve Southerners," among them the poet Allen Tate and the novelist Robert Penn Warren, mounted a defense of what it saw as a pre-capitalist, agricultural social order against the incursions of Northern industrialism, as embodied in the mill towns and profit-grasping rapacity of the "New South." Faulkner would have some sympathy with that position, as we can see from his account of the all-consuming Snopes clan in The Hamlet and its successors; and while the Agrarians themselves might have recognized Anse Bundren's mendaciousness, they would also have accepted his sense of an opposition between the "hard-working" farmer and "them that runs the stores in the towns" (63). But any comparison between Faulkner and the Agrarians offers more contrast than connection. If As I Lay Dying is an exception in his work in depicting a world largely without black people, the Agrarians did their level best to write the black presence out of the Southern past as a whole. Their version of the South was one almost entirely without the stain of slavery—that capital investment on which Southern agriculture depended—and their idealization of the yeoman farmer was simplistic on other grounds as well. I've chosen an excerpt from Andrew Nelson Lytle's essay "The Hind Tit" to serve as a counterpoint to Faulkner's picture of rural life. Years later Flannery O'Connor would say, when asked how it felt to write in Faulkner's shadow, that "Nobody wants his mule and wagon stalled on the same track the Dixie Limited is roaring down."[2] I'll Take My Stand remains an important reference for any student of the period, and no one would claim that As I Lay Dying approaches the status of documentary. Nevertheless a comparison of Lytle's description of country life to Faulkner's account of the Bundrens is enough to suggest that even a dozen Southerners all working together couldn't manage to clear that wagon.

A very different account of a farm family's world comes to us in James Agee's Let Us Now Praise Famous Men, his collaboration with the great photographer Walker Evans. The project began as a magazine assignment, a Depression-era attempt to document a world of rural poverty. That Depression was not yet an unmistakable fact at the time Faulkner wrote As I Lay Dying; as has often been noted, he began the book on the day after the 1929 crash, but it took some months for the scale of the disaster to become clear. Yet Faulkner did not need the Depression to understand poverty, and though the Bundrens own their land, they still have much in common with the families of Alabama sharecroppers whose lives Agee chronicles. Agee's prose is at times florid, and in places shows Faulkner's own fingerprints; still he finds a kind of poetry in the stark, bare world of the Gudger family and their neighbors.

My last selections address other aspects of the novel. Thomas Clark's Pills, Petticoats and Plows is an invaluable guide to the material culture of Southern life in the first years of the twentieth century. Reading it

---

2. Flannery O'Connor, "Some Aspects of the Grotesque in Southern Fiction," Mystery and Manners (New York: Farrar Straus & Giroux, 1969), p. 45.

will suggest that Faulkner has in the Bundrens given us a family whose lives, forty miles away from the nearest significant town, have lagged several decades behind their times. Early in the novel we find a memorable description of Anse Bundren's shoes, which look "hacked with a blunt axe out of pig iron" (8). So I have taken a passage from Clark that suggests the importance of those shoes, and another on funerals that touches on the question of home-built coffins.

At the end of the novel Faulkner shows us Darl Bundren, bound in a straitjacket, on the train for Mississippi State Insane Hospital at Jackson. His family has commited him to the asylum as a way to avoid a suit over his destruction of Gillespie's barn. Nobody knows how clear an image Faulkner had of the hospital, or its treatment of the insane; of the future, if any, that he envisioned for the novel's central character. But he often talked about his characters as if they were alive, as if he might at any moment hear some news about them that would give him another story to tell, and I have often wondered about the world to which Darl is consigned. The pages I've selected from the Hospital's report to the Mississippi legislature will at least give us the start of a picture; a picture in some places reassuring, and in others horrific.

CARSON McCULLERS

The Russian Realists and Southern Literature[†]

In the South during the past fifteen years a genre of writing has come about that is sufficiently homogeneous to have led critics to label it "the Gothic School." This tag, however, is unfortunate. The effect of a Gothic tale may be similar to that of a Faulkner story in its evocation of horror, beauty, and emotional ambivalence—but this effect evolves from opposite sources; in the former the means used are romantic or supernatural, in the latter a peculiar and intense realism. Modern Southern writing seems rather to be most indebted to Russian literature, to be the progeny of the Russian realists. And this influence is not accidental. The circumstances under which Southern literature has been produced are strikingly like those under which the Russians functioned. In both old Russia and the South up to the present time a dominant characteristic was the cheapness of human life.

Toward the end of the nineteenth century the Russian novelists particularly Dostoievsky, were criticized harshly for their so called "cruelty." This same objection is now being raised against the new Southern writers. On first thought the accusation seems puzzling.

† From *Decision* 2 (July 1941): 15–19. Reproduced by permission of Pollinger Limited and The Estate of Carson McCullers. Carson McCullers (1917–1967) was a Georgia-born novelist. Her works include *The Heart Is a Lonely Hunter* (1940) and *The Member of the Wedding* (1946).

Art, from the time of the Greek tragedians on, has unhesitatingly portrayed violence, madness, murder, and destruction. No single instance of "cruelty" in Russian or Southern writing could not be matched or outdone by the Greeks, the Elizabethans, or, for that matter, the creators of the Old Testament. Therefore it is not the specific "cruelty" itself that is shocking, but the manner in which it is presented. And it is in this approach to life and suffering that the Southerners are so indebted to the Russians. The technique briefly is this: a bold and outwardly callous juxtaposition of the tragic with the humorous, the immense with the trivial, the sacred with the bawdy, the whole soul of a man with a materialistic detail.

To the reader accustomed to the classical traditions this method has a repellent quality. If, for instance, a child dies and the life and death of this child is presented in a single sentence, and if the author passes over this without comment or apparent pity but goes on with no shift in tone to some trivial detail—this method of presentation seems cynical. The reader is used to having the relative values of an emotional experience categorized by the author. And when the author disclaims this responsibility the reader is confused and offended.

Marmeladov's funeral supper in *Crime and Punishment*[1] and *As I Lay Dying,* by William Faulkner, are good examples of this type of realism. The two works have much in common. Both deal with the subject of death. In both there is a fusion of anguish and farce that acts on the reader with an almost physical force. Marmeladov's violent death, Katerina Ivanovna's agitation about the supper, the details of the food served, the clerk "who had not a word to say for himself and smelt abominably"—on the surface the whole situation would seem to be a hopeless emotional rag-bag. In the face of agony and starvation the reader suddenly finds himself laughing at the absurdities between Katerina Ivanovna and the landlady, or smiling at the antics of the little Pole. And unconsciously after the laughter the reader feels guilty; he senses that the author has duped him in some way.

Farce and tragedy have always been used as foils for each other. But it is rare, except in the works of the Russians and the Southerners, that they are superimposed one upon the other so that their effects are experienced simultaneously. It is this emotional composite that has brought about the accusations of "cruelty." D. S. Mirsky, in commenting on a passage from Dostoievsky says: "Though the element of humor is unmistakably present, it is a kind of humor that requires a rather peculiar constitution to amuse."[2]

---

1. 1866 novel by Fyodor Dostoyevsky (1821–1881)
2. D. S. Mirsky (1890–1939), *A History of Russian Literature: From the Earliest Times to the Death of Dostoyevsky (1881).* (New York: Knopf, 1927), p. 347.

In Faulkner's *As I Lay Dying*, this fusion is complete. The story deals with the funeral journey made by Anse Bundreen to bury his wife. He is taking the body to his wife's family graveyard some forty miles away; the journey takes him and his children several days and in the course of it the body decomposes in the heat and they meet with a mad plethora of disasters. They lose their mules while fording a stream, one son breaks his leg and it becomes gangrenous, another son goes mad, the daughter is seduced—a more unholy cortege could hardly be imagined. But the immensities of these disasters are given no more accent than the most inconsequential happenings. Anse throughout the story has his mind on the false teeth he is going to buy when he reaches the town. The girl is concerned with some cake she has brought with her to sell. The boy with the gangrenous leg keeps saying of the pain, "It don't bother me none," and his main worry is that his box of carpenter's tools will be lost on the way. The author reports this confusion of values but takes on himself no spiritual responsibility.

To understand this altitude one has to know the South. The South and old Russia have much in common sociologically. The South has always been a section apart from the rest of the United States, having interests and a personality distinctly its own. Economically and in other ways it has been used as a sort of colony to the rest of the nation. The poverty is unlike anything known in other parts of this country. In social structure there is a division of classes similar to that in old Russia. The South is the only part of the nation having a definite peasant class. But in spite of social divisions the people of the South are homogeneous. The Southerner and the Russian are both "types" in that they have certain recognizable and national psychological traits. Hedonistic, imaginative, lazy, and emotional—there is surely a cousinly resemblance.

In both the South and old Russia the cheapness of life is realized at every turn. The thing itself, the material detail, has an exaggerated value. Life is plentiful; children are born and they die, or if they do not die they live and struggle. And in the fight to maintain existence the whole life and suffering of a human being can be bound up in ten acres of washed out land, in a mule, in a bale of cotton. In Chekhov's *The Peasants*,[3] the loss of the samovar in the hut is as sad, if not sadder, than the death of Nikolai or the cruelty of the old grandmother. And in "Tobacco Road,"[4] Jeeter Lester's bargain, the swapping of his daughter for seven dollars and a throw-in, is symbolical. Life, death, the experiences of the spirit, these come and go

---

3. Anton Chekhov (1860–1904), short-story writer and playwright; "The Peasants" (1897).
4. Best-selling novel (1932) by Erskine Caldwell (1903–1987).

and we do not know for what reason; but the *thing* is there, it remains to plague or comfort, and its value is immutable.

Gogol is credited to be the first of the realists. In *The Overcoat* the little clerk identifies his whole life with his new winter cloak, and loses heart and dies when it is stolen. From the time of Gogol, or from about 1850 until 1900, imaginative writing in Russia can be regarded as one artistic growth. Chekhov differs certainly from Aksakov and from Turgenev, but taken all in all the approach to their material and the general technique is the same. Morally the attitude is this: human beings are neither good nor evil, they are only unhappy and more or less adjusted to their unhappiness. People are born into a world of confusion, a society in which the system of values is so uncertain that who can say if a man is worth more than a load of hay, or if life itself is precious enough to justify the struggle to obtain the material objects necessary for its maintenance. This attitude was perhaps characteristic of all Russians during those times, and the writers only reported exactly what was true in their time and place. It is the unconscious moral approach, the fundamental spiritual basis of their work. But this by no means precludes a higher conscious level. And it is in the great philosophical novels that the culmination of Russian realism has been reached.[5]

*   *   *

*** Dostoievsky, Tolstoi[6] and the minor moralists, brought to Russian realism one element that had hitherto been obscure or lacking. That is the element of passion.

Gogol has an imaginative creativeness that is overwhelming. As a satirist he has few equals, and his purely technical equipment is enormous. But of passion he has not a trace. Aksakov, Turgenev, Herzen,[7] Chekhov, diverse as their separate geniuses are, they are alike in lacking this particular level of emotion. In the work of Dostoievsky and Tolstoi it is as though Russian literature suddenly closed its fist, and the whole literary organism was affected; there was a new tenseness, a gathering together of resources, a radically tightened nervous tone. With the moralists Russian realism reached its most fervent and glorious phase.

From the viewpoint of artistic merit it would be absurd to compare the new Southern writers with the Russians. It is only in their

---

5. Nikolai Gogol (1809–1852) author of "The Overcoat" (1842). Ivan Turgenev (1818–1883) author of *Sketches from a Hunter's Album* (1852) and *Fathers and Sons* (1862); Sergei Aksakov (1791–1859), author of *Family Chronicle* (1959).
6. Leo Tolstoy (1828–1910); *War and Peace* (1869); *Anna Karenina* (1877).
7. Alexander Herzen (1812–1870), editor and political theorist.

approach to their material that analogies can be drawn. The first real novel (this does not include old romances) to be written in the South did not appear until after 1900, when Russian realism was already on the decline. *Barren Ground,* by Ellen Glasgow,[8] marked the beginning of an uncertain period of development, and Southern literature can only be considered to have made its start during the past fifteen years. But with the arrival of Caldwell and Faulkner a new and vital outgrowth began. And the South at the present time boils with literary energy. W. J. Cash in *The Mind of the South*[9] says that if these days you shoot off a gun at random below the Mason-Dixon line you are bound by the law of averages to hit a writer.

An observer should not criticize a work of art on the grounds that it lacks certain qualities that the artist himself never intended to include. The writer has the prerogative of limiting his own scope, of staking the boundaries of his own kingdom. This must be remembered when attempting to appraise the work now being done in the South.

The Southern writers have reacted to their environment in just the same manner as the Russians prior to the time of Dostoievsky and Tolstoi. They have transposed the painful substance of life around them as accurately as possible, without taking the part of emotional panderer between the truth as it is and the feelings of the reader. The "cruelty" of which the Southerners have been accused is at bottom only a sort of naïveté, an acceptance of spiritual inconsistencies without asking the reason why, without attempting to propose an answer. Undeniably there is an infantile quality about this clarity of vision and rejection of responsibility.

But literature in the South is a young growth, and it cannot be blamed because of its youth. One can only speculate about the possible course of its development or retrogression. Southern writing has reached the limits of a moral realism; something more must be added if it is to continue to flourish. As yet there has been no forerunner of an analytical moralist such as Tolstoi or a mystic like Dostoievsky. But the material with which Southern literature deals seems to demand of itself that certain basic questions be posed. If and when this group of writers is able to assume a philosophical responsibility, the whole tone and structure of their work will be enriched, and Southern writing will enter a more complete and vigorous stage in its evolution.

8. Ellen Glasgow (1873–1945), Virginia novelist; *Barren Ground* (1925).
9. W. J. Cash (1900–1941), journalist and historian; *The Mind of the South* (1941).

FRED HOBSON

Benighted South[†]

If the 19th-century South was viewed by romantics, North as well as South, as the primal garden, Eden before the Fall, the 20th-century South—at least to many image makers—has often been something quite different. To be sure, the Benighted or Savage South had its origins in the 19th century: William Lloyd Garrison had referred to it as the "great Sodom" and Frederick Law Olmsted,[1] Harriet Beecher Stowe, and other northern writers had written harshly of it. But in the early 20th century—more particularly in the decade of the 1920s—the idea that the South was savage or barbarian took hold even more strongly than before. The new image of the Benighted South was a result partly of actual events in the South during the 1920s and partly of the writings of social critics and novelists who focused attention on the dark side of the contemporary South. The writers did not, as traditional southerners often charged, invent the negative southern image: the events did that. The Scopes evolution trial in Dayton, Tenn., in July 1925;[2] the anti-Catholicism shown during Al Smith's presidential campaign in 1928; textile strikes and violence in Gastonia and Marion, N.C., and in Elizabethton, Tenn., in 1929; the rise of the modern Ku Klux Klan and numerous lynchings, outbreaks of nightriding, and other manifestations of racial injustice—these events drew the attention of national journalists such as H. L. Mencken and Oswald Garrison Villard; of prominent magazines such as the *Nation*, the *New Republic*, and the *Century*; and of social scientists such as Frank Tannenbaum of Columbia University, who wrote the aptly entitled *Darker Phases of the South* (1924). The Yankee crusade against the romantic southern image was carried out on several fronts: Tannenbaum concentrating on social ills; Villard and W. E. B. Du Bois, the black editor of the *Crisis*, focusing on racial matters; and Mencken in general command, attacking intellectual and cultural sterility. Mencken's essay, "The Sahara of the Bozart" (1920), was the most trenchant—

[†] From *The Encyclopedia of Southern Culture*, eds. William Ferris and Charles Reagan Wilson (Chapel Hill: University of North Carolina Press, 1989), pp. 1100–1101. Copyright © 1989 by the University of North Carolina Press. Used by permission of the publisher.

1. Frederick Law Olmsted (1822–1903), landscape architect and designer of New York City's Central Park among others, traveller in the antebellum South, and author of *The Cotton Kingdom* (1861). William Lloyd Garrison (1805–1879), editor of the Abolitionist newspaper, the *Liberator*.

2. Court case challenging a Tennessee law that made it illegal to teach any theory that denied the Biblical account of creation. High school biology teacher John Scopes was found guilty, and fined. Dramatized by Jerome Lawrence and Robert Edwin Lee as *Inherit the Wind* (1955) and later filmed.

and readable—indictment of the South, contributing more than any
other work to the popular image of the Benighted South.[3]

But the outsiders were hardly alone in portraying the South of the
early 20th century as uncivilized, unsanitary, and violent. A native
group of journalists and literary figures was perhaps even more effective in this role, presumably because they, as southerners, knew
whereof they spoke. North Carolina newspapermen Gerald W. Johnson and W. J. Cash sent essay after essay to their mentor, Mencken, at
the *American Mercury*, and the subjects of their essays were southern
racism, religious barbarism, and intellectual sterility. Southern editors took their stands against racism and religious bigotry and won
Pulitzers for their courage. As George B. Tindall has written, a "fifth
column of native Menckens and Tannenbaums" found "an almost
ridiculously simple formula for fame": they revealed "the grotesqueries
of the benighted South."

Southern novelists were perhaps even bolder, or at least more
graphic. Beginning in the early 1920s, writers such as T. S. Stribling
of Tennessee and Clement Wood of Alabama, and slightly later Erskine Caldwell of Georgia, portrayed Dixie as a land of poverty, sloth,
ignorance, and racial injustice. Stribling's Tennessee hillbillies and
corrupt folk of northern Alabama were depicted in *Birthright* (1922),
Teeftallow (1926), *Bright Metal* (1928), and his late trilogy, *The Forge*
(1931), the Pulitzer Prize–winning *The Store* (1932), and *The
Unfinished Cathedral* (1934). Caldwell became famous for his pictures of depraved poor whites in *Tobacco Road* (1932) and *God's
Little Acre* (1933). And on their heels came greater, less exclusively
regional writers, whose portrait of the South, for all its artistry, was
judged by reviewers to be no more flattering. In *Look Homeward,
Angel* (1929) Thomas Wolfe—in the words of one reviewer—"spat
upon" the South. Wolfe's fictional town of Altamont—based closely
on his hometown of Asheville, N.C.—he described as a "barren
spiritual wilderness," which maintained a "hostile and murderous
intrenchment against all new life." If Wolfe's South was intellectually
barren and culturally sterile, that of William Faulkner was downright
frightening. Between 1929 and 1936 the young Mississippian burst
forth with a series of novels portraying a South of decaying gentry,

---

3. "Down there a poet is now almost as rare as an oboe-player, a dry-point etcher or a meta-
physician. It is, indeed, amazing to contemplate so vast a vacuity. One thinks of the inter-
stellar spaces, of the colossal reaches of the now mythical ether. Nearly the whole of
Europe could be lost in that stupendous region of worn-out farms, shoddy cities and paralyzed cerebrums: one could throw in France, Germany and Italy, and still have room for
the British Isles. And yet, for all its size and all its wealth and all the 'progress' it babbles
of, it is almost as sterile, artistically, intellectually, culturally, as the Sahara Desert. There
are single acres in Europe that house more first-rate men than all the states south of the
Potomac; there are probably single square miles in America." From "The Sahara of the
Bozart" in *Prejudices, 2nd Series* (New York: Alfred A. Knopf, 1920). H. L. Mencken,
Baltimore-based journalist (1880–1956).

idiocy, religious fanaticism, murder, rape, and suicide. *The Sound and the Fury* (1929) depicted the decline and fall of the Compson family, antebellum aristocrats who could not cope with the new order. *As I Lay Dying* (1930), Faulkner's tragicomic story of the attempt of a dirt-poor Mississippi family to bury their wife and mother, seemed to reinforce the worst image of southern degradation brought out by the journalists of the 1920s. *Sanctuary* (1931) was even more depraved—and, because it was sold to Hollywood, even more influential in creating the image of a savage South. *Light in August* (1932) presented a gallery of southern grotesques and eccentrics. *Absalom, Absalom!* (1936), perhaps Faulkner's greatest novel, pictured a dark and violent antebellum South. And Faulkner's conniving poor whites, the Snopeses, were yet to come in *The Hamlet* (1940), *The Town* (1957), and *The Mansion* (1959).

By the mid-1930s the depiction of the South in contemporary fiction had become so sordid that even that earlier iconoclast, Gerald W. Johnson, was moved to call this latest Dixie-in-print "The Horrible South." Faulkner, Stribling, Caldwell, and Wolfe were "real equerries of Raw-Head-and-Bloody-Bones . . . the merchants of death, hell, and the grave . . . the horror-mongers-in-chief." *Sanctuary,* Johnson insisted, "put me under the weather for thirty-six hours." Yet, as Johnson maintained, the new picture of the South was a necessary corrective to the romantic picture of the Old, an antidote to Thomas Nelson Page.[4] The South of 1930 was not so bad as its writers suggested—but the South of 1830 had never been so good.

The image of the Benighted South remained firmly entrenched in the national mythology throughout the 1930s. The Scottsboro[5] case of the early 1930s and President Roosevelt's pronouncement in 1938 that the South was "the Nation's No. 1 economic problem" insured that. Events of the next two decades did little to modify the image, and those of the 1960s brought the South the same widespread negative attention it had attracted in the 1920s and 1930s. Now Oxford and Selma and Birmingham were in the news, not Dayton and Gastonia and Scottsboro, but the result was the same: Yankee reporters again flocked South and reported that Dixie remained benighted, savage, somehow out of touch with modern civilization.

Only with the end of the civil rights movement—and the rise of the Sunbelt of the 1970s—did the image of a Benighted South begin to fade. In truth, perhaps the coming of interstate highways and widespread air-conditioning had as much to do with the new positive image of Dixie as the departure of lynching and the decline

---

4. Thomas Nelson Page (1853–1922), prolific Virginia writer whose works depict an antebellum world of happy slaves and benevolent masters.
5. 1931 Alabama case in which nine black teenagers were convicted of raping two white women on the basis of false testimony. All eventually went free, but after years on death row.

of racial segregation. In any case, as the South entered the last two decades of the 20th century, it was bolder and more confident than before, possessing shining new cities, a new base of wealth dependent on oil, aerospace, real estate, and leisure, and a working knowledge of the power of public relations. The image of the Benighted South it had consigned, in large part, to its past.

ANDREW NELSON LYTLE
The Hind Tit[†]

*   *   *

Let us set his holdings at two hundred acres, more or less—a hundred in cultivation, sixty in woods and pasture, and forty in waste land, too rocky for cultivation but offering some pasturage.* * * This example is taken, of course, with the knowledge that the problem on any two hundred acres is never the same: the richness of the soil, its qualities, the neighborhood, the distance from market, the climate, water, and a thousand such things make the life on every farm distinctly individual.

The house is a dog-run with an ell running to the rear, the kitchen and dining-room being in the ell, if the family does not eat in the kitchen; and the sleeping-rooms in the main part of the house. The dog-run is a two- or four-crib[1] construction with an open space between, the whole covered by one roof. The run or trot gets its name from the hounds passing through from the front to the rear. It may or may not have a floor, according to the taste or pride of the occupant. This farmer will have it floored, because his grandfather, as he prospered, closed in the dog-run with doors, making it into a hall; added porches front and rear, weather-boarded the logs, and ceiled the two half-story rooms. His grandfather belonged to that large number of sturdy freemen who owned from three to five hundred acres of land and perhaps a slave or two in better days. But owning a few slaves did not make him a planter. He and his sons worked alongside them in the fields. Of farmers so situated in the South there was one to every twelve and one-tenth of free population.

† From *I'll Take My Stand: The South and the Agrarian Tradition*, by Twelve Southerners (New York: Harper & Brothers, 1930), pp. 217–23. Reprinted by permission of Louisiana State University Press. Andrew Nelson Lytle (1902–1995), critic, novelist, and editor of the *Sewanee Review*. "Hind tit" is a proverbial phrase for a raw deal; the runt of a litter of pigs gets crowded to the back and has to suck at its mother's hind tit, where the milk is less plentiful. Here the phrase denotes what Lytle feels both has been and will continue to be the fate of the (white) South in the world of modern industry.
1. An enclosure; here denoting a unit of construction and used as a synonym for "room."

There is a brick walk running from the porch to a horse block, lined on either side with hardy buttercups. From the block a road marked off by tall cedars goes out to the pike gate, two hundred yards away. The yard is kept grazed down by sheep, and occasionally the stock is turned in, when the pastures are burned in a drought. The house needs paint, but the trees are whitewashed around the base of the trunks to keep insects off and to give a neat appearance to the yard.

Over the front doorway is a horseshoe, turned the right way to bring luck to all who may pass beneath its lintel. The hall is almost bare, but scrubbed clean. At the back is a small stairway leading to the half-story. This is where the boys sleep, in their bachelorhood definitely removed from the girls. To the left is the principal room of the house. The farmer and his wife sleep there in a four-poster, badly in need of doing over; and here the youngest chillurn sleep on pallets made up on the floor.

The large rock fireplace is the center of the room. The home-made hickory chairs are gathered in a semicircle about it, while on the extreme left of the arc is a rough hand-made rocker with a sheep-skin bottom, shiny from use, and its arms smooth from the polishing of flesh, reserved always for "mammy," the tough leather-skinned mother of the farmer. Here she sets and rocks and smokes near enough for the draught to draw the smoke up the chimney. On the mantel, at one end, is dry leaf tobacco, filling the room with its sharp, pungent odor. A pair of dog-irons rests on the hearth, pushed against the back log and holding up the ends of the sticks which have burnt in two and fallen among the hot ashes. The fire is kept burning through the month of May to insure good crops, no matter how mild and warm its days turn out to be. The top rock slab is smoked in the middle where for generations the wind has blown suddenly down the chimney, driving heavy gusts to flatten against the mantel and spread out into the room. A quilting-frame is drawn into the ceiling, ready to be lowered into the laps of the women folks when the occasion demands, although it is gradually falling into disuse. Beneath it, spreading out from the center of the floor, a rag rug covers the wide pine boards which, in turn, cover the rough-hewn puncheons that sufficed during the pioneer days. From this room, or rather, from the hearth of this room, the life of the dwelling moves.

If this is the heart of the house, the kitchen is its busiest part. The old, open fireplace has been closed in since the war, and an iron range has taken its place. This much machinery has added to the order of the establishment's life without disrupting it. Here all the food is prepared, and the canning and preserving necessary to sustain the family during the winter is done.

The cooking is a complicated art, requiring mastery over all its parts to burden the table with victuals that can be relished. Each meal is a victory over nature, a suitable union between the general principles of cookery and the accident of preparation. The fire must be kept at the right temperature (without a thermometer), or the bread won't rise; too much lard, or too little, will spoil the pastry; and since the test of all cooking is the seasoning, which can never be reduced to exact rules but is partly intuitive, too many pinches of salt may ruin the dish. The farmer's wife learns to satisfy the tastes of her particular family, but she can never set two meals on the table exactly alike. She never overcomes nature; her victories are partial, but very satisfying, for she knows her limitations.

The kitchen leads out to the back ell-shaped porch. Upon its banister, or, if there is no banister, upon the wash-table, a bucket of water and its gourd, a tin pan, soap, and towel wait to serve the morning toilet. The towel will hang on a folding rack fixed to the wall. This rack may also serve long strings of red peppers drying in the air. A bell-post rises up near the kitchen to ring the boys in from the fields at dinner-time. In the back, behind the kitchen, is the smokehouse and several outhouses. Iron kettles for washing tilt to one side in the ashes of an old fire, some distance away. An ash-hopper made from a hollow log, no longer in use, lies up against the buggy-house, having gone the way of the kitchen fireplace. The lye for soap- and hominy-making is now bought in town.

Convenient to the kitchen is the woodpile, made of different-sized sticks, some for the stove, split and cut to the right length, and some for the fireplaces, back logs and front sticks. The wood has been cut in the early fall, just as the sap begins to go down, not too early and not too late, but just at the right time, so that the outer surface will be dry and will catch quick, while the inside remains sappy and hard, burning slowly. It takes a great deal of study and intelligence to keep the fires going steadily.

Before dawn the roosters and the farmer feel the tremendous silence, chilling and filling the gap between night and day. He gets up, makes the fires, and rings the rising bell. He could arouse the family with his voice, but it has been the custom to ring the bell; so every morning it sounds out, taking its place among the other bells in the neighborhood. Each, according to his nature, gets up and prepares for the day: the wife has long been in the kitchen when the boys go to the barn; some of the girls help her, while the farmer plans the morning work and calls out directions.

One or two of the girls set out with their milk-pails to the barn, where the cows have been kept overnight. There is a very elaborate process to go through with in milking. First, the cow must be fed to occupy her attention; next, the milker kneels or sits on a bucket and washes the bag which will have gotten manure on it during the night (she kneels to the right, as this is the strategic side; the cow's foot is somehow freer on the left). After the bag is clean, the milking begins. There is always a variation to this ritual. When the calf is young, the cow holds back her milk for it; so the calf is allowed to suck a little at first, some from each teat, loosening the milk with uniformity, and then is pulled off and put in a stall until his time comes. There is one way to pull a calf off, and only one. He must be held by the ears and the tail at the same time, for only in this manner is he easily controlled. The ears alone, or the tail alone, is not enough.

This done, the milking begins. The left hand holds the pail, while the right does the work, or it may be the reverse. The hand hits the bag tenderly, grabs the teat, and closes the fingers about it, not altogether, but in echelon. The calf is then let out for his share. If he is young and there are several cows, it will be all that is left, for careful milkers do not strip the cow until the calf is weaned. The strippings are those short little squirts which announce the end, and they are all cream.

The milk is next brought back to the house, strained, and put in the well to cool. This requires a very careful hand, because if it happens to spill, the well is ruined. The next step is to pour up the old milk and let it turn—that is, sour—for churning. Some will be set aside to clabber for the mammy whose teeth are no longer equal to tougher nourishment. What she does not eat is given to the young chickens or to the pigs.

After breakfast the farmer's wife, or one of the girls, does the churning. This process takes a variable length of time. If the milk is kept a long time before it is poured up, the butter is long in coming. Sometimes witches get in the churn and throw a spell over it. In that case a nickel is dropped in to break the charm. The butter, when it does come, collects in small, yellow clods on top. These clods are separated from the butter-milk and put in a bowl where the rest of the water is worked out. It is then salted, molded, and stamped with some pretty little design. After this is done, it is set in the well or the spring to cool for the table. The process has been long, to some extent tedious, but profitable, because insomuch as it has taken time and care and intelligence, by that much does it have a meaning.

Industrialism gives an electric refrigerator, bottled milk, and dairy butter. It takes a few minutes to remove it from the ice to the table, while the agrarian process has taken several hours and is spread out over two or three days. Industrialism saves time, but what is to be done with this time? The milkmaid can't go to the movies, read the signboards, and go play bridge all the time. In the moderate circumstances of this family, deprived of her place in the home economy, she will be exiled to the town to clerk all day. If the income of the family can afford it, she remains idle, and therefore miserable.

The whole process has been given in detail as an example of what goes on in every part of an agrarian life. The boys, coming in to breakfast, have performed in the same way. Every morning the stock must be fed, but there is always variety. They never shuck the same ears of corn, nor do they find the mules in the small part of the stall, nor the hogs in the same attitudes, waiting to be slopped. The buckets of milk did not move regularly from cow to consumer as raw material moves through a factory. The routine was broken by other phenomena. Breakfast intervened. One morning the cow might kick the pail over, or the milkmaid might stumble over a dog, or the cow come up with a torn udder. It is not the only task she performs, just as feeding the stock is not the only task done by the boys. The day of each member of the family is filled with a mighty variety.

*   *   *

JAMES AGEE

The Gudger House[†]

*   *   *

In front of the house: its general structure

Two blocks, of two rooms each, one room behind another. Between these blocks a hallway, floored and roofed, wide open both at front and rear: so that these blocks are two rectangular yoked boats, or floated tanks, or coffins, each, by an inner wall, divided into two squared chambers. The roof, pitched rather steeply from front and rear, its cards met and nailed at a sharp angle. The floor faces the earth closely. On the left of the hall, two rooms, each an exact square. On the right a square front room and, built later, behind it, using the outward weatherboards for its own front wall, a leanto kitchen half that size.

At the exact center of each of the outward walls of each room, a window. Those of the kitchen are small, taller than wide, and are glassed. Those of the other rooms are exactly square and are stopped with wooden shutters.

† From James Agee and Walker Evans, *Let Us Now Praise Famous Men: Three Tenant Families* pp. 138–40, 150–55. Copyright 1939, 1940 by James Agee. Copyright 1941 by James Agee and Walker Evans. Copyright © renewed 1969 by Mia Fritsch Agee and Walker Evans. Reprinted by permission of Houghton Mifflin Harcourt Publishing Company. All rights reserved.
   This classic of Depression-era reporting grew out of a 1936 assignment that Agee (1909–1955) and the photographer Walker Evans (1903–1975) undertook for *Fortune* magazine. They spent eight weeks living with three white tenant-farm families in rural Alabama, families here renamed Gudger, Woods, and Ricketts. The magazine eventually did not print the story, and Agee reworked and expanded his copy into a style—grand, anguished, and mannered—that both reminds one of Faulkner himself and calls attention to Agee's own troubled position as an upper-middle-class witness to the life of the poor. The passages I've selected here are among the book's most restrained; they provide an inventory of the Gudgers' material world. This book aside, Agee is best known for his film criticism and his posthumous Pulitzer Prize–winning novel, *A Death in the Family* (1957).

From each room a door gives on the hallway. The doors of the two front rooms are exactly opposite: the doors of the rear rooms are exactly opposite. The two rooms on either side of the hallway are also connected inwardly by doors through their partition walls.

Out at the left of the house, starting from just above the side window of the front room, a little roof is reached out and rested on thin poles above bare ground: shelter for wagon or for car.

At the right of the house, just beneath the side window of the front room, a commodious toolbox, built against the wall. It is nailed shut.

The hallway yields onto a front porch about five feet long by ten wide, reaching just a little short of the windows at either side, set at dead center of the front of the house. A little tongue of shingles, the same size, is stuck out slightly slanted above it, and is sustained on four slender posts from which most of the bark has been stripped.

Three steps lead down at center; they are of oak: the bottom one is cracked and weak, for all its thickness. Stones have been stacked beneath it, but they have slid awry, and it goes to the ground sharply underfoot. Just below and beyond it is a wide flat piece of shale the color of a bruise. It is broken several ways across and is sunken into the dirt.

The forty-foot square of land in front of the house, the 'front yard,' is bare of any trees or bushes; there is nothing at all near the house of its own height, or bestowing of any shade. This piece of land is hunched a little on itself in a rondure. Through the dry haze of weeds and flowering fennels its dead red yellowness glows quietly, a look of fire in sunlight, and it is visible how intricately it is trenched and seamed with sleavings of rain; as if, the skull lifted off, the brain were exposed, of some aged not intellectual being who had lived a long time patiently and with difficulty.

Where we stand, square toward the front, the house is almost perfectly symmetrical. Its two front walls, square, balanced, each of a size, cloven by hallway; the lifted roof; at center of each wall, a square window, the shutters closed; the porch and its roof and the four little posts like candles:

Each window is framed round with a square of boards.

Ten or twelve feet out in this yard, and precisely in line with these front windows, as if they were projections of them, and of about the same size, two hollow squares of wood are laid upon the earth and are sunk level with it: and these are in fact two projections and are related with these windows, and indeed are windows, of a sort: for they are intended to let through their frames from the blank wall and darkness of the earth a particular and gracious, pleasing light; they are flower-beds. The one at the left is sprung through with the same indiscriminate fennels of the yard; the one on the right, the same. But here among this rambling of bastardy stands up, on its weak stem, one fainting pale magenta petunia, which stares at its tired foot; and this in the acreage of these three farms is the one domestic flower.

*   *   *

The hallway

Structure of four rooms

The hallway is long courses of weatherboard facing one another in walls six feet apart, featureless excepting two pair of opposite doors, not ceiled, but beneath the empty and high angling of the roof: perhaps because of the blankness of these walls, and their facing closeness relative to their parallel length, there is here an extremely strong sense of the nakedness and narrowness of their presence, and of the broad openness, exposing the free land, at either end. The floor is laid along beams rather wide apart. In all the rear end it yields to the ground under much weight: the last few feet lie solid to the ground, and this is a strong muck in wet weather.

The one static fixture in the hallway is at the rear, just beyond the kitchen door. It is a wooden shelf, waist-high, and on this shelf, a bucket, a dipper, a basin, and usually a bar of soap, and hanging from a nail just above, a towel. The basin is granite-ware, small for a man's hands, with rustmarks in the bottom. The bucket is a regular galvanized two-gallon bucket, a little dented, and smelling and touching a little of a fishy-metallic kind of shine and grease beyond any power of cleaning. It is half full of slowly heating water which was not very cold to begin with: much lower than this, the water tastes a little ticklish and nasty for drinking, though it is still all right for washing. The soap is sometimes strong tan 'kitchen' soap, sometimes a cheap white gelatinous lavender face soap. It stands on the shelf in a china saucer. The dipper again is granite-ware, and again blistered with rust at the bottom. Sometimes it bobs in the bucket; sometimes it lies next the bucket on the shelf. The towel is half a floursack, with the blue and red and black printing still faint on it. Taken clean and dry, it is the pleasantest cloth I know for a towel. Beyond that, it is particularly clammy, clinging, and dirty-feeling.

A few notes of discrimination may be helpful:

The towels in such a farmhouse are always floursacks. 'Kitchen' towels are of another world and class of farmer, and 'face' and 'turkish' towels of still another.

By no means all poor farmers use any sort of 'toilet' soap. Some seldom use soap at all. When they use other than kitchen soap, it is of one of about three kinds, all of them of the sort available in five-and-tens and small-town general stores. One is 'lava' or 'oatmeal' soap, whose rough texture is pleasing and convincing of cleanliness to a person who works with his hands. The white soaps smell sharply of lye: again, the odor is cleansing. Or if the soap is more fancy, it is a pink or lemon or purple color, strongly and cheaply scented and giving a big lather. No cheap yet somewhat pleasantly scented soap such as lux is used.

Rather more often than not, the basin and the dipper are plain unenameled tin. I expect, but am not sure, that this is a few cents cheaper. In any case the odor, taste, and shiny, greasy texture soon become strong. The use of enamel ware is a small yet sharp distinction and symptom in 'good taste,' and in 'class,' and in a sort of semi-esthetic awareness, choice and will. The use of gray as against white is still another discriminative. That they bought small sizes, which are a very few cents cheaper, speaks for itself. So does the fact that they have afforded still another basin, not quite big enough for its use, to wash their feet in.

At times, there is also a mirror here, and a comb; but more often these are on the bedroom mantel.

The hall and front porch are a kind of room, and are a good deal used. Mrs. Gudger and her children sit in the porch in empty times of the morning and afternoon: back in the rear of the hall is the evening place to sit, before supper or for a little while just after it. There are few enough chairs that they have to be moved around the house to where they are needed, but ordinarily there is a rockingchair on the porch and a straight chair in the rear of the hall next the bedroom door. This rockingchair is of an inexpensive 'rustic' make: sections of hickory sapling with the bark still on. On the hard and not quite even porch floor the rocking is stony and cobbled, with a little of the sound of an auto crossing a loose wooden bridge. Three of the straight chairs are strong, plain, not yet decrepit hickory-bottoms, which cost a dollar and a half new; there is also a kitchen-type chair with a pierced design in the dark scalloped wood at the head, and the bottom broken through.

When we first knew the Gudgers they had their eating-table in the middle of the hall, for only in the hall is there likely to be any sort of breeze, and the kitchen, where nearly all farm families eat, was so hot that they could at times hardly stand to eat in it. This was only an experiment though, and it was not successful. The hall is too narrow for any comfort in it for a whole family clenched round a table. If it were even two feet wider, it would be much more use to them, but this would not have occurred to those who built it, nor, if it had, would anything have been done about it.

Four rooms make a larger tenant house than is ordinary: many are three; many are two; more are one than four: and three of these rooms are quite spacious, twelve feet square. For various reasons, though, all of which could easily enough have been avoided in the building of the house, only two of these rooms, the kitchen and the rear bedroom, are really habitable. There is no ceiling to either of the front rooms, and the shingles were laid so unskillfully, and are now so multitudinously leaky, that it would be a matter not of repairing but of complete re-laying to make a solid roof. Between the beams at the eaves, along the whole front of the house, and the top of the wall on which the beams rest, there are open gaps. In the front room on the right, several courses of weatherboarding have been omitted between the level of the eaves and the peak of the roof: a hole big enough for a cow to get through. The walls, and shutters, and floors, are not by any means solid: indeed, and beyond and aside from any amount of laborious calking, they let in light in many dozens of places. There are screens for no windows but one, in the rear bedroom. Because in half the year the fever mosquitoes are thick and there are strong rainstorms, and in the other half it is cold and wet for weeks on end with violent slanted winds and sometimes snow, the right front room is not used to live in at all and the left front room is used only dubiously and irregularly, though the sewing machine is there and it is fully furnished both as a bedroom and as a parlor. The children use it sometimes, and it is given to guests (as it was to us), but storm, mosquitoes and habit force them back into the other room where the whole family sleeps together.

*　*　*

Odors

The Gudgers' house, being young, only eight years old, smells a little dryer and cleaner, and more distinctly of its wood, than an average white tenant house, and it has also a certain odor I have never found in other such houses: aside from these sharp yet slight subtleties, it has the odor or odors which are classical in every thoroughly poor white southern country house, and by which such a house could be identified blindfold in any part of the world, among no matter what other odors. It is compacted of many odors and made into one, which is very thin and light on the air, and more subtle than it can seem in analysis, yet very sharply and constantly noticeable. These are its ingredients. The odor of pine lumber, wide thin cards of it, heated in the sun, in no way doubled or insulated, in closed and darkened air. The odor of woodsmoke, the fuel being again mainly pine, but in part also, hickory, oak, and cedar. The odors of cooking. Among these, most strongly, the odors of fried salt pork and of fried and boiled pork lard, and second, the odor of cooked corn. The odors of sweat in many stages of age and freshness, this sweat being a distillation of pork, lard, corn, woodsmoke, pine, and ammonia. The odors of sleep, of bedding and of breathing, for the ventilation is poor. The odors of all the dirt that in the course of time can accumulate in a quilt and mattress. Odors of staleness from clothes hung or stored away, not washed. I should further describe the odor of corn: in sweat, or on the teeth, and breath, when it is eaten as much as they eat it, it is of a particular sweet stuffy fetor, to which the nearest parallel is the odor of the yellow excrement of a baby. All these odors as I have said are so combined into one that they are all and always present in balance, not at all heavy, yet so searching that all fabrics of bedding and clothes are saturated with them, and so clinging that they stand softly out of the fibers of newly laundered clothes. Some of their components are extremely 'pleasant,' some are 'unpleasant'; their sum total has great nostalgic power. When they are in an old house, darkened, and moist, and sucked into all the wood, and stacked down on top of years of a moldering and old basis of themselves, as at the Ricketts', they are hard to get used to or even hard to bear. At the Woods', they are blowsy and somewhat moist and dirty. At the Gudgers', as I have mentioned, they are younger, lighter, and cleaner-smelling. There too, there is another and special odor, very dry and edged: it is somewhere between the odor of very old newsprint and of a victorian bedroom in which, after long illness, and many medicines, someone has died and the room has been fumigated, yet the odor of dark brown medicines, dry-bodied sickness, and staring death, still is strong in the stained wallpaper and in the mattress.

* * *

THOMAS D. CLARK

From Pills, Petticoats and Plows: The Southern Country Store[†]

* * *

Most important of all the items of men's clothing, however, were shoes. Shoes have ever been the southern farmer's great concern. Walking behind plows in the sandy soils of the South, across plowed fields, or along muddy roads was always a trial even in the most

---

[†] From *Pills, Petticoats and Plows: The Southern Country Store* (Indianapolis and New York: Bobbs-Merrill, 1944), pp. 209–12, 264–69.

favorable circumstances. But until the late nineties the common everyday shoe was the formless brogan which sold at wholesale prices for seventy-five and ninety cents and were retailed at the high credit prices of $1.25 to $2.25. This shoe was designed by the cobblers of Massachusetts whose itinerate salesmen followed the backroads after the Civil War looking for customers.

Until after 1880 few shoes of the common stock type were made specifically for left and right feet. Lasts were straight, and it made no difference which one of a new pair of shoes was put on first. Southern stores sold the crudest type of work shoes. Although there were several kinds of shoes on the market, the most popular with the country trade was the brogan. This work shoe came tied in pairs according to approximate sizes, and they were tumbled into bins to be fished out and fitted as they were called for.

This shoe was made either of split or hard oak tanned leather. Soles were fastened on with hardwood pegs, and seldom if ever did the manufacturer go to the trouble either to trim the pegs or to pad the soles. Brogan toes were broad and plain without any stitching to break the lines. It was universally poorly made and highly uncomfortable. Seams were often bound with heavy harness brads, and buckles were used instead of strings in about half of the shoes sold. After the first day or two of wear, these shoes became hard with deep creases across the toes, and around the ankles. Thus it was that for fifty years the American shoe manufacturer perpetrated upon the southern country a foot agony which caused a good portion of the population to go barefoot as much as possible. "Breaking in" a pair of shoes was a torturous ordeal. Often some tough-footed friend would oblige by wearing a pair of shoes just long enough to give them a hint of shape.

A pair of shoes for a two-year-old was as heavy and sturdy as is the modern heavy-duty adult shoe. Toes were boxed in with brass and copper strips, and heavy uppers came well above the ankles. Manufacturers had not mastered the art of making light flexible shoes. Despite its poor quality and general unsuitability the famous old "brass toe" was an object of sentiment which older generations of southerners recall with affection. In reality their sentimentality, however, is a bit of subconscious wonderment over the fact that they were able to wear such shoes and live with any degree of happiness.

Thus it was that from the cradle onward the problem of wearing shoes was vital. Certainly the history of the propagation and spread of hookworm is partly due to the failure of shoe manufacturers to supply country merchants with decently designed shoes of good quality and at reasonable prices.

*   *   *

In all the long story of maladjusted styling and poor quality, there was no racial discrimination in the matter of wary feet. Both the white man and the Negro were victimized. The fact that the Negro's feet hurt him, however, became a humorous matter. Locally he was chided for the wide gashes which gave bony toe joints and sensitive bunions relief. These slit brogans became a bit of everyday stock for the blackface minstrels which traveled through the South. The white man most often endured his suffering without resort to the knife.[1] * *

* * *

There were actually few customers for coffins in the rural South prior to 1910. Death like birth was pretty much a homemade affair, and because of its eternal element of misfortune the burden was spread out to as many people as possible. Neighbors contributed to the financing of the costs of materials, and making coffins was almost always a labor of charity. A tenant farmer's child took sick with the "summer complaint" and within a day or two it was dead. Crops were "in the grass," help was scarce, and the moment was the most unfortunate one of all for a child to die. The father had no money, and the margin of credit on his lien note failed to take into consideration the certainty of death. Thus it was that burying the dead in a majority of cases became a community responsibility.

Fixtures were bought from stores and carpenter-farmers spent hours shaping oblong, hexagon or curved-end boxes into caskets. The ends of death were served with the most careful workmanship possible. Hour after hour hot water was poured over pine, walnut and oak boards, and triangular slits were cut halfway through to facilitate the bending. The monotonous pounding of the bending hammer was heard on many a sultry southern night. Blinking lanterns lighted the activities of the cabinetmakers as they moved around from one detail to another. Laboriously the handmade boxes took form to receive an army of victims of consumption, pneumonia, croup, measles, skin diseases, fevers and debility. Long steel tacks were set in place. Heavy screws with ornamental heads decorated with classical designs of cypress and garlands marked the bends and joints. There were other nails in the shape of crosses which held the lining in place, and sometimes were driven into a line of beading around the lids. When they were set in place against a background of black cloth and dark stained woods they presented a striking and dolorous appearance of funereal adornment.

---

1. See Agee, pp. 269–71, for another description of the countryman's shoe; and note that one of his poor whites, the man he calls Ricketts, has slashed them in the way Clark describes.

Coffin hardware was sold wholesale by distributors located in the larger centers. Wholesale houses like Belknap in Louisville supplied fixtures in completely assembled bundles. There were four handles and a plate bearing the legend "At Rest," "Our Darling" or "Our Babe." Sometimes the handles bore imprints of lambs at rest against a background of Elysian fields, and the lid screws were leaden roses in a half-blown stage. For adult coffins there were various designs. There was the legend "Mother" for married women's coffins; the inevitable square, compass and "G" for the Masonic fraternity; the open Bible and letters I.O.O.F. for the Odd Fellows; and the rugged lengths of tree trunks and axes for Woodmen of the World.

At Whitakers, North Carolina, Hearne Brothers and Company specialized in supplying stores with a large assortment of hardware. Their large illustrated catalogue was a graphic document of burial artistry for the years following the Civil War. Page after page portrayed designs of varying types of fixtures, and every one of them conveyed an intensity of sorrow. The last four or five pages of the books were devoted to tools and equipment for merchants who wished to become undertakers.

The Hearne Brothers' catalogue was of more than ordinary interest. For the boys sitting around the stores it furnished a fearful diversion from the usual course of idle conversation. Perusing its pages was in fact a theft of a surreptitious glimpse at the face of life's greatest inevitability. These catalogues sometimes figured in folk beliefs. Many persons believed that looking at such things as coffin fixtures was flirting with death itself. Especially was this true of the weary colored customers who timidly pushed up to the store, or eased up to the porches to take a moment of ease only to have a coffin book opened in their faces. The realistic illustrations of coffins and fixtures sent half-frightened customers home to ponder such things in their subconscious minds and to awaken at night in the midst of dreams of death. The belief was strong that to dream of coffins and open graves was to be in imminent danger of a dreadful accident.

*   *   *

Burial customs in the rural South in the postwar years were closely patterned after the spirit of the times. Funeral directors were unknown. When a person died he deserved better treatment than to fall into the hands of unctuous and patronizing professional undertakers even if he had possessed the money to pay burial costs. The corpse was "laid out" by neighbors, local carpenters and cabinet-makers made the coffin, a near-by store supplied the materials, and friends kept the wake and dug the grave. In all the thousands of hapless victims recorded in the vital statistics of the census reports before 1915, a remarkably small percentage of them were carried to their final resting places by anyone other than neighbors. The only charges ever made in death were those which found their way on to the ledgers as entries for fixtures, linings and shrouds. Between 1865 and 1915 it was not an unreasonable thing from a financial standpoint to die. Seldom did an ordinary casket cost more than five to twenty-five dollars, graves were dug by obliging friends, there was seldom a hearse, and the wake nearly always turned out to be a semi-social affair.

* * *

Graves were dug in light clay or deep sandy loam by volunteer laborers. They were usually four to six feet deep with a narrower pit the size of the casket. Lowering a coffin into the grave was always a mechanical problem. The most common practice was to use buggy lines with buckles stripped off so that when the casket came to rest at the bottom the straps could be pulled out from one side. Then there were the patent straps which hooked into a bracket on the side of the boxes and once the box rested on the bottom of the grave the straps were slackened and the brackets were released. Often stores kept these straps and lent them throughout their territory for use.

Once the casket was in place the boards were placed over the shoulders and the grave was ready to be filled. Throwing the first shovels of dirt into the box was a heartless operation. Always there was an inhumane maliciousness in the monotonous rumble of dirt over the boards. This was, without exception, the most morbid of all the experiences of human life in the South. As one shovelful of dirt after another poured down on top of a vacuous coffin, and the sound rolled back in a hollow roar, the very emptiness of most of life in the region itself was echoed in its starkest degree of depravity. The rising sound of fresh dirt over a grave was in reality the last full measure of the bitter sting of death.

* * *

C. D. MITCHELL, M. D., SUPERINTENDENT

Thirty-Sixth Biennial Report of the Mississippi State Insane Hospital, Jackson, Mississippi

From July 1, 1925 to June 30, 1927[†]

Movement of Population

* * * [W]ith the beginning of the hospital year, July 1, 1925, we had in the hospital 1,952 patients, 878 were white and 1,074 were negroes; 894 were males and 1,058 were females.

There were admitted in the two years, including first admissions, and patients returned who had been either in this or some other institutions 2,249, making a total of 4,201 patients cared for and treated during the biennium. Of these admissions, 1,052 were white, and 1,197 were colored; 1,247 were males and 1,002 were females. During the biennium 1,384 patients were paroled home, 801 of whom were white and 583 colored; 881 were men and 503 were women. During the past two years 193 white patients died, and 480 colored, leaving in the Institution at the close of the year June 30, 1927, 2,244 patients.[1]

The character of the patients brought us differ but little from those admitted in former years.

The Dementia Praecox group predominates, 111 of this class of patients being received. 200 were old feeble, helpless arteriosclerotics whose days at best were but few; 154 were diagnosed General Paralysis; 104 were Epileptics and 53 Mental Deficients.

Of the patients who died many were helpless and in a dying condition when brought to the hospital. 126 died before they had been in the hospital a week, 144 of those who died were over 70 years of age, 100 died of Tuberculosis, 95 of Pellagra, 89 of General Paralysis and 70 of Apoplexy.

The death rate among the white population compares favorably with that of any other institution, but the death rate among the negroes is far too high.

Because their buildings are jammed up against the back doors of the white wards we are compelled to keep them closely confined

---

† From "Thirty-Sixth Biennial Report of the Mississippi State Insane Asylum, Jackson, Mississippi. From July 1, 1925 to June 30, 1927" (Jackson, MS: 1929), pp. 11–12, 13–14, 17, 19–20, 27–28.

1. The maximum capacity of the hospital at this time was 1,600. See Laura D. S. Harrell, "Medical Services in Mississippi," in R. A. McLemore, *A History of Mississippi*, vol. 2 (Hattiesburg: University and College Press of Mississippi, 1973), p. 527.

because it would never do to permit the two races to intermingle, and the freedom of the grounds and lawn is given to the white people, and consequently the colored people are denied the liberties and freedom, and outside exercise to which they are entitled, and which would greatly aid and hasten their recovery. The wards in which they are confined are dark and dreary and illy ventilated, and terribly over-crowded; and it is impossible to make them habitable. Wards which were made to care for 60 patients have twice that number on them. When we get to our new hospital with its wards properly located and arranged where they can get the care and treatment to which they are justly entitled, the death rate among the negroes will be cut in two.

During the last two years 250 negroes died who should not have died; who would have lived and been mentally restored could they have been on wards such as will be provided for them at the new hospital. This alone seems to me would justify the action of the Legislature in building a new hospital.

* * *

Medical Reports

* * *

We are still keeping a strict surveillance over restraint and seclusion. It is very unusual for any patient to be placed in seclusion and only as they become a menace to others and then for short periods. No restraint of any kind is being used, and the old time camisoles or strait jackets have been utterly abolished. In fact, it would be a revival of prehistoric custom to resort again to such ingenious inhumanities. The use of hydrotherapy, tonic and soothing baths, continuous baths and the like are worthy therapeutic substitutes for the former mechanical methods of subjugation.

The limited parole of patients is extended to include all patients who can be trusted about the grounds. There is no doubt that one of the main deterrents in the improvement of many patients is the unnecessary restrictions which heretofore have been placed around patients with mental diseases. It is a striking fact that as more humane and sympathetic methods are being employed in the hospitals of this type the patients themselves are beginning to realize their mental condition, and co-operate more readily in their treatment. There have been numerous men and women (during the past two years) who have personally applied for admission to obviate the necessity of court action, but the hospital was unable to receive them through lack of the State Law permitting the same. This is one of the laws which could be added to the statutes which would be of inestimable benefit to some afflicted patients who so keenly realize the necessity for treatment but dislike the notoriety and implied stigma of court commitment. All our efforts should be directed towards making it easier for patients of their own volition to get into State hospitals as the prognosis for recovery increases in direct relation as the treatment is insituted early in the development of the mental symptoms. All types of mental disease are potentially curable if treatment can be obtained early and the old saying, "Once insane, always insane" is a mistaken view to be taken of the mentally afflicted.

* * *

Occupational Therapy

This department has been considerably enlarged during the past two years. We are convinced that every patient should have some form of employment and recreation and as many as possible are enrolled in classes where they receive the type of occupation considered beneficial in the treatment of their mental symptoms. Through the co-operation of the physicians and nurses, this department has become an important part of the hospital organization and this treatment is given to as many of the patients as can be taken care of in the classes. The classes are graded; a new patient is assigned to that class seemingly best suited to his mental capacity and is advanced as improvement is shown.

Many of the classes are Habit Training Classes—the day's program including calisthenics, games, walks and singing classes as well as graded occupations. Patients attending O. T. Centers for part of the day join Playground Therapy Classes at other hours. These Playground Therapy activities are an important part of the Occupational Therapy department, providing both pleasure and benefit for the patient and the schedule is carefully arranged so that all patients may have opportunity to participate in these classes as well as in other forms of occupation. Practically all patients except bed patients and those employed in hospital industries join in calisthenics on the porches at 8:00 A.M. The Playground Schedule is varied according to the season, most of the year all classes can be held out doors. A weekly dancing class and twice weekly singing lessons under trained instructors are enjoyable and helpful parts of the week's schedule which includes all sorts of games, drills, etc.[2]

2. As part of their occupational therapy patients worked under supervision at one of the hospital's enterprises. Examples include a dairy, hay and corn fields, a market garden, a sewing room, an ice plant that supplied the state capitol, and a carpenter's shop that among other things made whatever coffins the hospital might need. Mitchell notes that during the two years covered by this report the hospital's poultry and hog farm "furnished to the patients" 105,450 dozen eggs, and slaughtered 457 hogs. The sewing room appears to have made most of the clothes and linen the patients required, and "represented quite a saving to the State."

* * *

Social Service

* * * Of prime importance in the therapeutic value of the State Hospitals are the results shown in individual cases whereby their mental trends are so directed and stabilized that after a short stay as a patient they are able to leave the institution itself and resume their place in the world, still, however, under the influence and supervision of the hospital.

In the readjustment process a great deal has to be accomplished in securing the proper community attitude toward the discharged patient. So often insanity is considered a disgrace rather than an illness and where such an opinion prevails the lot of the patient is indeed a sad one, and when any eccentric conduct is observed, the patient is immediately and frequently unnecessarily, returned to the hospital. If the patient on discharge can realize the attitude of the family life with its every day problems and can be encouraged to meet friends on the former social status a great many of the readmissions to the hospital can be prevented.

Readjustment of family relationships, industrial conditions, social surroundings and community irritabilities, all of which frequently play other roles as causative factors in mental breakdowns can avert many a commitment and assist in the restoration to normal mental trends. While in the hospital, discouraged by the loss of friends and their counsels, neglected by the family who so often unconsciously forget the little amenities, and the realization of the possible outcome of the mental illness, the recovery of many a patient is retarded by these factors and thus it is that the Social Worker, reestablishes assurance and ambition, interesting the friends and relatives in the patient and readjusting the broken threads connecting the patient with Life, has her important place in the treatment of all such cases.

* * *

New Hospital

The last Legislature, appreciating the deplorable condition of the insane, the most pitiable of God's creatures, who were kept in buildings similar to jails, horribly arranged and terribly overcrowded; appreciating the fact that the people were locked behind iron bars, helpless to help themselves and in constant danger of being burned alive; realizing that these unhappy people, wards of the State, were not getting what they were entitled to and what they had a right to expect, were wise enough and brave enough and generous enough to pass a bill authorizing the building of a new hospital on the Rankin County Farm. This one Act of this Legislature will tell more for human happiness than all the legislation for the past quarter of a century.

This hospital is now under construction and when completed will be the most modern, most complete and best hospital in this country. It will be a credit to the State; a blessing to her afflicted people, and a pride to all patriotic Mississippians.[3]

*   *   *

Respectfully submitted,

C. D. MITCHELL, M. D., Superintendent.

3. The new hospital was opened in 1935 (Harrell, 528).

CRITICISM

Sustained criticism of *As I Lay Dying* dates from 1950, when Olga W. Vickery published an account of the novel in the journal *Perspective*. It was quickly reprinted in *William Faulkner: Two Decades of Criticism* (1951), a book co-edited by Vickery herself that attempted, in the immediate wake of Faulkner's Nobel Prize, to establish a brief initial canon of criticism. This volume draws upon Vickery's revised, 1959 version of her essay, as it appeared in her own book-length study of Faulkner's *oeuvre*. The essay suggests that we see the Bundrens' journey as a blackly comic travesty of ritual, and as such it provides one pole of the novel's critical history. The other is that offered by Cleanth Brooks in his 1963 *William Faulkner: The Yoknapatawpha Country*. Brooks acknowledges the novel's dark comedy and its strain of folk humor but nevertheless asks us to recognize the Bundrens' journey as a form of heroic action.

Most subsequent readings of the novel begin by assuming the relevance—indeed the truth—of both Vickery's and Brooks' arguments. Each offers something like a tour of the novel's world, and each stands as an example of what I call "normative" criticism: clearly written introductory accounts that are intended to order the common reader's experience. No one will find these essays "wrong" and almost everyone will still find them useful, but at this distance they seem to me normative in another sense as well. They smooth out the book's difficulty, as though they have through long familiarity forgotten its abrupt and overwhelming strangeness. Calvin Bedient's essay therefore provides a useful corrective, one that captures the shattering first impression that this book can make upon a reader. It is in a way a modernist reading: a piece that not only attends to Faulkner's modernism, but that also offers a similarly dislocating and furious experience of its own. And much the same can be said of the articles reprinted here by Eric Sundquist and André Bleikasten, the latter an account of the novel's setting, its logged-off, riverine wasteland.

Faulkner scholarship very quickly became an industry, and as such mirrors developments in academic literary criticism as a whole. Sundquist's immensely sophisticated essay is the last important piece on the novel to stand in a direct line of descent from the New Criticism of the 1950s and 1960s. Later criticism either comes to us inflected by developments in literary theory, or situates the novel within its cultural and historical context; the best scholarship of course does both. The work of Jacques Derrida and Mikhail Bakhtin, among others, is implicit in Stephen M. Ross discussion of the novel's verbal texture, his analysis of the very different ways in which its different characters speak. Doreen Fowler's "Matricide and the Mother's Revenge" set the course for the many feminist readings the novel has received in recent years; an account, inspired by Jacques Lacan, of the price that Addie Bundren exacts for her death. Patrick O'Donnell's "Between the Family and the State" explores *As I Lay Dying* in terms of its depiction of power and authority, of ideology and control, an argument derived in part from the work of the Marxist philosopher Louis Althusser.

Richard Gray's "A Southern Carnival" is drawn from what seems to me the most comprehensive recent account of Faulkner's work. It too is a normative reading, in a way that suggests the domestication of theory: a useful tool, but one that no longer carries the totalizing claims of earlier decades. Yet by now the norms have changed, and Gray's Bakhtinian account of the novel offers a fresh look at an old problem. It makes sense of but does not resolve the difficulties of this "disconcerting" tale, disconcerting because it never quite allows us "to be sure what we are reading." Over the years many of the book's readers have noted that Darl Bundren appears to have fought in the Great War, but John Limon is the first to make something interesting out of it. His "Addie in No Man's Land" defines Faulkner's attitudes towards war, modernity, and the connection between them; a work of cultural history that begins with a wry description of the critic's own work in the classroom. Finally, Donald M. Kartiganer's essay returns us to the novelist: a shrewd account of the differences between *As I Lay Dying* and Faulkner's other work, a reading that defines the book's precise location in both the author's career and in his life itself.

Throughout these essays I have substituted page references to this Norton Critical Edition for the authors' original citations from earlier editions of *As I Lay Dying*.

OLGA W. VICKERY

The Dimensions of Consciousness†

As I Lay Dying possesses basically the same structure as *The Sound and the Fury* but in a more complex form. Instead of four main sections, three of which are dominated by the consciousness of a single character, there are some sixty short sections apportioned among fifteen characters. Each of these brief chapters describes some part either of the funeral preparations or of the procession itself, even as it explores and defines the mind of the observer from whose point of view the action is described. Accordingly, the clear sweep of the narrative is paralleled by a developing psychological drama of whose tensions and compulsions the characters themselves are only half-

† From *The Novels of William Faulkner: A Critical Interpretation* (Baton Rouge: Louisiana State University Press, 1959), pp. 50–65. Reprinted by permission of Louisiana State University Press.

aware. The need to co-operate during the journey merely disguises the essential isolation of each of the Bundrens and postpones the inevitable conflict between them. For the Bundrens, no less than the Compsons, are living each in a private world whose nature is gauged in relation to Addie and to the actual events of the journey to Jefferson. The larger frame of reference, provided in *The Sound and the Fury* by the impersonal, third person narration of the fourth section, is here conveyed dramatically through eight different characters who comment on some aspect of the funeral in which they themselves are not immediately involved. Their diverse reactions to and judgments of the Bundrens chart the range of social responses, passing from friendliness to indifference to outraged indignation.

As in *The Sound and the Fury*, each private world manifests a fixed and distinctive way of reacting to and ordering experience. * * *

* * *

* * * Each of the Bundrens is concerned with Addie's death and with her funeral, events which are by no means identical. As Doctor Peabody suggests, the former is a personal and private matter: "I can remember how when I was young I believed death to be a phenomenon of the body; now I know it to be merely a function of the mind— and that of the minds of the ones who suffer the bereavement." (26) Thus, it is Addie not as a mother, corpse, or promise but as an element in the blood of her children who dominates and shapes their complex psychological reactions. Their motivation lies within her life, for she is the source of the tension and latent violence which each of them feels within himself and expresses in his contacts with the rest of the family. Obsessed by their own relationships to Addie, they can resolve that tension only when they have come to terms with her as a person and with what she signifies in their own consciousness.

In contrast to her death, her funeral is a public affair, participated in and, indeed, supervised by the neighbors as well as the family. On this level she is simply the corpse which must be disposed of in accordance with a long established ritual of interment. While the neighbors prepare themselves to comfort the bereaved, the Bundrens are expected to assume the traditional role of mourners, a role which carries with it unspoken rules of propriety and decorum. Only Anse, for whom Addie never existed as an individual, finds such a role congenial. His face tragic and composed, he easily makes the proper responses to condolences and recites his litany of grief, though somewhat marred by his irrepressible egotism. There is even a sense in which Anse thoroughly enjoys the situation since as chief mourner he is, for once in his life, a person of importance. It is not, however, that simple for Addie's sons, who find that the conventions of mourning and burial can neither channel nor contain their grief.

Thus, Cora Tull, the self-appointed champion and arbiter of propriety, finds that each of them fails, at some point, to behave in a fitting manner.

Because the agonizing journey to Jefferson does fulfill the promise to Addie, because it does reunite her in death with her family, some critics have seen in it an inspiring gesture of humanity or a heroic act of traditional morality. In reality, however, the journey from beginning to end is a travesty of the ritual of interment. Any ritual, as Addie herself suggests, can become a travesty, even though it has been ordained and sanctioned in its fixed order from the beginning of time. Since there is no virtue attached simply to the meticulous repetition of its words and gestures, it is the individual who must give meaning and life to ritual by recognizing its symbolic function. But the spirit which should give meaning to Addie's funeral is either absent, as in Anse and Dewey Dell, or in conflict with it, as in Cash and Darl. As this becomes clear, the series of catastrophes that befall the Bundrens becomes a source of macabre humor, for it is only when the ritual is disengaged from its symbolic function that the comic aspect becomes apparent.

Awareness of the difference between empty and significant ritual, framed in terms of the word and the act, dominates Addie Bundren's dying thoughts. She concludes that any experience—love, marriage, motherhood, bereavement—can be either an intensely felt reality or a mere conventional form of speech and behavior. The ritual of the word attempts to impose an order and a significance on experience, while the ritual of the act allows them to emerge from it. While Anse talks about his trials and his grief, Cash, Darl, and Jewel, each in his own way, express the meaning of love and bereavement through their actions which frequently come in conflict with accepted and acceptable forms of behavior. This contrast, sustained throughout the funeral journey, is a confirmation of Addie's perception of "how words go straight up in a thin line, quick and harmless, and how terribly doing goes along the earth, clinging to it, so that after a while the two lines are too far apart for the same person to straddle from one to the other." (100) Words need not, however, be empty providing they are grounded in non-verbal experience. It is when this condition is not met that they tend to be separated from and ultimately to replace the act. There are, as Addie realizes, both "the words [that] are the deeds, and the other words that are not deeds, that are just the gaps in peoples' lacks." (100–101)

Addie and Anse themselves represent the two polar opposites of action and words which must be meshed if their relationship is to be meaningful. The word by itself leads to a paralysis of the ability to feel and act; the act by itself results in excessive and uncontrolled responses to various stimuli both internal and external. Addie and

Anse, however, are not able to effect this fusion of word and act. Because they are "husband" and "wife," Anse feels no need to establish a personal relationship which would give significance to those words and to the ritual of marriage. He is completely blind to Addie's intense desire for life and to her conviction that language is a grotesque tautology which prevents any real communication.

The birth of Cash confirms her feeling that words are irrelevant and that only physical experience has reality and significance. Through the act of giving birth she becomes part of the endless cycle of creation and destruction, discovering that, for the first time, her "aloneness had been violated and then made whole again by the violation." (99) Yet accepting Cash as the sign of her own passionate involvement in experience implies a total rejection of Anse who is now father as well as husband in name only. Because Addie accepts the fact that she and Anse live in different worlds, her second child, Darl, comes as the ultimate and unforgivable outrage. Addie, however, quickly disowns the thought of Anse as the deliberate agent of her betrayal; they have both been "tricked by words older than Anse or love." (100) Precisely what these words are is not clear, but what they signify for Addie is quite apparent. Primarily, she realizes that the ritual of the word does have its repercussions in the world of experience, and on this basis she is able to distinguish between the empty words of Anse and the words which are deeds.

Her sudden and brief affair with Whitfield constitutes Addie's attempt to explore this new relationship between words and acts, for it encompasses even as it differentiates between two quite distinct conceptions of sin. As a word, sin is the opposite of virtue and leads inevitably to damnation. It is this aspect which Addie stresses when she thinks of sin as garments which she and Whitfield wear in the face of the world and which they remove "in order to shape and coerce the terrible blood to the forlorn echo of the dead word high in the air." (101) But as an act, sin may be a step toward salvation. Accordingly, Whitfield becomes "the instrument ordained by God who created the sin, to sanctify that sin He had created." (101) The adultery thus becomes a moral act, not, of course, in the sense of "good" or "virtuous," but in the sense that it re-establishes the reality of moral conduct and of the relationship between God and man. This reality is neither linguistic nor factual in character; instead, it consists of the possible, the hypothetical, the conceivable, all, in short, that follows from the capacity for unrestricted choice. Significantly, Addie sees in Jewel, the child of her sin, a sign of grace: "'He is my cross and he will be my salvation. He will save me from the water and from the fire. Even though I have laid down my life, he will save me.'" (97) Through sin Addie seeks to find and enact her own humanity, and if her solution seems extreme, so is her provocation. For the alternative, as she

sees it, is the moral myopia of those who live by words "because
people to whom sin is just a matter of words, to them salvation is just
words too." (102)

*   *   *

Because Anse lives by words alone, Addie has no influence over
him except when she ironically exacts a promise which is a word but
which will compel him to act. All that saves him from equating the
deed with the word and the intention with the achievement of it is
his own desire for new teeth and Jewel's savage determination to perform the promised act. At the first sign of difficulty he falls back on
his inexhaustible stock of moral platitudes to isolate himself effectively from the horrors of the journey, to avoid any exertion on his
part, and to maneuver others into acting for him. Incapable of for-
mulating any plan or initiating any action, he depends on his sons to
overcome each new obstacle. If they fail, there are always the neighbors to come to his rescue. Certainly the neighbors can do nothing
but help when confronted by his covert pleas couched in the language of forbearance: "'I ain't asking you to risk your mule. It ain't
your dead; I am not blaming you.'" (79) His words create an image of
himself as the meek and magnanimous victim forgiving a cruel and
heartless world. To refuse him help after this is to admit the validity
of his remarks and therefore, by implication, their own hardhearted-
ness. They see through his verbal camouflage, but since it is based on
emotional and moral clichés to which the response is predetermined,
they are helpless before it.

From the beginning the distance between what Anse says and what
he does is ironically and humorously emphasized. The irony is, however, most apparent in the scene of Addie's burial. Having had his
promise to her fulfilled for him, he makes a short funeral oration. His
words and his sentiments as he expresses his grief, though a trifle
marred by self-pity, are appropriate to the occasion and to his role as
chief mourner: "'The somebody you was young with and you growed
old in her and she growed old in you, seeing the old coming on and it
was the one somebody you could hear say it don't matter and know it
was the truth outen the hard world and all a man's grief and trials. You
all don't know.'" (135) But it is simply a verbal sincerity, unrelated to
the act and therefore to the kind of truth that arises out of and
touches the heart directly and immediately. Lacking these, his words,
like his expression, constitute "a monstrous burlesque of all bereavement." (45) The lament for Addie is followed by his unwillingness to
buy a shovel for digging her grave; and even before her body has been
placed in it, he has found a new wife to reassure him in his old age.
These ironic incongruities are profoundly in keeping with Anse's character. Cushioned by words and conventional sentiments against the

harsh impact of reality, he is the only one of the Bundrens completely unchanged by Addie's death or by the funeral journey. The horrors which drive Darl into insanity and leave their mark on the others pass him by so that he avoids agony and insight alike.

In contrast to his father, Cash undergoes certain very clear and definite changes as a result of Addie's death and funeral. Apparently reflecting Addie's rejection of words at the time of his birth, Cash begins by being silent, absorbed in his work, and curiously remote from the tensions and violence of the rest of the family. It is only after something concrete has been accomplished that he speaks. As a carpenter, Cash is concerned with working with his hands and building well; as Addie's son, he uses those hands and that skill to express what she means to him. Thus, the construction of the coffin becomes an act of love, understood as such by Addie, in which emotion tempered by reason is manifested in a concrete form. The sense of proportion which guides his hands also distinguishes his behavior and makes him the inevitable peacemaker in the family. Yet admirable as these characteristics are, Cash is, at the outset, a curiously stiff and one-sided figure. By devoting all his energy to and expressing his emotions through his work, he leaves no room for the cultivation of imaginative or linguistic potentialities. If Anse represents words without action, Cash is action in search of a word. Accordingly, a whole realm of human awareness and response is closed to him.

Cash does, however, develop a more comprehensive understanding of himself and his world. His exclusive preoccupation with concrete tangible objects yields to a more flexible, imaginative vision. The violence he suffers is, if not the cause, then the means of this profound transformation. The twice broken leg and the pain which he accepts without protest, as Addie had accepted the violence of his birth, pave the way for the extension of his range of awareness and for his increased sensitivity both to events and to people. The process is accelerated by the fact that his traditional mode of response, constructive action, is suddenly denied him. Lying helplessly on the coffin, his leg encased in cement and jarred by every turn of the wheel, he is forced to seek new forms of expression.

The increasing range of Cash's awareness is suggested by his growing sympathy with Darl. Facing the flooded river, they "look at one another with long probing looks, looks that plunge unimpeded through one another's eyes and into the ultimate secret place." (82) In that moment crossing the river becomes more than a problem of finding ways and means; Cash begins to realize that the prolonged journey is, in effect, destroying the significance it should affirm. During their stay at the Gillespies', Cash and Darl once more share the same revulsion and repudiation of the family's obsession with fulfilling the letter of the promise to Addie. Although it is Darl who sets fire to the barn, Cash accepts the responsibility as his own because he is the elder and because he too had contemplated the same violent act. Accepting this responsibility is one more step in his recognition of the complexity of those moral and emotional qualities which inhere in men's actions. Accordingly, he alone comprehends that the judgment of Darl's attempt to destroy the coffin and of Jewel's grim efforts to save it must depend upon whether the body is viewed realistically or symbolically. Darl's action issues from his conviction that the corpse has long since become an offense to God and man, Jewel's from the equally strong emotional conviction that the coffin contains his mother. Combined with his own firm foundation in action and the concrete details of his trade, this increase of sensitivity and imaginative perception makes Cash the one character in the novel who achieves his full humanity in which reason and intuition, words and action merge into a single though complex response.

Darl, the second son and the most complicated of the Bundrens, faithfully reflects and dramatizes Addie's attitude at the time of his birth. She had believed, a belief later qualified, that reality lay only in physical experience and that the word and the act were polar opposites. Feeling Darl to be an outrage, she had denied him a place in her affections and in her world. Consequently, Darl's is a world of consciousness exclusively, and this, of course, renders his connection with the external world increasingly precarious and insecure. He exists in a kind of limbo where the firm, defining shape of objects and of people is continually dissolving. Only by a painful process of reasoning can he establish the physical existence of himself, his mother, and the loaded wagon: "Yet the wagon *is*, because when the wagon is *was*, Addie Bundren will not be. And Jewel *is*, so Addie Bundren must be. And then I must be, or I could not empty myself for sleep in a strange room." (47) This attempt to define objective reality is an index of Darl's separation from it.

But the same absence of defining and limiting outline permits Darl to penetrate the minds of others and to intuit those secret thoughts of which they themselves are scarcely aware. Twice, while he himself is absent, he apprehends the actions of Cash, Anse, and Dewey Dell as they cluster around the dying Addie and describes them with startling vividness. And at every moment he is able to expose, with merciless accuracy, the secret thoughts and motives of others. He knows that Jewel is the son of Addie's sin, a fact with which he repeatedly taunts the latter by asking, "Who is your father, Jewel?" More important, he knows that the horse Jewel caresses and curses is a surrogate for Addie. Similarly, he is aware of Dewey Dell's pregnancy. In both cases his knowledge forces them to face certain facts about themselves and their world. Unwilling to do so, Jewel relieves his mounting frustration in the violence of curses, while Dewey Dell finds temporary release in a fantasy of murder. Both join in the vicious physical attack on Darl when they arrive in Jefferson. Addie's rejection of him is thus repeated: with the exception of Vardaman, who is too young to know what is happening, each of the Bundrens contributes to the decision to send Darl to Jackson. As Cash's final, unacrimonious assessment suggests, the rejection is inevitable: "This world is not his world; this life his life." (149)

* * *

Yet Darl's delusion is grounded in the conviction that the funeral has become an unbearable travesty of filial piety. Addie's imagined but not unreasonable request prompts him to abandon his usual role as spectator. Thought and action are fused, though in a particularly violent way. Depending on one's point of view, his action becomes a sign either of a deranged mind or of an acute moral sensibility, an ambiguity recognized by Cash who reflects: "Sometimes I ain't so sho who's got ere a right to say when a man is crazy and when he ain't. Sometimes I think it ain't none of us pure crazy and ain't none of us pure sane until the balance of us talks him that-a-way." (134) Action, the basis of individual moral conduct, is subject to social judgments and these are implemented through language. Hence, though Cash understands and is sympathetic to Darl's gesture of protest, he is forced to conclude that society's judgment is the only possible one.

Although Jewel is the most closely connected with Addie and the most active during the journey, only one section is devoted to his stream of consciousness. The reason for this is that his world is least accessible to public scrutiny since it consists of a welter of emotions, centering on Addie, which cannot be communicated. These emotions are not subjected to the control of reason but are translated immediately into actions which, unlike Cash's carefully planned moves, are the products of spontaneous reflexes. Whether the results of such actions are destructive or constructive in any given instance is a matter of chance. Thus, his is the blame for perpetuating the horrors of the journey and his the credit for forcing it to a successful conclusion. It is significant that when the stimulus to action is removed, when Addie's corpse is buried and Darl committed to an insane asylum, Jewel's fury subsides except for brief spasms of irritation caused by some word or gesture of Anse's.

Because Jewel is himself largely unconscious of his own motives and emotional compulsions, it is Darl who expresses them. As Darl keeps reiterating, Jewel has no father. Addie, then, becomes the sole center of his emotional life. There is, however, no way in which

Jewel's violent feelings can be channelled into socially acceptable rituals. Seeing, as usual, only the surface meaning of actions, Cora Tull mistakes his despair for indifference. But when Jewel's own thoughts are revealed, they are seen to be devoted entirely to Addie. He imagines the two of them defiantly and violently isolated from the world and its interference. Most of Jewel's subsequent actions are, in effect, attempts to make this fantasy a reality and so to claim exclusive possession of Addie. Dewey Dell, Vardaman, and Anse, he simply ignores; but each time he meets Cash it is to override the latter's caution with his own impetuous activity. As for the neighbors, they are kept at a distance by his coldness and his deliberate insults. Even the genuinely helpful and sympathetic Tull is repulsed. Only Darl cannot be excluded from his private world and he is finally eliminated by being sent to Jackson.

This process of exclusion merely intensifies Jewel's emotional attachment to Addie without providing a release for it. The latter he finds in the wild horse which he tames and on which he can lavish his love and inflict his hatred. Because the horse is actually his possession, he can and does isolate himself and it from all contact with others. No one except himself is permitted to feed, care for, or even touch it. In a sense, the horse perpetuates Addie's emotional relationship with Jewel. Because of this identification, Jewel insists on bringing the horse with him despite Anse's protests and Darl's oblique taunts. And when he finally sells it to pay for a new team, the full intensity of his feeling reverts to Addie. This explains why he is almost prevented by his concern for the horse from rescuing Addie's coffin out of the river, whereas during the fire all his energies are directed solely toward saving it.

In sharp contrast to Jewel, Dewey Dell seems the least concerned with Addie's death and funeral. Addie, however, had revealed the same impersonal and unemotional attitude toward Dewey Dell when she stated that she had given Dewey Dell to Anse in order to "negative" Jewel. In a way, Dewey Dell has no need of Addie because she herself is recreating Addie's past and discovering that pregnancy is both a state of mind and a physical fact, both a word and an action. But unlike Addie, she is determined, if possible, to effect their separation. Thus, she will not name her condition even to herself because to do so would be to transfer her pregnancy from her private world of awareness to the public world of fact.

Yet it is only by admitting the physical reality of her pregnancy and by making it, at least to some extent, public that she can do anything to terminate it. The problem is focussed for her by the presence of Peabody. By destroying the physical evidence of her pregnancy, Peabody would become a witness to its reality, a reality which would be perpetuated in his consciousness. She avoids telling Peabody, but

Darl, unfortunately, already knows. Her desire to destroy Darl and with him his knowledge is first expressed in fantasy: "I rose and took the knife from the streaming fish still hissing and I killed Darl." (69) This is followed by her savage physical attack on him and by her determination to have him sent to Jackson. Darl's departure does not, of course, solve anything for Dewey Dell, but it does postpone the need for immediate decision and action. Because there is no one present who knows of her pregnancy, she can act, for the time being, as if it did not exist. As she sits on the wagon, placidly munching a banana, her mind relapses into its normal state, that of the minimal level of conscious thought.

The limitations of Vardaman's mind are of a different order; they are those of the youngest child, who is bewildered by a phenomenon completely new to him. Out of the various sensations that he experiences and the facts that he observes while Addie is dying, he attempts to define for himself the meaning of death. He can do this only by constructing analogies to what he already knows or remembers. But because Vardaman is limited largely to sensations, he is not able to pass from the concrete to the general and abstract. What begins as an analogy ends as an identification. Addie and the fish are linked by death and therefore, according to his own particular logic, what happens to one happens to the other: "Then it wasn't and she was, and now it is and she wasn't. And tomorrow it will be cooked and et and she will be him and pa and Cash and Dewey Dell and there won't be anything in the box and so she can breathe." (39) Eventually the dead fish and the dead mother fuse into a single thought: "My mother is a fish." Knowing that he himself is the cause and instrument of the fish's death, Vardaman seeks to find the agent responsible for Addie's death. Selecting Doctor Peabody, he gains his revenge by mistreating the doctor's horses.

Still arguing from analogy, Vardaman remembers the lack of air in the corn crib and assumes that his mother, now confined in the coffin, must feel a similar lack. Drilling holes in the coffin thus becomes a reasonable and humane act, an expression of his concern for his mother. Though certain of Vardaman's acts seem to border on the insane, he himself is not. He is a child, sensitive and even intelligent, who is exposed to a tremendous shock. And in meeting it, he has neither precedent nor advice to guide him. It is, therefore, almost inevitable that he should arrive at a distorted conception of death and that his actions, having their source in that concept, should appear grotesque and incongruous. Certainly Vardaman suffers from a delusion but an understandable one since it permits him to dissociate his mother from the horrors of physical death and decay: *"My mother is not in the box. My mother does not smell like that. My mother is a fish."* (114)

Through the interaction of the characters the complexity of the
central situation is evoked, and through an understanding of those
complexities, the motivation and hence the credibility of the characters is established. At the end, we see them in terms of their relationship to Addie and to each other, "sitting bolt upright in [their]
nakedness, staring at one another and saying 'Now is the truth.'"
(77) The private world of each of the Bundrens has been exposed,
partly by their own actions and partly by Darl's constant probing.
With his departure and the burial of Addie's corpse, the period of
tension ends. The new wife, the gramophone, the memory of the toy
trains, and the bananas do not replace Addie, but they do indicate a
shift in the family's focus of consciousness. It is through the incep-
tion of such new patterns that the characters seek to avoid too close,
protracted, and painful a scrutiny of the meaning of life and death.

Addie's death and her funeral are construed in terms of the family's varied levels and modes of consciousness, but they also possess
a wider frame of reference, for the actions of the Bundrens project
both death and funeral into the public world. It is in this capacity of
responding to the Bundrens and their funeral procession that Faulkner introduces his eight reverberators. Mosely and MacGowan reveal
two contrasting attitudes to Dewey Dell's pregnancy. The former
responds to her request for pills with self-righteous moral indignation; the latter unhesitatingly takes advantage of what he conceives
to be an essentially comic situation. Between them they indicate the
range of possible social reactions to and judgments of her condition.
Quite obviously, neither Mosely nor MacGowan is concerned with
Dewey Dell as a person; they respond only to the fact that she is
clearly somewhat stupid, pregnant, and unmarried.

In Samson, Armstid, and Tull, the purely social and moral judgment
is tempered by personal knowledge of the Bundrens. They are, in
fact, themselves implicated to some extent in the funeral. There is a
kind of humorous despair in their frustrating knowledge that Anse
has and will continue to take advantage of their neighborliness. Tull,
for example, remarks: "Like most folks around here, I done help him
so much already I can't quit now." (20) Each of these men describes
a stage in the journey to Jefferson in terms of his contribution to it.
Significantly, as individuals, they are appalled by the horrifying physical aspects of Addie's decaying body; but as neighbors, they feel obli-
gated to offer their help in continuing the journey. With the burning
of Gillespie's barn, however, the limits of neighborliness are reached.

In contrast to the three men, Cora Tull and Whitfield see the Bundrens solely in terms of their own ethical systems. It is fitting, therefore, that Addie's soliloquy, with its emphasis on the separation of the
word and the act, should be flanked by their moralizing and empty
rhetoric. Fearing that he will be forced at last to face Anse, Whitfield

is intent upon finding the right words for framing his confession. Yet the moment he learns that Addie has not betrayed their secret, all thoughts of confession leave his mind. He is once more free to act as if he had never violated the moral code of his community since the public world is still unaware of his guilt. As for the sin against God, a verbal apology is sufficient: "He will accept the will for the deed, Who knew that when I framed the words of my confession it was to Anse I spoke them, even though he was not there." (104) Confession, repentance, and even penance are carried out in his mind, thereby obviating any necessity of embracing them in an act. Anse's own formula of verbal evasion is thus, ironically, turned against him.

Whitfield's account of his relationship with Addie is rendered wholly in terms of ethical and religious clichés from which all human passion and meaning has been carefully deleted. Similarly, everything about Addie, her family, and her death is but another moral lesson to be interpreted by Cora Tull as she elbows her way to heaven. Having learned her ethics by rote, Cora has no difficulty in affixing praise and blame or in predicting salvation or damnation for all whom she meets. Though she consigns Addie and her family to the latter category, she is consistently and determinedly helpful. Her help, however, is offered in the name of duty not love, and it is meant, whether she realizes it or not, to be one more step in establishing her own virtue and her own right to salvation. Kindness such as Cora's is essentially selfish, debasing both the giver and the recipient and destroying the possibility of any personal relationship between them. In her eyes even family ties are moral rather than emotional. As a result, Cora is totally unaware, in any real sense, of those agonizing and exalting human experiences which stand outside her rigid system of ethics, resisting and disrupting its smooth simplification of existence.

Of all the characters who observe and comment on the actions of the Bundrens, Doctor Peabody is the most judicious. Although Tull's remarks often contain shrewd assessments of specific events, it is Peabody who grasps their broader significance. His insight is the result of long and varied experience with people compelled to face the realities of pain, suffering, and death. Thus, when he makes separate evaluations of life, love, and death, his statements serve as a general guide for interpreting the actions of the family. His is the compassionate but detached vision of the country doctor-cum-philosopher. Yet when he is suddenly confronted with the Bundrens in Jefferson, he loses his philosophic objectivity. Overwhelmed by the massing of concrete horrors and sensations, he reacts with bitter indignation.

While acting as reverberator for the actions of the Bundrens, these eight characters offer release from the tension through humorous or ironic remarks. Because only the actions of the Bundrens and not their thoughts and emotions are perceived, they become grotesques.

What is horror and pain for the family becomes farce for those who are not themselves involved and who merely observe with the physical eye. For the Bundrens, the journey seethes with unresolved tensions; for the townspeople of Mottson, it is only a ridiculous or macabre spectacle. This intermingling of humor and horror, which is part of the very texture of As I Lay Dying, issues out of the Bundrens' conviction that their actions are eminently reasonable and out of the spectators' conviction that the Bundrens and their coffin have long since passed beyond the realm of reason, logic, or even commonsense. The juxtaposition of the two views gives rise to a complicated and ambivalent feeling of hilarity and despair. Confronted with the irrational, the rational mind finds itself bewildered and uneasy, indignant and outraged, or simply wryly amused. As the funeral journey is prolonged, all these attitudes are exhibited.

The interplay of seriousness which reaches toward tragedy and of humor which is practically farce is part of the complete success of As I Lay Dying. In a sense, it reinforces the theme of the separation of words and acts by insisting on at least these two modes of response to the same set of characters and events. At the same time, it precludes any easy generalizations about the funeral journey itself. Any event or series of events elicits various and, at times, contradictory responses. The meaning of an experience as distinct from a word exists in the consciousness of the individual observer. Accordingly, it is only when one becomes conscious of the mingling of humor and pathos, of the relation of the Bundrens to Addie, and of the observers to the action that the full complexity of As I Lay Dying is plumbed and Faulkner's easy mastery of it recognized.

CLEANTH BROOKS

Odyssey of the Bundrens[†]

The author's fondness for As I Lay Dying is easily understood. The writing in this novel is as good as Faulkner has ever done, and the book constitutes a triumph in the management of tone. Faulkner has daringly mingled the grotesque and the heroic, the comic and the pathetic, pity and terror, creating a complexity of tone that has proved difficult for some readers to cope with. To ignore this complexity is to find in the novel simply an exploitation of horror for the sake of its shock value or for the sake of a grotesque comedy. Even

---

† From *William Faulkner: The Yoknapatawpha Country* (New Haven and London: Yale University Press, 1963), pp. 141–66. Reprinted by permission of Louisiana State University Press.

the reader who is able to see that the novel concerns itself with a heroic action is likely to have his difficulties. Appreciating the heroic, he may wonder whether his comic response is appropriate, or, sensing the comic value of the absurd and anticlimactic incidents, he may come to doubt his earlier intimations that the action was in fact heroic.

* * *

In view of the prevailing tendency to "sociologize" Faulkner, it may be just as well to say here and now that Faulkner is not portraying a quaintly horrifying Southern folkway. Few, if any, families in rural Mississippi would have attempted to do what the Bundrens did. Consider how all the non-Bundren characters within the novel regard the expedition. They are shocked and horrified—the women especially. Lula Armstid exclaims: "It's a outrage. [Anse] should be lawed for treating her so" (108). Rachel Samson bursts out to her husband: "You and [Anse] and all the men in the world that torture us alive and flout us dead, dragging us up and down the country—" (67). Samson thinks to himself: "I got just as much respect for the dead as ere a man . . . and a woman that's been dead in a box four days, the best way to respect her is to get her into the ground as quick as you can" (66).

A primary question, therefore, must be why the Bundrens carry out their strange and difficult task, for it not only cuts across the community's sense of what is fitting, but runs counter to the shiftless husband's lethargy and irresponsibility, is opposed by at least one of the brothers, and involves the whole family in hardship, loss, danger, and injury. The reader will not find an obvious answer. When neighbors remonstrate with Anse, he replies that "it's Addie I give the promise to. Her mind is set on it" (65), though we do not take very seriously Anse's concern for his wife. Early in the novel we learn of other motivations for taking Addie's body to Jefferson: Anse longs for a set of store-bought teeth and Darl imagines Anse saying, when Addie dies, "God's will be done. Now I can get them teeth" (30). The daughter, Dewey Dell, who knows she is pregnant, is desperately anxious to get into town so that she can buy an abortion drug. And there are things in town which tempt even the moderate Cash and the child Vardaman. Did the Bundren family, then, simply drift into its heroic action? Did they accomplish it unwittingly and for the least heroic of motives?

One would like to postpone for the time answers to such questions, but I suggest that as we look about for answers, we will be forced to consider the possibility that one of Faulkner's principal themes in *As I Lay Dying*—perhaps the principal theme—is the nature of the heroic deed, with an examination both of what fosters it and of the various things that would inhibit it, including not only common sense, selfishness, and cowardice, but romantic self-consciousness.

Yet we should not dismiss out of hand the claims of honor, heavily as we may be constrained to qualify them in view of Anse's character. The code of honor receives heavy stress in this novel. The need of the male to prove himself * * * comes to a high focus in this story of the Bundren family. It is not enough simply to bury the mother reverently and with some show of decent grief; the promise she has exacted must be honored to the letter: come fire or flood, hell or highwater, her body must be taken to the spot which she has designated as her final resting place, and no circumstance, not even the most frustrating, is allowed to cancel the obligation. By any rational test, the undertaking is quixotic, but in carrying it out, two of the children, Cash and Jewel, exhibit true heroism—Cash in his suffering, Jewel in his brave actions. Both brothers go far beyond the claims of rationality and common sense. Their brother Darl, of course, does not. His role is that of the critic of the action, who does not believe in honor and has the supreme lucidity of the mad.

※　　※　　※

Because Darl is by far the most articulate of the Bundrens, because his speech is endowed with a certain poetry, and because he voices what is probably the reader's own revulsion against the Bundrens' foolish and horrible journey, it is very likely that Darl will appear to be the representative intelligence of the novel and the mouthpiece of the author. By contrast, the decent, patient, unimaginative Cash—the good workman, proud of his work and careful of his tools—may well appear as dull and unfeeling, hopelessly prosaic. Nor is the typical reader likely to find Jewel other than antipathetic. For Jewel is the high-strung man of action, impatient, ardent, flamboyant, and heroic, but only in some kind of terribly brainless way. Yet the reader will be mistaken if he accepts Darl's account of things as necessarily true and if he sees in Darl's judgments and valuations necessarily those of the author. The novel is not nearly so simple.

With regard to the burial journey, Darl, the lunatic, is indeed the only one of the three older brothers who is thoroughly "sane," and in general he is the one who knows the truth—about Dewey Dell's secret thoughts, about his mother's special attachment to Jewel, and about the various secret motivations of the members of his family. But Darl's truth is corrosive and antiheroic, and in its logic perhaps finally inhuman. Does he really grieve for his mother at all? It would be hard to say. In a sense, he knows too much about her and too much about the absurdity of reality to have any emotional commitment.

Darl represents, among other things, the detachment and even callousness which we sometimes associate with the artist. Darl is pure perception. He intuits almost immediately Dewey Dell's pregnancy, and his sister, realizing this, resents and fears him. Darl sees through his father's clumsy pretenses. He chides Jewel for his childishly immoderate attachment to his horse. Twice he tries to stop the outrageous journey to the Jefferson cemetery. In general, in spite of all his poetry, he is a rationalizing and deflating force—the antiheroic intelligence.

*   *   *

It is important to notice the author's own detachment in this matter. Though Darl, with his gift for language and his penchant for almost clairvoyant observation, must represent much that is dear to Faulkner himself, Faulkner is, as we shall see, perfectly willing to judge against Darl on point after point. Indeed, Faulkner, probably more than any other author of our time, is willing to see the limitations of the artistic temperament and to refuse to believe that it has a monopoly upon truth. Or perhaps Darl as artist has too much truth—sees the complexity of human motivations so thoroughly that all action is paralyzed and all risks rendered quixotic because no motivation is so pure and no goal so desirable as to be worth the necessary risk. There are passages in the novel that would seem to support this interpretation, and yet there are other passages in which Darl's prophetic and preternatural vision gives way to a bitterness and pettiness as in his baiting of his brother Jewel.

Yet Darl, even if we are not to assume that he has all the truth, certainly does possess some of the truth, and Faulkner avails himself of Darl's imagination nineteen times in the novel. Far more passages are given to Darl than to any other character in *As I Lay Dying*. Moreover, it is in these passages—in which we are within Darl's mind—that Faulkner employs some of his most interesting technical devices and departs furthest from a merely naturalistic presentation of events. The scene of Addie's death, so meticulous in its detail, so convincing in its realism, is actually a fictitious construct imagined by Darl as he rides on the wagon with Jewel, miles from home. (This is not to say, of course, that Darl's vision of what happened was necessarily untrue.) So also is the fine scene in which Darl imagines Cash working into the night through the rainstorm on their mother's coffin. Even after Darl has suffered his breakdown and is on the train headed for the state insane asylum, laughing with the laughter of the mad, his description of the scene in which two deputies sit by him on the train is brilliantly done. Such clarity of vision is not impaired by Darl's madness and may even find in that special kind of madness its necessary condition.

*   *   *

* * * Like Jewel and Cash, Vardaman runs counter to the claims of common sense; but he does so in the way in which a child, confused and disturbed, would. He is suffering from a traumatic shock. Because the two exciting experiences, the catching of the big fish and his mother's death, happen so close together, the events somehow coalesce in his mind and he can say "my mother is a fish." Vardaman bores holes in his mother's coffin in order to give her air. His attempt to liberate her from the coffin is "crazy" of course, but it has nothing to do with Darl's kind of madness.

Though only Darl opposes the journey, its successful prosecution depends upon the positive efforts of two of the children, Cash and Jewel. They are willing to pay the price for honoring their mother's request. Anse, it is true, appears to honor it. He evidently enjoys refusing to let his neighbors talk him out of the trip to Jefferson with his wife's body. * * * Anse is the selfish man who has a lifetime habit of leaning on other people. Anse knows that he can depend on his children to make good his promise. His statement to Cash, "There is Christians enough to help you," is characteristic. In this general connection it is interesting to note what Darl has to say about him. Darl imagines his father leaning above his mother's deathbed and pictures him thus: "his humped silhouette partaking of that owl-like quality of awry-feathered, disgruntled outrage within which lurks a wisdom too profound or too inert for even thought" (29).

One is tempted to say that in this novel Addie and Anse have exchanged roles. It is Anse who has the profound inertia that Faulkner usually associates with woman, who is apparently unaggressive, pliant, and resilient, but with tireless persistence tends toward her elected goal and is never finally deflected from it. Addie one is tempted to call another example of Faulkner's masculinized women. * * * [S]he insists upon the impractical and heroic gesture, and though she could hardly have foreseen how difficult the journey with her coffin would be, it is obviously her still-vital, implacable energy that enables her family to complete their mission and holds them together as a family until her body is finally deposited in the stipulated grave. But the word "masculinized" risks distorting Addie's character. She is completely feminine to the extent that she expresses herself in and through her children. She has fulfilled herself in breeding up and nurturing the children whom she is forcing to become heroes.

Addie is also feminine in Faulkner's sense in being completely committed to the concrete fact. She has seen through all illusions. She despises words. One thinks of the one long, terrible expression allowed her in this novel in which she tells the story of her life. What Addie lacks, and what she yearns for, is some kind of communion. Even before her marriage to Anse, she has felt this emptiness of despair. She switches the children she teaches, in a desperate attempt, as she puts it, to say to them: "Now you are aware of me! Now I am something in your secret and selfish life, who have marked your blood with my own for ever and ever (98)."

* * *

Since Addie does not believe in the spiritual—not, at least, in any of its conventional senses—she can make the assertion of her identity only in terms of the body. Her body then becomes of inordinate importance to her, first through her children—two of whom she jealously claims as a peculiar expression of her body, having no part of Anse but "being of [her] alone"—and now that she is dead, as a token of her final repudiation of Anse. Her dead body becomes a monstrous token—the only available token—of her fierce identity when, through the pledge that she forces from her shiftless husband, she manages to endow it with an almost vampire-like personal will. The body will die only on its own terms: it will not rest—or allow her family rest— until it has been delivered to its chosen resting place.

Addie's grim but exultant confession ends with a significant sentence: "One day I was talking to Cora. She prayed for me because she believed I was blind to sin, wanting me to kneel and pray too, because people to whom sin is just a matter of words, to them salvation is just words too" (102). Addie's salvation was not of mere words. It involved the substantiality of the body. The Jordan which it had to cross in order to enter into salvation was the flooded river from which Cash and Jewel save her coffined body. The fire of hell which she had to escape was the quite literal fire of the burning barn from which Jewel lugs the coffin. The salvation was a tangible one, not that of some wordy prayer that was to bring her before a heavenly Father but the actual placing of her now foul body beside the bones of her literal earthly father. * * *

* * *

Addie has good reason for her disgust at mere words—not only from her experience with her husband but also from her experience with her lover. The passage assigned to Whitfield follows immediately after Addie's. In it Whitfield tells what went on in his mind when he heard that Addie was dying and when, as her pastor, he was summoned to her bedside. His colloquy with himself beautifully illustrates Addie's point about those who live by mere words. When the minister hears of Addie's impending death, he wrestles with his spirit and finally gathers strength to make a full confession to the deceived husband; but in spite of his talk about feeling that he has now been received again into God's holy peace and love, it is plain that he continues to dread the confession that he must make. Thus, when he reaches Tull's house and hears that Addie is already dead, he is greatly relieved. He says to himself: "I have sinned, O Lord. Thou knowest the extent of my remorse and the will of my spirit. But He" (and the shift from second to third person is significant) "is merciful; He will accept the will for the deed, Who knew that when I framed the words of my confession it was to Anse I spoke them, even though he was not there (104)." * * *

Whitfield's confession, then, is only a matter of words. It is never fulfilled in deeds. Whitfield enjoys the credit of full confession and reacceptance without undergoing any of the suffering and opprobrium that would have ensued from an actual confession to Anse and Anse's neighbors.* * *

The various commentators on *As I Lay Dying* have made rather heavy work in dealing with Addie. She is sometimes seen as a "good" woman, much put upon, whose story is one of pathos and suffering, and sometimes as a wicked woman, deliberately punishing the members of her family by playing a horrible joke upon them. Neither of these views is very perceptive. Addie is indeed a destructive force, but she is responsible for whatever of heroic temper the Bundrens achieve. She is a wicked woman, if you like (certainly a woman who has been warped and perverted), and she uses her energies for questionable purposes, but the Lady Macbeths and the Medeas—to name more celebrated and august members of Addie's sisterhood—have all been such mixed cases.

Though Addie Bundren has so small a speaking part in this novel, she possesses something of tragic complexity as well as tragic intensity. If she is perverted, her energy, her willingness to suffer, and her complete honesty with herself provide complicating virtues. In any case, she possesses a tremendous intensity, and her corrupting body is throughout the nine days' journey, in some sense, the most vital thing that rides upon the Bundren wagon.

*   *   *

Addie cannot be fully understood, however, unless we take into account her husband. Anse Bundren is one of Faulkner's most accomplished villains. He lacks the lethal power of a Popeye and the passionate intensity of a Percy Grimm, but the kind of force that he embodies has to be reckoned with. It is deceptively slight, as delicately flexible as a root tendril but, like the tendril, powerful enough to break a boulder. Anse resembles most nearly Flem Snopes[1]—in his coolness, his sheer persistence, his merciless knowledge of other human beings and of how much they will put up with. A nice example is the way in which he gets from Dewey Dell the money her lover has

1. Characters in Faulkner's other novels: Popeye appears in *Sanctuary*, Percy Grimm in *Light in August*, and Flem Snopes in the trilogy made up of *The Hamlet*, *The Town*, and *The Mansion*, as well as in other works [*Editor*].

given her for an abortion drug. The girl frantically tries to save her money. But Anse is like a ferret working his way toward the trapped rabbit. When Dewey Dell in her desperation tells her father, "If you take it you are a thief," Anse has his rhetoric ready at command: "My own daughter accuses me of being a thief. My own daughter." And reminding her that he has fed her and sheltered her, he laments that "my own daughter, the daughter of my dead wife, calls me a thief over her mother's grave" (147). Besides, it is only a loan. "God knows, I hate for my blooden children to reproach me. But I give them what was mine without stint. Cheerful I give them, without stint. And now they deny me. Addie. It was lucky for you you died, Addie." (147).

*   *   *

Our attitude toward Anse—fury at his cheapness and pusillanimity, disgust for his essential callousness and cruelty, baffled admiration for the stubborn vitality which like that of some low order of organism allows him to fatten on what would starve nobler creatures and survive blasts that would kill more sensitive organisms, and, not least, a sense of simple awe at the sheer thickness of his skin—all of these attitudes qualify and determine the kind of comic figure that Anse is. But we must not underestimate him. He is not contemptible, a mere insect that one could and would like to squash underneath the foot. He represents a force probably necessary to the survival of the human animal though it is terrifying when seen in such simple purity.

The grim comedy that attaches to Anse does not, however, call in question the heroic quality of the Bundren adventure. Indeed, this novel beautifully exemplifies how comic elements such as Anse, the human buzzard, and horrifying elements, such as the actual buzzards, are in fact used to undergird the epic mode. The account of the river-crossing, surely one of the finest descriptive achievements in American literature, will illustrate.

Faulkner was skillful in his choice of the people who describe the crossing. It is a fine stroke to have Tull, the practical, earthy, and common-sense countryman, tell part of it. Tull is cynical about the Bundrens' motives for insisting on crossing the river: "Just going to town. Bent on it. They would risk the fire and the earth and the water and all just to eat a sack of bananas" (81). But Tull can make us see the flooded stream: "The water was cold. It was thick, like slush ice. Only it kind of lived. One part of you knowed it was just water, the same thing that had been running under this same bridge for a long time, yet when them logs would come spewing up outen it, you were not surprised, like they was a part of water, of the waiting and the threat" (79).

But Faulkner also has Darl, whose perceptions are always instinct with poetry, describe the scene: "What had once been a flat surface was now a succession of troughs and hillocks lifting and falling about us, shoving at us, teasing at us with light lazy touches in the vain instants of solidity underfoot" (85). And Darl, describing the catastrophe says: "Cash looked back at me, and then I knew that we were gone. But I did not realize the reason for the rope until I saw the log. It surged up out of the water and stood for an instant upright upon that surging and heaving desolation like Christ" (85–86). Why like Christ? It would be hard to say, though the similitude seems inevitable and right. Is Darl remembering the passage in which the alarmed fishermen on Galilee see their Master incredibly walking upon the waves? But with the difference that this erect object, incredibly footing the water, moves toward them not to reassure but to threaten and astound? Perhaps so, or perhaps the force of the similitude is more general. The log, standing for an instant upright, is like Christ simply in its hint of supernatural portent, an astonishing assertion out of the mere flux of anonymity. (Later, Cora is to call the log "the hand of God.")

The passage that follows, which details the destruction caused by the log as it bears down upon the team and which depicts Jewel's surging horse and the mules for a moment shining black out of the water just before they are overturned—all of this is done with the fidelity that one expects from the dedicated observer, the habitual spectator, for that, as we have seen, is all that Darl is. Cash and Jewel agonize and struggle; Darl does not.

It is also a fine stroke on Faulkner's part to have the child Vardaman describe what happened just after the drowning of the mules and the coffin's slipping off into the water. Vardaman's account has the clarity of detail of the innocent eye, but also the confused subjectivity of Vardaman's anxiety. For the child it will be intolerable if Darl doesn't catch the coffin. Surely he will come up with it out of the water. His failure to do so will be unbearable: "Then his hands came up and all of him above the water. I can't stop. I have not got time to try. I will try to when I can but his hands came empty out of the water emptying the water emptying away" (87). But we also need, for our total comprehension, Tull's objective account as he tells his wife about it later. He puts it laconically: "How Darl jumped out of the wagon and left Cash sitting there trying to save it and the wagon turning over" (88).

* * *

The force exerted by the dead woman in holding her family together is underscored by our sense of the divisions within the family. One might argue that each of the Bundren children is making the journey alone, each shut up in his own consciousness and unable to communicate with the others. Jewel cannot understand Cash and is exasperated by what he takes to be Cash's insensitivity and callousness. He is outraged that Cash chooses to work on his mother's coffin near a window through which his mother can see him at his work. Between Jewel and Darl there is active hostility. Darl is bitter and even cruel in taunting Jewel for having a horse for a mother. The intensity of Jewel's love for his horse and the sacrifice that he has made to obtain it give special edge to the taunt. Yet there is no question that Jewel loves his mother and even Darl recognizes this, as, for example, when he observes what he calls "the furious tide of Jewel's despair" (57).

The lack of communication extends through the family. Dewey Dell is unable to speak to anyone about her plight. There is a desperate need to talk to someone about her problem and yet there is literally no one to whom she can talk. The only person who is aware of her pregnancy is Darl, and him she fears and hates with a blind fury. Once their mother's body has been put into the grave, Dewey Dell joins Jewel in leaping upon Darl as they seize him in order to turn him over to the officers.

Jewel, too, is a passionate person who has no one with whom he can talk. Granted that there is a kind of nameless understanding between him and his mother, still it is nameless and unuttered, and his inarticulate poetry, the ardor and passion which he can express only through violent action, find no release in words—in part because there is no one with whom he can converse.

Cash, of course, has no poetry in him, articulate or inarticulate, and perhaps in him of all the family there is the least need for expression or for a sympathetic and understanding listener. Yet if Cash bears his relative isolation with patience and with no special sense of pain, he is nevertheless a baffled and lonely man. He reflects that he was born almost ten years before the three youngest children and therefore feels closest to Darl, but it is plain that he and Darl have very little in common. Cash shakes his head in puzzled reproach when he learns that it was Darl who set fire to Mr. Gillespie's barn. He is shocked when Dewey Dell and Jewel leap upon Darl in fury to turn him over to the officers, and when Darl breaks down into his crazy laughter, Cash is indeed at a loss. He says: "I be durn if I could see anything to laugh at" (137).

The essential isolation of the characters is unobtrusively enforced by the fact that each part of the novel is presented through the consciousness of a particular character. We are always within one mind, never in some domain of objectivity and commonly held values. Often we are in the minds of sensitive observers like Darl and the child Vardaman. Darl has nineteen sections; Vardaman, ten. The sections assigned to all the rest of the family amount to only fourteen, and of these, Jewel, the heroically active son, has only one.

Faulkner's method of presentation allows us, on occasion, not only to penetrate into the depths of a character but to see him externally as others see him. Sometimes this external view is that of another member of the family; at other times, that of an outsider like Dr. Peabody or the druggist MacGowan. This technique of multiple presentation has everything to do with the solidity and power of *As I Lay Dying*. The author does not commit us to the experience and sensibility of one character whom we see only from the inside and whose world we apprehend only from his point of view. Instead, Faulkner has attempted the much more difficult role of putting us in some kind of sympathetic rapport with an individual character and yet constantly forcing this character back into the total perspective of the world—the world of the family and the larger world of the community.

The presentation of Dewey Dell will illustrate. She looks at first glance like a rather stupid and selfish young woman, as in some sense she is. Yet in spite of her somewhat bovine simplicity, Dewey Dell has her secret terrors, her pathos, and even her shy dignity. When Dr. Peabody comes to see her mother, she yearns toward his knowledge: "he could do so much for me and he don't know it" (35). But she is afraid to tell him what her problem is and feels to the full her alienation: "It's because I am alone" (35). Later she reflects: "I don't know whether I am worrying or not. Whether I can or not. I don't know whether I can cry or not. I don't know whether I have tried to or not. I feel like a wet seed wild in the hot blind earth" (38).

Incidentally, the reader must not be put off because Dewey Dell—and all the other characters for that matter—frequently in these interior monologues use words and expressions which we feel are beyond their education and background. This is one of the conventions which must be accepted in a reading of *As I Lay Dying*. The language with which the author provides the character to express his innermost thoughts is not necessarily the same language the author has him use when he speaks to another character. It would certainly not occur to Dewey Dell to *tell* anyone that she felt like a "wet seed wild in the hot blind earth."

*   *   *

But Faulkner allows us to see Dewey Dell through other eyes—those, for example, of the rather straight-laced Mottson druggist, who notices that "she was pretty in a kind of sullen, awkward way," and who finally * * * dismisses Dewey Dell with an admonition: "I haven't got anything in my store you want to buy, unless it's a nipple. And I'd advise you to buy that and go back home and tell your pa, if you have one, and let him make somebody buy you a wedding license." The author also lets us see Dewey Dell through the eyes of MacGowan, the less scrupulous druggist in Jefferson, who sees her as looking "pretty good" for a country girl, "one of them blackeyed ones that look like she'd as soon put a knife in you as not if you two-timed her" (139).

The account of MacGowan's prescription for what Dewey Dell has called the female trouble and of the "treatment" he gives her is comedy in the tradition of the medieval fabliau, but I find that it intensifies the pathos of the situation rather than canceling it.

Jewel, too, has an inner life—though little of it is revealed in interior monologue. He is high-strung and fractious, youthfully intolerant, lacking imaginative sympathy, shortsighted, and ignorant. Yet because of its real ardor and passion, his inner life has its beauty. The horse that Jewel finally sells so that his father can buy the team to complete the journey to Jefferson is his most precious possession. We cannot know how much this sacrifice costs him until we have from Darl the story of how Jewel paid for his horse, slipping out each night to work by lantern light in a neighbor's field and the next day working in his father's field. Darl first thinks that Jewel's nightly expedition has to do with a woman, but Cash, to whom Darl confides the secret, follows Jewel one night and learns the truth. But Cash does not let the rest of the family know what Jewel is doing; he just quietly takes over some of Jewel's work. The secret is not divulged until the morning that Jewel rides up on his pony. Anse is quick with his reproaches: "You went behind my back and bought a horse" (78). But Addie is overcome: "'I'll give—I'll give—give—' Then she began to cry. She cried hard, not hiding her face, standing there in her faded wrapper, looking at him and him on the horse" (78). And that night Darl finds his mother sitting beside the bed where Jewel was sleeping in the dark. "She cried hard, maybe because she had to cry so quiet" (78). In saving the coffin from the river and from the burning barn, Jewel acts in character and makes use of his special talents. His sacrifice of his horse is less expected. In a sense it is the most heroic thing that he does.

It is Cash, however, who gains most from a multiple focus on his personality. Jewel possesses something of the poetry of action. Darl has the lucidity of the mad. But Cash's dignity and integrity scarcely shine forth—they are virtues too dull to shine—and we are hardly in a position to appreciate them until we have regarded Cash from a number of angles. More than one critic has been misled by Cash's inarticulate expression and his homely metaphors, drawn from the carpenter's trade, into taking him at the lowest discount. But Cash is no materialist; he is simply a very quiet and limited man, whose ideals are not showy but who has great power to endure and a great capacity to suffer without whining or complaining.

Cash also possesses more imaginative sympathy than may at first be evident. We have remarked upon the way in which he simply assumes a number of Jewel's duties when he realizes that his younger brother, in his passion to possess the horse, is attempting something beyond his powers. And Cash is sympathetic with Darl. He almost

grasps the motives for Darl's actions on the journey. * * * The real difficulty with depicting a character like Cash, so patient, so uncomplaining, so passive in his acceptance of hardship, is that the reader
may regard him as simply weak and stupid, and may laugh rather
than sympathize with him. Faulkner's solution is to allow us to laugh
at Cash. He does not play down the irreverent and mocking attitudes, but stresses them, makes them part of the total view, and thus
wrests Cash's dignity out of the very jaws of comedy.

There are only five sections attributed to Cash, and the first three
of these are brief and quite objective: Cash's justification for making
the coffin "on the bevel," a short scrap of his conversation with Jewel,
and an additional remark about the coffin's not balancing. The only
meditative and ruminative passages allowed him are two that occur
quite late in the novel.

Cash, then, begins as a kind of flat caricature, like a character in a
humors play. We see him first working away at the coffin to the chuk,
chuk, chuk of his adze, just outside the room in which his mother is
dying. He is still a comic figure of a sort when he lies injured beside
the flooded river, his tools carefully arranged beside him, with the
wretched Anse muttering, "A fellow might call it lucky it was the
same leg he broke when he fell offen that church" (94). The horror of
the grotesque contends with the comedy of the grotesque when the
family, under Anse's direction, pour sand and cement around Cash's
broken leg in order to set it in a crude cast. Later, when Cash is in
agony, Darl recounts: "So we poured the water over it. His leg and
foot below the cement look like they had been boiled. 'Does that feel
better?' we said. 'I'm obliged,' Cash said. 'It feels fine'" (123).

The problem of tone comes to a head in the exchange between
Cash and Dr. Peabody. The doctor, having managed to get the home-
made cast off the leg and having reset the broken bone, proceeds to
say what he thinks of the way in which Cash has been treated. He
remarks that a man might conceivably get into a position where he
would let a veterinarian like Bill Varner patch him up as if he were a
mule (this has happened earlier in the novel) but, he continues, "I
be damned if the man that'd let Anse Bundren treat him with raw
cement ain't got more spare legs than I have" * * * As the doctor
works grumpily over the leg, he assures Cash that maybe next summer he can hobble around fine on this leg: "Then it won't bother
you, not to speak of. . . . If you had anything you could call luck, you
might say it was lucky this is the same leg you broke before." And
Cash answers: "Hit's what paw says" (138).

What does the doctor feel toward Cash? Pity? Admiration? Sheer
amazement at his patience, irritation at his stolidity? Perhaps something of all of these. But not contempt, I should think. Cash has
earned his right to be allowed to suffer in his own way. He is too

sturdy and too solidly based to deserve any emotion elicited by weakness or moral pettiness.

The truth of the matter is that Dr. Peabody would probably not himself be able to describe precisely what his attitude toward Cash is. Our attitude toward Cash, of course, is not necessarily Dr. Peabody's, nor is our attitude toward any other member of the family that of our attitude toward Cash. And yet the problem that we have just been considering is a sort of paradigm of the larger problems raised by the novel. As Vernon Tull or Samson might put it, the Bundrens' exploit leaves us not knowing whether to laugh or to cry. And more is involved than simple indecision or a stalemate between these opposed attitudes. Both the pathetic and the comic have scope in this situation: folly intermingles with heroism, and the total perspective in which we are invited to view the Bundrens' odyssey accommodates what would usually be regarded as hopelessly conflicting attitudes.

In the total perspective the contradictions prove to be only apparent. The surface of the Bundren life shows squalor, crassness, selfishness, and stupidity, but beneath the surface there are depths of passion and poetry that are terrifying in their power. The very drabness of the surface is the guarantee of the genuineness of the passion. These people are not rhetoricians who talk themselves into their transports. One of them has the poetry of madness; one of them, the poetry of the child. But the others are almost inarticulate, and the two brothers who dare most and suffer most lack the wordiness that their mother despised.

Faulkner has been concerned in all his books with what the human being can endure, what he can dare, what he can accomplish. The story of how the Bundrens managed the burial of Addie Bundren affords him a very special vantage point from which to contemplate the human capacity for both suffering and action. The heroic adventure involves a mixture of motives and a variety of responses. There is the child who only partially comprehends what is occurring and responds to what he sees with astonishment and fear. There is the young woman so much obsessed with her own problems that she can reflect upon the adventure only as a possible answer to her own need. There is the parasite Anse, who does not even know that he is asking his children to be heroes, and if he could understand it would not care. There is Darl, who knows too much and feels too much to take in more than the nauseating horror and fear that the act costs. There is the patient Cash, who never sees that he is doing more than his bounden duty. There is Jewel, perhaps the least reflective member of the group, violent and even brutal, whose heroism is so pure and unself-conscious that he is not aware that it is heroism. It burns like a clean flame that exhausts itself in the process, leaving no sooty residue.

As a commentary upon man's power to act and to endure, upon his apparently incorrigible idealism, the story of the Bundrens is clearly appalling—appalling but not scathing and not debunking. Heroism is heroism even though it sometimes appears to be merely the hither side of folly. Man's capacity to spend himself in a cause is always a remarkable thing and nowhere more so than when it springs from an unlikely soil and when it is not aware that it is remarkable. For a summarizing statement on *As I Lay Dying,* one might appeal to one of the choruses in *Antigone*: "Wonders are many, and none is more wonderful than man." *As I Lay Dying* provides a less exalted but not unworthy illustration of Sophocles' judgment.

CALVIN BEDIENT

Pride and Nakedness: *As I Lay Dying*†

The force of *As I Lay Dying* is in its opacity. Faulkner's novel has the particularity of real experience, and this is so rare a quality in modern art that we have forgotten how to appreciate it. So untranslatable, so irreducible to symbol and idea is the detail of the novel that one looks for analogies in painting and music; and even the sporadic explosions of reflective rhetoric in the book convey little more than a momentary and frustrated impulse to the "universal": they remain essentially opaque. For example, the construction "How do our lives ravel out into the no-wind, no-sound, the weary gestures wearily recapitulant: echoes of old compulsions with no-hand on no strings: in sunset we fall into furious attitudes, dead gestures of dolls" (120) has no value whatsoever as literal statement or meaning, particularly in the context, where it lies disconnected, florid, and obtrusive, like a bouquet found abandoned in the dust. These words function, instead, precisely as "furious attitude," as an expressive verbal gesture, a mood-painting; they are as immediate in interest as the sudden clenching of a hand or the swirls in a Van Gogh cypress.

In the sense intended by William Golding in *Free Fall, As I Lay Dying* is patternless, "translating incoherence into incoherence,"[1] from life to art. The novel has a wonderful immunity to schematization; it is innocent of both a moral and a morality, and it seems to breathe out rather than posit a world view. Faulkner's novel does have, to be sure, a narrative movement and structure—a movement that, considering the fragmentation of narrative method, is remark-

† From *Modern Language Quarterly* 29 (1968): 61–76.
1. Penguin Books (Harmondsworth, 1963), p. 7.

ably steady, and a structure that is timeless, that answers to some unchanging psychological need: the journey undertaken and, despite great perils, completed. And yet, regardless of this, the book is open, both in the sense of making room for the incidental (indeed, the trivial) and in the sense that it does not understand itself: it is essentially spectacle.

As I Lay Dying is to be "seen," not understood; experienced, not translated; felt, not analyzed. The malignity it portrays, both of the land and sky and of man, is aesthetic. Here suffering is above all a spectacle—to us, to the neighbors of the Bundrens (the chorus to the collective protagonist), and even to Anse Bundren, who looks upon each new misfortune as a show of the Opponent's ingenuity, the staging of Destiny. Is there, indeed, an organizer behind the spectacle? The novel does not help us to an answer. What it unfolds before us is simply the autonomy of misfortune: the brutal fact of its monotonous regularity and astonishing variety, of its farcical absurdity, of its tragedy; and questions of cause are not raised—they are extraneous. There is thus in the novel a fundamental silence that is truly terrible. For what is more mysterious, finally, than immediacy? Explanations tranquilize wonder, and *As I Lay Dying* contains no explanations.

The nakedness of form in this novel is the aesthetic equivalent of an act of courage; and despite its strong element of farce, the book is like tragedy in its refusal to mediate between destructive contradictions. The openness of *As I Lay Dying* is thus almost morally exhilarating; and yet it is appalling, too. For like its own Darl Bundren, the novel lacks defenses; it takes the world upon its flesh like a rain of arrows. Can one imagine a Faulknerian Utopia? His books do not hold their heads so high as hope. *As I Lay Dying* is a prolonged cry of astonishment; everything within it is recorded as if with a soundless gasp. "Outrageous," say the neighbors when they are assailed by the odor of the rotting corpse; and the word echoes and expands until it has embraced everything in the book.

One could argue that *As I Lay Dying* is patternless to a fault—that it is, in places, confused and self-destroying. The crucial monologue of Addie Bundren, for instance, is a marvel of dazzling unintelligibility. Why does she call herself "three" (herself, Cash, and Darl) when, as she says, Darl is her husband's child and not her own? By Cash's birth, she remarks, her "aloneness had been violated and then made whole again by the violation: time, Anse, love, what you will, outside the circle." (99). But if Cash is still inside the circle with Addie, is her aloneness truly intact? Very often, the illogic of the characters is extreme, grotesque; it is not merely puzzling, but dizzying, and throws the mind down. And yet this grotesquerie possesses a kind of beauty—precisely the beauty of opacity. Like the pyrotechnic rhetorical reflections, the logical absurdities have a stubborn and assertive density that makes them analogous to the squiggles and clots of paint on modern canvasses; the book is entirely of a piece, opalesque all through.

It is for this reason that the thematics of *As I Lay Dying* are difficult to approach—or better, that it is questionable to speak of a thematics at all. At any rate, there is clearly no Ariadne's thread that will lead one through the labyrinth. But of course it is far from my intention to claim—what would after all be self-defeating—that the book cannot be discussed. The problem is that it can be discussed endlessly, since its patternlessness results, not in emptiness, but precisely in a continuous, turgid thickness of meaning, the significant indefiniteness of life itself. My purpose is simply to explore one of the dialectics of the novel as this is manifested in both the content and the form. I shall be bolder and assert that this dialectic is at the center of the book—not its theme, but its axis; not what the novel is "about," but a significant part of its substance and the determining principle of its form.

II

In *As I Lay Dying* life is conceived as the antagonist, living is "terrible," the protagonist self is alone: a naked and isolated consciousness in a broad land. This nakedness, this dreadful isolation, is already a kind of defeat, a form of abjectness, so that the utmost to be expected from the mind in its continual conflict with the world is simply a capitulation without dishonor: a surrender of everything, if need be, except pride. It is true that there are or appear to be, in the Faulknerian world, other "answers" to aloneness—for example, Vardaman's mental revision of a reality his emotions cannot accept, and the physical "violation" of Addie's aloneness that comes with childbearing. Yet Vardaman's answer is transparently desperate, and Addie's seems to have the effect, not of breaking through her aloneness, but of expanding it; the circle of isolation remains inexorable. Thus the third term of this existential dialectic, the solution which remains after all others have failed, is pride, for pride is the only answer that stands upon, rather than attempts to evade, our inescapable nakedness.

The most remarkable quality of the very remarkable Bundrens— country people who feel their difference from "town folk"—is their fierce, their unexpected, their magnificently sustaining pride. Even Anse Bundren really seems to believe that he would be "beholden to none" (132)—though in truth, of course, he often is. Like wounded animals that have instinctively found the herb that will cure them, the Bundrens have discovered pride; and each is typical, each is "universal," precisely in bearing, not as an idea but as a fact, the wound of nakedness, the solitary confinement and essential impotency of conscious being.

The fact and awareness of isolation is the very bedrock in Faulkner; it is given out direct as an odor. And it is the strength and beauty of *As I Lay Dying* that the form of the novel itself amplifies, that it is an aesthetic equivalent for, this truth. For each of the numerous monologues constitutes a new demonstration of the obvious: the fundamental isolation inherent in the very structure of consciousness.

Now let us take note of an apparent contradiction in the form and, at the same time, of its echo in the content. Obviously, each monologue is implicitly isolated, hermetically sealed from the others; yet the result of their grouping is, nonetheless, an appearance of mutual cooperation. *As I Lay Dying* is a composite narrative, a kind of unwitting group enterprise; and undeniably this apparent aspect of the form is as expressive as the actual technique of the accretion of fragmentary monologues. Considered as a whole, the novel expresses, through its form, Faulkner's profound feeling for the human group, above all for the family, which is presented as constituting its own fate: a kind of involuntary and inescapable group confinement, the inexorable circle in expanded form.

Human coherence in Faulkner, whether of the family or of the larger community, is presented chiefly as a response to the onslaughts of an opposing world. In the Bundrens, Faulkner lays bare the most primitive of the motives to community: society as a principle of survival. Shy and aloof as a herd, the Bundren family is held together, not by love, but by pride; which is its instinctive response to danger, including unfavorable public opinion. And if this herd is self-destructive, still it prefers its cannibalism to exposure to the world, to a nakedness synonymous with defeat.

The Faulknerian family is thus a kind of exacerbating protective covering, a hair shirt, to the "abject nakedness" of the individuals composing it. This accounts for the fact that family ties are so horrendously tense in Faulkner: they are the crackling bonds of a bitter necessity. At bottom, the Faulknerian family is a compulsive effort to end, to disguise, nakedness; but since nakedness is inescapable, this effort issues in hate. Thus if nakedness leads to community, it is also true that community leads to an aggravation of nakedness. The effort returns upon itself. Like the aesthetic form of the novel, the family only *appears* to transcend or resolve the fundamental isolation of the individual; in actuality, it is a terrible and frustrating unit of interlocking solitudes, atomic in structure like a molecule.

Yet the family is no more, if no less, terrible than nakedness. In the absence of other consolations, it may afford at least an illusion of "confidence and comfort"—words Darl uses when he defines the meaning that the coffin has for Addie (4). Let us note that the coffin and the family are analogous forms, or better, that a dreadful yet desired confinement and covering is the form that accounts for both. Peabody helps us to this perception when, seeing Anse and Addie together, he observes of the latter:

> She watches me: I can feel her eyes. It's like she was shoving at me with them. I have seen it before in women. Seen them drive from the room them coming with sympathy and pity, with actual help, and clinging to some trifling animal to whom they never were more than pack-horses. That's what they mean by the love that passeth understanding: that pride, that furious desire to hide that abject nakedness which we bring here with us . . . [and] carry stubbornly and furiously with us into the earth again. (27)

This little-noticed but important passage obviously extends into a paradigm of the behavior of the Bundrens on the journey to Jefferson, for they too, in their furious desire to hide their abject nakedness, drive from them those coming with sympathy and pity. More subtly, it explains the importance to Addie of the coffin, over the construction of which she attends, from her bedroom window, with an anxious and severe observation. To her, the coffin is a substitute for her family; it represents but a change of coverings.

Of course, for a while after death Addie clings to the family itself, and it is in this sense that she is not yet dead, that the entire journey takes place while she still lies "dying." Through her magnificent will, which is the instrument of her pride, she is thus doubly protected on her way to the grave, even in death covering her nakedness in the fierceness of her "modesty," which is but the pride, as it were, of her privacy. "For an instant," as the coffin is loaded on the wagon, "it resists, as though volitional, as though within it her pole-thin body clings furiously, even though dead, to a sort of modesty, as she would have tried to conceal a soiled garment that she could not prevent her body soiling" (57). It is as if even death could not conquer Addie's pride, though it constitutes the final and absolute nakedness. By means of the promise Addie exacts from her family to bury her in Jefferson, she prolongs even into death their customary relationship to her while she was living, which was to protect her, to encircle her with "her own flesh and blood." She is thus not so much carried as attended to Jefferson. Nor does she "die" until she is placed in the ground. Then at last she is abandoned and—as she might have foreseen—immediately forgotten, replaced at once by a new "Mrs Bundren." By that time, however, she has punished her family just as she had intended[2]—punished it by keeping it to herself a little longer,

---

2. "But then I realised that I had been tricked by words older than Anse or love, and that the same word had tricked Anse too, and that my revenge would be that he would never know I was taking revenge. And when Darl was born I asked Anse to promise to take me back to Jefferson when I died . . ." (100).

and in suffering, and for the reason that she had needed it, just as, in the instance of the deceit she practices for Jewel, she hated him "because she had to love him so that she had to act the deceit" (78).

In Faulkner, then, pride binds but at the same time lacerates; there is a distance between people which, except in rare instances, cannot be closed, which, indeed, is maintained by pride itself. For pride is an expression of the aggressive instinct, a response and counterantagonism to the antagonism of destiny, to the painfully naked structure of being. The community that pride creates is at best an illusory one— the Bundrens on the road to Jefferson. And this deceptive community, overlaying a stark and irremediable personal nakedness, is mirrored in the form of the novel, which is real in its parts—its lonely monologues—but illusory as a "whole." In both the characters and the form that presents them, it is isolation that is basic and substantive.

III

Turning from the relationship of form to content, let us consider the two characters of the novel who embody the extreme ends of Faulknerian being: Darl Bundren, in whom nakedness has an absolute form, and his brother Cash, in whom pride attains to a constructive, humane, and stabilizing limit.

Alone among the Bundrens, Darl lacks the ingredient, the enzyme, of pride. Stricken in his very being, he is a demonstration of our natural emptiness, of a nakedness powerless to hide itself behind an "I." What is more, the vacuum of identity in Darl, unlike that of the mystic or the artist, cannot be seized upon and converted into a positivity; for although Darl is invaded by others as the mystic is inundated by God and the novelist possessed by his characters, those who occupy Darl do not replenish him, and naturally his consciousness deteriorates by a law of diminishing returns. Hopelessly open and undefended, at times even plural and familial, Darl's mind leaps barriers of space and flesh, flowing everywhere like the floodwaters of the river— but flowing because unformed, because it has no home in itself, no principle of containment.

This bitter gift and fatality, this plurality of being, Darl carries like a cross. If he is a freak, he is also a victim, and knows with characteristic lucidity what has made him the casualty he is. When Vardaman says, "But you *are*, Darl," the latter replies: "I know it. . . . That's why I am not *is*. *Are* is too many for one woman to foal" (58). The point is that, unlike Jewel (whose "mother is a horse"), Darl has never been a foal, that is, sponsored; and as he here observes to Vardaman, it is his fate to be everyone except himself. He is *de trop*, a consciousness inhabiting the world as a kind of excess, baseless, and, as a result, pitilessly empowered to trespass upon the privacy of others.

Darl exists, but, because he is unloved, he cannot become *himself*; at least this is the explanation that he himself seems to favor. As Ortega has noted, love is choice in its very essence, a vital preference of this being over that one, a corroboration of the beloved;[3] and Darl knows that he has never been affirmed. "Jewel *is*," Darl thinks at one point, "so Addie Bundren must be"; for the created postulates the creator. But Darl maintains that he has no mother, and the absence of the creator throws into doubt the reality of the created:

> In a strange room you must empty yourself for sleep. And before you are emptied for sleep, what are you. And when you are emptied for sleep, you are not. And when you are filled with sleep, you never were. I dont know what I am. I dont know if I am or not. (46)

By thus equating being with consciousness, which sleep annihilates, Darl removes from existence its stability, giving it the flickering reality of a dream. "And so," he concludes, "if I am not emptied yet, I am *is*." Only on that condition. For Darl has, he feels, no identity ("I dont know what I am") and thus no cord of continuity capable of withstanding the unraveling power of sleep. So the ending of the monologue falls with the force of a metaphor: "How often have I lain beneath rain on a strange roof, thinking of home."

Further, Darl's consciousness, in this passage, casts upon the world itself a desubstantiating shadow, so that for him objects too may appear suddenly orphaned:

> Beyond the unlamped wall I can hear the rain shaping the wagon that is ours, the load that is no longer theirs that felled and sawed it nor yet theirs that bought it and which is not ours either, lie on our wagon though it does, since only the wind and the rain shape it only to Jewel and me, that are not asleep. (46)

More than this, their being is also subject, like his, to abrupt cancellation: "And since sleep is is-not and rain and wind are *was* [the load] is not" (46–47). And although for the present the wagon "*is*," it too will surrender its reality when it has carried Addie Bundren to Jefferson: "when the wagon is *was*, Addie Bundren will not be" (47). For Darl, then, being springs from the mother ("Jewel *is*, so Addie Bundren must be"); disjoined from Addie, the world and Darl appear equally unauthored, existing without authentication, hovering on the verge of extinction.

Mercilessly unclouded by egoism, Darl's mind is the perfect mirror of what surrounds him, which it reflects with a terrible clarity. It is only his own identity that is obscure to Darl—the failure of the mirror

---

3. José Ortega y Gasset, *On Love: Aspects of a Single Theme* (New York, 1957), p. 20.

to reflect itself. In this novel, shapelessness is the condition against which the characters must define themselves, and Darl cannot find his own shape. It is thus his destiny to be, not himself, but the world. Since Darl neither acts (he is called "lazy"), nor possesses anything that he can call his own, nor is loved, he must fall back upon intro- spection to give him identity. But, as Husserl observes, consciousness is itself empty; we must be conscious *of* something to be conscious at all;[4] and when Darl turns in upon himself, he finds nothing there. Tragically, Darl is not made present to himself as an *object* until he is acted upon, literally apprehended by the world and conducted to the insane asylum at Jackson (for, to be acted upon, one must exist). But the Darl then given birth is a monster, a belated and violent creation, who rightly laughs at the brutal comedy of his birth, and who, with heart-breaking irony, is at last all affirmation: "Yes yes yes yes yes" (146). At this parturition, the suspected absurdity of the world finally declares itself unequivocally. Appallingly, it answers to expectation. And yet to be so well served is, after all, a kind of mercy. For Darl has at last discovered certainty: "Yes yes yes yes yes."

If, on the one hand, Darl remains, even to the end, a transparent perceiver, he has become, on the other, a pure opacity. It is true, of course, that Darl was never perfectly transparent; earlier there is in him, for instance, the darkness of the body ("I could lie with my shirt- tail up . . . feeling myself without touching myself, feeling the cool silence blowing upon my parts" [8]), and what appears to be an inces- tuous feeling for Dewey Dell asserts itself, through metaphor, on the train to Jackson. Ethereal as he is, moreover, Darl possesses, in addi- tion, that subterranean, savage charge of energy which is necessary for life itself: "He and I look at one another," Darl says of Cash, "with . . . looks that plunge unimpeded . . . into the ultimate secret place where for an instant Cash and Darl crouch flagrant and unabashed in all the old terror and the old foreboding, alert and secret and without shame" (82). Yet Darl *is* abashed at this naked core: that is his tragedy. Limitless, unclaimed, despairing of attaining shape, his very being longs to be undone: "If you could just ravel out into time. That would be nice. It would be nice if you could just ravel out into time" (121). This decreation, however, is not permitted to Darl, whose fate it is to *see,* and who must endure even in madness a perception as pitiless as it is crystalline.

There is, of course, one point at which Darl *acts*: his setting fire to the barn that contains his mother's corpse. When this attempt fails, Darl is found, in tears, lying on the coffin, his passivity resumed, his mind more hopeless than ever. Darl's laughter at his seizure by the

---

4. See Edmund Husserl, *Ideas* (New York, 1967); Jean-Paul Sartre, *Being and Nothingness* (New York, 1964), p. ii.

asylum authorities, Cash's insight, "This world is not his world; this life his life" (149), and the tearful resurrender to nonentity over the putrescent body of his mother, taken together, suggest how unbearable the world must appear to a being absolutely naked to it, between whose capacity to suffer and the power of the world to inflict pain no selfhood and no love have intervened.

Though Darl's consciousness is so attentive and catholic that it seems at times to be a form of love, it is, for the most part, as neutral as photographic film. For Darl loves no one—except perhaps, in an unspeakably tormented way, Addie Bundren (as the barn-burning obscurely suggests)—and, until the end, he affirms nothing at all. On those few occasions when he displays strong feeling toward others, he is barbed and vindictive; for even he has a component of egotism, though only so much as is requisite for suffering. And just as he bitterly resents the woman who has caused his emptiness, so he resents those of her children who are enviably intense and narrow with their own being: Jewel and Dewey Dell. If Darl taunts them, he does so because they are so self-absorbed, because they *can* be self-absorbed, and from his aggressive insinuations one may understand that he would like to induce in them a portion of his own pain. Jewel and Dewey Dell, both truly flagrant and unabashed, are equally exposed to Darl, the first through the inexpressible intensity of his feeling for his mother, which renders him rigid, and the second, who is pregnant, through the unwelcome violation of her aloneness. Nor is it by chance that Darl gains and wields like a weapon secret knowledge of each: his clairvoyance is sharpened by his envy. At the end, when these two throw themselves upon Darl with ferocity, they are simply reasserting the privacy of their identities. The very fact that they have identities to defend proves their existential superiority to Darl; a battle between unequal opponents, the scene is cruel.

Perhaps Darl is finally a standing condemnation of the world. If "this world is not his world, this life his life," is it not because it is unloving where he wants its love, random where he wants its reason, savagely obtuse where he needs its understanding? Darl is not better than the world, only—by a kind of ontological error—more generous: though he receives nothing from his surroundings, he gives himself to them, just as he lends his eyes to the land that fills them. Doubtless, Cash is being sentimental when he says, "Sometimes I think it aint none of us pure crazy and aint none of us pure sane until the balance of us talks him that-a-way" (134); and yet clearly this is true of Darl. Until he is seized, he is not truly insane; but then, sitting on the ground and laughing, bitter and manic, he does grant the world its victory and surrenders to the unreason at its heart. In his last monologue, which is tantamount to a ferocious, uncontrollable parody of all those earlier monologues in which his mind had seemed to belong to the family itself, he watches and attends "our brother Darl" (146) on his departure to Jackson, and is puzzled by his laughter. Now that he sees "Darl," now that Darl exists for him, he cannot comprehend him. And perhaps he senses, as he speaks of our brother Darl in his cage in Jackson, that ultimately such laughter is beyond understanding.

It is against this dreadful nakedness that pride, in Faulkner, assumes its value. If Darl is our innate nakedness *in extremis,* impotent to defend itself, Cash exemplifies the pride that saves us and is itself the substance of identity; for the identity a man asserts is simply that part of himself he thinks well of.

As I Lay Dying brings to mind Conrad's *Heart of Darkness,* not only in the land that shapes "the life of man in its implacable and brooding image" (27) and in the tensions it establishes between the shaped, moral surfaces of the mind and subterranean psychic energies (tensions aggravated, moreover, by a journey through a violent land), but also in its cautious celebration of the worker as hero. For Cash, like Marlow, is man defining himself, declaring his human dignity through the perfection of his work. Both heroes labor precisely in order to avoid being shaped by the violent land, or better, to avoid being shapeless; and in work each discovers the reality of himself. Whereas Marlow knows that work is man's defense against himself, a noble self-avoidance, Cash senses merely that the man is the work— an important but lesser insight. What Marlow tries to defend himself against is the darkness in himself; the darkness in Faulkner's novel, by contrast, is of the world. It is more than human, though it encompasses the human; and Cash is heroic (unassumingly and narrowly heroic) not so much in mastering himself as in contesting the amorphousness, the appalling anonymity, of existence itself.

For in the world depicted in Faulkner's novel, the hero's role must be to shape and to define. We see in Cash literally a rage for efficiency as he labors at the coffin, "his face sloped into the light with a rapt, dynamic immobility above his tireless elbow" (44), working on into the night and the rain unfalteringly, as if "in a tranquil conviction that rain was an illusion of the mind" (45). But neither at this time nor any other (a truth not generally grasped) does Cash's devotion to the perfection of his work dehumanize him: he is never the equivalent, say, of Conrad's Chief Accountant, whose books are kept in dazzling yet mean order only yards above a grove of death. On the contrary, Cash is always a figure nearer to Marlow, provincial and less profound, but humane and wise. Cash builds the coffin where his dying mother can see him because he loves her, as Jewel jealously perceives ("It's like when he was a little boy and she says if she had some fertilizer she would try to raise some flowers and he taken the bread pan and brought it back from the barn full of dung" [10]); and such dogged, mechanically rationalized, and in the circumstances impractical efficiency indicates that his labor is basically an act of pride, the purpose of which is to assert the human in the teeth of its negation—the nothingness awaiting life, the shapelessness surrounding it. After Addie's death, when Cash (his ears deaf to the practical words of his father, his face composed) stands "looking down at her peaceful, rigid face fading into the dusk as though darkness were a precursor of the ultimate earth, until at last the face seems to float detached upon it, lightly as the reflection of a dead leaf" (29), he takes in at once what he and his mother are up against and returns immediately to work. Against such dematerialization of the human, the construction of the coffin, which looks so merely mechanical, is actually a passionate protest, a fierce assertion of human value. Built under the inimical pressure of time, but nonetheless perfected beyond practical reason, the coffin is to death what *As I Lay Dying* itself is to the artless world: a product of love, a preserving form, and in its craftsmanship a predication of human dignity.

From first to last Cash is the most human of the Bundrens—and also the most humane. The notion that Cash develops during the course of the narrative "from unimaginative self-containment to humane concern"[5] has taken hold despite obvious objections: the gross improbability of such a development in a man in his late twenties within a nine-day period and, more important, the textual evidence to the contrary. "The increasing range of Cash's awareness," writes Olga Vickery, "is suggested by his growing sympathy with Darl."[6] But, on the contrary, the point to note is that Cash's sympathy with Darl, which was strong from the first, actually meets with a check as the novel progresses: it comes up against a moral judgment.

For though Cash's pride is not in itself dehumanizing, it necessitates, as a safeguard, a morality that is inevitably rigid. Of the kinds of strength represented in the novel—the violence of feeling in Addie and Jewel, the imperturbable, maudlin self-centeredness of Anse, the wild-seed egoism of Dewey Dell, the rational stability of Cash—it is only the latter which is moral in tendency, leading to the correction of life by mind. The strength of Cash is ultimately the strength of conviction. When he declares that men who cannot "see eye to eye with other folks" must be considered crazy (135), clearly he is assuming a kind of tacit social contract, according to which men work and construct their buildings and shape their lives with the understanding that others will not hinder them or destroy the fruits of their labor. Those who fail to honor this contract are morally blind, that

5. Irving Howe, *William Faulkner*, 2nd ed., rev. (New York, 1962), p. 188.
6. "The Dimensions of Consciousness: *As I Lay Dying*," in *William Faulkner: Three Decades of Criticism*, ed. Frederick J. Hoffman and Olga W. Vickery (East Lansing, 1960), pp. 239–40.

is, "crazy." "I dont reckon nothing excuses setting fire to a man's
barn and endangering his stock and destroying his property," Cash
says. "That's how I reckon a man is crazy" (135). What Cash opposes
is not simply the destruction of material property, for property is
never simple. There is always the man *in* the property to take into
account, the value it possesses from having absorbed part of the
human life that shaped it: "there just aint nothing justifies the deliberate destruction of what a man has built with his own sweat and
stored the fruit of his sweat into" (137).

Like Marlow, then, Cash values a good job because it creates human
value, or rather, it is valuable because it is a human creation. The
meaning of work is that it is an essentially human expression; and
its value is that it allows a man to be proud of himself as a creator.
But where Marlow also values work for its binding effect—workers
become brothers—Cash, an American very much on his own, prizes
work solely as a source of human identity and pride. Life as it gets
lived, certainly as the Bundrens live it, is a "shoddy job" (137), a judgment that includes not only Darl's burning of the barn, but also the
attack made upon Darl by Jewel and Dewey Dell. To Cash, a neat job
does more than testify to man's capacity for shaping; it is also a symbol of discipline and decency, of a renunciation of aggression. Thus
for Cash, life, like the building of a barn, is what you make of it, and
the shamefulness of the present, its shoddiness, really stems from a
failure of pride, of man's imagination of his value. Only recently,
Cash implies, have people moved away "from the olden right teaching that says to drive the nails down and trim the edges well always
like it was for your own use and comfort you were making it" (135).
Why is this teaching "right"? Because a man defines himself, not by
what he builds, but by the way he builds it: "it's better to build a tight
chicken coop than a shoddy courthouse, and when they both build
shoddy or build well, neither because it's one or tother is going to
make a man feel the better nor the worse" (135). And if ultimately
the self-definition of man matters, it is because, naked as man is, he
has nothing else to claim as his own.

Both Marlow and Cash are forced to judge as evil the actions of
men of whom they almost feel themselves to be accomplices, for just
as Marlow acknowledges the "fascination of the abomination,"[7] so
Cash had thought more than once that "one of us would have to do
something" (134) to get rid of the corpse. In noble contrast to the
vicious men around them, each judges with a sense of necessity, in
the name of civilization, and at real cost to himself. But it is precisely

---

7. Joseph Conrad, *Heart of Darkness*, in *Three Short Novels*. Bantam Book (New York,
1960), p. 5.

here that we come up against the negative limits of pride; for the final
relationship of Cash to Darl is one of unbending (though not insensi-
tive) pride to abject nakedness. The response the book itself makes
to Darl's nakedness, the response it elicits from the reader, is that
of a disarmed compassion unadulterated with judgment. "It was bad
so," Cash says of Darl's laughter. "I be durn if I could see anything
to laugh at. Because there just aint nothing justifies . . . deliberate
destruction . . ." (137). The point is not that Cash is incapable of
perceiving abject nakedness, for it is this that he describes when
he says, "It's like there was a fellow in every man that's done a-past
the sanity or the insanity, that watches the sane and the insane doings
of that man with the same horror and the same astonishment" (137).
What is significant is that Cash cannot *afford* his own insight into
abjectness. For compassion dissolves pride, it is utterly passive—at its
fullest, it is a recognition of man's ultimate, existential defeat. On
the other hand, though the novel carries us beyond Cash into the
impotent heart of understanding, into a compassion beyond social
principle and responsibility, it will not allow us to judge pride, either.
What it says, rather—even through the fact that Cash, the techni-
cian, has broken his leg for the second time and lies helpless as Darl
is apprehended—is that finally the world is too much even for the
proud and that there is no limit to the demand life makes upon our
compassion.

IV

Let us return to our examination of the relationship between form
and content in Faulkner's novel. We have noted in the subject matter a polarity of nakedness and pride, and in the aesthetic form an
answering nakedness. Let us now see whether there is also, in the
technics of the novel, a complementary pride.

As I Lay Dying is primarily naturalistic in technique. The device
of the narrative soliloquy is a means of presenting the mind in its
immediacy, and in this sense it directly serves the ends of realism.
Let us acknowledge, further, that the basic impulse underlying the
book is unmistakably a yearning for reality. And yet it would be
untrue to claim that Faulkner's novel lacks all traces of the dehumanization often observed in modern art. In his seminal essay on
this trend, Ortega pungently remarked that all style involves dehumanization, for style necessarily deforms reality; and it was the aim
of modern poetry, as Ortega saw it, to substitute style for reality.[8] I
have remarked already upon the turgidity and opacity of Faulkner's

8. *The Dehumanization of Art and Other Writings on Art and Culture*, Doubleday Anchor
Book (Garden City, N.Y., 1956), pp. 23, 32.

rhetorical style. Now let us take this observation to its limit: Faulkner's metaphorical prose is, at its densest, not so much a mimetic instrument as the preening expression of the pride of the imagination in itself. This is to say that Faulkner's very language is proud, and proud precisely as a defiantly "free" response to the threat always present in the perilous nakedness of the self and the world.

When, for example, Darl says of the vultures that they hang in the sky "in narrowing circles, like the smoke, with an outward semblance of form and purpose, but with no inference of motion, progress or retrograde" (131), or when Peabody defines death as "no more than a single tenant or family moving out of a tenement or a town" (26), the language gets in the way of the reality it describes, or better, the language here secretly flouts and overcomes reality, achieving a proud independency. Or consider the description of Vardaman's face at his mother's death: "From behind pa's leg Vardaman peers, his mouth full open and all color draining from his face into his mouth, as though he has by some means fleshed his own teeth in himself, sucking" (29). It is the simile that is primary, and the reality referred to exists principally as a pretext for the image: an image which is, in truth, not a description but an invention, a subjective idea. In all these instances, Faulkner's prose is distended to make room for the imagination. And the result is a style at once grotesque, as though somehow maimed, and proud, as if totally free to make of itself what it will.

The very grotesqueness of the style is a demonstration that language is not free, that it is governed by certain laws. And as a rule Faulkner's language bends, if not bows, to necessity, admitting the authority of reality. But plainly Faulkner's style is impatient of law, and harbors a resentment toward the duty of mimesis. In its attempts to liberate itself, it moves toward its own self-defeat, at times failing to convey any meaning at all. Proud as it is, it represents, like Cash's pride, an ambiguous triumph over nakedness: its strength is at the same time an impotence, a refusal to admit, and perhaps an inability to tolerate, the naked power of the world. As in the polarity, then, between proud and naked being in the novel, there is between the openness of the form and the opacity of the style an unremitting tension, a contradiction that testifies, on the one hand, both to man's hunger for reality and to his nerve for the truth, however invidious it may be, and, on the other, to his proud and imaginative spirit—to his ambition to create an object, whether a building or a prose, that is his own.

ANDRÉ BLEIKASTEN

The Setting†

> That's the one trouble with this country: everything, weather, all,
> hangs on too long. Like our rivers, our land: opaque, slow, violent;
> shaping and creating the life of man in its implacable and brooding
> image. [27]

Such is Faulkner's earth: a space where things are held in endless
abeyance, where nothing has a beginning or an ending; a viscous,
reptilian time, whose treacherous slowness is broken by sudden
outbursts of violence; a nameless and omnipresent force which has
been creating and molding man in its image according to the same
immutable laws for thousands of years. The earth is the primal
matrix, the original crucible in which all life develops, "the hot blind
earth" in which the wet seed germinates (38); it is also "the dead
earth in the dead darkness" (38), the ultimate dust to which all life
descends.* * *

Man is born of mud. A manifold complicity binds him to the soil
which bears and nourishes him, to the powers of sun, night, fire,
water, and wind. Yet this complicity is first and foremost that of an
age-old struggle. The peasant knows this better than anyone, since
he confronts the earth in his daily work and has learned to beware
of its wild and cunning whims: "It's a hard country on man; it's
hard" (63). Like all Faulkner's novels, As I Lay Dying pits man against
the world around him, against what the novelist used to call his environment. But the conflict is reduced here to its most elementary
form. The world against which the Bundrens measure themselves
has little in common with the one full of social, racial, and historical
fatality in which the destiny of Faulkner's patrician families is played
out. Their immediate opponent is Nature, and as in "Old Man"[1] it is
against her—against the fury of elements, against the violence of
fire and water—that the battle is waged.

The setting for the action is therefore far from being an inert
backdrop before which the characters come and act out their drama.
It is an agent in its own right and on the same footing as the characters. If we momentarily leave aside its psychological and philosophical complexities and consider As I Lay Dying in its epic or allegorical

---

† From Faulkner's As I Lay Dying. Rev. and enlarged edition. Trans. from the French by
  Roger Little, with the collaboration of the author (Bloomington: Indiana University Press,
  1973), pp. 100–114.
1. A part of Faulkner's The Wild Palms, often printed separately, that tells a story of the
  1927 flooding of the Mississippi River [Editor].

simplicity, little remains but the description of Man—a collective hero represented both by the Bundren family and by the farmers who lend a hand—locked in single combat with Nature. And so close is their embrace that the two adversaries can be hardly distinguished from each other. The traditional distinction between character and setting thus becomes nearly pointless. The scene comes to life and takes part in the action; conversely, the characters tend to lose their individual outlines and to blend with the landscape. This tendency to describe men and things as if they were cut from the same cloth is frequent in Faulkner; perhaps it is even more conspicuous in *As I Lay Dying* than in the other novels. Here all barriers between the animate and the inanimate, the human and the nonhuman, the subjective and the objective, are removed: the world is within man, and man is everywhere within the world.

Stasis and Motion

The strangeness of this magical universe manifests itself first of all in a perpetual oscillation between movement and immobility, in their irresoluble contradiction. *As I Lay Dying* depicts moving figures in a space which is itself moving: the Bundrens' wagon trundles obstinately along the road; Jewel wheels on horseback around the funeral cortège; the buzzards circle in the July sky. But nature also moves: a storm bursts, torrential rain sweeps down, the river overflows and its raging water carries all before it. Few of Faulkner's novels give so intensely the sensation of a seething world, and rarely does the novelist keep his paradoxical wager better: "to arrest motion, which is life, by artificial means and hold it fixed so that a hundred years later, when a stranger looks at it, it moves again, since it is life."[2]

Some passages in the book are pure kinetic poems. Consider for instance this lyrical evocation of Jewel and his horse:

> When Jewel can almost touch him, the horse stands on his hind legs and slashes down at Jewel. Then Jewel is enclosed by a glittering maze of hooves as by an illusion of wings; among them, beneath the upreared chest, he moves with the flashing limberness of a snake. For an instant before the jerk comes onto his arms he sees his whole body earth-free, horizontal, whipping snake-limber, until he finds the horse's nostrils and touches earth again. (9)

Yet as much as by movement, Faulkner seems fascinated by immobility (the word "motionless" recurs many times in the novel). Or rather

---

2. *Lion in the Garden: Interviews with William Faulkner, 1926–1962*, ed. James B. Meriwether and Michael Milgate (New York: Random House, 1968), p. 253.

what fascinates him is the passage, sudden or imperceptible, from one to the other, as the continuation of the above extract shows: "Then they are rigid, motionless, terrific" (9). Any movement is followed by a halt. In Faulkner, however, immobility is scarcely ever absolute or final. Stillness is almost always throbbing with latent motion; it is movement beginning or ending, energy dying or gathering its forces. Often it is simply the lull before the storm:

> They stand in terrific hiatus, the horse trembling and groaning. Then Jewel is on the horse's back. He flows upward in a stooping swirl like the lash of a whip, his body in midair shaped to the horse. (9)

This leads us to the self-contradictory concept, well attested in literature and especially in the plastic arts so often referred to by Faulkner, of "dynamic immobility." Darl uses this very expression when describing Cash at work:

> Cash works on, half turned into the feeble light, one thigh and one pole-thin arm braced, his face sloped into the light with a rapt, dynamic immobility above his tireless elbow. (44)

The moment described here is one of those "frozen moments"—frequent in Faulkner's work and of which there are some fine examples in *As I Lay Dying*—when characters turn into statues and the scene suddenly becomes a tableau. They are equivocal moments * * * suggestive of the continuation of movement even while arresting it; moments of suspension set apart from the flux of time and, as it were, from reality itself (cf. 127: "They are like two figures in a Greek frieze, isolated out of all reality by the red glare"). If so many scenes seem to dissolve into unreality, it is because immobility and motion are equally deceptive appearances. Any immobility is false immobility; any movement becomes mere make-believe. Before Vardaman's eyes, Peabody's horses wheel without moving, like horses on a merry-go-round:

> I strike at them, striking, they wheeling in a long lunge, the buggy wheeling onto two wheels and motionless like it is nailed to the ground and the horses motionless like they are nailed by the hind feet to the center of a whirling plate. (33)

The riddle of motion and immobility is the spatial and physical translation of the metaphysical enigma of time and timelessness. This is probably the reason that Faulkner finds it so exciting. Again and again he reverts to it and attempts to capture it in words. And there are moments indeed when revelation seems near. In *As I Lay Dying*, * * * it happens that the paradoxical conjunction of motion and stasis reaches a kind of perfection, that motion becomes so slow as to be the mere tremor of immobility. Then space and time exchange their

attributes; time becomes space, space time—not the time of events
but a time accumulated like that of memory, bewitched like that of
dreams, fluid and static; a time marking time. As Darl, sitting on the
wagon, watches Jewel on his horse, the road between them no longer
measures distance but time:

> We go on with a motion so soporific, so dreamlike as to be unin-
> ferant of progress, as though time and not space were decreasing
> between us and it. (62)

Similarly, at the time of the crossing, when Darl is looking at his family on the other bank, the separating interval seems temporal rather
than spatial:

> It is as though the space between us were time: an irrevocable
> quality. It is as though time, no longer running straight before
> us in a diminishing line, now runs parallel between us like a
> looping string, the distance being the doubling accretion of the
> thread and not the interval between. (85)

Metamorphosis

Through this baffling dialectic of space and time, through this giddy
interplay of stasis and motion, in which reality is no sooner mentioned
than it is conjured away, Faulkner's universe offers us one of its
central paradoxes: dynamic immobility, petrified turbulence, "fury in
itself quiet with stagnation" (94).

In *As I Lay Dying* this paradox assumes cosmic proportions; the
novel often suggests a world threatened by paralysis, on the point of
lapsing back into inertia, nearing its end, yet at the same time, as we
have already noted, it also conveys a sensation of prodigious activity.
Motion, what Darl calls "the myriad original motion" (94), is at work
not only across the universe but in the universe, in the heart of the
elements, substances and beings that it compels to transform themselves, sweeping them along in the flux of incessant change. Nothing
has yet been fixed in its function and identity; everything is fleeting
and flowing. Metamorphosis governs all.

The climactic river scene is the most revealing in this respect.
Water, the element of metamorphosis *par excellence*, springs to life.
Tull, for instance, describes it in the following way:

> The water was cold. It was thick, like slush ice. Only it kind of
> lived. One part of you knowed it was just water, the same thing
> that had been running under this same bridge for a long time,
> yet when them logs would come spewing up outen it, you were
> not surprised, like they was a part of water, of the waiting and
> the threat (79).

The same animism even more markedly informs Darl's description of the scene. Beneath the murmuring, swirling surface of the water, Darl senses the disturbing presence of some marine monster up from the deep, a slumbering Leviathan which moves in its sleep and threatens to wake at any moment:

> Before us the thick dark current runs. It talks up to us in a murmur become ceaseless and myriad, the yellow surface dimpled monstrously into fading swirls travelling along the surface for an instant, silent, impermanent and profoundly significant, as though just beneath the surface something huge and alive waked for a moment of lazy alertness out of and into light slumber again. (82)

* * *

Nothing, it seems, is left to define the hierarchy of nature's categories, or to distinguish reality from unreality. The inanimate comes to life, matter becomes dematerialized and ghostlike: a log surges out of the water, standing "for an instant upright upon that surging and heaving desolation like Christ" (86), and "upon the end of it a long gout of foam hangs like the beard of an old man or a goat" (86). Men turn into animals, looking like birds, dogs, horses, or cattle, while animals become human. The buzzard Samson sees in his barn after the Bundrens have left is almost taken to be a human being, and he watches it go away like "a old bald-headed man" (67). Jewel's horse, during the river crossing, flounders in the water, "moaning and groaning like a natural man" (89). It is particularly in the teeth of disaster and death that the kinship of man and beast is acknowledged; they communicate then in their common terror and, in *As I Lay Dying* as in Picasso's *Guernica*, are seen to adopt identical attitudes and expressions. All the world's anguish is reflected in the mules' sad and terrified eyes:

> Looking back once, their gaze sweeps across us with in their eyes a wild, sad, profound and despairing quality as though they had already seen in the thick water the shape of the disaster which they could not speak and we could not see. (85)

* * *

Between man and animal, as between man and things, continual and unpredictable exchanges of properties occur. *As I Lay Dying* sucks us into the whirlpool of a protean world whose only law seems to be change and which achieves unity only through the countless analogies these exchanges tirelessly weave between one realm and another. From metaphor one moves to metamorphosis and from meta-

morphosis back to metaphor: everything becomes "profoundly significant" (82); not only *are* things something other than themselves, but
they *say* something else as well. Everything cross-refers to everything
else through a mysterious network of often startlingly close corre-
spondences. Thus the dead fish hiding in the dust, "like it was
ashamed of being dead, like it was in a hurry to get back hid again"
(19), foreshadows "that pride, that furious desire to hide that abject
nakedness which we bring here with us" (27) of which Peabody
speaks with regard to Addie. And the sun, "a bloody egg upon a crest
of thunderheads," the evening of the storm, is like a cosmic counter-
part to Addie's corpse, a broken egg in her coffin (24).

The most disturbing feature is not that inert objects enjoy a strange
life of their own, but that this strangeness has something human
about it in which man recognizes obscurely the image of his own
destiny. Even the random shapes of nature sometimes resemble
human ones, as in this sentence where the configuration of the place
suddenly appears like the sketch of some anatomy: "The path looks
like a crooked limb blown against the bluff" (25). The human figure
in return sometimes seems to reproduce the shapes and forces of
the universe. Dewey Dell, as we have seen, is described by Darl as
a miniature cosmos; her "mammalian ludicrosities" are "the horizons
and the valleys of the earth," (94) and her leg "measures the length
and breadth of life" (60). The human and the cosmic are in the relationship of reciprocal metaphor. In this fluctuating world everything
thus ends by being absorbed into the unity of a single vision.

The Apocalypse

All this turmoil might presage the birth of a new cosmos. Yet it does
not take us long to discover that there is no question here of a gene-
sis. The world depicted in *As I Lay Dying* is not one emerging from
primeval chaos but one preparing to return to it.

In the first sections, it is true, we are still on firm ground, in a
clearly ordered space which the eye can master and take in and size
up at its leisure. Darl's opening monologue describes the setting with
an almost geometrical precision (3–4). But soon the scene starts to
crack up, and we slip into an unfamiliar dimension, where the ordinary laws of perception no longer obtain. The acoustics are upset: in
the Bundrens' house on the hill sounds travel most oddly; voices are
heard nearby, disembodied and sourceless: "As you enter the hall, they
sound as though they were speaking out of the air about you" (13).
Sounds have a strange habit especially of "ceasing without departing":

> Cash labors about the trestles, moving back and forth, lifting
> and placing the planks with long clattering reverberations in
> the dead air as though he were lifting and dropping them at the

> bottom of an invisible well, the sounds ceasing without depart-
> ing, as if any movement might dislodge them from the immedi-
> ate air in reverberant repetition. (44)

By some inexplicable power of remanence, sounds linger in endless
reverberation, remain as traces even when they are no longer audi-
ble. Everything that strikes the senses seems destined to persist
beyond its disappearance. Few words in this novel recur more often
than "fading": nothing is ever fully present, nothing completely
vanishes; sounds and sights are in a state of perpetual suspension,
oscillating between receding presence and nearby absence, as can
be also seen from Darl's singular description of shadows:

> Upon the impalpable plane of [the air] their shadows form as
> upon a wall, as though like sound they had not gone very far
> away in falling but had merely congealed for a moment immedi-
> ate and musing. (44)

Concrete things are dematerialized; shadows acquire substance. A similar phenomenon occurs in the scene where the Bundren brothers
carry Addie's coffin to the wagon; when the "box" slips from Darl's
hands, it slides "down the air like a sled upon invisible snow, smoothly
evacuating atmosphere in which the sense of it is still shaped" (57).
And just as sounds, shadows, and objects do, so events leave a wake:
after the crossing, when the wagon has finally been hauled out of
the river, "it is as though upon the shabby, familiar, inert shape of the
wagon there lingered somehow, latent yet immediate, that violence
which had slain the mules that drew it not an hour since" (90).

Another significant anomaly, particularly evident in the night
scenes, is the frequent reduction of space to two dimensions. For
transparent space in which perspectives are clearly ordered is substituted an opaque space, with neither depth nor relief, against which
objects appear flat. In the scene of Addie's death this flattening is twice
suggested: when Vardaman leaves the bedside, we see his pale face
"fading into the dusk like a piece of paper pasted on a failing wall"
(29), and a page later, the dying woman's face is similarly blurred in
the twilight, floating in the darkness, "detached upon it, lightly as the
reflection of a dead leaf" (29). This transformation of volumes into
surfaces is particularly noticeable with regard to characters, who are
sometimes reduced by Faulkner to the insubstantial fragility of silhou-
ettes. But it is also to be found in descriptions of the setting. Thus, in
the other night scene, which shows us Cash busy finishing the coffin,
one finds the following simile: "Upon the dark ground the chips look
like random smears of soft pale paint on a black canvas" (44). As in
the death scene, space is reduced to two dimensions, but the chromatic range is likewise reduced to two contrasted shades: pale strokes

on a black background. The allusion to painting is again revealing; it refers us back to a world of fiction and illusion, one which vacillates between reality and the representation of reality.

This breakdown of perceptions, these distortions of space may be found in many of Faulkner's books, yet rarely have they been used to better effect. Added to so many other suggestions of impending chaos, these singularities are most useful in heightening the apocalyptic atmosphere peculiar to *As I Lay Dying*. This atmosphere already pervades the scene in the opening sections; as in Shakespeare's tragedies, the world seems to be out of joint and is presented from the beginning in an eerie light. Nature holds its breath in expectation of the catastrophe portended by the sinister omens everywhere visible. Before Addie's death, the storm gathers, threatening, on the horizon; light takes on a copper hue, the air smells of sulphur, and the sun is covered with blood (24). The hallucinating night scene already quoted, where Cash saws the last planks for the coffin by the feeble light of a lantern (44–47), is similarly Shakespearean: the atmosphere is electric; noises, lights, shadows, and the whole landscape assume a supernatural aspect, and again there is the reek of sulphur. Hell is not far away.

As I Lay Dying conjures up Hell as much as the Last Judgment. *Another* world, beyond the range of normal experience, fabulous and terrifying, comes to life, and one cannot tell whether it is given up to demoniacal violence, to the wrath of the Old Testament God, or to the cruel whims of that evil demiurge whom Faulkner sometimes invokes in his novels. When the rain, awaited and feared for so long, finally starts to fall, it sweeps down with a sudden violence suggestive of the biblical Deluge: the drops are "big as buckshot, warm as though fired from a gun; they sweep across the lantern in a vicious hissing" (44). The rainstorm is the first manifestation of the cosmic forces which are going to be unleashed against the Bundrens. It might also be a warning against the folly of their undertaking, like the signpost at a turning of the road which "wheels up like a motionless hand lifted above the profound desolation of the ocean" (62). These dark omens announce the coming catastrophe and proclaim the imminence of the descent into Hell. The wagon is soon to become Charon's ferry: the river crossing, like that of the Styx or Acheron, marks the Bundrens' entry into the underworld. We are now in Death's other kingdom. Everything points to its menacing presence: Addie's coffin swallowed by the raging floodwaters, the floating corpses of pigs and mules (89, 86), the desolate, haunted wasteland around them. * * * The accounts given by the principal witnesses of the scene complement and confirm each other; Darl, the visionary dreamer, and Tull, the man of earthy common sense, both give the impression of escaping from an unprecedented cataclysm. Darl describes the scene as an Apocalypse:

that single monotony of desolation leaning with that terrific quality a little from right to left, as though we had reached the place where the motion of the wasted world accelerates just before the final precipice. (85)

Tull speaks as someone who has seen the jaws of Hell open:

The bridge shaking and swaying under us, going down into the moiling water like it went clean through to the other side of the earth, and the other end coming outen the water like it wasn't the same bridge a-tall and that them that would walk up outen the water on that side must come from the bottom of the earth. (79)

The fiendish savagery of the elements reaches a paroxysm here. For the Bundrens it is the decisive ordeal. Not the last, of course, since after the ordeal by water they have to undergo the ordeal by fire. But Darl's description of the barn fire does not have the same sustained apocalyptic intensity; it is more spectacular than visionary, and attention focuses more on the heroic figure of Jewel than on the scene itself, as though man had momentarily regained the upper hand over the elements.

Water rather than fire seems to be the dominant element in *As I Lay Dying*. For it is water that translates most appropriately into the register of the perceptible the obsession with chaos and death which wells up from the whole novel. Water is not simply the prime agent for metamorphosis; while allowing changes of form, it also contains the threat of a regression to the formless. As in "Old Man," the Apocalypse is envisioned here as a liquid catastrophe, and as in *The Sound and the Fury* and *Sanctuary* images of dissolution recur so often that they become one of the significant motifs of the novel. The motif appears first * * * in connection with Addie's death:

a runnel of yellow neither water nor earth swirls, curving with the yellow road neither of earth nor water, down the hill dissolving into a streaming mass of dark green neither of earth nor sky. (29)

The confusion of elements is also noted by Tull:

a fellow couldn't tell where was the river and where the land. It was just a tangle of yellow. . . . (71)

Vardaman takes up the motif in his description of the horse:

It is as though the dark were resolving him out of his integrity, into an unrelated scattering of components. . . . I see him dissolve . . . and float upon the dark in fading solution. (33–34)

* * *

Dissolving may be connected with another motif in the novel: uprooting. Each existence draws its life-force from the earth, and the most eloquent symbol of life in *As I Lay Dying* is the "wet seed wild in the hot blind earth" (38). Dying, then, means being torn from the native soil, and Addie's death certainly suggests such an uprooting: Jewel compares his mother's hands to unearthed roots (10), and when she dies, her face seems to float in the dusk, light and detached, like "the reflection of a dead leaf" (29). Significantly enough, it is in Darl's monologues that references to uprooting or, more generally, to a loss of contact with the earth are most numerous. * * *

* * *

as if the road too had been *soaked free of earth* and floated upward. . . . (83)

* * *

Jewel and Vernon are in the river again. From here they do not appear to violate the surface at all; it is as though it had *severed* them both at a single blow. . . . (94)[3]

That Darl should see images of uprooting everywhere need not surprise us: they reflect his own rootlessness. Similarly, the world of metamorphosis mirrors his nonidentity and the vision of the Apocalypse his inner collapse. Through the scenes he describes it is his own vertigo he tries to pinpoint and fix in words. In *As I Lay Dying* no space is uninhabited, for every place here is haunted by the presence of a consciousness. The characters project themselves into the landscape and make it throb with their desires and anxieties. Thus Dewey Dell finds signs of her expectancy in everything she sees, whether a pine clump (36) or a signboard (69). It is true that reality is not interiorized to the same extent in all the monologues; the theater in which the drama is enacted is not a mere shadow theater, and the scene eventually acquires, thanks mostly to the contribution of the peripheral narrators, a semblance of objective existence. Yet it is through the descriptions most charged with subjectivity that the setting is made memorable. Darl's combine the quiver of sensitivity with an unfailing acuity of perception. In the novel he stages the show. Through his eyes the scenery leaps to life. It is not enough to say that his evocations are the richest and most suggestive. The setting of the book is invented in his look, created through his words.

---

3. Emphasis to these passages added by author [*Editor*].

ERIC SUNDQUIST

Death, Grief, Analogous Form: *As I Lay Dying*†

> You know if I were reincarnated, I'd want to come back a buzzard.
> Nothing hates him or envies him or wants him or needs him. He is
> never bothered or in danger, and he can eat anything.
> —Faulkner, *1956 interview*

Faulkner's desire to be reincarnated as a buzzard[1] may appear to
betray the kind of grotesque humor that *As I Lay Dying* (1930) has
been rightly accused of indulging. It is a noteworthy gloss not simply
because the novel's own buzzards pose a constant threat to the rotting corpse of Addie Bundren as it is borne on its funeral journey to
Jefferson, but also because Faulkner's identification with the birds,
when viewed in the context of the problems of narrative form posed
by the novel, indicates immediately a grand, if macabre, detachment
from his materials. Such a detachment from materials that are both
dead and yet potently living—or to be more exact in terms of the
book, from materials that are in the process of dying—suggests an
analogy that is relevant to all of Faulkner's work (and, from the vantage of 1956, to his great fictional design itself) but has particular
interest for *As I Lay Dying* since the novel itself seems curiously
detached from his other major works. Although its mood is that of
savage burlesque, and thus represents a continuation of the intimate
family brutalities Faulkner had already explored in *The Sound and
the Fury* and would make more violently shocking when he revised
Sanctuary, As I Lay Dying is rather a tender book. It can, more than
any of his major novels, be read independently, and it is his most perfect and finished piece of fiction. Perhaps because of this, however,
it is nearly a compendium of the problematic techniques that Faulkner had discovered in the sudden creative illumination of *The Sound
and the Fury* and would relentlessly pursue throughout the remain-
der of his career. It is a virtual textbook of technique, one that displays all his talents and their inevitable risks as they support and
drive one another to the perilous limits of narrative form Faulkner
would require for his great novels on the prolonged tragedy and grief
of the South.

Complaints about Faulkner's rhetoric—its gratuitous contortions,
its motiveless expanse, its tactless mix of pathos and ridicule—are

---

† From *Faulkner: The House Divided* (Baltimore and London: Johns Hopkins University
  Press, 1983), pp 28–43. © 1983 The Johns Hopkins University Press. Reprinted with permission of The Johns Hopkins University Press.
1. Jean Stein, "William Faulkner: An Interview," *Paris Review* (Spring 1956), reprinted in
  Frederick J. Hoffman and Olga W. Vickery, eds., *William Faulkner: Three Decades of Criticism* (New York: Harcourt, Brace & World, 1963), p. 72. [See p. 187 of this Norton Critical Edition (*Editor*).]

common even among his admirers. Most often, such complaints proceed from one of two assumptions: that the author or narrator (the two are easily confused) has fallen victim to his own fantasies of technique; or that a character or speaker (these two are also easily confused) has been allowed a command of language utterly incommensurate with his place in the novel's realistic or representational scheme. In some notable instances the two difficulties are merged, as in the following passage from *As I Lay Dying*, in which the young boy Vardaman, "speaking" both as one of the book's fifteen main characters and as one of its equal number of narrators, describes an encounter with his brother's horse in the barn:

> It is dark. I can hear wood, silence: I know them. But not living sounds, not even him. It is as though the dark were resolving him out of his integrity, into an unrelated scattering of components— snuffings and stampings; smells of cooling flesh and ammoniac hair; an illusion of a co-ordinated whole of splotched hide and strong bones within which, detached and secret and familiar, an *is* different from my *is*. I see him dissolve—legs, a rolling eye, a gaudy splotching like cold flames—and float upon the dark in fading solution; all one yet neither; all either yet none. I can see hearing coil toward him, caressing, shaping his hard shape— fetlock, hip, shoulder and head; smell and sound. I am not afraid. (33–34)

Vardaman's narration presents an outrageous example of the kind of writing that has understandably led Martin Green to complain that Faulkner's rhetoric often appears to exist "*in vacuo*," that there is a "gap between it and the writer" so apparent as to leave him completely "alienated" from it.[2] What Green's complaint assumes, however, is in this case exactly what the form of *As I Lay Dying* so astutely challenges—a narrative consciousness formed by a supposed union between the author and his language, a union formalized and made conventional by the standard device of omniscient, or at least partly omniscient, narration, which the novel explicitly discards and disavows.

Vardaman's episode with the horse insists that we experience it as alienated language—alien in the sense of being disembodied, traumatically cut off from the conscious identity of character on the one hand and author on the other. The episode is remarkable but, in the context of the book's unique rhetorical problems, not extraordinary. And it has thematic significance insofar as the book is obsessively concerned with problems of disembodiment, with disjunctive relationships between character and narration or between bodily self and

---

2. Martin Green, *Re-Appraisals: Some Commonsense Readings in American Literature* (New York: W. W. Norton & Company), p. 174.

conscious identity. At extremity, Vardaman's trauma leads to the novel's shortest and most comically wrenching chapter—"My mother is a fish"—and therefore suggests an intimate analogy between the absence of an omniscient narrator, a controlling point of view, and the central event of the book: the death of Addie Bundren, with respect to which each character defines his own identity. The relationship between absent omniscient narrator (or author) and dead mother does not, of course, consist of an exact parallel. Addie Bundren appears in the book, not only dying but speaking her own story in one chapter that appears more than a hundred pages after her literal death. It is important here to distinguish literal from figurative death, for the book's title—its adverb capable of being construed as *while, how,* or even *as if*—endorses the fact that Addie's death as it is experienced (one might speak of the phenomenology of her death) occurs over the course of the book and in relation to each character, thus rendering the distinction both necessary and hazardous. The title contains this possibility, moreover, by intimating an elegiac past tense where the collected acts of individual memory (the speaking "I" of each narrator) are disembodied and merged with the dying "I" of the mother, and by playing on the colloquial use of *lay* as an intransitive verb, so as to blur further the distinction between past and present events, a blurring sanctioned and exacerbated by the mixing of narrative tenses among the book's fifty-nine chapters. The action of the book occurs, that is, as Addie *lies* dying and as she *lay* dying, with each narrative "I" participating in the dissolution of her "I" by reflecting and partially embodying it.

It is in this respect that the dying maintains a figurative power far succeeding the literal event of Addie's death; and the chronological displacement of her single monologue alerts us to the possibility not only that we must understand the death itself to function as an act of temporal and spatial disembodiment, but that Addie's speech, as it were logically disengaged for the corporeal self that could have uttered it, is an extreme example of the way in which the novel's other acts of speech should be interpreted—as partially or wholly detached from the bodily selves that appear to utter them. One thinks for immediate comparison of Whitman's "Crossing Brooklyn Ferry," in which the speaker's violation of temporal and spatial boundaries generates the frightening sense of a truly disembodied, ever-present voice; but more so than Whitman's poem, the voices of *As I Lay Dying*, because they are detached even more obviously from a bounded authorial self, raise doubts about the propriety of referring to the novel's narrative acts as monologues. Such doubts are readily apparent in the example of Vardaman's encounter with Jewel's horse, where the utterance seems disembodied from the conscious identity of author and narrator alike. Yet it also works to enforce our understanding of Vardaman's traumatic reaction to his mother's death and by doing so provides an analogy for the narrative form of the entire novel. The horse that is resolved "out of his integrity, into an unrelated scattering of components . . . an illusion of a co-ordinated whole of splotched hide and strong bones within which, detached and secret and familiar, [there is] an *is* different from my *is*," is emblematic, even symptomatic, of the body of Addie, in process of being resolved out of her integrity, the "*is*" of her self-contained identity; and it is emblematic of the "body" of the novel, itself disintegrated and yet carefully producing the "illusion of a coordinated whole."

Because the relationship between the bodily self and the conscious identity of Addie remains an issue throughout the book, because the self must continue both *to be* and *not to be* the corpse carried along on its self-imposed journey to Jefferson (a possibility disturbingly underscored by Anse's comic refrain "her mind is sot on hit" (27), one is tempted to speak of the body of the book as existing in an analogously fragile state and maintaining its narrative form despite the apparent absence of that substance one might compare to, or identify with, a central point of view embodied in an omniscient narrator. The horse's phenomenal dissolution and "float[ing] upon the dark" recalls other instances in the novel in which objects as experienced are detached from their fixed physical limits: for example, Addie's face in death, which "seems to float detached upon [darkness], lightly as the reflection of a dead leaf" (29), or the flooded ford, where the road appears to have "been soaked free of earth and floated upward, to leave in its spectral tracing a monument to a still more profound desolation" (83)—all of which contribute to our experience of the novel itself as an object whose uttered parts are radically detached from fixed limits and fully identifiable sources. The novel, like the family whose story it tells, is held together in the most precarious fashion, its narrative components adhering and referring to an act that is simultaneously literal and figurative, just as the body of Addie is neither exactly corpse nor conscious self. The logic thus presents itself of speaking of the novel too as a corpse, as a narrative whose form is continually on the verge of decomposition and whose integrity is retained only by heroic imaginative effort.

Some early readers, misunderstanding the nature of Vardaman's reaction to his mother's death, took him to be another idiot, like Benjy Compson. Although one would not need Faulkner's certification to deny such a claim, the explanation he once provided is important. Vardaman reacts as he does, Faulkner pointed out, because he is a child faced with the intimate and perplexing loss of his mother, because "suddenly her position in the mosaic of the household [is]

vacant."[3] This is true for all members of the novel's family, for whom
Addie, at least in the portion of their history presented in the novel
(the portion detached, as it were, from the fuller one we imagine by
interpretive projection), is the center that no longer holds, that is
defunct and yet lingers in stages of tenuous attachment. Vardaman's
confusions between his mother and the fish, and between her seeming imprisonment in the coffin and his own recollection of being
momentarily trapped in the corn crib—

> It was not her because it was laying right yonder in the dirt. And
> now it's all chopped up. I chopped it up. It's laying in the
> kitchen in the bleeding pan, waiting to be cooked and et. Then
> it wasn't and she was, and now it is and she wasn't.

> "Are you going to nail her up in it, Cash? Cash? Cash?" I got
> shut up in the new crib the new door it was too heavy for me it
> went shut I couldn't breathe because the rat was breathing up
> all the air. I said "Are you going to nail it shut, Cash? Nail it?
> *Nail* it?" (39)

—provide the most moving instances of the psychological disorienta-
tion that affects each of the Bundrens in his or her own way. And
they bring into focus the two central problems of bodily integrity
and conscious identity with which the novel is concerned: How can
a body that still *is* be thought of as *was*? How can I, whose self has
depended upon, and been defined in relation to, another self, now
understand the integrity of my own identity? Vardaman, child though
he is, consistently asks the most difficult and sophisticated questions about death in the book. He asks where Addie has gone; he in
effect questions the farcical funeral journey, which is founded particularly on Addie's command to Anse that she be buried in Jefferson
and sanctioned generally by the technically absurd and paradoxical
notion on which funeral ceremonies are based—that the corpse
both *is* and *is not* the self of the person; and he alone, innocently
though mistakenly, assigns an agency to Addie's death by blaming
Doctor Peabody, whose visit coincides with her death no less reason-
ably than the chopping up and eating of the fish.

Peabody's role in the novel is important quite aside from the comic
relief provided when his obese body (again tangentially calling our
attention to the importance of corporeal form in the novel) must be
hauled up the steep hill to the Bundren house by means of a rope;
important because, as Faulkner himself remarked, it gives "a nudge of

---

3. Frederick L. Gwynn and Joseph L. Blotner, eds., *Faulkner in the University: Class Conferences at the University of Virginia, 1957–1958* (1959; reprint ed., New York: Vintage-
   Random, 1965), p. 110. [See p. 191 of this Norton Critical Edition (*Editor*).]

credibility to a condition which was getting close to the realm of unbelief." Bringing in Peabody from what Faulkner called "comparatively the metropolitan outland" allows the reader to admit of the Bundrens that "maybe they do exist. Up to that time they were functioning in this bizarre fashion almost inside a vacuum, and pretty soon you wouldn't have believed it until some stranger came in as a witness."[4] Faulkner's explanation is a perfect indication of one of the novel's more instrumental effects: that in the absence of a controlling narrator the characters, who as narrators themselves participate in the dissolution of the book's integrity and yet by that very act define and maintain its fragile form, do indeed, as Darl says, "sound as though they [are] speaking out of the air about your head" (13) and appear to be acting in a virtual vacuum—the vacuum left both by the "author" who is not, as it were, present and by the integrated form that we as a consequence imagine would be there if he were. Without attaching too much importance to Faulkner's remarks we might nonetheless consider Peabody's appearance, apart from its other functions, in some measure a response to Faulkner's anxiety about the vacuum created by his own authorial absence, one that is bound up with the vacuum created by Addie's death. That is to say, the need to imagine a narrative rendered coherent by the controlling presence of an author—an authoritative *voice*—is not unlike the need to imagine, and the stricken reluctance to let go belief in, the integrated self of one who has died. Both needs may well be spoken of as conventional, as being formed by prior or habitual expectations, though it is precisely for that reason that both are so psychologically demanding.

Although Peabody need not necessarily be thought of as a figure for the author (a conventional way of meeting this demand), part of his role as witness consists of a most telling remark about the action of death in the novel: "I can remember how when I was young I believed death to be a phenomenon of the body; now I know it to be merely a function of the mind—and that of the minds of the ones who suffer the bereavement." (26) Of the two qualifications by which Peabody's remarks proceed, the second is the most striking and the most definitive with respect to the form of the novel; while the distinction raised by the first—that body and consciousness may present separable forms of identity—is one simultaneously entertained and held in abeyance by the book, the insistence that death demands the intimate participation of other minds virtually explicates the reactions of Addie's family to her demise and, correspondingly, the disintegrated yet tenuously coherent form of the novel. What dies in death, Peabody suggests, is not simply the body or even the mind attached

---

4. Gwynn and Blotner, eds., *Faulkner in the University*, pp. 113–14. [See p. 193 of this Norton Critical Edition (*Editor*).]

to the body. Rather—and here again one might speak of the phenomenology of death—what dies are the connections between one
mind and others. Thus it is that Addie dies not within a single, temporally bounded moment, but rather lies dying throughout the book,
in that her death is not complete until the book ends. But even this is
not a satisfactory way of putting it. For, although one could claim that
her death is complete once she is buried, once her command is fulfilled, this would ignore the fact that many if not almost all the monologues, whether they are in the present or past tense, need to be
understood as occurring, or continuing to occur, *after* the chronological end of the action. The process of detachment that grief involves
must, that is, be understood as continuing beyond the physical limits
of the story.

Peabody's definition suggests, moreover, that the mind that dies, the
integral "I," depends on others for its dying (a metaphysical version of
Addie's devoutly upheld command), and thus also undergoes a process
of detachment. If this is so, then the self or the "I" existing prior to
physical death is a self composed of others. Such a self is not isolated
or solitary but communal; or, one should say, its integrity depends
upon being integrated and its identity upon being constituted by identification, by a form of psychological or emotional analogy that works
to extend the boundaries of identity. It is in death, as the novel tells us
time and again, that this paradox is made manifest, that the need to
imagine an integral self becomes most apparent even as the possibility
of doing so passes away, a passing physically symbolized, as in Addie
Bundren's case, by a decomposing corpse. And it is the action of grief,
the refusal to let go those connections that once formed an integral
self, that most painfully attests to the illusion of identity upon which
our notions of self are founded. The "I" that lies dying, then, is the "I"
of Addie and it is not; it is the "I" of each family member and it is not.
As in the case of Anse, of whom Dewey Dell says, "he looks like right
after the maul hits the steer and it [is] no longer alive and dont yet
know that it is dead" (36), it is the "I" that each in his connection to
her has formed and that now resists its own detachment and isolation
even as it takes place. These paradoxes have their perfect analogous
expression in the narrative form of the book, which both insists upon
and yet prohibits our imagining that the fragmentary, disembodied
episodes are—or to be more exact, *were once*—connected to the body
or self of a story presented by a single controlling narrator. In taking
this further risk, Faulkner perfects the formal strategy that the story of
Caddy, lost in the grief-stricken maze of *The Sound and the Fury*, had
suggested: like Addie, *As I Lay Dying* is both integrated and disintegrated; like each member of the family, each narrative episode participates in composing that integrated self at the same time it works out
its own psychological detachment from it.

The theatrical collection of voices that the novel resembles not only reminds us that consciousness is largely memory, that the self is a fusion between a body with clear limits and a mind with unpredictable ones, and that the psychological chronology of our lives is easily more chaotic than that of the conventional novel; it does so by reminding us as well that although the novel, like any system of belief, offers an illusion of integrated form that may well be an improvement upon life, it is one that is precarious and requires our belief in things that do not exist. Or, as William Gass has remarked, "theories of character are not absurd in the way representational theories are; they are absurd in a grander way, for the belief in Hamlet (which audiences often seem to have) is like the belief in God—incomprehensible to reason—and one is inclined to seek a motive: some deep fear or emotional need."[5] *As I Lay Dying* is an exemplary case, because it is markedly a book in which characters exist on the basis of the briefest and most fragmentary physical descriptions and in which dialogue is constantly reported and often dislocated by narrative voices that, while they are careful to record identical dialects differently, nonetheless seem utterly severed from the peculiar bodily selves that ostensibly produce them. Vardaman's willingness to confuse the body of his mother with the body of a fish begins as a matter of temporal comparison (before the fish was "not-fish" Addie was still "is"), but issues eventually in a spatial or corporeal integration of the two, dislocating one and the other from fixed limits in order to conceive a new form of identity. Vardaman's notion is absurd; yet it is only an extreme and traumatic form of the logic of analogy on which the book depends, a logic demanded by Faulkner's presenting his characters with powers of articulation that are literally inconceivable, by his splicing of reported action and dialogue with stream-of-consciousness narration, and, of course, by his dislocation of conventional prose limits through frequent violation of the rules of grammar and punctuation.

Among the three children most disturbingly affected by the death, Vardaman, perhaps because of the mechanism of transference, seems in some respects best able to maintain a hold on his own identity. He does so by a continual, prosaically simplified enumeration of his connections to, and understanding of, the actions around him. Darl seems technically his opposite and stands in much the same relation to him as Quentin does to Benjy in *The Sound and the Fury*. Although his sympathy with Vardaman becomes so pronounced that they ultimately listen together to the coffin, where Darl says Addie is "talking to God" and "calling on Him to help her [. . .] lay down her life" (124), Darl moves uncomfortably toward the tormented self-conscious posturings

5. William Gass, "The Concept of Character in Fiction," in *Fiction and the Figures of Life* (New York: Alfred A. Knopf, 1970), p. 37.

of Quentin Compson. Unable to contain his consciousness within the boundaries of sanity, Darl expresses his madness through hallucination and clairvoyance. As Tull puts it, "it's like he had got into the inside of you, someway. Like somehow you was looking at yourself and your doings outen his eyes" (72). In his clairvoyant knowledge of Dewey Dell's pregnancy and Jewel's illegitimacy; in narrating the events of Addie's actual death from a physical point that makes it impossible; and at last, on his way to a Jackson insane asylum, in speaking of himself in the third person, Darl tempts us to identify him with the omniscient author. But while Faulkner himself on one occasion associated Darl's visionary madness with artistic power,[6] it is important to note that this too is an instance of the novel's reluctance to meet the anxiety of omniscience. That is, by suggesting a link between omniscience and madness, Faulkner reveals what the novel backs away from as a form of disembodiment so extreme as to be terrifying and debilitating.

The tranquil side of Darl's madness, subtly and exactly expressed in his contention that "it would be nice if you could just ravel out into time" (121), is countered by the more nightmarish character who, as Dewey Dell reports, "sits at the supper table with his eyes gone further than the food and the lamp, full of the land dug out of his skull and the holes filled with distance beyond the land" (17). In psychological terms, the person of Darl offers the danger that the conventional boundaries between internal and external will become irremediably confused; while in terms of the novel, the character of Darl, who as Tull remarks "just thinks by himself too much" (41), offers the danger that Addie's dying will be swallowed up by his consciousness, that her "I" and those of the other characters will become inseparable from his own. Darl's omniscience is thus presented as a paradox that parallels, and takes its cue from, the paradox of death as it is explored in the novel: just as Addie's death calls into question the boundaries of the self by defining that self as a series of connections that appear even as they are disintegrated, Darl's intense consciousness, like that of an omniscient author-narrator, defines a self whose identity risks being lost in the act of becoming saturated with the ability to be connected to other minds. The very form of the novel requires, of course, that the characters be understood as minds, as

6. See Gwynn and Blotner, eds., *Faulkner in the University*, p. 113: "Who can say how much of the good poetry in the world has come out of madness, and who can say just how much of superperceptivity the—a mad person might not have?" Faulkner even appeared to have apprehended an unconscious power in the character of Darl that, instead of leading to a fuller identification between author and character, rather disengaged them. "You can't make [a character] do things once he comes alive and stands up and casts his own shadow," Faulkner claimed. "I couldn't always understand why [Darl] did things, and when we would quarrel about it, he always won, because at that time he was alive, he was under his own power" (Ibid., pp. 263–64). [See pp. 192, 202 of this Norton Critical Edition (*Editor*).]

instances of narration or storytelling, but by constantly exposing as impractical our desire to fix the limits of each character's conscious identity, the novel also constantly refers us to the one identity, the one mind—that of the author—that has become so illusive as to be felt to be missing altogether.

In speaking of a corpse like Addie's that continues to seem both dead and alive, the difficulty of choosing between grammatical forms— *she* and *it*, *is* and *was*—keeps in view the central problem of bodily integrity, a problem explored insistently by the novel's blurring of boundaries between the animate and the inanimate, as in Anse's monologue on roads, Darl's on the river and the wagon, or Dewey Dell's on the dead earth. There are other examples we must turn to, but in all cases such blurrings increase our dependence on the rhetorical terms of the novel, preventing us from doubting the legitimacy of the absurd ritual journey as it unfolds and keeping us attached to the startling possibility of Addie's continued integral power. In this respect the most unnerving yet effective device is the sudden appearance more than halfway through the book, and chronologically (though it makes little sense to speak of it so) some four days after her death, of Addie's single monologue, one of the most emotionally charged pieces of writing in the novel and perhaps the one that comes closest to stating internally a theory of its narrative form.

The importance of Addie's diatribe against "words"—and particularly the word *love*—lies not simply in her belief that "words dont ever fit even what they are trying to say at," that we have "to use one another by words like spiders dangling by their mouths from a beam, swinging and twisting and never touching" (99), for these remarks add virtually nothing to the overwhelming effect already generated by the novel that this is the case. Nor does Addie's enumeration of her pregnancies and the manner in which each balances out or revenges another accomplish much more than providing a partial key to the various relationships of antagonism and devotion that exist among her children. While these relationships are important and finally have much to do with analogies one might draw between the family and the book as integrated forms, the instrumental significance of Addie's monologue arises rather in those sections of her utterance that may be said most to resemble the brooding, silenced voice of the narrator (or author) and are therefore most likely to be misread as moments of sheer invention for the sake of invention on Faulkner's part. The implied or explicit correlation between words and bodies that appears throughout Addie's monologue recalls similar dramatizations of Faulkner's authorial agony in *The Sound and the Fury*, dramatizations that in each case also prefigure the intimate analogy between creation and grief in Faulkner's most passionate explorations of wasted love and historical loss, *Absalom, Absalom!* and *Go Down, Moses*.

The technical wonder of *As I Lay Dying* and its relative thematic isolation among Faulkner's major novels may obscure its place in the development of his handling of loss and grief. The book elaborates those intimacies of loss that *The Sound and the Fury* had broached, but here the simultaneous rage and sentimental indulgence that unbalance the Compson's story are modified and merged; and the emotion spent in the sublimation of erotic passion in the earlier book, and later spent in the sublimation of the equally passionate tragedies of race, is brought to focus and distanced in the novel's extraordinary technique. This technique, fracturing that universal presence by and in which we constitute the essence of a story, defines grief as a characteristic of Faulkner's narrative form itself, a characteristic, that is to say, in which his forms find their fullest expressive power—that of articulating what is lost but lingering on the verge of memory, what will never be but *might have been*, what passionate word or act is harbored in that which remains, for fear or shame, unspoken or unactualized. While suggesting that the decaying corpse of Addie is emblematic of the burden of the Southern past, Faulkner at the same time comes closer to a full evocation of that feminine presence he everywhere associates with creative desire, its failure, and the resulting grief; identifying himself with that presence and yet barely screening his apparent hatred of it, he portrays in Addie the figure of *mothering* conspicuously absent in *Sartoris, The Sound and the Fury*, and *Sanctuary*—the figure his later novels will seek to actualize in a crossing of races and whose essence is the literal embodiment of the loss, the separation, and the grief Faulkner finds at the heart of cultural and familial history and acts out in the lives and form of fictional narrative.

Words like *motherhood, love, pride, sin,* and *fear*, Addie suggests, are just "shape[s] to fill a lack," shapes that, when the need for them arises, cannot adequately fill the void left by an accomplished act or a past event. Words "fumble" at deeds "like orphans to whom are pointed out in a crowd two faces and told, That is your father, your mother," and they resemble, in Addie's mind, the names of her husband and children, whose names and bodies imperfectly fill the lack in her bodily self they have caused:

> I would think: The shape of my body where I used to be a virgin is in the shape of a   and I couldn't think *Anse*, couldn't remember *Anse*. It was not that I could think of myself as no longer unvirgin, because I was three now. And when I would think *Cash* and *Darl* that way until their names would die and solidify into a shape and then fade away, I would say. All right. It doesn't matter. It doesn't matter what they call them. (100)

Although it might be too much to claim that the confused and some-times contradictory remarks of Addie's monologue immediately explain anything, they do reveal that the novel, as John K. Simon has pointed out, is "the story of a body, Addie's, both in its existence as an unembalmed corpse and as it was—at least partly—conceived for passion."[7] That is, her remarks clarify what Addie implies and what Dewey Dell, in her own first pregnancy, has begun to discover—that the connection between sexual "lying" and lying dying is an intimate one, and that the violation is not simply sexual but generational, as Dewey Dell understands: "I feel my body, my bones and flesh begin-ning to part and open upon the alone, and the process of coming unalone is terrible" (36).

Pregnancy for Dewey Dell and for Addie involves a confusion of identity that inverts the one expressed in the process of death, in which the impossibility of conceiving of the self as a singular identity is made paradoxically conspicuous in the sudden need to preserve those connections that define the self even as they pass away. Standing at the other end of death, as it were, "the process of coming unalone" initiates in their most apparent physical form the connections without which one cannot fully imagine ever having been a lone, identical self existing apart from conscious and bodily ties to others. In extremity, the "coming unalone," the becoming more than one "I," leads to a threat of utter extinction through saturation, as in the case of Darl, whom we might think of as figuratively invaded by, and thus con-sciously "bearing" in distorted shape, all the novel's characters and events; or it leads to an extinction in which consciousness is com-pletely severed from its own "I," as in Darl's meditation on sleep and in the nightmare that Dewey Dell's pregnancy, in conjunction with her mother's death, leads her to recall:

> When I used to sleep with Vardaman I had a nightmare once
> I thought I was awake but I couldn't see and I couldn't feel I
> couldn't feel the bed under me and I couldn't think what I was
> I couldn't think of my name I couldn't even think I am a girl
> I couldn't even think I nor even think I want to wake up nor
> remember what was opposite to awake so I could do that. (69)

It is this predicament that Addie speaks of metaphorically when she cannot remember the shape of her body when virgin, cannot even articulate the word that might describe it. Words, that is, are inade-quate not so much because they fail to "fit even what they are trying to say at," but because they fail to describe or fill the blank space that only the act of conceiving the need for a word can make manifest as

7. John K. Simon, "The Scene and Imagery of Metamorphosis in *As I Lay Dying*," *Criticism* 7, no. 1 (Winter 1965): 14.

irreparably lost or passed. Words are for something we are not or can no longer be: or as Peabody remarks, in a humorous variation on this potent analogy, when "it finally occurred to Anse himself that [Addie] needed [a doctor], it was already too late" (25).

As I Lay Dying speaks pointedly to the need for establishing and maintaining conscious attachments symbolically incorporated in bodily ties by constant reference, in both actual and formal terms, to the loss of the originating mother. Darl's claim that he has no mother and that the illegitimate Jewel has a horse for a mother; Dewey Dell's psychological merging of death and childbearing (both in her rhetorical association with Addie as mother and in her conceiving of the funeral journey as a means to get an abortion); Cash's obsession with Addie's coffin, as though its perfection and preservation will somehow save the bodily integrity of Addie; Jewel's heroic actions to save that coffin and its body from flood and fire; and Vardaman's transfiguration of mother into fish—all of these reactions identify grieving as foremost a process of detachment, of disembodiment, in which the act of *expression* is central. Supported by the chaotic chronology of the novel, which prevents us from knowing "where" the characters are speaking from, the community of voices itself participates in the paradoxical action that grieving is, an action that expresses connections in order both to make them and let them go. Like the voices of the women singing at the wake described by Tull, the voices of the novel that tell Addie's story (including her own) seem to "come out of the air, flowing together and on in sad, comforting tunes. When they cease it's like they hadn't gone away. It's like they had just disappeared into the air and when we moved we would loose them again out of the air around us, sad and comforting" (53).

This is true whether we conceive of the characters as talking, as thinking, or—in some instances—even as writing their stories; and the confusion as to which is the more appropriate conception makes it clear that grief seldom has an appropriate form or a distinct chronology. What Faulkner once spoke of as characteristic of his entire work is particularly relevant to As I Lay Dying: "The fact that I have moved my characters around in time successfully, at least in my own estimation, proves to me my own theory that time is a fluid condition which has no existence except in the momentary avatars of individual people. There is no such thing as *was*—only *is*. If *was* existed, there would be no grief or sorrow."[8] The form of the novel keeps *is* from becoming *was* as Addie's corpse is kept dying beyond the physical death and—because the stories have no fixed temporal origins but rather are desperately detached from them—even beyond the supposed chronological end of the action, Addie's burial

8. Stein, "William Faulkner: An Interview," p. 82.

and Anse's remarriage. Grief itself seems disembodied from its object precisely because the boundaries of that object have ceased to have specific meaning and now receive abnormally deliberate, if displaced, attention. The dislocation of conscious attention that grief can produce makes Vardaman's psychological transferences from mother to fish, for example, or Cash's from body to coffin plausible and even necessary, and helps explain what André Bleikasten has referred to as Faulkner's possession by the "demon of analogy" in the novel.[9] The action of grief responds to and reflects the demand for analogy, for the possibility of relocating the lost integrity of one object in another as a way of expressing the maintenance of emotional connections that are threatening to disappear.

Because the novel refuses to settle on a point of view, a narrative focus that gives immediate coherence to the story, but on the contrary forces us to develop that coherent identity by an act of imaginative identification, piecing it together from disparate parts, it too might well be regarded as a family without a mother, as it were, without a single source from which we can clearly say the parts have sprung. And yet of course we do say just that: we say Faulkner is the author, these all are parts of him, products of his creation. To say this, however, is both necessary and speculative, for the parts—disembodied from the act that apparently produced them—are in their own way as much orphaned as Addie's own children or the words that she speaks of as filling a lack left by a deed that has passed. The self that produced them, or the integral point of view that we imagine as controlling them, has "come unalone" in that act, which is now a lack filled by shapes. We know and need it only in retrospect; because this is the case, the process of grieving that the Bundrens undergo—a process in which their breaking of connections with Addie at once defines her self as composed of them yet requires each of them to lie dying along with her—is analogous to the narrative unfolding of "Faulkner's story," a process in which the shape of the book is built up by accumulation and connection but paradoxically participates in the disintegration of that imagined single form, leaving each episode in isolation, tenuously attached to the others and at the same time orphaned—referring to, yet failing properly to "fill" and complete, the lack that they make manifest. Because they exist in the novel's form as disembodied both from the bodies that utter them *and* from the one body that we must understand as having once produced them, the narrative episodes do indeed seem a collection of voices in the air.

As I Lay Dying is best understood, then, as a book in which death is the story and the story is a death, a book in which the authorial

9. André Bleikasten, *Faulkner's As I Lay Dying*, trans. Roger Little (Bloomington: University of Indiana Press, 1973), p. 39.

"I" also lies dying; that is, he is dead as Addie is dead, dead as a single identity but still alive in the episodes that continue to refer themselves to that identity and continue to constitute it even more emphatically in our desire to locate Faulkner's own "language," his own "story," in the voices of his characters. To speak of the book as a corpse is to recognize that such an expression is at once appropriate and inadequate, for just as Addie's corpse is not what dies (except on one occasion) in the book, the words that fill the book, like the family that continues to fill and be filled by Addie Bundren, are alive, however disembodied, fragmented, and comically bereaved. The expressions of grief that work out their own disembodiment from a lost, decomposing object by the insistent desire for analogous experience find analogy in the novel's form, which, like the action of grief, relocates the limits and power of that object in the stories of which it is now composed. Those expressions continue to have and to acquire meaning, and continue to make connections, despite the absurdity of doing so and appearing to act, as Faulkner recognized, in a virtual vacuum.

It is a measure of the novel's magnificent power that it leads us to recognize Faulkner's mastery in the very situation in which we are tempted to say he has surrendered control of the book, has himself become disembodied as "author." Wright Morris has spoken quite rightly of such examples of stylistic power in Faulkner's work as moments in which "the technique is so flawless that the effect is incandescent. Craft and raw material are in such lucid balance that it seems the craftsman himself is missing."[1] A more appropriate way of characterizing *As I Lay Dying* is difficult to imagine, for Faulkner is indeed missing—missing as Addie is missing, nonetheless commanding our attention and our attempts to account for his seemingly invisible control. His own notorious remarks (in the preface to *Sanctuary*) about the ease and speed with which he wrote the novel are no doubt slightly overstated; but Faulkner's admission on another occasion that the novel is an example of that creative situation in which "technique charges in and takes command of the dream before the writer himself can get his hands on it"[2] corresponds to our sense that the book's craft and material, its form and substance, like the form and substance of Addie, are working in brilliant accord, at once engagingly distinct and emotionally inseparable.

It is such power, charged by the activity of grieving that expresses itself analogically, that compels us to seek analogues for the author

1. Wright Morris, *The Territory Ahead* (1957; reprint ed., Lincoln: University of Nebraska Press, 1978), p. 177.
2. Stein, "William Faulkner: An Interview," p. 72. [See p. 188 of this Norton Critical Edition (*Editor*).]

in the work, connections between Faulkner and Peabody, Faulkner and Darl, Faulkner and Addie, for example—or perhaps just as appropriately, as the lucidity of Faulkner's technique may suggest, between the author and Cash, the patient, meticulous builder of Addie's coffin. Faulkner's many references in letters and interviews to himself as a craftsman, as a user of "tools" and materials and a virtual builder of tales, makes the analogy unavoidable; though this analogy is not as immediately central as the formal analogy between Faulkner and Addie, it amplifies that one by bringing into focus the relationships between body and coffin, and perhaps more notably between coffin and book, as objects of extraordinary fragility and devotion. Against flood, fire, and scavenging buzzards, the coffin, though hiding it from view, preserves its rotting cargo long enough to get it buried in Jefferson—preserves the integrity of the object it both literally contains and figuratively renders absurd *as* an object in the same way that the form of the book, elaborately pieced together, both literally contains its central event, Addie's death, and figuratively renders absurd the physical limits of that event. Darl's early characterizations of his dead mother's body as "spent yet alert" (30), "volitional," or "lightly alive, waiting to come awake" (46), as well as the novel's continual unpredicated reference to the coffin and its body as "it" (or to both as "her"), all work to blur the distinction between body and container, the animate and the inanimate, in a fashion that is completely analogous to the novel's formal blurring of distinctions between its own structure of expression and the ongoing event that is expressed. The coffin "contains" the object of the family's quixotic devotion as absolutely and precariously as the book "contains" the dying of Addie Bundren. Like the book, the coffin is both the shape filled by the fragile self of Addie and a "shape to fill a lack," the lack that death makes manifest and *is*, but in which those of whose minds it is a function refuse fully to believe.

The coffin and the book, each in its way, maintain the integrity of Addie's bodily self. But if we keep in mind the example of gentle Cash, who admits that there is "a fellow in every man that's done a-past the sanity or the insanity, that watches the sane and the insane doings of that man with the same horror and the same astonishment" (137), the coffin and the book must also be seen as maintaining, in moral terms, the integrity of the funeral journey—and against rather overwhelming odds. For quite aside from the preposterous physical threats to the journey, the family's own intentions are continually betrayed as shallow and self-serving. Anse wants new teeth and a new wife; Dewey Dell wants an abortion; Cash wants a gramophone; and Vardaman wants to eat bananas and see a toy train. Only Jewel and Darl seem immune from mixed motives for reaching Jefferson, the one determined to complete the burial, the other determined to prevent it. Although the effort may succeed precisely because of these base intentions, it is also the case—as in Vardaman's wish to see the train, which he says "made my heart hurt" (125)—that the intentions themselves may have become bound up with the forms of analogous experience and expression that grief both makes possible and necessitates. There seems no other explanation for Faulkner's most masterful stroke in the novel, the complete deletion of the actual burial of Addie, the act that her command set in motion and to which the entire action of the book is devoted. Yet as Vardaman unwittingly suggests early on when he asks Dewey Dell, "Did [Addie] go far as town?" (39) it is not the burial that matters but the journey, the heroic effort to sustain the fragile community of the family in the face of physical and psychological trauma. Each of the Bundrens participates in the journey as he or she participates in the dying of Addie; each journeys and each dies, and in doing so testifies to the continued integrity of the dead mother, memorializing the passing of the body by expressing the emotional ties that continue to compose the self.

The novel's treatment of the corpse of Addie must thus be understood in the same light as Vardaman's boring of holes through the coffin into her face—as an act of love whose grotesque expression is at once perversely comic and at the same time utterly sincere. What the book poignantly exposes is the precarious nature of ritual expression, particularly that of funeral rituals, in which an absurd possibility—that the corpse of the person nonetheless *is* the person—is maintained not because anyone believes it but because no one can immediately, emotionally deny it. The trauma of grief, in which death most clearly *is* a function of other minds, makes the irrational conventional; and the elegy that the expression of grief may become must itself, as the novel certainly does, harbor the eventuality of seeming comic or grotesque. It is "only when the ritual is disengaged from its symbolic function," Olga Vickery has remarked of the novel, "that the comic aspect becomes apparent." Vickery goes on to note that the distinction between empty and significant ritual is not unlike the distinction Addie's monologue draws between words and deeds,[3] an analogy that is completely appropriate if—and only if—we understand words to be capable of more than Addie admits; that is, only if we understand words, the shapes that fill a lack, as the possible expression of an identity that is most intensely and passionately present even as it passes away. The ritual of the book threatens at every point to become disengaged from its symbolic function and

3. Olga Vickery, *The Novels of William Faulkner: A Critical Interpretation* (Baton Rouge: Louisiana State University Press, 1959), p. 53. See pp. 236–48 in this Norton Critical Edition.

thus to appear simply absurd or grotesque; yet this is perfectly in keeping with the various characters' precarious and traumatic attachment to the central object of the ritual, and moreover in perfect keeping with the novel's formal disengagement of its narrative expression from a controlling consciousness, a consciousness that would more clearly and conventionally stabilize the meaning of the death and its ritual enactment. The absurdity of the characters' reactions, as well as the absurdity of the journey itself, register in unmediated form the paradox of death that the book struggles so hard to contain.

At one point Darl describes Anse's face as having been "carved by a savage caricaturist [in] a monstrous burlesque of all bereavement" (45). If one is tempted to say that this applies equally well to each of the characters, and that Faulkner's modern parable produces only a travesty of its characters' efforts and a virtual parody of itself, it must be kept in mind that, because parody works by a form of analogy that is more successful the more fragile are the boundaries between the mockery and the object, the tale of the Bundrens is one that preserves that fragile equilibrium and expresses it formally in the extenuated distinctions between voice and character, between corpse and self, and in this case most of all between the conventions of ritual and their burlesque. "There's not too fine a distinction between humor and tragedy," Faulkner once remarked, for "even tragedy is in a way walking a tightrope between . . . the bizarre and the terrible."[4] It is difficult, of course, to read *As I Lay Dying* as tragedy, but its bizarre and terrible humor keeps before us the fact that comedy itself is often a means of releasing pressure and relieving anguish. The contortions of language that break down boundaries between the outrageous and the awful, that is to say, are not unlike the emotional trauma associated with death, for the instability of the expression of grief makes it particularly susceptible to the potential comedy of analogy.

Such contortions tend easily toward the tall tale; but then Faulkner, in an age dominated by "The Waste Land" and by Hemingway's cold-blooded and often futile heroism, might well have felt the necessity of exaggeration in order to render a parable of heroic effort in the modern world. Of course much of Faulkner's fiction tends toward the tall tale, but what is extraordinary about *As I Lay Dying*, particularly when we recall that it follows *The Sound and the Fury* and falls between the composition and revision of *Sanctuary*, Faulkner's most unrelentingly brutal parable of the modern world, is that the comedy itself could come to seem the finest, most passionate expression of grief and— with precarious extremity—of love. In this respect, the novel projects a world of tragic compassion Faulkner would not find again until

4. Gwynn and Blotner, eds., *Faulkner in the University*, p. 39.

Absalom, Absalom! and *Go Down, Moses*, in which the intimate entanglement of grief and love, and the scattered family passions they reflect, are so anguished as to appear almost beyond redemption. For the moment, however—perhaps the only certain moment in his career—Faulkner's own compassion became brilliant, powerful, and unabashedly moving.

STEPHEN M. ROSS

[Mimetic Voice]†

As I Lay Dying is a virtual laboratory for experimentation with mimetic voice. Few texts interrogate so insistently—yet without abandoning—our shared expectations about the recording of speech. * * * Throughout its fifty-nine sections the novel employs, almost with a vengeance, the conventions of speech presentation to evoke truly "hearable" voices. The polyphonic sections, each headed by the name of one of the fifteen first-person narrators, exhibit striking variations in tone: we hear the dialect of poor white Mississippi farmers, the talk of small-town shopkeepers, tense and fast-paced narrative, richly metaphoric digression, and philosophically charged speculation burdened by Latinate diction and convoluted syntax. In narrative sections that range from one sentence ("My mother is a fish") to ten pages of elaborate Faulknerian rhetoric, *As I Lay Dying* forces us to treat unspeakable discourse as the speech of improbable characters—in one section a carpenter numbers his reasons for building a coffin "on the bevel," in another a decomposing corpse reminisces. The novel is fundamentally spoken; voices emerge from an eloquence of the spoken word that permits shifts into and out of differing registers of fictional discourse. Faulkner described *As I Lay Dying* as a tour de force, and from the perspective of mimetic voice it is truly that.

* * *

Nowhere is the truth of Barthes's emphatic assertion that *"the character and the discourse are each other's accomplices"*[1] more ingeniously borne out than in *As I Lay Dying*. While this principle operates in all fictional discourse, and particularly in the conventions of appropriate speech that govern mimetic voice, the collaboration between voice and character in *As I Lay Dying* takes a perverse form: consciousness emerges not from appropriate speech, but from the *in*appropriate

---

† From *Fiction's Inexhaustible Voice: Speech and Writing in Faulkner* (Athens and London: University of Georgia Press, 1989), pp. 111–29. © 1989 by the University of Georgia Press. Reprinted by permission of the publisher.
1. Roland Barthes, *S/Z*, trans. Richard Miller (New York: Hill and Wang, 1974), pp. 178.

disruption of mimetic voice. In those moments when mimetic voice "breaks down," when speech is dis-illusioned, we discover character. The illusion of speech unconventionally generated in a title, where some "I" speaks of lying and dying, generates a power of voice that transcends mimesis.

As I Lay Dying constructs its verbal world, and its characters' expressive identities, by first generating convincing mimetic voice and then either heightening or disrupting the illusion of speech in a manner that articulates a given speaker's consciousness in its relation to others. Faulkner's typical rhetorical gesture places the reader within imaged speech and then disturbs the discursive illusion so that the mimetic voice we hear translates into another register, another mode of voice—the phenomenal, the psychic, even the oratorical. Faulkner makes speech an index to character not, as in conventional realistic fiction, by recording it "faithfully" and "consistently," but by disrupting such verisimilitude. The text renders identity as a felt and constantly changing verbal relationship to others. The fictional entities whose names we know (Darl, Cash, Tull) possess personalities distilled out of their speech; but because their speech defines them in relation to others, their talk escapes the gabble of idiolects to move into a shared, communal field of verbal expression, a not always harmonic choir of living voices.

The monologues differ greatly, especially on first reading, in the degree to which each experiments with conventional presentation of speech. Faulkner employs this strategy in virtually all the monologues, not merely in those most obviously imitative of a character's stream of consciousness. It is easy to see, for example, how he translates the illusion of speech into a more purely *written* discourse in Cash's first section, where he lists the reasons he built the coffin on the bevel. The numbered list transforms a potentially spoken explanation into a visual, documentary analog of Cash's orderly mental habits. To illustrate the play with mimetic voice, however, I will examine a less patently odd section, one that heightens rather than disrupts familiar conventions of mimetic voice, yet where individual expressive identity nonetheless emerges from within the text's field of verbal relationships.

By any standard of verisimilitude readers certainly hear Peabody and Anse Bundren speaking in Peabody's first section:

> He and Anse are on the porch when I come out, the boy sitting on the steps, Anse standing by a post, not even leaning against it, his arms dangling, the hair pushed and matted up on his head like a dipped rooster. He turns his head, blinking at me.
>
> "Why didn't you send for me sooner?" I say.
>
> "Hit was jest one thing and then another," he says. "That ere corn me and the boys was aimin to git up with, and Dewey Dell

a-takin good keer of her, and folks comin in, a-offerin to help
and sich, till I jest thought . . ."
        "Damn the money," I say. "Did you ever hear of me worrying
a fellow before he was ready to pay?"
        "Hit aint begrudgin the money," he says. "I jest kept
a-thinkin . . . She's goin, is she?" The durn little tyke is sitting
on the top step, looking smaller than ever in the sulphur-colored
light. That's the one trouble with this country: everything,
weather, all, hangs on too long. Like our rivers, our land: opaque,
slow, violent; shaping and creating the life of man in its implacable and brooding image. "I knowed hit," Anse says. "All the while
I made sho. Her mind is sot on hit." (26–27; ellipses in original)

* * * The section opens in a typically colloquial manner with a temporal marker ("When Anse finally sent for me . . .") plus Peabody's
expressions of how he came to be involved and what he thought
and said about the events he relates to us. Peabody's section itself,
and different speech acts reported by Peabody, are differentiated and
clearly identified by speech tags, paragraphing, and punctuation. The
name "Peabody" at the section's beginning, and the colloquial speech
tags "I say" and "he says" within the monologue, attribute words to the
appropriate speakers. Peabody's discourse transcribes his own town
dialect (evincing rhythms of speech and an occasional "damn" or
"durn," but virtually no phonetic spelling), and Peabody mimics Anse's
country white dialect: " 'Hit was jest one thing and then another,' he
says. 'That ere corn me and the boys was aimin to git up with, and
Dewey Dell a-takin good keer of her.' "
        In most ways, then, this passage typifies Faulkner's methods of cre-
ating mimetic voice, both characters' voices and those of character-
narrators. But certain oddities in Peabody's expression emphasize two
identifying traits in his relations with the Bundrens. When Peabody
quotes Anse we note the extreme version of country white dialect.
Anse's talk has a high density of phonetic spelling, higher than in
most other speech in *As I Lay Dying;* indeed, Anse in other sections
does not exhibit much eye dialect at all—no "hit," no "jest," and so on.
"She'll want to start right away. I know her. I promised her I'd keep the
team here and ready, and she's counting on it" (11). This technique
[allows] the density of dialect to vary in accord with the narrator who
reports it. * * * Peabody, as an educated town professional, reinforces
the distinction between his own speech and Anse's by stylizing Anse's
country pronunciation; other narrators, like Tull or Darl, transcribe
"it" instead of "hit" in Anse's speech because they inhabit the same
dialectic level as Anse, whereas Peabody is the "superior" speaker. In
his frustration with Anse and his disdain for Anse's laziness, Peabody
parodies (deliberately, we can assume) Anse's country talk. The

mimetic consistency of imitated dialect here (as elsewhere in Faulkner) gives way to the need to establish a sociolinguistic hierarchy, which in turn helps define Peabody's expressive identity.

The illusion of speech is strong in Peabody's narrative partly because of its colloquial mannerisms. Faulkner simultaneously augments his voice with passages that contain hints of the allusive intertextual oratorical voice, either because of the diction or because they propound general ideas attributable to an authoritative "literary" presence more than to Dr. Peabody the fictional character. "Like our rivers, our land: opaque, slow, violent; shaping and creating the life of man in its implacable and brooding image." Such a description does not so much violate the verisimilitude of Peabody's verbal capabilities (as passages in Darl's and Vardaman's sections do) as it intensifies the expressive purpose Peabody must serve through his voice.

There are hints, too, of Peabody's internal, psychic voice. His colloquial narration turns subtly into interior monologue in two ways. First, past-tense narration switches to present tense in the course of the section. The recounting of events gives over to the recording of impressions as he experiences them. The opening recounts the past, as Peabody tells what he thought "when Anse finally sent for me." When he arrives at the Bundren farm ("When I reach the spring") the tense shifts in accord with his arrival in the family's presence. Not only does the present-tense narration indicate more immediate "mental" experience than does the conventional story-telling past tense, but also the *shift* in itself signifies Peabody's emergence from an objectively distant posture vis-à-vis the Bundrens into a concerned if frustrated sharing of their experience of Addie's death. * * * Peabody's narration also turns into psychic voice in his attention to Addie's eyes and to Vardaman, that "durn little tyke." Peabody notes, in highly impressionistic imagery, how Addie looks at him "like [her eyes] touch us, not with sight or sense, but like the stream from a hose touches you, the stream at the instant of impact as dissociated from the nozzle as though it had never been there" (25–27). Peabody reacts to Vardaman throughout the section, always aware of him (though only once referring to him by name), always noting his whereabouts in each shift of scene, even though focusing his conscious attention elsewhere. "The boy overtakes us"; "She looks at me then at the boy"; "He and Anse are on the porch when I come out"; "The durn little tyke is sitting on the top step." Peabody senses what later sections will bear out, that Vardaman regards him with terrified loathing because he believes Peabody's arrival has caused his mother's death.

The transcription of excessive dialect, the hints of an augmenting oratorical voice, and the record of interior impression all disturb the surface of mimetic voice in Peabody's section to place him appropriately within the cluster of voices weaving their self-referring discourse around the dying Addie. The novel sustains its strategy of mixing voices throughout, though the tactics vary considerably, depending always on a speaker's relation to the Bundrens and to Addie's death. Tull, for example, like Peabody, occupies an intermediate position between the outside observers, who relate only one incident in the funeral journey, and the family members; his expressive identity reflects a shifting degree of closeness to the Bundrens, a modulating participation in their acts and emotions.

Unlike Peabody, Tull shares the Bundrens' country white dialect, both in his narration and when he quotes the Bundrens' speech. Though highly colloquial, Tull's speech shows little eye dialect, and only dialect words like "holp" or "mought" reflect a sound different from Peabody's more standard town speech. That Faulkner revised most of the extreme dialect out of the novel suggests his careful arrangement of relative dialect levels, as he reduced the stylizing effect of dialect and retained only words like "ere" or "a-hammering" that would be heard even by a speaker with the same speech habits.

Tull's expressive identity, therefore, unlike Peabody's, does not differ from the Bundrens' in speech sounds or in the class distinctions implicit in dialect. His closeness to the family varies instead along a temporal axis reflected in verb tense. Faulkner manipulates the grammatical relationship between the time of enunciation and the time of the reported action in order to modulate Tull's physical and emotional involvement in Addie's death. Shifts between past and present narrative tenses signal concomitant changes in the intensity of Tull's involvement: when Tull is actually with the Bundrens, both physically and psychically, he employs present tense; when he is, or feels, separated from them, when he thinks about the family as from a distance, as an observer instead of a participant, he uses past tense. In his first section Tull sits on the Bundrens' porch waiting with Anse: he is present and involved, though like Anse he passively sits. In his second section, however, when at home and thinking about Vardaman, he tries to comprehend the boy's actions more than he participates in them. He looks back on what happened the night Addie died, remembering and puzzling over the elemental injustice of Vardaman's grief. In this section Faulkner keeps Tull physically as well as temporally separated from events at the Bundren farm by bringing him back home ("It was long a-past midnight when we drove the last nail, and almost dust-dawn when I got back home and taken the team out and got back in bed" (42) before letting him tell us that Vardaman drilled holes in the coffin to let his mother breathe. None of the narration in this section occurs while Tull is at the Bundrens'. His thoughts, more than Vardaman's actions, constitute the real subject of his talk, so he renders these in a gnomic present ("Now and then a fellow gets to thinking. About all the sorrow and afflictions in this world" (41), while he recapitulates events in past tense.

* * *

* * * Tull's voice generates time in its own expressive terms, not in terms of the needs of the plot; time becomes a *product* of Tull's voice more than something external that his discourse reflects or imitates in his choice of tense. Tull's third section, the funeral, begins with a brief exchange rendered in past tense with Armstid and Quick about Peabody's team, then shifts to present as Tull's attention focuses on Anse ("Anse meets us at the door"). Present narration continues until Tull describes the coffin, and how the women laid Addie in it backward; the drawing of the "clock-shape" calls sudden attention to Tull's account as retrospective and even as *written*, for one cannot say ⬡. When Tull's attention turns to Cash, and he tries to console him about the way the women have ruined his work, he continues to report the talk of the other men. His attention to Cash pushes that talk into the background, however, so Faulkner puts the voices in italics and removes speaker identification, as Tull is not listening closely enough to note who speaks which lines. Tull then reports the funeral itself, but only as it affects him, that is, as he feels the power of phenomenal voice:

> In the house *the women begin to sing.* . . . *The song ends*; the voices quaver away with a rich and dying fall. *Whitfield begins.* His voice is bigger than him. It's like they are not the same. It's like he is one, and his voice is one. . . . *Somebody in the house begins to cry.* It sounds like her eyes and voice were turned back inside her. . . . *Whitfield stops at last. The women sing again.* In the thick air it's like their voices come out of the air, flowing together and on in the sad, comforting tunes. When they cease it's like they hadn't gone away. . . . *Then they finish.* . . .
> *On the way home Cora is still singing.* (53; my italics)

This passage records movement through time marked by the voices Tull hears (the women singing, Whitfield eulogizing, Cora still singing) instead of by minutes and hours; time passes in the presence of voice. Tull's impression of the funeral becomes the time "span" here, with each change in voice (the sentences I have emphasized) serving as a temporal marker. * * *

The italicized portion that follows the description of the funeral has a detached quality similar to that of the italicized dialogue going on in the background when Tull talks to Cash. The attempt to persuade Anse to get started for Jefferson seems more half remembered than immediately experienced by Tull, as if only fragments remained in his awareness. The past tense helps create this impression, as does the jumbled sequence within the passage (Tull refers to Anse as still waiting after he tells us the boys have returned home and the family has started for Jefferson). Only bits and pieces have stuck in Tull's memory; these are all we get because these suffice to indicate the incident's importance to Tull. The past tense in the final portion of the funeral section, when the Tulls find Vardaman fishing at the slough, not only creates a slight mental distancing from the farm and funeral (the Tulls are now a mile away), but it also is consistent with the past-tense narration in Tull's second section in which he puzzles over Vardaman's behavior. Tull certainly experiences Vardaman in the immediacy of the moment, and thus we might expect present-tense narration, but the boy assumes a significance in the expressive voicing of Tull's consciousness almost always as someone pondered rather than someone faced in the present instant without time for speculation.

Peabody's section exhibits a change in tense from past to present concomitant with Peabody's arrival at the Bundren farm. Faulkner extends this tactic in Tull's fourth section when Tull joins the Bundrens at the river. By beginning with past and changing to present tense, Faulkner causes the past to continue into the present; what was and what is blend into a single progression of Tull's enunciation. The movement in enunciatory time tracks Tull's gradual passage from his own cotton field to the riverside, from the moments prior to his joining the family to his sharing their examination and crossing of the flood-swollen waters. The opening sentence states in simple, definite past tense that he rode from his field to the river: "After they passed I taken the mule out and looped up the trace chains and followed" (71). When he arrives and first describes the Bundrens looking at the river, Tull uses more indefinite verb forms that depict a continuing past time: "was setting," "was watching," "was looking" (71). And before talk commences in the present tense, Tull describes the river in a frequentative tense that refers to repeated action going on in the past and carrying on into the future: "Sometimes a log *would* get shoved over the jam and float on, rolling and turning, and we *could* watch it go on to where the ford used to be. It *would* slow up" (71, my italics). Only then does true present-tense narration begin: " 'But that don't show nothing,' I say. . . . We watch the log. The gal is looking at me again" (71). The narrating discourse makes no simple jump from past to present but traces out a controlled progression in enunciation, in voiced experience, from past, through continuous past, to frequentative past, to present tense.

In his fifth section Tull crosses the submerged bridge with Anse, Dewey Dell, and Vardaman, and because of his direct participation in the action we might expect present-tense narration. But Tull vocalizes this moment more as an observer than as a participant: "Like it couldn't be me here, because I'd have had better sense than to done what I just done. And when I looked back and saw the other bank and saw my mule standing there where I used to be and knew that I'd have to get back there someway, I knew it just couldn't be. . . . When I looked back at my mule it was like he was one of these here spy-glasses and I could look at him standing there and see all the broad land and my house sweated outen it" (79–80). Tull's last section (88–89) brings Cora's judgment of Anse, plus Tull's rejection of that judgment, to bear on the events at the river. The Tulls look back on what Vernon has just been through, so they use past tense. The final portion of the section, after the brief dialogue with Cora, describes an action in a vivid, narrative past tense since this experience in Tull's memory demonstrates the irrelevance of Cora's contradictory explanation for the incredible scene Tull has witnessed—Jewel holding the wagon alone against the current, saving his mother (as she predicted) from the flood waters.

*   *   *

Faulkner manipulates the grammar of represented speech in order to symbolize consciousness—not merely to express it, but to constitute it out of voice. Faulkner maneuvers conventional mimetic voice into providing material for states of mind. This is particularly evident in how narrators report the speech of other characters: divergence from standard narrative practice in reporting dialogue signals a variance in the narrator's attitude, stance, and subliminal position vis-à-vis others. Not only does a character possess mimetic voice in his or her own right as a narrator, but each narrating character creates the illusion of others' speech in how he or she reports it. So the *creation* of the illusion of speech becomes an act undertaken by characters and indicative of each narrator's unique position in the verbal world—that verbal world analogous to the fictional world of the farm and Addie's death. This tactic constitutes [a] double disturbance of mimetic voice's verisimilitude: both the narrator's speech and the quoted speech sound (and sometimes look) unconventional.

Voice in *As I Lay Dying* also interrogates the metaphysics of *individual* consciousness, revealing characters' secret selves by immersing them in a *communal* discourse, making their private thoughts a function of how they hear, respond to, and render each other's speech. Ultimately, *As I Lay Dying* depicts a community of voices more than a series of isolated souls. * * * Even as voices emerge from obsessed and grieving individual minds, they remain in crucial ways still a part of the Bundren family and the broader Yoknapatawpha region. This is not at all to deny that Faulkner in some sections conveys his characters'

"secret obsessions, bringing into the light of language all the unspoken obscurity seething within [their] tortured mind[s]."[2] Rather it is to
assert that the text expresses even the most private of concerns in the
disharmony of a discourse shared with others. Voice is personal, yet
also separated from person, to be heard always in relation to others:
* * * The illusion of speech eludes us, as one moment we hear a character named Darl saying "I reckon" in the idiom of his region, in
another we hear a narrator named Darl comparing Addie's coffin to a
"cubistic bug." Indeed, consciousness itself in *As I Lay Dying* often
seems a matter more of communal awareness than of psychological
idiosyncracies—and this is perhaps to say that, rather than being
revealed by interior speech, consciousness *equals* speech used by and
shared by the narrating figures. The sharing is evident at the level of
dialect, as the closer the speaker is to Addie's death the fewer dialect
distinctions his or her speech evinces in relation to others also close
to Addie. The sharing is evident, too, on the level of imagery. Not only
do the characters perceive the same phenomena, they employ the
same metaphors to describe them: four different speakers liken the
sound of Cash's sawing to snoring—though each couches the image
in a slightly different manner: "It sounds like snoring" (Cora 6);
"Cash's saw snores steadily" (Peabody 27); "the saw begins to snore
again" (Darl 29); "the saw sounds like it is asleep" (Vardaman 39).
The metaphor's articulation does not individualize the speaker's consciousness so much as it individualizes a manner of talking: mimetic
voice moves gracefully between the ineffable uniqueness of individual consciousness and the communal language. * * * Often individuality manifests itself only in talk, in how one speaker expresses
something, not in any content of the psyche. Tull's and Darl's
descriptions of the flood-swollen river show a shared awareness rendered unique and appropriate to each only by mimetic voice, the illusion of the speech through which the image is expressed:

> The water was cold. It was thick, like slush ice. Only it kind of
> lived. One part of you knowed it was just water, the same thing
> that had been running under this same bridge for a long time,
> yet when them logs would come spewing up outen it, you were
> not surprised, like they was a part of water, of the waiting and
> the threat. (Tull 79)

> Before us the thick dark current runs. It talks up to us in a mur-
> mur become ceaseless and myriad, the yellow surface dimpled
> monstrously into fading swirls travelling along the surface for
> an instant, silent, impermanent and profoundly significant, as
> though just beneath the surface something huge and alive

waked for a moment of lazy alertness out of and into light slumber again. (Darl 82)

The verbal images of the river as alive and threatening, as well as some aspects of syntax, are all virtually the same here—yet how different the passages "sound." The differences can be isolated only with reference to imitated talk, to mimetic voice.

The presence of public stories further enhances the sense of a shared communal discourse that serves to constitute character. The speakers farthest distant from the Bundrens narrate, appropriately, in conventional past tense with no incursion into present. Samson, Moseley, Armstid, and MacGowan sound like colloquial storytellers speaking in varieties of Yoknapatawpha dialect appropriate to their stations—the farmers Samson and Armstid speak in country white idiom ("durn," "sholy," "outen," etc.), while Moseley and MacGowan, the two druggists, are town colloquial speakers. * * * All four sections exhibit strong features of vocalization, as if told orally, without any trappings of interiorization except that no audience is explicitly dramatized. * * * All begin in oral narrative fashion with phrases that establish the time and place of the events. Samson keeps trying to remember the name of the MacCallum twin he was talking to ("Rafe's twin; that one it was" [64]), and Moseley accounts for how he learned part of the story ("It was Albert told me about the rest of it" [117]). These anecdotal touches enhance the public quality of the outsiders' narratives, placing them at some remove from the family, expressing varieties of the community's accumulated oral lore. We can readily imagine their tales being told and retold, passed along from farmhouse to store to village throughout the county.

By both enhancing and challenging conventional illusions of speech, by defining "person" as participant in an ever-changing and hearable choir of voices, and yet by simultaneously disrupting expected correlations between voice and person, As I Lay Dying recalls us to the problematic status of verbal representation in general and of mimetic voice in particular. As I Lay Dying signifies the existential power of voice and its uncertainty and flux. Addie Bundren's central monologue * * * expresses the frustration of a life within language. * * * To Addie, words are meaningless, empty sounds that the weak substitute for active confrontation with the forces of the real world. She has lived her life as a desperate struggle to unite her private self with the inaccessible outside world; she has sought to push herself into the elemental flux of life, to mingle her own life force with "the wild blood boiling along the earth." She has sought some ultimate and final acknowledgment from mankind and the universe itself, some recognition that she truly does exist. As a school teacher, before marrying Anse, Addie would whip her pupils to make them feel her in the most private reaches of their souls where her words could never reach: "And I would think with each blow of the switch: Now you are aware of me! Now I am something in your secret and selfish life, who have marked your blood with my own for ever and ever" (98). It is this kind of intense recognition that Addie wants to give and to receive by accepting a man; she wants someone to batter his way (like Donne's three-personed God)[3] into her soul, to break down the walls that keep her separated from "the terrible blood" she can feel at night in the spring when the geese fly overhead. When such a fusion with nature's vital forces or with some other human being fails to come to her, Addie grows bitter. Having married Anse in hopes of a violent commingling, she discovers, ironically, that the attempt to fuse herself with life has intruded on her own selfish privacy by causing her to bear a child.

Addie blames words for her dissatisfaction and for her failure to perceive, before she married and gave birth, the emptiness of Anse Bundren's version of life. She feels tricked into the sterile void between the desired mystical union with life and the violation of herself that such a union entails. Anse, instead of sweeping her headlong into the "doing," deceived her and made her feel "that living was terrible." She realizes that "words are no good; that words dont ever fit [even] what they are trying to say at. When [Cash] was born I knew that motherhood was invented by someone who had to have a word for it because the ones that had the children didn't care whether there was a word for it or not" (99). Although she accepts Cash as her punishment for ever believing in Anse, she cannot excuse Darl, the second child: "Then I found I had Darl. At first I would not believe it. Then I believed that I would kill Anse. It was as though he had tricked me, hidden within a word like within a paper screen and struck me in the back through it" (99–100). Words (like "love," perhaps) have kept Addie from ever feeling genuinely alive: "I would think how words go straight up in a thin line, quick and harmless, and how terribly doing goes along the earth, clinging to it, so that after a while the two lines are too far apart for the same person to straddle from one to the other" (100). And so Addie takes Rev. Whitfield as a lover because loving him is purely and simply a deed, without words, and through her action she and he can "shape and coerce the terrible blood to the forlorn echo of the dead word high in the air" (101).

Addie's own harsh and urgent talking denies that language can help one deal with one's human condition, that words can ever bridge the gap between oneself and the world outside. Addie's *voice*, however, the voice of a corpse, demonstrates the irony of human

---

3. From his Holy Sonnet 14, "Batter my heart, three-personed God" [*Editor*].

existence in language, for by voicing her need and her deed Addie belies her own claim for "reality" over "words." Nowhere is Faulkner's comic-tragic irony stronger. In taking Rev. Whitfield, a master of the hypocritical word, as her lover, Addie gives in to language, to "hearing the dark land talking of God's love and His beauty and His sin; hearing the dark voicelessness in which the words are the deeds." For the novel bestows no identity outside of voice. The text mocks Addie's metaphor of "the land talking the voiceless speech" as she speaks it in her monologue bracketed between Cora Tull's and Whitfield's sanctimonious hypocrisy.

Speech betrays Addie Bundren doubly, and more than she could ever know or say, by enshrining her subjective "self" in a mere dead echo of a voice. The transcendent subject, that presence we call consciousness, is here, as it often is in Faulkner, deconstructed by its own verbal devices. Voice, imitated in expressive written speech, releases subjectivity for the reader's scrutiny and sympathy. Yet voice empties or drains consciousness as well, replacing its energy with the hardened shell of imitated discourse. Faulkner knew, of course, that voice creates character—the subject—but he also knew that voice erases transcendental subjectivity for the sake of its own production. For Addie Bundren, to speak is to fail to live or do; to speak is to fail to exist, to become an empty shape that cannot fill its own lack; it is to go mad, like the voluble Darl. By entering into the novel's discourse, Addie joins the chorus of voices "fumbling at the deeds like orphans," and thereby reveals that her deed, her "salvation" was itself "just words too." By giving Addie speech Faulkner at one and the same time creates her in voice and undercuts her voiced word. Dead as a person, speaking to us only from what Beckett's Molloy calls "the tranquility of decomposition,"[4] Addie is truly a "dead sound," ironically given life, as are all the fiction's characters, only in her voice. Dewey Dell unwittingly but aptly sums up her mother's fate when she says that Darl "told me ma is going to die without words" (17).

DOREEN FOWLER

Matricide and the Mother's Revenge: *As I Lay Dying*[†]

The phrase, "As I lay dying," seems to have haunted Faulkner. Not only did he use it as the title of his novel about the Bundrens, but

---

4. Samuel Beckett, *Molloy*, trans. Patrick Bowles (New York: Grove Press, 1959), pp. 28–29.
† Courtesy of *The Faulkner Journal* 4:1&2 (Fall 1988/Spring 1989). Copyright 1991. Reprinted with permission.

years earlier he had applied it to a fragment which he would later recast and publish as "Spotted Horses." When questioned about the source of the title, Faulkner quoted a line from *The Odyssey* which occurs as Agamemnon, in Hades, relates to Odysseus the manner of his death: "As I lay dying, the woman with a dog's eyes would not close for me my eyelids as I descended into Hades." As for the relevance of these words to Faulkner's novel, scholars have frequently observed that Agamemnon's speech stresses the indignity of death, a theme certainly evident in *As I Lay Dying*.

I propose that Faulkner titled his novel *As I Lay Dying* because this allusion to Agamemnon's murder evokes matricide and a mother's revenge. Agamemnon's murder, described briefly in *The Odyssey*, is dramatized in a later text, the first play of Aeschylus's trilogy, the *Oresteia*, where Agamemnon is murdered by his wife, Clytemnestra, to avenge the death of their eldest daughter, Iphigenia, sacrificed to the gods for a wind to sail to Troy. As the eldest daughter, Iphigenia is a mother-surrogate; and, when Clytemnestra kills Agamemnon, she avenges her own foreshadowed death, which follows when Orestes repeats his father's act and slays Clytemnestra. In *As I Lay Dying*, Clytemnestra reappears in the form of Addie Bundren, another murdered mother who demands a price for her death.

According to Luce Irigaray, the myth of the murder of the mother, and not the murder of the father as Freud claims, is the founding myth of western culture.[1] In *Le Corps-à-corps avec la mère*, Irigaray contends that when Freud in *Totem and Taboo* writes that human culture is founded on the murder of the father by the primitive horde of his sons, Freud forgets—or represses—an older murder, the murder of the mother, which is represented by the myth of the murder of Clytemnestra by her son, Orestes. Aeschylus's trilogy dramatizes a myth found in virtually all of the texts of our culture: the death or absence of the mother makes possible the construction of patriarchal culture. In Aeschylus, Iphigenia must die so that her father can lead his army into battle.

* * *

In *Bearing the Word*, Margaret Homans also finds that this disturbing myth is central to all Western culture; she explains that the Freudian theory of the stages and processes of human development is based on Freud's reading of classical myths, in particular the myth of Oedipus, and that Lacanian theory, which derives from Freud, is a psychoanalytical retelling of the myth to which our culture had

---

1. Luce Irigary, *Le Corps-à-corps avec la mère* (Ottawa: Pleine Lune, 1981).

long subscribed—that the mother's death is the price of patriarchal culture.[2]

In Lacanian terms, at first all children are engaged in an imaginary dyadic relation with the mother in which they find themselves whole.[3] * * * For the child to acquire language, to enter the realm of the symbolic, the child must become aware of difference, for, as Saussure explains, a sign has meaning only because of its difference from other signs.[4] In other words, for the child to be a speaking subject he / she must separate from the mother and repress the desire for union with the mother. To quote from Toril Moi's useful paraphrase of Lacan, "The speaking subject that says 'I am' is in fact saying 'I am he (she) who has lost something' and the loss suffered is the imaginary identity with the mother and the world."[5] The appearance of the father drives the desire for original unity with the mother underground, opening up the unconscious. According to Lacan, only the repression of this desire, only the loss of the mother, makes possible desire, law, language, and the civilized order. In Lacanian theory, then, as in myth, the murder of the mother is constructed as a positive step toward establishing identity.

* * * I propose to show that in *As I Lay Dying* Faulkner creates a feminine voice that * * * issues a challenge to paternal structures of meaning. * * * Addie Bundren rebels against a patriarchal order that mandates the mother's death: she rejects her father's teaching that "the reason for living was to get ready to stay dead a long time" (98), and locates the meaning of existence in the body and the living world: "I believed that the reason was the duty to the alive, to the terrible blood, the red bitter flood boiling through the land" (101). With these words, Addie sets herself up in opposition to a life-repressive social order. Whereas patriarchal law identifies life with death, the origin in the mother with the end, Addie lives for "the alive," for the fluid, chaotic, elemental existence that the father's law would stifle. She lies awake at night "hearing the dark land talking the voiceless speech" (101); she acknowledges the material world, naming her daughter, Dewey Dell, for the land.

As opposed to patriarchal culture which repudiates what Lacan calls the Imaginary, a state in which the boundaries of the self are

2. Margaret Homans, *Bearing the Word: Language and Female Experience in Nineteenth-Century Women's Writing,* (Chicago: University of Chicago Press, 1986).
3. In this article Fowler only once refers to a specific moment in the work of the French psychoanalytic theorist Jacques Lacan (1901–1981), but in her later *Faulkner: The Return of the Repressed* (Charlottesville and London: University Press of Virginia, 1997) she draws upon both *The Four Fundamental Concepts of Psychoanalysis* (ed. Jacques-Alain Miller, trans. Alan Sheridan. New York: Norton, 1981) and the 1977 selection from his work called *Ecrits* (trans. Alan Sheridan. New York: Norton) [*Editor*].
4. Ferdinand de Saussure (1857–1913), Swiss linguist whose work provides a foundation for much twentieth-century literary theory [*Editor*].
5. Toril Moi, *Sexual/Textual Politics: Feminist Literary Theory* (London: Methuen, 1985), p. 99.

lost and all is one, Addie embraces the Imaginary. With the birth of her first child, Addie knows "that living was terrible and that this was the answer to it" (99). In childbearing, Addie experiences an immersion of self in the other; one with Cash, she says that "the land . . . was now of [her] blood and flesh" (100).

The sense of completeness that Addie knows as a mother is readily explained by Nancy Chodorow's theory of maternity. In *The Reproduction of Mothering*, Chodorow argues that a woman's entry into the symbolic is different from a man's, that whereas the son is threatened with castration if he continues his union with the mother, the daughter is not; that the daughter instead identifies with the mother, and she does not enter the symbolic as wholeheartedly or as exclusively as the son.[6] Moreover, the daughter, like the son, longs to recover the lost unity with the mother, and for the daughter this is done by becoming a mother herself and recreating with her child the lost tie she experienced with the mother. The woman yearns for babies to recreate the original unity and presence. This, then, is what Addie experiences when she bears her first-born, Cash: "I knew that it had been, not that my aloneness had to be violated over and over each day, but that it had never been violated until Cash came. Not even by Anse in the nights" (99).

Given that Addie embraces a pre-oedipal period when no difference exists between self and world, it is not surprising that both she and her daughter-double are consistently identified with matter. * * * [T]o Jewel, Addie's hands look like "two of them roots dug up" (10); according to Peabody, beneath the quilt Addie's body is "no more than a bundle of rotten sticks" (26); and Darl scornfully describes Dewey Dell's breasts as "those mammalian ludicrosities which are the horizons and valleys of the earth" (94). And precisely because the maternal is identified with the material, patriarchal law denies the mother's existence. Both this identification with matter and this denial are implied in Addie's statement that she "would hate [her father] for having ever planted [her]" (98). If Addie's father "planted" her, then Addie's mother is the land, in which the seeds grow. But the mother herself is never named. She is the repressed referent, the origin that imbues all symbols with meaning, but is herself absent. Like the connection to matter, the connection to the mother is not spoken, and so Addie's mother is referred to only with a metaphor, an allusion to the land.

The same denial of the mother as matrix is inscribed in "The Eumenides," the last play of the *Oresteia*. At the conclusion of Aeschylus's drama, Orestes is tried for matricide and, although he

6. Nancy Chodorow, *The Reproduction of Mothering: Psychoanalysis and the Sociology of Gender* (Berkeley: University of California Press, 1978).

has cut his mother's throat, he is found not guilty of a crime on the grounds that "the mother is no parent of that which is called her child, but only nurse of the new-planted seed that grows. The parent is he who mounts."[7] Here also the mother is both identified with the earth and denied; in the words of Apollo, "no parent." Only the father is acknowledged.

The attempt to assert the primacy of the father and to dematerialize the world with the mother is the central project of patriarchal culture in *As I Lay Dying*. But nature continually threatens to deconstruct the male symbolic order and to return it to an original unity and presence. For example, at Addie's funeral, the farmers discuss the rain that will wash out of the earth the seed they have labored to plant.

> *It's a fact. Washed clean outen the ground it will be. Seems like something is always happening to it.*
>
> *Course it does. That's why it's worth anything. If nothing didn't happen and everybody made a big crop, do you reckon it would be worth the raising?*
>
> *Well, I be durn if I like to see my work washed outen the ground, work I sweat over.*
>
> *It's a fact. A fellow wouldn't mind seeing it washed up if he could just turn on the rain himself.* (52; italics in original)

Their seed has been swept away: nothing has been made of their creative efforts. Even more important, however, the comment of one farmer indicates that it is precisely this "nothing" that imbues the symbolic order with meaning. "*If nothing didn't happen . . . , do you reckon it would be worth raising?*" "Nothing" is the absent center, the loss of selfhood associated with the dyadic unity with the mother; and, without this "nothing" their signifiers would have no meaning.

Addie, like the land, is that "nothing," that loss of difference, which is the denied literal behind all signifiers. After bearing Cash and Darl, she says "I was three now" (100). As her name suggests, Addie is not single, separate, and distinct; she is a plurality that threatens difference, the difference upon which language, culture, and authority are established. For this reason, time and time again in *As I Lay Dying* Addie is erased and replaced by a symbol, and each erasure reenacts the original separation from the mother, the cutting of the umbilical cord, leaving behind an absence. Addie recalls this original separation from Jewel: "With Jewel—I lay by the lamp, holding up my own head, watching him cap and suture it before he breathed" (102). The physician, an agent of patriarchal law, cuts the umbilical cord, severing "Jewel—I," and then he sutures the rupture

---

7. Aeschylus, *The Eumenides*, trans. Richmond Lattimore (Chicago: University of Chicago Press, 1953), p. 158.

left in Jewel by his mother's absence. Significantly, the word "suture" is a signal term in film theory and psychoanalysis. In the context of Lacanian film criticism, "suture" is the supplementation of an absence, the joining of a gap by representation. Jewel has been severed from his mother, and the stitches cover over, represent, what has been lost—fusion with the mother.

Like the stitches which shore up the gap in Jewel, language is also "a shape to fill a lack" (99), another substitute for the loss of the original unity and presence. For good reason, then, Addie hates words. Addie recognizes what Saussure has pointed out, the arbitrariness of language, a system of signs that substitutes for an absent referent. She understands that

> words are no good; that words dont ever fit even what they are trying to say at. When he [Cash] was born I knew that motherhood was invented by someone who had to have a word for it because the ones that had the children didn't care whether there was a word for it or not. I knew that fear was invented by someone that had never had the fear; pride, who never had the pride. (99)

More, Addie hates language because it is based on separation and difference—"we had to use one another by words like spiders dangling by their mouths from a beam, swinging and twisting and never touching"—and she whips the school children to abolish this distance and difference: "and . . . only through the blows of the switch could my blood and their blood flow as one stream" (99).

Lacan states that "there is no woman but excluded by . . . the nature of words."[8] More simply stated, to become a speaking subject, to enter the realm of the symbolic, the child must renounce his/her desire for the mother and generate substitutes for her that are permissible within the Law of the Father. Accordingly, in *As I Lay Dying*, Vardaman, Jewel and Cash each erases the mother and substitutes for her a sign—a fish, a horse, and a coffin.

Vardaman's choice of a symbol, a fish, suggests clearly the elemental threat that is identified with the mother. Fish inhabit water, and, according to Mircea Eliade, are infused with its power to return the speaking subject to an original formlessness.[9] Given this association of water and the fish with the power of nature to threaten the symbolic order, when Vardaman kills the fish, he is asserting his control over elemental life: he aims "to show it to ma," as evidence of his manhood, his ability to master the physical world. He has plumbed the depths of the water, the source, and captured and killed its inhabitant, emblem of the fluid, transforming powers of nature. Because these

8. Jacques Lacan, *Encore: Le seminaire livre XX* (Paris: Seuil, 1975), p. 68.
9. Mircea Eliade, *Patterns in Comparative Religion*, trans. Rosemary Sheed (1958), (New York: New American Library, 1974), p. 207.

powers are also identified with the mother, the slaying of the fish ritually reenacts the slaying of the mother, the emergence of the speaking
subject. Addie, a reminder of the original presence and loss of self,
like the fish, must die. Her absence gives meaning to the symbolic
order; in this way, like the fish which is "cooked and et," she sustains
the male symbolic order.

Jewel erases his mother and replaces her with his horse, or, in Darl's
words, "Jewel's mother is a horse" (58). This substitution allows Jewel
to satisfy his conflicting feelings for his mother. On the one hand,
when, at 15, Jewel purchases a horse by doing without sleep—
cleaning up Lon Quick's forty acres of new ground at night after
working all day—Jewel is denying the body, and this denial formalizes
his assertion of the father's authority and law over the material world
and the maternal body. On the other hand, as Cash and Darl suspect
when they notice Jewel slipping out at night, Jewel is also satisfying
his desire for a woman, but not by fornicating with a local girl as Cash
and Darl at first think; Jewel is satisfying his desire for his mother
with the horse he works to buy. Upon the horse he can project his
conflicting feelings for the mother's body. He caresses the horse
and beats it into submission alternately, expressing the contradictory
desires to return to an original wholeness and to separate the self
from the world and assert the authority of the father's law.

Addie is distanced and replaced yet again by the coffin which Cash
builds to "her measure and weight" (52). Like Vardaman's fish and
Jewel's horse, the coffin, which contains Addie's corpse, is meant to
enclose and dispose of the threat to conscious patriarchal authority
and identity posed by the mother's body. The building of the coffin
externalizes the struggle between male symbolic authority and the
fluid, chaotic world of matter. Cash carefully calculates all physical
forces exerted by Addie's corpse in order to make the coffin "balance."
The balance Cash is trying to achieve recreates the ever fragile and
precarious construction of male authority over the natural world, a
delicate equilibrium which is particularly threatened by motherhood.
It is motherhood—symbolized by Addie's reversed, head-to-foot position in the coffin like a fetus in the mother's womb, a position imposed
by "them durn women" (52)—that disturbs the "balance," and reveals
that the father's law is always on the brink of collapsing back into the
world.

Each of these erasures and figurations of Addie thinly disguises
a desire for her death. The repressed, unspeakable meaning behind
these substitutions occasionally erupts in the text. Watching Cash
build the coffin for his mother's corpse, Jewel bursts out, "Good God
do you want to see her in it" (10). Similarly Darl invades Dewey Dell's
"secret self" and confronts her with her own buried desire: "You want
her to die so you can get to town: is that it?" (24). In fact, because
patriarchal culture is built on the death of the mother, secretly each

one of them does desire her death. Like the vultures that trail Addie's corpse, her family members would feed on her dead body. Only with her death can they enter the symbolic order, emblemized by Jefferson. The trip to town becomes an extended metaphor for their entry into the symbolic, patriarchal identity, and subjecthood. To acquire language, law, and culture, Addie must become an "it" buried in a hole that is "filled and covered" (137).

Addie's revenge on her family for this denial is to represence the repressed literal, her body and the material world. At one level, Addie's funeral journey reverses women's subordination within language. If women are the repressed referent that imbues all forms with meaning or, in Homans's terms, if women are made "to bear the word," with her funeral journey, Addie inverts this order and makes her family bear the literal, carrying her body overland, retrieving her from the flooded river and the burning barn. But Addie's funeral journey not only acknowledges her body and its death, it also asserts the value of the material world by objectifying how the symbolic order depends on the literal. Addie literally delivers from the original formlessness Cash and Jewel, the children who attempt to represence her body even though it means defying the law of the father and risking the annihilation of the self. In particular, Addie rescues and is rescued by Jewel, her illegitimate son, whose very existence, because he is her child and not Anse's, exposes the lie of the biological primacy of the father and affirms what culture would deny— that the mother is. "And Jewel is," Darl says, "so Addie Bundren must be" (47).

For example, crossing the river, which is swollen like the body of a pregnant woman, externalizes the attempt of patriarchal authority to subdue chaotic elemental forces identified with the mother. In these threatening waters, boundaries between human and animal and between human and material collapse: Jewel's horse "moan[s] and groan[s] like a natural man" (89); Cash, spewed up on the bank, looks like "a old bundle of clothes" (89); and the current against their bodies feels "like hands molding and prodding at the very bones" (91). The flooded river, then, as Darl observes, is the "myriad original motion," which threatens to dissolve the temporary "clotting" (94), which is the self. The bridge over the river functions like language; like "a shape to fill a lack," it attempts to bridge the gap over the repressed physical world, and, by walking over the half-sunk bridge, Anse, Dewey Dell, Vardaman, and Tull avoid—repress—the transformative powers of nature. Darl, Jewel, and Cash, on the other hand, enter the water with Addie; and when Cash, who, as the eldest son, is an avatar of the father, fastens the rope to the wagon and hands one end to Darl and the other to Jewel, he is symbolically reconnecting the severed umbilical cord. Thus as they enter the flooded river, they are all three ritually immersed, returned to an original formlessness that preceded the emergence of the subject.

The log, on which "a long gout of foam hangs like the beard of an old man or a goat" (86) and which Cora calls "the hand of God" (88), figures the father, whose law decrees the denial of this loss of boundaries. When the log strikes the wagon and overturns it, "like it had been sent there to do a job and done it and went on" (88), its "job" is to enact the Law of the Father: the mother is to be obliterated and the son who refuses to relinquish the mother is threatened with castration and death. In his role as father, Cash attempts to enforce this law. He orders Darl to "[l]et the rope go" (86) and to "[j]ump clear" (86); and he unties the rope which connects Jewel to his mother, recreating the original separation of mother and child, the cutting of the umbilical cord.

In this reenactment of the primal repression of the mother, Darl obeys patriarchal law, drops the rope, severs the bond joining him to the mother, and allows her body to be submerged. Jewel, on the other hand, defies the father's law and risks the dissolution of the subject by recreating the original fusion with the maternal body. He reenters the flood, finds the wagon with Addie's coffin, and reties the rope that joins him to the mother. Cash's role is dual. In his role as father-surrogate, he attempts to cut the cord attaching Darl and Jewel to Addie; but, in his role as son, he clings to Addie's body as it is immersed in the primal substance, risking a return to the formlessness of preexistence.

The trial by water ends with the triumph of the elemental, "the alive," over the father's law. Addie's body is represented and the cut cord is reconnected. The rope, tied fast once again to the wagon containing Addie's body, signals a return to fusion with the mother and the world of matter, as Tull's metaphor for the taut rope seems to acknowledge: "Like it was a straight iron bar stuck into the bottom and us holding the end of it" (89).

Throughout the river episode, the value of the material world is asserted. When Addie's family members are engulfed by the furious current, they are saved from being swept away by the ford, "the hard earth" (79), "*the vain instants of solidity underfoot*" (85). It is the earth that defends their integrity; and the sons who value the literal emerge with their identities intact. For example, Jewel, who violates the father's law and reenters the "surging and heaving desolation" (86), returning to the mother and risking the dissolution of the self, is not reabsorbed into primal matter. Rather, as always, Jewel is "wooden" and "rigid" (105). The son who holds fast to the mother's body emerges unscathed, solid. Cash, who, in his role as father, orders the son to relinquish his bond to the mother, and, who, in his role as son, clings to the maternal body, is both punished and saved.

He emerges from the flooded river with his identity intact, borne on a substitute for Addie, Jewel's horse, but with a broken leg. Cash had attempted to divide the child from the mother's body, to assert difference, which is signified, according to Lacan by the phallus; and, for initiating the endless process of differentiation, a phallus-substitute, his leg, is broken. The broken leg symbolizes the power of the authentic to dismantle a patriarchal order which is defined by difference and exclusion.

While Jewel emerges with Addie and Cash surfaces with an Addie-substitute, Jewel's horse, Darl arises from this ritual immersion empty-handed. His empty hands objectify that he has no attachment to his mother to deny. Unlike his brothers who have severed the bond to the mother and covered the gap with a symbol—the coffin, the horse, the fish—Darl has no substitute for Addie. As Darl recognizes when he says, "I cannot love my mother because I have no mother" (55), long before he could renounce his mother, Addie renounced him; and, without a mother to deny and to replace, he cannot say "I am": "I dont know what I am. I dont know if I am or not" (46). The speaking subject defines itself as separate from the repressed other, the mother who is identified with the body and the world. Patriarchal identity depends on this separation and negation to assert difference. Without a mother to deny Darl is unbounded, fluid; he flows into others, invading their secret selves. In this way, by renouncing Darl, Addie concretizes how the patriarchal order depends on her. As Bleikaston has noted,[1] because Darl is not grounded in the authentic, with disturbing regularity, he observes images of uprooting, reflecting his own disembodied state: "Above the ceaseless surface they stand—trees, cane, vines—rootless, severed from the earth" (82). Without the mother to deny, patriarchal culture's symbols are not grounded in the literal and are as empty as Darl's hands as they emerge from the flood, emblem of the waters of the womb: *"empty out of the water emptying the water emptying away"* (87).

Barred from denying the original matrix, identified with the mother's body, Darl attempts to take possession of Addie and to negate her by setting fire to the barn and incinerating her corpse. The burning barn, like the flooded river, objectifies unleashed elemental forces that threaten to dismantle the patriarchal order; and, in the fire as in the flood, Jewel once again violates the father's law and risks the disintegration of the self by affirming the value of the literal. In the "dissolving" (127) barn, "enclosed in a thin nimbus of fire" (128), he calls to Darl to help him prevent their mother's body from being consumed: "For an instant he looks up and out at us through

---

1. Andre Bleikasten, *The Ink of Melancholy: Faulkner's Novels from* The Sound and the Fury *to* Light in August (Bloomington: Indiana University Press, 1990), p. 187.

the rain of burning hay like a portière of flaming beads, and I can see his mouth shape as he calls my name" (128). Darl, intent on denying and displacing the mother in accordance with patriarchal law, refuses, leaving Jewel singlehandedly to rescue Addie. As he works to represence Addie's corpse, Jewel is releasing his repressed desire for the mother's body and the material world; and, as an exponent of the unconscious, he incarnates his dark, repressed self and appears to be flat and one-dimensional, like a shadow, "running against the glare like that figure cut from tin" (127). In this trial by fire, like the trial by water, the child who acknowledges his forbidden yearning and embraces Addie's body is saved by Addie. Jewel rides out of the conflagration borne on Addie's corpse: "Without stopping it overends and rears again, pauses, then crashes slowly forward and through the curtain. This time Jewel is riding upon it, clinging to it until it crashes down and flings him forward and clear" (128). Addie translates into an actual event how the symbolic order depends on the literal: she literally carries Jewel out of the consuming flames. When Jewel escapes the burning barn carried on Addie's coffin and when Cash rides to Jefferson, emblem of the symbolic order, again borne on Addie's coffin, Addie objectifies how the symbolic is supported by the literal. Too late, even Darl admits his dependence on the maternal body: in the aftermath of the fire, Vardaman finds Darl weeping, lying on the box which contains Addie's corpse.

When Darl sets fire to the barn sheltering Addie's coffin, he simultaneously enforces patriarchal law and threatens it. On one hand, by attempting to incinerate Addie's corpse, Darl means "to hide her away from the sight of man" (124), in accordance with the Law of the Father. In his role as displaced father, Cash supports Darl's attempt to erase Addie— "And me being the oldest, and thinking already the very thing that he done: . . . how it would be God's blessing if He did take her outen our hands and get shut of her in some clean way" (134)—even as he recognizes that Jewel's efforts to represence her body violate patriarchal law: "and it seemed . . . that when Jewel worked so to get her outen the river, he was going against God in a way" (134). On the other hand, by burning [Gillespie's] barn Darl poses a threat to the father's authority. The barn is a cultural construct, and, by setting fire to it, Darl unleashes the power of nature to dismantle the patriarchal order. For this infraction, in Cash's judgment, Darl must be punished: "Because there just aint nothing justifies the deliberate destruction of what man has built with his own sweat and stored the fruit of his sweat into" (137).

With the burning of the barn, then, the folks who branded Darl "queer" at last have concrete evidence that he poses a threat to the social order. Rejected by Addie, he has never been able to establish the boundaries of self; unbounded, he embodies a lack of separation from the other and from the world. Ironically, because he has been rejected by the mother, he is like the mother; he too is a reminder of fusion with the encompassing material world. His eyes are "full of the land" (17); he sees and represences the literal that patriarchal culture denies and covers over with symbols: "his eyes gone further than the food and the lamp, full of the land dug out of his skull and the holes filled with the distance beyond the land" (17). Darl, then, releases the repressed; he penetrates the unconscious and makes the conscious mind aware of chaotic, subversive, instinctive forces. He taunts Jewel, for example, by hinting broadly about Addie's adulterous liaison, Jewel's illegitimacy, Jewel's incestuous desire for his mother, and Jewel's figuration of Addie as a horse. Darl's ability to mine the unconscious mind is perceptively analyzed by Cash:

> I see all the while how folks could say he was queer, but that was the very reason couldn't nobody hold it personal. It was like he was outside of it too, same as you, and getting mad at it would be kind of like getting mad at a mud-puddle that splashed you when you stepped in it. (136)

For Darl, who lacks boundaries, the unconscious mind is an open book. He reads the repressed, as we readers, whom Cash directly addresses, read Faulkner's novel. Through no will of his own, but like a mud puddle spattering mud, Darl restores what culture displaces—material existence. Darl, then, like his mother, threatens the foundation of patriarchal culture by representing a loss of difference from the world of matter. Therefore, he suffers the same fate as Addie; he is denied and expelled: "Our brother Darl in a cage in Jackson where, his grimed hands lying light in the quiet interstices, looking out he foams" (146).

When the representatives of the law come to take Darl away and imprison him, even before the state officials can act, Dewey Dell and Jewel hurl themselves on Darl. One of the lawmen must restrain Dewey Dell, while Jewel holds Darl down, saying, "Kill him. Kill the son of a bitch" (137). Dewey Dell's and Jewel's violent attack on Darl can be explained in two ways. At one level, they represent patriarchal culture's repudiation of Darl. Darl is an exponent of the repressed unconscious which, according to patriarchal law, must be silenced and excluded. In other words, they hate him for represencing their own denied selves, and they desire his death as they desire to efface their own brutish instincts. But, from another perspective, this attack also represents matriarchal culture's vehement rejection of Darl. Seen this way, Darl, who has attempted to erase Addie's body, enacts the archetypal role of Orestes, the son who murders the mother; and Jewel and Dewey Dell are Faulkner's formulation of the Furies, the maternal spirits, who in the *Oresteia* torment Orestes for the murder of the mother. Both Dewey Dell and Jewel are well chosen avatars of maternal fury. Dewey Dell, now that she has been denied her abortion, will become the displaced mother; and Jewel, Addie's illegitimate son, born outside of patriarchal law, has proven himself again and again the champion of his mother's body. The dual roles played by Jewel and Dewey Dell, simultaneously representing both patriarchal and matriarchal cultures, are not contradictory but rather reinforcing; together, they stress the completeness of Darl's alienation. Darl is renounced by both patriarchal and matriarchal culture, by both Anse and Addie, and this double rejection leaves him utterly estranged, as Cash recognizes when he offers this epitaph for his exiled brother: "This world is not his world; this life his life" (149).

From the beginning, Addie's revenge focused on Darl. She formulated her revenge with his birth: "And when Darl was born I asked Anse . . . to take me back to Jefferson when I died" (100); and his expulsion occurs almost simultaneously with her own final displacement. Having just lowered Addie's body into a hole and covered it with earth, the Bundrens permit Darl to be handcuffed and carried away to a state asylum. Addie accomplishes her revenge on patriarchal culture in two ways by rejecting Darl. First, she successfully asserts the value of the repressed literal by denying Darl the opportunity to renounce his tie to his mother's body. Second, like the archetypal avenging mother, Clytemnestra, Addie exacts equal justice. Clytemnestra slays Agamemnon for slaying her daughter-double, Iphigenia. Similarly, to avenge her lifelong exclusion, Addie insures that Darl is excluded. Ultimately, Addie's revenge is to make Darl suffer the mother's endlessly reenacted fate: he is sacrificed to insure the continuance of the social order.

While Addie takes her revenge on Darl and represences the repressed literal in the course of her protracted interment, in the end, her victory is limited, for she is never able to put a stop to patriarchal culture's figuration of her. The symbolic order is built on representation, an endless series of inadequate substitutions for the full and present satisfaction experienced in an imaginary symbiotic unity with the mother. With the mother renounced, the family generates substitutes for her. For example, the Tull sisters predict that with Addie's death her sons will marry; these wives will serve as substitutes for the mother, since, as Chodorow explains, men recreate the early bond with the mother with the heterosexual relationship with a wife.[2] Anse also replaces Addie with a wife, the duck-shaped woman, the new Mrs. Bundren, who usurps even Addie's name.

Throughout the arduous journey to bury Addie in Jefferson, even as Addie repeatedly attempts to ruin representation by stripping her

2. Chodorow, 20, 199.

family members of their substitutes for her, her family replace their substitutes with more substitutes, reenacting the primal trade—the exchange of the maternal body, symbol of the material world, for law and language. In the flooded river, for example, the mules which carry them toward Jefferson, emblem of the symbolic order, are drowned and Cash's cherished tools, substitutes for his real desire, are swept away. But the Bundrens are undeterred by this dismantling of representation, and persist in favoring the figurative over the literal. Cash lovingly embraces his returned tools, and the Bundrens replace the lost mules by swapping their substitutes for more substitutes. For mules to carry them to their cultural Mecca, Jefferson, Anse trades their replacements for a lost fusion with the mother and with the world: Anse's money for new teeth, Cash's money for a "talking machine," and Jewel's horse. The diminishing nature of their substitutions, how with each trade they trade down, is most clearly demonstrated at the novel's conclusion, when Dewey Dell tries to placate Vardaman by offering him bananas as a replacement for the electric train in the store window: *"Wouldn't you rather have bananas?"* (144). Just as the bananas are an inadequate substitute for the train that made Vardaman's "heart hurt" (125), so also the train is a sorry substitute for an original plenitude with no lacks or exclusions of any kind. In other words, the Bundrens vainly attempt to plug up the gap at the center of their being with substitute after substitute, metaphor after metaphor. The whole endeavor of patriarchal culture, to repress the physical world and then to permit its controlled return in a permissible form, is ritually reenacted by the Bundrens' trip to Jefferson, as Tull observes with devastating acuity: "They would risk the fire and the earth and the water and all just to eat a sack of bananas" (81). In the end, the ultimate absurdity of the symbolic order's displacement and figuration of authentic existence is summed up in the novel's closing cartoon-image—with Addie safely underground, the Bundrens munch bananas in their wagon which stands on the square, the Jefferson courthouse at their back—but the only appreciative witness is Darl: "Dewey Dell and Vardaman on the seat and Cash on a pallet in the wagon bed are eating bananas from a paper bag. Is that why you are laughing, Darl? . . . Yes yes yes yes yes yes yes yes" (146).

PATRICK O'DONNELL

Between the Family and the State: Nomadism and Authority in *As I Lay Dying*†

*　*　*

* * * Many of the critical readings of the novel [*As I Lay Dying*] partake of an enchantment with the supposed mysteries of metaphor and desire that found the novel by "agreeing" with Faulkner, as it were, that at its center there lies the enigma of Addie, to be variously and partially explained by family members and critics alike, but never to be fully penetrated. Addie, variously, is mother, origin, language, spirit, body, consciousness, writing, the unconscious, the feminine, desire personified, life, death, voice, the unutterable. She is, in such readings, both what escapes signification and what signifies; she is the icon of "meaning" expressed in the form of figures (Vardaman's famous "My mother is a fish") and the critical explication of them. Addie holds the family together; even in death—perhaps especially in death—she gives the Bundrens, Faulkner, and his readers a purpose, a hermeneutic road, or intersection of roads, to follow.

But the novel tells yet another story—one that stands as a commentary upon the conditions of signification and reading I have outlined. As much as it is given over to figuring forth the ineffable nature of Addie's interiority, *As I Lay Dying* also makes a public display of the Bundrens and their intimate relations: the private agreement between Addie and Anse regarding her burial in Jefferson, for example, is theatricalized in the novel, brought out into the open, and witnessed as the fulfilling of a civic contract by neighbors and strangers alike. The Bundren family moves from the private and (to Peabody's dismay) somewhat inaccessible realm of house and farm to the public space of the Jefferson cemetery and the urban streets. Like temporary Snopeses, the Bundrens progress from country to city, but there is a price to pay for this ritual progression and the public fulfillment of a contract: Darl's insanity. Driven mad, his internal demons released for all to see, he is made a ward of the state. In the novel's comic strategy, he is sacrificed to the state so that, in several senses, the Bundrens may complete their arrangements, move through the city, and return home largely intact. It is upon this overlooked aspect of the novel—its negotiation and legitimation of the family's continuance within the bounds of state authority—that I will concentrate my remarks in this essay.[1]

---

† From *The Faulkner Journal* 4:1&2 (Fall 1988/Spring 1989). Copyright 1991. Reprinted with permission.
1. My notions of "state authority" and "state apparatus" in this essay are informed by Louis Althusser's concept of the subjects as organized and interpellated, or "hailed," within the structures and striations of the "State."

* * *

* * * For the duration of their journey to Jefferson * * * the Bundrens are migrants or nomads whose presence offers scandal on the public byways. The ostensible purpose of the journey is to fulfill a contract Addie has insisted upon after the birth of Darl—a contract exacted in the privacy of the family and one that will return her to her "own kind": in Anse's words, as he argues with Jewel about the necessity for a well-crafted casket and the need to transport Addie's body in the Bundren wagon, "She'll rest easier for knowing it's a good one, and private. She was ever a private woman. . . . With that family burying-ground in Jefferson and them of her blood waiting for her there, she'll be impatient. . . . We would be beholden to no man . . . me and her. We have never yet been, and she will rest quieter for knowing it and that it was her own blood sawed out the boards and drove the nails. She was ever one to clean up after herself" (12). Anse here reaffirms the self-sustained, nuclear family as the location for the fulfillment of "private" desires and the return unto itself. Yet, in the execution of this private, incestuous contract (blood returning to blood, kind to kind), against his own wishes and his hatred of the road, Anse incurs obligations at every step, and the Bundrens' meandering journey becomes a topic for communal discussion and advice, thus falling within the public venue—policed, as it were, under the eye of the public. In the novel's ironic logic, the obsession with personal privacy that dictates the need for the ritualistic journey gives rise to the exposure of Addie's decaying body to the population, and allows for the conversion of private desire into commodified want, Addie's burial being the excuse for a journey to town where new wives and graphophones can be acquired. Thus, the very road that serves as the vehicle for the fulfilling of Addie's need for privacy subverts that desire in that it leads to, and is one of the * * * marks of, the *polis*, the State.

As it unfolds, the Bundrens' nomadic journey falls ever more under the jurisdiction of the State as the pilgrimage comes to a halt in front of the Jefferson courthouse after having endured an extensive series of encounters with representatives of state institutions— the doctors, police, clergy, and merchants who bring the Bundrens into the public domain. Moreover, to a remarkable extent, the Bundrens assume contractual obligations and encounter manifestations of the law on the road to Jefferson. Countering Anse's refrain that he "dont begrudge" the funeral procession to Addie, that he will be "beholden to no one," there is the protracted negotiation with Snopes over a new team of mules, the purchase of a new set of teeth after Anse has appropriated the money Dewey Dell had been saving for an abortion, and the acquisition of a new Mrs. Bundren (this last the result of a "deal" that begins with Anse borrowing spades from a then unknown woman in order to dig Addie's grave). * * * [T]he upshot of Addie's death is a net capital gain to the Bundren family: new teeth, new mother, a graphophone. * * * Hence, the fulfillment of the private contract of blood and kin between Addie and Anse leads to a series of public negotiations involving the exchange of money and the exertion of state authority, both directly, in the removal of Darl to the state mental asylum in Jackson, and indirectly, through Anse's appropriation of surplus capital (here, acting as paternal stand-in for the state). At the same time, Anse's marriage to the new Mrs. Bundren comically suggests that the public institution of marriage is one in which the partners, themselves, are a form of capital in circulation, eminently exchangeable and replaceable. The novel's logic thus reveals that capital gain and the exertion of state authority through one of its institutions—be it marriage or the madhouse—are part of a singular process that confers upon the characters of *As I Lay Dying* a "civic" identity.

Once the Bundrens hit the road (or even before they do so, as Cash's meticulous preparations would suggest) they are given over to the state, and they become objects of public scrutiny to be differentiated according to custom. The paradoxical nature of their situation enhances the novel's comic effect, for they are limned by the public as nomads and outcasts while the funeral procession, itself, increasingly signifies the official fulfillment of an intimate contract. When Anse takes an entire day to bargain for the mules with Snopes, leaving Addie's corpse in the Armstids' barn where it attracts turkey buzzards, Lula Armstid comments, "It's a outrage. . . . He should be lawed for treating her so" (108); later, when Jewel rides away on his horse "looking like some kind of spotted cyclone," Armstid notes that "they was tearing down the road like the Law might have been behind them" (111). Indeed, the law is literally behind the Bundrens in Mottson when Moseley retails an encounter between Anse and the local marshal:

> It was Albert told me about the rest of it. He said the wagon was stopped in front of Grummet's hardware store, with the ladies all scattering up and down the street with their handkerchiefs to their noses, and a crowd of hardnosed men and boys standing around the wagon, listening to the marshal arguing with the man. He was a kind of tall, gaunted man sitting on the wagon, saying it was a public street and he reckoned he had as much right there as anybody, and the marshal telling him he would have to move on; folks couldn't stand it. It had been dead eight days, Albert said. They come from some place out in Yoknapatawpha county, trying to get to Jefferson with it. It must have been like a piece of rotten cheese coming into an ant-hill,

> in that ramshackle wagon that Albert said folks were scared
> would fall all to pieces before they could get it out of town, with
> that home-made box and another fellow with a broken leg lying
> on top of it, and the father and a little boy sitting on the seat
> and the marshal trying to make them get out of town.
>
> "It's a public street," the man says. "I reckon we can stop to
> buy something same as airy other man. We got the money to
> pay for hit, and hit aint airy law that says a man cant spend his
> money where he wants." (117–18)

This encounter with a physical embodiment of the law illustrates
the complexities of the Bundrens' position in relation to the authority
of the State. They are, at this stage of the journey, nomadic aliens
coming from the outside ("from some place out in Yoknapatawpha
county") and their presence constitutes a violation of the official order
in several senses. Legally, they are certainly in violation of whatever
county health and sanitation laws pertain (as the marshal says to
Anse, "Dont you know you're liable to jail for endangering the public
health?" (118); morally, they are offensive to the community of Mottson because its members perceive them to be degrading the putrefying body of the mother by parading it, as it were, in public; in terms of
class, they represent an intrusion of what is perceived to be back-
woods poverty, stupidity, and irrationality into the village with its comparatively "enlightened" customs and economic hierarchies. * * *
Yet at the same time that he is bringing the illegal corpse and all
that it represents into town, Anse cites the law in the attempt to justify his passing through: the exchange of capital, the public coin (in
this case, proffered in order to buy cement for Cash's broken leg)
makes Anse, temporarily, an equal citizen in Mottson, just as the
financial and personal transactions that take place in Jefferson "justify," in a sense, the horrendous trials of the procession. Accordingly,
in discussing with Jewel the reasons for selling his horse, Anse refers
to a higher authority as he rationalizes continuing the (by now) farcical journey as originally planned:

> For fifteen years I aint had a tooth in my head. . . . God knows
> it. He knows in fifteen years I aint et the victuals He aimed for
> man to eat to keep his strength up, and me saving a nickel here
> and a nickel there so my family wouldn't suffer it, to buy them
> teeth so I could eat God's appointed food. I give that money. I
> thought that if I could do without eating, my sons could do
> without riding. God knows I did. (111)

Anse justifies the continued journey and makes procedural rules for
it on the basis of practical need, but that need itself is justified by
divine law which has become an end in itself. Anse claims that he
wants to buy the teeth so that he can eat "God's appointed food,"

thereby undergirding his argument with an appeal to the need for fulfilling the demands of the highest symbolic order, often manifested among the nomads of another testament in the form of dietary laws.[2] In instances such as these, there is a negotiation taking place between the nomadic and the stately, the abject and the official, as Anse legitimates the journey by converting it into a journey *toward* law and capital.

Anse might be regarded as engaging in a major revision of his cultural identity in *As I Lay Dying*, for the legalistic rhetoric he employs in Mottson stands in glaring contradiction to the antiauthoritarian statements regarding roads, taxation, and draft boards that he makes at the beginning the journey. Anse recalls saying to Addie that there is "no luck" in roads because they run counter to divine intention (note how he has changed his mind about this by the time he reaches Mottson), though they do seem to fulfill certain nomadic desires:

> And so He [God] never aimed for folks to live on a road, because which gets there first, I says, the road or the house? Did you ever know Him to set a road down by a house? I says. No you never, I says, because it's always men cant rest till they gets the house set where everybody else that passes in a wagon can spit in the doorway, keeping the folks restless and wanting to get up and go somewheres else when He aimed for them to stay put like a tree or a stand of corn. (22)

Specious as the logic of Anse's argument appears to be, it makes sense in terms of the seeming opposition, but actual connection that exists between nomadism and the State, private and public in the novel. In his cultural analysis, civil authority makes and maintains the roads, which map the private onto the public realm ("men cant rest till they gets the house set where everybody that passes in a wagon can spit in the doorway"), and which organize or striate the nomadic: wandering, the desire to "get up and go somewheres else," is in Anse's view motivated and orchestrated by the road.

More disturbingly for Anse, the road provides public access to the officers of the State who invade the land and the realm of privacy. As he puts it, men put the road "where every bad luck prowling can find it and come straight to my door, charging me taxes on top of it. Making me pay for Cash having to get them carpenter notions when if it hadn't been no road come there, he wouldn't a got them" (22). Here, the road is both the purveyor of state authority and "knowledge," or

---

2. The comment is informed by [Julia] Kristova's discussion of the relation between dietary laws and the maintaining of the barrier between the abject and the social order in *Powers of Horror*, "Semiotics of Biblical Abomination," trans. by Leon S. Rondiez (New York: Columbia University Press, 1982), pp. 90–112.

what exists in *As I Lay Dying* as "technocracy," that is, the organization of knowledge into "carpentry" which Anse suggests has invaded
Cash's consciousness via the road, transforming him into a taxable
commodity. Anse does not stop to consider that Cash's vocational
training, while bringing the tax man, has also ensured the survival of
a family that can barely eke out a living on its impoverished farm.
But this is not an examination of survival as such; rather, Anse is
arguing that the coming of the road has resulted in a transformation
of a heretofore private, "natural" existence (however fallacious this
notion may actually be) into a public life, subject to civic laws and
duties, as is the road itself.

Ultimately, for Anse, the road brings the law and the military:

> And Darl too. Talking me out of him, durn them. It aint that I
> am afraid of work; I always is fed me and mine and kept a roof
> above us: it's that they would short-hand me just because he
> tends to his own business, just because he's got his eyes full of
> the land all the time. I says to them, he was alright at first, with
> his eyes full of the land, because the land laid up-and-down
> ways then; it wasn't till that ere road come and switched the
> land around longways and his eyes still full of the land, that
> they begun to threaten me out of him, trying to short-hand me
> with the law. (22)

As I have suggested, Darl is the sacrifice paid to the State so that the
Bundrens can complete their epic journey and continue with business as usual. In the view he posits here, as a way of explaining
"what happened" to Darl after being drafted into World War I as a
pretext for what will happen to him on the journey, Anse articulates
several illusory differences: between the verticality of divine authority and the horizontality of civil authority (the land laid "up-and-
down ways" as opposed to "longways"); between the "natural" and
the "cultural" (Darl's eyes "full of the land" as opposed, implicitly, to
what he will see once the road takes him); between the private and
the public; between the land, which is sacred and amorphous, and
the road, which profanes and striates the land. These oppositions to
which Anse holds as temporal markers of pre-cultural and cultural
conditions will be collapsed as a result of the journey itself, for it
reveals through its contradictions and travesties to what extent the
foundation and continuation of state authority *depends* upon the
maintenance of such false oppositions, and upon the incorporation
and exclusion of a mode of being outside or before "culture." The
Darl whose eyes are full of the land is the same Darl who is declared
to be insane by the novel's end, and whose insanity or otherness is
institutionalized—bordered off—and accepted as part of the recon-
figuration of the commodified Bundren family which returns home

with a brand new wife and mother. The disciplining of Darl, then, the limning of his eccentricity, is a necessary part of the process that brings the roads to the Bundrens and the Bundrens to Jefferson. In Anse's logic, Darl's strangeness and madness are ways of comprehending the always already completed movement into the realm of capital. His figuring of Darl's "being" as before or outside of that movement in the oppositions of land and road is the articulation of a loss of nature ("his eyes full of the land") that can only be compensated for—and Anse comes increasingly to accept this view as the journey progresses—through the legal exchange of commodities. It is a loss, like the loss of Addie, upon which anything can be inscribed, and it, in essence, offers the *excuse* for capital and all the striations that regulate its flow.

Thus, Darl becomes the necessary sacrifice who will be given over to the State to satisfy the legalities that ensue as a result of the Bundrens' peregrinations. The sacrifice of the nomadic—of him who would wander too far—is necessitated because, as I have suggested, there must be a simultaneous articulation, loss, and incarceration of something other (and in this, Darl is his mother's son, she in her coffin, he in his strait jacket), something outside the law, in order for the state to exert its authority as the entity which makes the distinction between the inside and the outside.* * *

* * *

As I Lay Dying has often been viewed as a comic or absurdist novel that portrays the complex psychological relations of a family whose story has universal ramifications. My reading suggests that in this novel Faulkner sacrifices psychological depth (embodied by Darl) to a comprehension of the family as a commodified entity that works—even in the fulfillment of its most private desires and intimate contracts—according to the law, within the confines of the State * * * [and] its systems of communication and exchange. At the center of the concept of the "nuclear family" (and Faulkner's families are implosive in this regard) there is the romance of desire, inwardness, privacy, and the illusion that there is a cultural order organized along different lines and protected from the social. In *As I Lay Dying*, Faulkner indicates that separation of the realms—private and public, family and State—is a fantasy that concurs with the ongoing processes of the state apparatus as desire is circulated and commodified. It is this recognition that, in some way, underlies Anse's complaint, "it seems hard that a man in his need could be so flouted by a road" (23), for he will come to discover that the road does not so much flout need as govern it, transforming desire into the law and custom.

RICHARD GRAY

[A Southern Carnival]†

* * *

One reason why As I Lay Dying is such a disconcerting story is because we, the readers, are never allowed to be sure what we are reading. There is, certainly, a vein of knockabout comedy at work here, derived ultimately from the traditions of Southwestern humour: inviting us into a world of henpecked husbands and bossy wives (the Tulls), people falling victim to cruel practical jokes (Dewey Dell and the chemist), or suffering bizarre forms of physical pain (Cash and the cement cast on his broken leg). Even the basic premise of the story, involving the transportation of a corpse, growing smellier by the minute, past a gallery of variously shocked and amused spectators, is like a graveyard joke out of one of the cruder Southern folk tales—or, for that matter, like those versions of 'grotesque' humour that Poe enjoyed so much and tried to imitate in some of his work. Co-existing with this, however, is a vein of feeling tapped from elsewhere in Faulkner's regional tradition, inviting us to see the characters in a quite different, heroic mould. The Bundrens' stoicism, the sheer tenacity they show in fulfilling their promise to Addie in defiance of fate, fire and flood, invites a comparison with those folk heroes who embodied Southerners' sense (and especially Southern poor folks' sense) of the troubles they had to face and the courage they needed to face them. The journey itself that forms the spine of the narrative, macabre though its physical consequences may be, is a trial of a kind, a way of testing strength and endurance; and the qualities the different members of the family reveal during the course of it seem intended to invite our respect along with our laughter. We are pained, impressed and amused—occasionally even at one and the same time. 'But I ain't so sho that ere a man has the right to say what is crazy and what ain't', observes Cash Bundren,

> It's like there was a fellow in every man that's done a-past the sanity or the insanity, that watches the sane and the insane doings of that man with the same horror and the same astonishment. (137)

Horror, astonishment, and more fundamentally the sense that we do not know how to feel or whether we can gauge a situation accurately: all this is likely to be incorporated into our response to a moment like

† From The Life of William Faulkner (Oxford and Cambridge: Blackwell, 1994), pp. 151–63. Copyright Richard Gray (University of Essex). Reprinted by permission of Wiley-Blackwell.

that one, say, in which Cash himself has the cement cast removed from his leg. It is the doctor, Peabody, removing the cast, who is describing the incident:

'Don't you lie there and try to tell me you rode six days on a wagon without springs, with a broken leg and it never bothered you.'
'It never bothered me much,' he [Cash] said.
'. . . And don't tell me it ain't going to bother you to lose sixty-odd square inches of skin to get that concrete off. And don't tell me it ain't going to bother you to have to limp around on one short leg for the balance of your life—if you walk at all again.
'Concrete,' I said, 'God Almighty . . . Does that hurt?'
'Not to speak of,' he said, and the sweat big as marbles running down his face about the colour of blotting paper.
'Course not,' I said. '. . . If you had anything you could call luck, you might say it was lucky it was the same leg you broke before. . . .'
'Hit's what paw says,' he said. (138)

A further complicating factor at work here, contributing to readerly discomposure, is the balladic quality of many of the sections. This is especially true of those moments when relatively minor characters like Vernon Tull or Samson take over the telling of the tale. They tell the story of the Bundren family and their journey to Jefferson—at least, as far as they encounter and know it—but, at the same time, they tell us about their own domestic rituals and how they and their neighbours pass the day in talk, rehearsing and recapitulating old tales, creating folk memory. It is surely no accident that Yoknapatawpha County is named in *As I Lay Dying*, since this is the first time in a completed novel that Faulkner shows how his characters 'name' their surroundings: which is to say, give them cultural identity by placing them within a communal story. The Bundren family are not only observed by their neighbours: they are situated within an accumulating store of legend, linked up in an apparently casual way to other people and other stories that are sometimes told, sometimes half-told, and sometimes simply referred to. The strategy is similar to that of a folksong or ballad, in which a particular story being remembered (and it does always seem that it is being remembered rather than invented) is given an additional depth and significance by the sense of the numerous other tales that lie behind it:

It was just before sundown. We were sitting on the porch when the wagon came up the road . . . 'What's that?' MacCallum says: I can't think of his name: Rafe's twin: that one it was. 'It's Bundren from down beyond New Hope,' Quick says. 'There's one of them Snopes' horses Jewel's riding.'

'I didn't know there was ere a one of them horses left,' Mac-
Callum says, 'I thought you folks down there finally contrived to
give them all away.' (64)

In effect, no work of Faulkner's comes as close as *As I Lay Dying*
does to illustrating the idea that the novel is an intentional and
conscious hybrid. Faulkner presents us here with a narrative that, to
the extent it draws on folk tale, folk epic, folk comedy and the ballad
is recognizably embedded in the traditional cultures of the South.
Where it appears to part company with those cultures, however, is
in Faulkner's evident willingness to mix genres: to move between
them, and sometimes collate them, in a way that openly invites 'horror
and . . . astonishment'. Voices join to tell us about their lives, to agree,
to present evidence or just to argue. No one voice can be regarded as
authoritative but equally no voice can be discounted either; consequently, the narrative assumes a character that is even more frankly
relativistic than most of Faulkner's major narratives are. All this is normally attributed to Faulkner's participation in modernism, with the
gloss that *As I Lay Dying* is a comic novel. To call the story of the Bundrens comic, though, is hardly to do justice to its radical shifts of tone,
the extent to which utterly contradictory emotions can be aroused
even by the rendering of one incident—such as the episode of Cash
and his cement cast. And while much of Faulkner's major fiction certainly invites the modernist comparison, it seems less apt here: the
disjunctions in *As I Lay Dying* are far more unnerving, at least to readers unfamiliar with folk culture, than they are in, say, *The Sound and
the Fury*. Instead of comic or modernist, perhaps this novel could
more usefully be seen in terms of carnival: those rituals of subversion,
barely organized riot and release, that every society—and every hier-
archical society, in particular—seems to require. What takes place in
carnival, according to Bakhtin, is 'a comical operation of dismember-
ment'. The audience is invited into a celebration of 'the social consciousness of the people' and the body as process: to witness the
linked realities of an unruly folk culture and 'the grotesque body'—
which is to say, 'the body in the act of becoming . . . never finished,
never completed'.[1] The key to the forms of the carnival is that they are
open, requiring participation: the audience is not so much apart from
as a part of the proceedings, required to 'walk round' and take in
events from all sides. Carnival offers the opposite of all those pieties
on which the official culture rests: fixed rituals, the prerogatives of

1. Mikhail Bakhtin, *Rabelais and His World*, trans. Helene Iwolsky (Cambridge, MA, 1968),
   p. 371. See also p. 94. [Mikhail Bakhtin (1895–1975), Russian scholar and literary theorist who argued that novelistic form was predicated upon the "dialogic" juxtaposition of
   different and often warring voices, languages, and levels of discourse. *The Dialogic Imagination* (1981); *Problems of Dostoevsky's Poetics* (1984) (*Editor.*)]

power and status, the respect and the closure that comes from distance. And its effect is not just to unsettle, it is to offer an alternative
view of life, as human subjects are forced into riotous proximity with
other, grotesque human subjects—and all are immersed in a dizzying
process of change.

All of this means that, as we read *As I Lay Dying,* we are unable
to pin down the Bundrens, to be sure about them even to the extent
that we are 'sure' about, say, the Compsons. Each member of the
family becomes as edgy, protean, and occasionally as baffling and
grotesque—that is, as contrary to our expectations—as people that
we know from our own intimate experience sometimes are. Take
Dewey Dell, the one girl in the family group, who is young, unmarried and pregnant: she is presented differently by every voice that
talks about or for her. Her youngest brother Vardaman, for instance,
tries to locate her as a replacement for Addie and so practically wor-
ships her. What she says must be right, he feels, because *she* says it:

> The hill goes off into the sky . . . In Jefferson it is red on the
> track behind the glass. The track goes shining round and round.
> Dewey Dell says so. (122)

Anse Bundren on the other hand, the head of the family, describes
Dewey Dell more as a thankless child—someone who will never
allow anything he does, however slight, to pass without criticism.
She is the guardian of the law for him as well, perhaps, but it is a law
seen more as a nuisance than a need—the law, in a way, as understood by the congenital lawbreaker.

For all their differences, there is a clear connection between the
assessments of father and brother; the woman, the reader may feel,
remains the same in principle—only the judgement passed on that
principle, the perspective from which it is seen, is altered. This is
hardly true, however, of a third version of Dewey Dell, voiced by a boy
who seduces her during the course of the journey. The story of his
seduction sounds as if it could have come straight out of folk comedy,
although folk comedy of a coarser, more robust kind than anything we
are likely to come across in the *written* culture of nineteenth-century
America. As assistant to the chemist in Jefferson, and so someone who
has gained a bogus medical status from his surroundings, the boy—
called MacGowan—persuades Dewey Dell that the only way she can
terminate her unwanted pregnancy is with 'a hair of the dog' that bit
her. One act of intercourse, he advises, will cancel out another and he
is ready to perform the service free of change when the shop is closed.
He obviously has no misgivings about this, no sense of guilt over the
trick he plays, and the reason is simple: he never thinks of Dewey Dell
as a person. She is merely a type for him, a nice, juicy country girl who

almost deserves to be duped as a punishment for her gullibility and
seductive good looks:

> She looked pretty good. One of them black-eyed ones that look
> like she'd as soon put a knife in you as not if you two-timed her.
> She looked pretty good. (139)

From the moment when Dewey Dell walks into the chemist's store,
she enters a world utterly different from the ones in which we have
seen her up until then, a world where a different set of relations
apply effectively turning her into a different person. It is like meeting an old friend unexpectedly in a strange place, perhaps, or with a
new group of companions. A side of him or her we had never noticed
before is suddenly exposed, and we are forced to reassess our assumptions of intimacy.

To talk simply about the characters who describe Dewey Dell from
the sidelines is, of course, to leave one, crucial series of voices unaccounted for: those that belong to Dewey Dell herself, as she debates
her situation in the world. The entire structure of *As I Lay Dying*
is restlessly dialectical, involving a continual and rapid movement
between character as object and character as subject—which means
that someone like Dewey Dell can bring her own expressions of
identity into the argument. She can tell us about dimensions of her
personality that no outside observer can properly know. Of course,
her voices do not always operate at a submerged level. Very often all
Faulkner does when he allows her to speak is remind us, in and
through the use of the vernacular, that she is a country girl, a being
defined on one level by her geographical and social surroundings. At
such times, she comes closest to the kind of person others describe—
as in this moment, when she talks about working in the fields with
the man who then impregnated her:

> The first time me and Lafe picked on down the row . . . We
> picked on, . . . the woods getting closer . . . and the secret
> shade . . . with my sack and Lafe's sack. Because I said . . . if
> the sack is full when we get to the woods it won't be me. I said
> if it don't mean for me to do it the sack will not be full . . . but
> if the sack is full, I cannot help it . . . And we picked on toward
> the secret shade and our eyes would drown together . . . (17)

This is not simply colloquialism, though: that last phrase, 'our eyes
would drown together', hardly belongs with the ordinary, everyday
idioms of country speech. With its help, the reader is being shifted
into a different dimension of voice, and of Dewey Dell's personality, and a more purely inward one at that. Here, words act as signs
for the unarticulated and otherwise inarticulable impulses running

through the character's consciousness: they are used as symbolic gestures rather than naturalistically—to chart, in Dewey Dell's case and others, how an apparently impassive character is actually drowning in his or her own subjectivity.

This is one of the main strategies Faulkner uses for disconcerting the reader: he pulls the verbal ground from beneath our feet, as it were, and from beneath the feet of the characters, forcing them and us to tumble down below the level of demotic speech into other, more dreamlike and dissociated, areas of language. Just when we think we have a clear picture of somebody like Dewey Dell, and can place her as an attractive, emotionally generous but rather simple-minded country girl, our assumptions are suddenly undermined— our snobbish detachment shown up for what it is—by the revelation of her inner fears and even despair. We move in under the equable surfaces of her behaviour to something else, a terror or sense of disaster by no means simple or simple-minded, that can only be expressed in the sort of language that works as much by rhythm and repetition as it does by any attempt at representation:

> I heard that my mother is dead. I wish I had time to let her die. I wish I had time to wish I had. It is because in the wild and out-raged earth too soon too soon too soon. It is not that I wouldn't and will not it's that it is too soon too soon too soon. (69)

And that is not all. In case we now start to feel secure, when Dewey Dell's conscious fears have been expressed, Faulkner will occasion-ally offer us another jolt. Without any warning, he will take an abrupt step down beyond this towards an even more incantatory and imagis-tic level of speech that is intended to recover Dewey Dell's subcon-scious for us—the secret, subliminal impulses that help make her what she is or prompt her to do what she does. Here her dimly real-ized fear of losing her identity, which includes her fear of death but goes beyond it, becomes a controlling factor:

> The dead air shapes the dead earth in the dead darkness, farther away than seeing shapes the dead earth. It lies dead and warm upon me, touching me naked through my clothes. I said You don't know what worry is. I don't know what it is. I don't know whether I am worrying or not. Whether I can or not. I don't know whether I can cry or not. I don't know whether I have tried or not. (38)

Thanks to all this, character is transformed into process rather than product, seen as a state of perpetual becoming: there is no possibil-ity of closure, no bedrock certainty here. A grotesque denial of any claims we might make for completeness, Dewey Dell—like the other major characters in *As I Lay Dying*—exists in the clash of voices, *between* the different consciousnesses that continually debate her. She, and they, offer the revelation that identity is made through activities of speech that can never be terminated or contained.

It is not always easy to live with the acceptance of this, the idea of identity as an intersubjective phenomenon realized through speech. Or, to put it more simply, we are generally happier with certainty: living with people we can pin down, and with a life that seems to have a settled meaning. The temptation to fix things is, consequently, always there: not only for the reader, as he or she struggles to 'know' the Bundrens, but for the characters themselves as Faulkner deploys them. In *As I Lay Dying*, people are constantly watching one another closely, as if the act of quiet, concentrated observation will put the observed in his or her place. As Addie Bundren dies, for instance, and 'all her failing life appears to drain into her eyes', she looks with simple ferocity at her family around her bed; they, in turn, look at each other or at her. The act of gazing seems intended to halt the processes of living, and dying, but it does not work here or anywhere else in the narrative. For the moment, under the pressure of the gaze, the subject may be translated into an object, apparently as solid and immobile as wood. But the figure frozen in time then moves again; the character that seemed 'made out of wood', 'with the rigid gravity of a cigar-store Indian', assumes a different, more fluid shape; the caravan, or carnival, passes on. This temptation to watch rather than participate, and so become incarcerated in one's own private world of observation, is shared by many of the characters. It is, however, Darl Bundren who carries it to an extreme. 'That's ever living thing the matter with Darl', comments Vernon Tull, 'he just thinks by himself too much.' He thinks; and he gazes. This permits him a special access to information at times, apparently. He seems to know, for example, when Addie is about to die, and to sense that Jewel is illegitimate and Dewey Dell pregnant. But it also deprives him of any sense of self-definition. Other members of his family feel the temptation simply to watch just as he does, and accordingly experience a slippage of identity; the temptation is embraced much more fiercely in his case, though, with the result that the slippage becomes complete disintegration, an utter lapse of being into nothingness. The extent of his slide can be measured: from those moments when he seems to see things hidden from others thanks to the sheer ferocity of his stare, through the weary nihilism to which his detached observations seem inevitably to lead ('how do our lives ravel out into . . . dead gestures of dolls'), to eventual dislocation of voice and consciousness. The last time this lonely watcher speaks, in fact, his voice seems to come from anywhere and nowhere: he is at once 'I', 'you', and 'he' as speech and mind slide into terminal division.

> Darl has gone to Jackson. They put him on the train, laughing,
> down the long car laughing, the heads turning like the heads of
> owls when he passed. 'What are you laughing at?' I said.
> 'Yes yes yes yes yes'
> Two men put him on the train . . . (146)

To some extent, Darl enables his creator to investigate both the lure
and the perils of privacy: like Faulkner, the second son of Addie and
Anse Bundren is on the outside looking in at the other characters, trying to work out what it is that makes them tick. He is the author as
observer, or even voyeur. Cash, in turn, is the author as craftsman,
quietly devoting himself to the job * * *; while Jewel, 'his whole body
earth-free' as he strains to tame and control his mount, summons up
more primitive ideas of the author as horseman, fighting to overcome
and direct instinctual energies. The dispersal of the author's sense of
himself through three different but related consciousnesses is symptomatic of something else besides autobiography: which is the shifting, metamorphic nature of *As I Lay Dying*—language and identity
are constantly slithering and blending in this novel. Vardaman, for
example, speaks of a sense of personal identity that seems to *depend*
upon intersubjectivity, identification with the other: 'Jewel is my
brother . . . Darl is my brother . . . I am. Darl is my brother.' And, at
another moment in the book, he talks of a fish that *is* his mother
that *is* his father that *is* Cash and *is* Dewey Dell:

> And now it's all chopped up. I chopped it up. It's laying in the
> kitchen in the bleeding pan, waiting to be cooked and et. Then
> it wasn't and she was, and now it is and she wasn't. And tomor-
> row it will be cooked and et and she will be him and pa and
> Cash and Dewey Dell and there won't be anything in the box
> and so she can breathe. (39)

In this fluid verbal environment, there is not so much intimacy as
identification—people and things *become* one another: 'My mother is
a fish.' 'Jewel's mother is a horse.' Which makes naming intolerably
difficult: nowhere else in Faulkner's work do characters have quite as
many problems finding or inventing the right sign, speaking things
into being, achieving even tentative, temporary articulation. In the
more obviously public areas of speech, these problems encourage the
habit of interpellation. Characters are constantly hailing one another,
trying to summon the other into a particular, fixed identification, a
definite, subject(ed) status: 'You, Cash!', 'You, Vardaman', 'You, Jewel!'
The corollary of this is that, when they cannot name, they feel they
cannot know. In a passage quoted earlier, for instance, Samson confesses in passing that he cannot remember the name of Rafe MacCallum's twin. The failure of naming dogs him so that, several pages after
this, it comes to occupy the foreground of his attention. Not to know

the name is not to know the man—to fail to identify and, to that extent, to lose control of the story:

> That MacCallum. He's been trading with me off and on for twelve years. I have known him from a boy up; I know his name as well as I do my own. But be durn if I can say it. (68)

In the more private arena, as far as voices in the mind are concerned, a similar failure to name usually provokes even more anxiety. There is real pain or panic felt nearly every time a character senses the forms of identification slipping away from him. To listen to Darl Bundren, for instance, talking about emptying himself for sleep, is the nearest verbal equivalent there is to watching a man trying to cling on to a greasy rock so as to save himself from drowning. The words slide and slither, and elide, even as he tries to pin them down, with the result that what begins as an attempt at self-identification—a struggle to fix and name the subject—ends in dizzying confusion, accompanied by desperate feelings of exile and loss:

> In a strange room you must empty yourself for sleep. And before you are emptied for sleep, what are you. And when you are emptied for sleep, you are not. And when you are filled with sleep, you never were. I don't know what I am. I don't know if I am or not . . . I can hear the rain shaping the wagon . . . And since sleep is is-not and rain and wind are *was*, it is not. Yet the wagon *is*, because when the wagon is *was*, Addie Bundren will not be. And Jewel *is*, so Addie Bundren must be . . . How often have I lain beneath rain on a strange roof, thinking of home. (46–47)

The failure to name that Darl is confronted with in this passage may hit him with particular force, but it is an experience that is by no means unique to him. On the contrary, not only do the other characters share it at times, the reader of *As I Lay Dying* is likely to do so as well, as he or she becomes immersed in a text that seems to delight in transgression: in the carnival world of this novel, the familiar boundaries of explanation are there it seems only to be breached, the rules exist only to be broken. Even motivation defies closure. 'God's will be done', says Anse Bundren when his wife dies, 'Now I can get them teeth.' And critics ever since have been struggling gamely to construct coherent motives for Anse: to offer a consistent interpretation of this and other statements, and the journey that follows them. This usually involves wagging a moralistic finger at this clearly failed father-figure: telling him off for his apparent weakness, selfishness and cant. To treat Anse in this way, however, is to fall victim to some fairly banal notions about character, and to forget the intersubjective space in which he, like all the other characters, lives. Character in *As I Lay Dying* is existence not essence: Anse is caught in the stream of his actions, not in some monolith of fixed motive. He is present in the flux of different discourses, the riot of voices that constitute the narrative; and, as a result, he resists any attempt the reader may make to insert him in a set framework of interpretation, a stable and finished world. So, he goes to Jefferson to honour a promise he made to Addie to have her buried there. *And* he goes there to buy a new set of false teeth and, with the help of his improved appearance, to acquire a second wife. In marrying once again, he finds the sort of helpmeet, or rather drudge, he requires. And he also obtains by way of a dowry the gramophone for which his oldest son has always pined. Anse's motives for travelling to Jefferson are no more the one or the other of these, than Anse himself is simply as one or the other voices in the novel describes him. 'Anse. Why Anse. Why are you Anse', asks Addie. And we never have a complete answer; since, like all the other characters in *As I Lay Dying*, he exists in constant metamorphosis, a climate of change. Thanks to the multiple voices of the narrative, we are invited to walk around him and take in his identity, what choices compel him, as a shifting, unfinalizable process. He offers, in short, a 'grotesque body' that resists closure: and we must accept that offer—not, like Darl, try to stand back, observe, then lower down on the observed some fixed explanatory grid.

The resistance to closure, the opposition to stable forms of explanation, is expressed most openly in the one section that is spoken by Addie Bundren, when she is already dead. Addie rehearses her past life—her childhood, her experience as a teacher, her marriage to Anse—and then tries to explain what it has all taught her, the lesson that somehow she now wants to pass on. 'I learned that words are no good', she says,

> that words don't ever fit even what they are trying to say at. When he [Cash] was born I knew that motherhood was invented by someone who never had to have a word for it because the ones that had the children didn't care whether there was a word for it or not. I knew that fear was invented by someone that had never had the fear; pride, who never had the pride . . . so when Cora Tull would tell me I was not a true mother, I would think how words go up in a thin line, quick and harmless, and how terribly doing goes along the earth, clinging to it . . . (99–100)

This, it seems, is a devastating assault on the harmful effects of language: the way that speech systems—like any system devised to organize experience and enable knowledge—can castrate the personality and paralyse experience, substituting for living a frozen series of signs. We talk, Addie suggests, and as we do so we impoverish and distort what we are talking about. Life, instead of being multidimensional, a various and constantly altering process, is turned into a fixed quantity, something made up out of the patterns of our syntax, the distinctions implicit in our vocabulary—in short, out of our own painfully restricted and restricting stock of 'words'.

To say all this, however, is to miss out the obvious. Addie is talking, telling us this. She herself is using words, and she is not just using them as, say, a postmodernist writer might do—in a negative way, that is, so as to locate their essential futility. She is actually trying to explain; she is struggling to forge an adequate style, even while she argues that a style adequate to any human occasion is impossible—including, it must be inferred, this one. The circularity here is dizzying. Addie is deriding words; she is using words; she is deriding her own use of them; she is, therefore, simultaneously demonstrating and denying her own point. She is saying and not saying: using language because she must (what else does she have?), but intimating that language conceals even more than it reveals and, in the process, calling into question her own use of language. It is difficult to think of a more subversive strategy, a more radical way of shifting the ground beneath the reader's feet. What at first sight looks like the 'message' of the book denies the viability of 'messages' from anyone, let alone 'messages' from a decaying corpse. There is no need to labour the point to see what is going on here: to add, for instance, that any woman who denies one child (Darl) and, by her own admission, 'gave' two others away emotionally (Dewey Dell and Vardaman) is hard to describe as 'a true mother'—which further casts into doubt Addie's claims to have 'learned'. What is clear from all this is that even the authority of an apparently authoritative statement about the unauthoritativeness of words is seen to be unauthoritative: the terms in which it is communicated at once support and subvert the communication. To this extent, the section devoted to Addie is true to the carnival spirit of the book as a whole, it can even be regarded as a kind of paradigm: here as elsewhere, one voice speaks but even in its speaking its silences and exclusions are noted—its truth, the reader can sense, is also a form of lying.

All of which is to say that meaning is to be found in *As I Lay Dying* where character is: in the warring space between voices, the process of debate. True to the discomfiting rituals of the carnival, the reader learns by being seduced by a particular voice, a certain way of looking at personality and behaviour, and then being quietly mocked or chided for permitting the seduction. Expectations are raised only to be reversed, so that a lesson can be carried to us on the back of our own shattered preconceptions. Do we think the Bundrens are involved in a heroic quest, like something out of Homeric legend? One remark by an observer, comparing the Bundren wagon as it comes into town to 'a piece of rotten cheese coming into an ant-hill', appears to persuade us that we are wrong. So can we assume the observer is right? Hardly, because no sooner has he spoken than we are back with the family again, sharing in their journey and in the agony that seems to give it epic proportions. One vocabulary is suddenly jettisoned for another one quite different and then, almost as soon as we have come to accept *that* as accurate, it too is discarded in favour of something else. The process is the thing: the ever unfinished passing of one form into another, the continual battling and eliding of voices. Even when we think we have reached journey's end, we are reminded how mistaken we are ever to believe that the process is ever finished, that closure is ever possible:

> 'It's Cash and Jewel and Vardaman and Dewey Dell,' pa says, kind of hang-dog and proud too, with his teeth and all, even if he wouldn't look at us. 'Meet Mrs Bundren,' he says. (149)

In comes another Mrs Bundren, trailing a fresh set of possibilities behind her—inviting the journey, and the story, to continue.* * * The feudal model of the South was predicated on a vision of the lower white orders that saw them as, at best, stout supporters of the system that repressed them or, at worst, a lesser breed without the law. The carnival impetus of this book, however, drawing on populist resources and the novelist's remembering of folk speech, describes something quite different: the ordinary white people of the South weaving an alternative reality together out of a continuous succession of vocal acts—a reality that, in its degradation as well as its energy, reminds us of the vital, grotesque underbelly of official culture. There are exclusions here too, of course. Black people are conspicuous by their absence: even as objects they hardly appear, and their voices take no part in the debate. But the achievement of *As I Lay Dying* is still considerable: in the war of their words, the clash of their voices, the poor white people of Yoknapatawpha make a place for themselves in this novel, into which they invite the reader to enter. They create their own transgressive space, an assertion of vulgar power and possibility, that mocks claims to authoritativeness and authority of any kind—including, quite clearly, our own.

JOHN LIMON

Addie in No Man's Land[†]

I teach *As I Lay Dying* pretty frequently, and occasionally I have taught it in a seminar on modernism. I pair it in this seminar with a book about modernism and the Great War, Modris Eksteins' *Rites of Spring*, which makes the haunting, invigorating, yet scattershot point that modernism was created in the same spirit in which Germany fought World War I.[1] The seminar meets for two-and-a-half hours each week, and for the first hour we kick around Eksteins' claim. We have previously screened a recreation of the Nijinsky-Stravinsky ballet that inspires Eksteins' title, so the class is prepared to see the merits and limitations of his thesis. Then I coyly introduce *As I Lay Dying*. I wonder, in short, whether the novel has any of the attributes that would qualify it for Eksteins' condemnation: is it irrational, violent, mythic, primitive, and so on? The students muse on this for a while. After a pause, I say: "Of course, there is a direct relation between *As I Lay Dying* and the Great War." Then I wait.

What happens, year after year, is nothing. Silence. After a while, students make a few haphazard and forlorn guesses about what I might mean. Finally, one student—it is one student per seminar who notices this—ventures: isn't it true that Darl, the central character of *As I Lay Dying*, actually fought in World War I? I remain poker-faced, and inquire, "What makes you think that?" Other students are staring at the responding student with mystification and awe. The responding student says, "Well, the book says so." Of course the student is right. Six or seven pages before the end of the book, Darl reveals that he has an obscene spy-glass that he brought home from France after the war (146).

It is time for the students in the seminar to rally; one of them, every year, now remembers that Darl informs us that he has spent many nights beneath strange rooftops, thinking of home (47). We had been given no reason to believe that these rooftops were the French orange kind, but it had seemed odd when Darl mentioned it: how long have any of the Bundren kids spent away from home? Not long, we would have thought. Other students begin to chime in: perhaps this news about his participation in the Great War *accounts* for Darl. He is the most literate of the Bundrens, the most sensitive; also the meanest and most vengeful. We now hold him responsible

† From *Faulkner and War*, ed. Noel Polk and Ann J. Abadie (Jackson: University Press of Mississippi, 2004). Adapted by the author for this Norton Critical Edition. Reproduced with permission of University Press of Mississippi.
1. Modris Eksteins, *Rites of Spring: The Great War and the Birth of the Modern Age* (New York: Anchor/Doubleday, 1989).

for the cement cast that does much to cripple his older brother, Cash; we now blame him because he is the one who ought to have some expertise in tending to injuries. Is his attitude toward the corpse of his mother—i.e., that it would be good to get rid of it, by burning if necessary—a soldier's callousness? The class is eager to rebound from its shame in not noticing that Darl was in the Great War by explaining, now, *everything* about Darl in terms of the war.

I am not the only one in the room to observe, but I am the only one in the room to make anything of the fact, that Darl, at the site of the very barn fire in which he tries to incinerate his mother's body, describes the coffin on sawhorses as "a cubistic bug" (126). This prompts me to wonder aloud where Darl had gone on his leaves. Did he, like many another American soldier, run into Gertrude Stein in Paris? She would have liked him: he would have awakened in her a nostalgia for American craziness. He would have seemed to her like the sort of budding young American writer, for Darl seems like a budding young writer, who needed to learn at her feet what the twentieth century signified. She might have taken him back to the rue de Fleurus, where he might have seen a wall full of Braques and Picassos. From then on he would have been inclined to see life as violently fragmented, like *As I Lay Dying*. I am enchanted by this vision of the friendship of Darl Bundren and Gertrude Stein, and I am hopeful that the modernism class finds the idea mildly amusing.

But here is the punch line of this story, which I admit here but never to my class, because it would have seemed as if I were toying with them. The punch line is that I find a lot of what I have just now elaborated silly. I do not think that the students were entirely wrong not to notice that Darl was a doughboy, and I do not think that the teacher was entirely right in allowing them to proceed as if that fact were the hidden key to the story. You can turn back, if you want, six or seven pages before the end of *As I Lay Dying* and reread the entire novel with Darl's unknowable French campaign in mind, but I do not recommend it.

In fact, there had already been a moment in the text when it seemed one had to return to the beginning and start over. I have read *As I Lay Dying* probably ten times now, but I remember the first time; I remember figuring out that the book revolved around Addie, the Bundren family matriarch, but that Addie would die without ever narrating (much as *The Sound and the Fury* revolves around Caddy, who is not allowed to preside over her own section). This seemed a fine literary prank; but the joke was on me, because almost immediately after I figured this out, I was humiliated to read the section in which Addie makes her preposterous, posthumous address. Not only does she speak, but she also provides the only way of making psychological sense of the involute Bundren family sickness. And not only does she make sense of the group psychopathology, she also explicitly provides the linguistic theory on which the book has been based. Not only that, she connects the psychology and the linguistic theory. When you read the Addie section, three-fifths of the way through *As I Lay Dying*, you had better start over. You had been reading things that were inexplicable.

We seem to find ourselves, reading this book, in the middle of a Borges story.[2] (Borges loved Faulkner, and a Borgesian retrospective misreading of Faulkner is easy to imagine.) We get three-fifths of the way through the novel to the Addie section, then start again; we get almost to the end of the novel, if upon rereading we move straight through the Addie section, discover that Darl had been in France, and start over again, again. Maybe it is possible to imagine an infinity of these recursive points, and thus a never-ending Zeno's paradox[3] reading of Faulkner that never quite reads the last word.

Well, maybe not. Thinking of Darl as a veteran provides, it turns out, not such a perfectly fitting key to Darl's aspect of the novel. For one thing: should Darl's psychology require a unique explanation? Though Darl is the only Bundren to be committed to the madhouse, there is plenty of madness loose in the household. Invoking the war even to explain Darl's particularly insidious method of madness fails the Occam's razor test.[4] It is one premise too many. Darl is covertly vengeful because his mother prefers Cash, her first born, and Jewel, son of her love affair with the minister Whitfield, and their relationship with their mother is the only thing in the world that matters to a Bundren son, though each son finds his own way to displace it. Darl wants to burn his mother's corpse as revenge against her and those who are still loyal to her desires. It seems likely that he went to the war, if it is licit to speculate far beyond the authority of the book, to flee his mother's relationship with Cash and, especially, Jewel. If this is so, then the war, far from explaining Darl, is reduced in dimension, as far as the novel is concerned, to just another gargoyle on the Bundren family structure.

This is very close to my precise view. If it were exactly my view, the essay would be over now and much admirable analysis would be supernumerary. But I think it is more accurate to assert that in *As I*

---

2. Jorge Luis Borges (1899–1986), Argentinian poet, fiction writer, and essayist, best-known in English for short stories such as "The Garden of Forking Paths" that delight in self-reflexive puzzle and paradox. *Ficciones* (1962), *Labyrinths* (1962). [*Editor*]
3. After the Greek mathematician Zeno of Elea (circa 450 BCE). In its simplest version the paradox takes this form: to reach any given point, one must first cover half the distance from one's starting point, then half again. And again, *ad infinitum*, in such a way that the goal is never reached (*Editor*)
4. After the English logician William of Ockham (1288–1348). Occam's razor holds that in choosing between hypotheses, one should select that which requires the fewest assumptions; in essence, choosing simple explanations over complicated ones wherever possible. [*Editor*].

Lay Dying, Faulkner has written a book with alternative locks for competitive keys. I shall argue that in seeing how the competition fares, we can find out something critical about Faulkner, and what is more, about modernism, and what is more, about the whole war-obsessed history of literature.

Oddly enough, the hypothesis that the Great War explains Darl is not as convincing as that the Great War explains As I Lay Dying, itself—its characteristic images, its form, its style. What is the reason for the sheer muddiness of As I Lay Dying, which is perhaps the muddiest book in all literature? Here is Darl's meditation on the mud that he and Jewel are slogging through, far away from Addie's death, which Darl nevertheless manages to envision and narrate:

> Overhead the day drives level and gray, hiding the sun by a flight of gray spears. In the rain the mules smoke a little, splashed yellow with mud, the off one clinging in sliding lunges to the side of the road above the ditch. The tilted lumber gleams dull yellow, water-soaked and heavy as lead, tilted at a steep angle into the ditch above the broken wheel; about the shattered spokes and about Jewel's ankles a runnel of yellow neither water nor earth swirls, curving with the yellow road neither of earth nor water, down the hill dissolving into a streaming mass of dark green neither of earth nor sky. (29)

Every writer on the human experience of World War I stresses its muddiness. The British trenches were muddy all the time; infantry lived in mud. They also died in mud; the apotheosis of muddiness in Paul Fussell's The Great War and Modern Memory is the battle of Passchendaele. The four million shells fired by the British over ten days prior to the battle did not weaken the enemy; rather it tore up the earth. Then "the rain fell and turned the dirt to mud. In the mud the British assaulted and the attack finally attenuated three and a half months later. . . . Thousands literally drowned in the mud."[5] What is the meaning of the muddiness? The only way to see the meaning in Fussell is to appreciate the gross, almost tautological, irony: the mud transfigured the very grounds of the attack.

In his short story "Victory," Faulkner was himself preoccupied with the muddiness of the Great War. In the fighting portion of that story, the word "mud" appears at least once on every page: the hero squats "in the mud with newspapers buttoned inside his tunic"; another, anonymous character on the same page, like the donkeys in As I Lay Dying, "slips in the greaselike mud, trying to cling to the crest of the kneedeep ditch"; three paragraphs later we are told that "platoon by

5. Paul Fussell, The Great War and Modern Memory (New York: Oxford University Press, 1975), 16. All further references to this edition, abbreviated MM, will be inserted in the text.

platoon they slip and plunge into the ditch and drag their heavy feet out of the clinging mud."[6] We have a right to conclude either that Faulkner's preoccupation with mud has its own origin in World War I, or else his personal obsession with mud finds in the trenches of World War I a catastrophic objective correlative. Either way, the question to which we must quickly proceed is: what does mud mean to Faulkner? In "Victory," a very strange story, I am not sure. What I can report is that the protagonist is severely punished for a failure of cleanliness; later, after he rejoins the army and frags[7] the officer who insisted on his punishment, he is obsessed with his own cleanliness, and the obsession does not abate even when he is poor and homeless after the war.

In *As I Lay Dying*, muddiness is met by its opposing principle—cleanliness that takes the form of rectilinearity, manifest in Cash's will to keep everything straight and tidy and hard and discrete. What he mainly attempts to keep impermeable and ruled is Addie's coffin: "a gout of mud, backflung, plops onto the box. Cash leans forward and takes a tool from his box and removes it carefully" (62). Cash's neatness and straightness seem to prevail in this skirmish, but as the body within the coffin rots, the ultimate victory would seem to belong to whatever deliquesces and leaks and permeates and stinks.

What fascinates Faulkner most in mud is its chromatic impurity, or more precisely say its excremental non-elementality. About Jewel's ankle swirls "a runnel of yellow neither water nor earth"; it curves with "the yellow road neither of earth nor water"; it dissolves into "a streaming mass of dark green neither of earth nor sky." The mud is rather like Thoreau's streaming mass of clay as it melts down the train embankment at Walden, but rather unlike the pond itself, which holds earth, water, and heaven in its reflection of the ideal harmonious inviolate beauty of the world. What mud means to Faulkner is that the world is nauseating (his Great War stories often feature vomit) because it cannot be contained, categorized, and idealized.

This again is a lesson that can be learned directly from World War I. If you read Eric Leed's remarkable book on the mythic structure of the war, *No Man's Land*, while thinking about Faulkner, you cannot avoid the sensation that Leed is writing about *As I Lay Dying*, though Faulkner is never mentioned in the study. Leed adopts the anthropologist Mary Douglas's notion of "pollution" to understand what the soldier in the trenches was experiencing. Leed quotes Douglas—"In short, pollution behavior is the reaction which condemns any object

---

6. William Faulkner, *Collected Stories of William Faulkner* (New York: Vintage/Random, 1995), 444–45.
7. A term dating from the U.S. war in Vietnam, though the practice itself is older. Assassinating an unpopular or oppressive officer from one's own unit; often, in Vietnam, with a fragmentation grenade. [*Editor*]

or idea likely to confuse or contradict our cherished classifications"—
and applies it to war:

> The most unsettling feature of the landscape of war, for many
> combatants, lay in the constant transgression of those distinc-
> tions that preserve both order and cleanliness. The men in the
> trenches lived with the rats that grew fat from eating the
> corpses of men and animals. The smell of the dead pervaded
> the front lines, penetrating even the deepest living quarters.
> The war literature is full of surprising encounters with corpses,
> complaints of being unable to prevent dirt, mud, and vermin
> from invading the most personal spaces.[8]

The feeling, while reading such a passage, which links categorical
confusion, rotting corpses, and mud, that I was reading Faulkner criticism was so strong that I began to think that the title of *As I Lay
Dying* was *No Man's Land* (for Addie dies partly to escape the men of
her family), and I began to fantasize a novel in the form of a memoir
written by a wounded, unevacuated, and finally dead but unburied
soldier in No Man's Land entitled *As I Lay Dying*.

It is of course one thing to imagine a world in which, generally,
boundaries and classifications are permeable, and another to imagine that the boundary between life and death is permeable. That is
what *As I Lay Dying* does imagine: Dr. Peabody pronounces that
Addie was dead ten days prior to her medical demise, during which
she supervises the construction of her own coffin, and in another
sense she stays alive for ten more days as she awaits, if that is the
right word, her burial. Once again, we may trace Faulkner's interest
in this Gothic horror to the Great War: his story "Crevasse" is about
the fear of burial alive—which seems to be the complementary pho-
bia to the fear of nonburial dead—in a cave in World War I. Again,
this is standard World War I horror: Leed discusses the invariant
dream of living burial after a shelling, "of being held motionless by
the weight of the earth" (NML 22). The front, Leed summarizes, "is
a place that dissolved the clean distinction between life and death"
(NML 21).

Not just Faulkner was writing, in the last years of the 1920s, about
the experience of seeing one's coffin or the aspects of one's grave
while one is still alive. In Erich Maria Remarque's *All Quiet on the
Western Front*, the narrator, on the way to the front, passes a shelled
schoolhouse. "Stacked up against its longer side is a high double wall
of yellow, unpolished, brand-new coffins. They still smell of resin,
and pine, and the forest. There are at least a hundred. . . . The coffins

8. Eric J. Leed, *No Man's Land: Combat and Identity in World War I* (New York: Cambridge
University Press, 1979), 18. All further references to this edition, abbreviated NML, will
be inserted in the text.

are really for us."[9] In Richard Aldington's *Death of a Hero*, a soldier "peered through [a shelled cottage window at the front] and saw that the whole of the inside had been cleared of débris, and was stacked with quantities of wooden objects. He shaded his eyes more carefully, and saw they were ranks and ranks of wooden crosses. Those he could see had painted on them R.I.P.; then underneath was a blank space for the name."[1]

Muddiness almost signifies death for Faulkner, as it seems to in the conjunction of muddy drawers and Damuddy's passing in *The Sound and the Fury*. More exactly, it seems to signify the incapacity for patrolling the boundary between life and death, or more exactly yet, it serves as the emblem for Faulkner's capacity for locating death in all life. Pregnancy feels to Dewey Dell like the invasion of her body by mud (or, as she says, guts); and after death, humans live in each other's minds like demons and ghosts, which is where and how they had always lived. In short, the way to feel death in life is to feel the incapacity for specifying where a self begins or ends. Temporally, this point is made by Faulkner's treatment of the fetus as a half-life, and of the moment of dying as a half-death. Spatially, the point is first made by way of Darl's capacity to inhabit a scene of death from which he is miles, and presumably years, removed. *As I Lay Dying* is a book not without boundaries, but with always trespassable boundaries, and in fact one of the strands of the plot, Dewey Dell's search for an abortion, has no ending, which means that the death we pursue cannot be killed off.

What is the appropriate linguistic theory for such a conception? Addie's speech provides it. Here is the point at which Faulkner's conception of reality implies his literary modernist project: the linguistic experimentation of *As I Lay Dying* derives from Addie's theories. When Addie thinks of her husband Anse, she homes on his name:

> Anse. Why Anse. Why are you Anse. I would think about his name until after a while I could see the word as a shape, a vessel, and I would watch him liquify [*sic*] and flow into it like cold molasses flowing out of the darkness into the vessel, until the jar stood full and motionless: a significant shape profoundly without life like an empty door frame; and then I would find that I had forgotten the name of the jar. (100)

This suggests that the way to produce an actual death—the once and for all kind—is to produce a name like a coffin. Naming is the only way to effect what Dewey Dell needs: it is the manufacturing of

9. Erich Maria Remarque, *All Quiet on the Western Front*, trans. A. W. Wheen (New York: Fawcett, 1929), 99–100.
1. Richard Aldington, *Death of a Hero* (Garden City, N.Y.: Garden City Publishing, 1929), 325.

containers to rigor mortis the amorphous, irreducible death-in-life and life-in-death of the viscous world.

This is the theory we need to understand some of the oddity of the way that *As I Lay Dying* was written. For example, the way words liquefy and coagulate and liquefy—like Anse in Addie's imagination, but not the labeled jar he flows into. In honor of Dewey Dell's pregnancy, the trees are said to be "swollen, increased as though quick with young" (44). Within a few pages, this phrase is echoed by the following linguistic flurry:

> "Yes, sir. It will rain some more."
> "It come up quick." (51)
>
> "It's been there a long time, that ere bridge," Quick says. (51)
>
> "A fellow can sho slip quick on wet planks," Quick says. (52)

This is either bizarrely incompetent writing or very interesting. I would choose interesting, particularly insofar as the word "quick" is a noun, an adjective, and an adverb, and refers simultaneously to birth, injury, and (because it is anticipated that the quick rain will wash the crop from the ground) abortion.

Or take what happens to the "bore" homonym-cluster, within one page of text:

> And the next morning they found [Vardaman] in his shirt tail, laying asleep on the floor like a felled steer, and the top of the box bored clean full of holes.
>
> And when folks talks [Anse] low, I think to myself he aint that less of a man or he couldn't a bore himself this long.
>
> Cora said, "I have bore you what the Lord God sent me." (42)

The homonyms suggest endurance, maternal nurturing, and violent maternal penetration. Also, tenses are confused, as they always are in Addie's virtuosic use of the word "lie" and cognates—"Then I would lay with Anse again—I did not lie to him" (101)—which muddles intimacy and isolation, body and spirit, verbal and physical intercourse, and past and future from the title of the novel onward.

Nouns in particular irritate Addie, as well they might, because the prestige of nouns keeps the world from liquefying or muddying. "[M]otherhood was invented by someone who had to have a word for it because the ones that had the children didn't care whether there was a word for it or not. I knew that fear was invented by someone that had never had the fear; pride, who never had the pride." And Anse "had a word, too. Love, he called it" (99).

We have neglected the Great War for a while, but here we are compelled to remember it. For every modernist worthy of the title had to consider, in the wake of the war, where all the high, noble locutions, nouns especially, had gone. Hemingway's dictum in *A Farewell to Arms* is famous: "abstract words such as glory, honor, courage, or hallow were obscene beside the concrete names of villages, the numbers of roads, the names of rivers, the numbers of regiments and the dates."[2] In this remark, we may register the distinction of Hemingway and Faulkner: Hemingway wants the names of rivers, Faulkner wants the river itself. That is, Hemingway wants less abstract, more concrete naming; Faulkner wants less abstract *and* less concrete naming, muddier half-naming. (The fallacy of misplaced concreteness in the cast almost mortifies Cash's living limb.) Another skew is that Hemingway wants to outlaw the word "courage," but does not deprecate, as Addie does, the word "fear": Hemingway's mode is disillusioned speech but Faulkner's is the border of the speakable. Still, what the two theories have in common is that words, unreformed, may elevate and etherealize the world, and Fussell—who provides a long list of recently outmoded words ("comrade" for friend, "steed" for horse, "peril" for danger, etc.)—assumes that the best place to learn about the treachery of ennobling nouns was the western front (MM 21–22).

Yet here, in the midst of an unexceptional summary of the linguistic effects of the Great War, the argument has to take its detour. The looming question about the psychological theory of the book (egos fail to quarantine body from body), the ontological theory of the book (the world is indivisible heavy flow), the linguistic theory of the book (words are not grammatical or semantic integers), and the formal theory of the book (narrative rides on streams of consciousness that overflow their banks) is why they are all announced by Addie, rather than Darl.

Granted that Addie is rather violent. In fact, she seems to resemble a type of soldier that Eric Leed is interested in. Leed's book is about the way that World War I invited soldiers into the dynamic of a rite of passage, isolating them, defamiliarizing the world for them, acquainting them with death, but failed to give them a world to return to, restored. The war was not a redemptive escape from the ordinary trials of life; it was a nearly infinite magnification of them. One way out was hysteria. Another was identification with the war machine, itself, as practiced by the soldier-litterateur, Ernst Jünger. Jünger is the sort of German, familiar to us from Klaus Theweleit's great book on the German Freikorps, *Male Fantasies*,[3] who writes passages like this:

> But now [in a breakthrough] we will rip away this veil [of trenches and fire power] instead of gingerly lifting its corner. . . . We will

2. Ernest Hemingway, *A Farewell to Arms* (New York: Scribner's, 1929), 185.
3. Klaus Theweleit, *Male Fantasies: Vol. 1: Women, Floods, Bodies, History*, trans. Stephen Conway (Minneapolis: University of Minnesota Press, 1987).

force open the closed door and enter by force into the forbidden land. And for us who have, for so long, been forced to accumulate in desolate fields of shell holes, the idea of this thrust into the depths holds a compelling fascination. We will demolish the dikes and break like a stormflood into the broad, untouched region. Every day new villages and cities appear to our gaze and rich booty falls into our fist. (NML 158–59)

Leed has recourse to Wilhelm Reich on sadism and masochism, especially sadism, to diagnose this, and he also intuits signs of the incestuous in Jünger's penetration of the forbidden. It is hard not to think of Addie, whose unorthodox, proto-incestuous pedagogical techniques were probably frowned upon even in her day. She would look forward to her students' mistakes, so she could "whip them. When the switch fell I could feel it upon my flesh, when it welted and ridged it was my blood that ran, and I would think with each blow of the switch: Now you are aware of me! Now I am something in your secret and selfish life, who have marked your blood with my own for ever and ever" (98).

You need blood, one way or the other, if you yearn to escape the ordinary entrenched weariness of your own life. We might be inclined to wish that Addie, rather than Darl, had been allowed to enlist to do so. But the fact is that Addie, unlike Jünger, and unlike all the German Freikorps writers quoted by Theweleit, does not thwart the vulnerability of her passions by an identification with the rigid and unyielding machine: she desires complete mutual confluence of liquescent flesh and liquescent flesh. This is precisely the seductive horror that the Freikorps steeled itself against. She proposed to find her joy not in war but in what we might have called, if she had not warned us away from the term, motherhood. Pregnancy is for her a kind of dying, in the Renaissance sense (it is dying for Dewey Dell in the usual sense); it is how Addie performs a ritual sacrifice of her identity to her passion.

I hope two things are clear. The first is that As I Lay Dying is nearly a perfect specimen of the Great War novel, written during the outpouring of Great War writing that commenced a decade after the armistice. The second is that the Great War is nearly irrelevant to it. It is from Addie's autobiography that we learn almost everything necessary to understand the Bundrens and the novel and the world they share. From Darl's war experience, we surmise nothing. Why write a war novel in which war is negligible?

My guess is that Faulkner began his career as a novelist on the principle that coming to terms with the Great War was the first obligation of the modernist. If you consider Faulkner's odd-numbered novels at the beginning of his career, you track a series that devolves to the cameo appearance of the war in As I Lay Dying. In his first novel, *Soldiers' Pay*, Faulkner teaches himself the technique of making his narrative spiral around an almost mute character, Donald Mahon, who is dead while still alive ("The man that was wounded is dead and this is another, a grown child"),[4] who is permitted a single passage in which to recall the circumstances of his wounding, and whose physical death seems a perfection of the immobility of his final days. That Donald was an aviator in the Great War makes his always waning afterlife typical of "all the dead pilots." Yet Faulkner will transfer all Mahon's moribundity to a woman whose earthbound adult experience consists of being a schoolteacher, a wife, once a lover, and five times a mother.

In the short story I just alluded to, "All the Dead Pilots," we are told that all the pilots are dead in the Donald Mahon–Addie Bundren sense, with one exception, John Sartoris, who was shot down.[5] And Faulkner's third novel, *Flags in the Dust*, is largely about Bayard Sartoris, who most resembles Jewel in *As I Lay Dying*, as he careers around town on horseback or in cars trying to replicate his brother John's spectacular destruction.[6] There is, however, a peculiar turn in the novel, by the end of which the subject is not so much Bayard's suffering as his great-aunt Miss Jenny's and his wife Narcissa's. Miss Jenny endured Grant's total warfare. Narcissa gives birth on the day her husband crashes a plane he is test-piloting and dies; this means, in Faulkner's view, that she has fought her war more successfully than the Sartoris men fight theirs. She surrounds her infant with "wave after wave of the strength which welled so abundantly within her as the days accumulated, manning the walls with invincible garrisons." With Faulkner's approval, apparently, Narcissa "thought how much finer that gallantry which never lowered lance to foes no sword could ever find, that uncomplaining steadfastness of those unsung (ay, unwept, too) women than the fustian and useless glamor of the men that theirs was hidden from" (FD, 349, 350). Only maternity, at this stage of the progression, earns the diction that the Great War outmoded for war and men.

This is not merely to congratulate women on a stalwart endurance that is non-violent. It is also to say that they live in a different historical time from men. Female days "accumulate" (in the case of Narcissa's pregnancy); Dewey Dell's pregnancy allows her to understand "what they mean by the womb of time: the agony and the despair of spreading bones, the hard girdle in which lie the outraged entrails of events" (69). These are the two moods of one temporal sense. Male

---

4. William Faulkner, *Soldiers' Pay* (New York: Liveright, 1926), 118. All further references to this edition, abbreviated SP, will be inserted in the text.
5. William Faulkner, "All the Dead Pilots," in *Collected Stories*, 511–31.
6. William Faulkner, *Flags in the Dust* (New York: Random House, 1973). All further references to this edition, abbreviated FD, will be inserted in the text.

temporality, on the other hand, can only seek climaxes. This means either that men achieve their climax in war, like Donald Mahon, who symbolically loses his virginity and his potency in a single act of air combat, and are condemned thereafter to a life of ebbing anti-climax, or they fail to achieve their climax in war, like Bayard Sartoris, and are impelled thereafter to seek it in a furious peacetime. Here is how aviator sex is described in *Soldiers' Pay* by Januarius Jones: "Do you know how falcons make love? They embrace at an enormous height and fall locked, beak to beak, plunging: an unbearable ecstasy. While we have got to assume all sorts of ludicrous postures, knowing our own sweat." His lack of self-conscious sweat makes the falcon's fall unfallen; it seems to be marked by a fearlessness of shameful lapsarian anti-climax: "The falcon breaks his clasp and swoops away swift and proud and lonely, while a man must rise and take his hat and walk out" (SP 227). Faulkner, like the virginal cadet Lowe, never flew this high; but as a "falconer," perhaps he had an instinct for proud and lonely falcon intercourse. Mahon actually experiences it; but he is a man, after all, and his deflation is always gravewards.

I once posited, grandiosely, that one of the reasons for the invention of literature was the failure of war to be beautiful; I hypothesized that one of the most urgent meta-themes of *The Iliad* was the decay of warfare from war-as-duel (symmetrical, bounded, swift, pure, lonely, complete) to asymmetrical, prolonged, squalid strategic combat.[7] John Keegan and Richard Holmes tell us that

> the onset of mass-produced weapons, something approaching which was made possible by the introduction of iron about 1200 B.C., confronted the champion of single combat with a threat he had not previously had to face. It was that of a body of enemies who, because they could match him both in quantity and quality of weapons, did not need to equal him in skill in order to beat him. Not, at least, if they were prepared to undergo collective training and to conform vigorously to drill and to orders during the course of action.[8]

Organized armies began to appear around 1000 B.C., about half way from the Trojan War to its epic, so that a warrior began to be transformed into a soldier. Previously, Keegan and Holmes write, "Hector and Achilles [had fought] as individuals, indeed, as the poet tells us, almost as performers under the eye of their assembled supporters" (S 25). What seems, however, to preoccupy Homer in *The Iliad* is the failure of the Trojan War to take the form of already

7. John Limon, *Writing After War: American War Fiction from Realism to Postmodernism* (New York: Oxford University Press, 1994).
8. John Keegan and Richard Holmes, *Soldiers: A History of Men in Battle* (New York: Viking, 1986), 23. All further references to this edition, abbreviated S, will be inserted in the text.

aesthetic duels of emblematic individuals: the Akhaian side cannot cohere; attempts at duels to epitomize and settle the conflict are foiled by partisan goddesses; when individual combat momentarily crystallizes, other soldiers often rush to the defense of the weaker warrior, shattering the duel; and occasionally the war decomposes into pure melee. The war fails to be beautiful, and Homer can only maintain the war as an aesthetic object by continually bowing to the ideal of combat beauty that has been lost.

What Faulkner was after, in his early life and early career as a novelist, was warfare that seemed to be the harbinger of all modernity but that actually allowed him to fulfill his Southern dream of pre-historic, pre-literary, personal, duel-like, beautiful combat. When he enlisted in the Royal Air Force in Canada to fight in the Great War, and when he pretended (after no combat experience) to be injured in a crash, he was looking to the most technologically advanced aspect of the (to date) most brutal and technologically revolutionary war to fulfill a dream of gallantry already antique at the time of Homer. The point of Faulkner's anachronism was to fulfill his dream of a better, or a redeemed, Civil War; a war in need of redemption, for one thing, because it had its own crucial role in the eternal falling away of war from the symmetrical, bounded, and complete form of the duel. Keegan and Holmes specify that

> in the middle of the nineteenth century, the technological equilibrium which had endowed the European infantryman with his battle-winning capacity was suddenly upset. New firearms, rifled to enhance accuracy at unprecedented ranges and then furnished with a magazine to decuple firepower, rendered close-order infantry tactics not merely ineffective but dangerous and self-defeating. The character of the battles of the American Civil War . . . had issued that warning in stark terms. . . . By the end of the first decade of the twentieth century it was clear to any dispassionate observer that the era of the primacy of man in warfare was drawing to a close and that the era of the primacy of the machine was at hand. (S 14)

Was the primacy of man in warfare, in retreat since 1000 B.C., absolutely at an end three millennia later in the first decade of the twentieth century, a single teasing decade before Faulkner went to Canada to seek it? Not quite, because until 1917, when "the development of fighting and flying in formation . . . replace[d] the Homeric combat of individual champions," the airplane had, ironically, revived the beauty of the duel as the last, best hope of heroic, aesthetic warfare.[9] Thus the Great War, at its beginning, and as conjured at the

---

9. B. H. Liddell Hart, *The Real War: 1914–1918* (Boston: Little, Brown, 1930), 316.

beginning of Faulkner's career, offered an authentic prolongation of hope to Faulkner for locating beauty within modernity. If this is your project, paradox will have to be your mode, and here is the central paradox of Faulkner's war writing: disillusion exists to maintain illusion. Aviators will have to be disillusioned by post-war, peacetime modernity as tribute to the illusion that properly aesthetic climaxes can still appear in modernized killing and dying.

As I Lay Dying, however, is a melee. (The simple ratio of the ancient duel is as demolished in it as the various quotients of the Greek elements.) It is uncertain where the alliances are (the family is united when it faces outward and antagonistic when it faces inward, like the Akhaians); it is certain that death is not final and climactic; the book is attrition in mud. And by the end of the book, very little has been settled.

Does war ever settle anything? The question is critical for literature because, if it does, then fiction is aesthetically inferior to history. The traditional American view is that war's capacity to settle things is its essence; even if the fighting is squalid and brutal, the closure is dramatic. William James considered the Civil War to be the perfect specimen: interrupting what would have been a protracted history of compromises on slavery, the Civil War simply abolished it. In "The Moral Equivalent of War," which might as well have been titled "The Aesthetic Equivalent of War," James, trying to imagine how war might be transcended, felt obliged to concede "the unwillingness of the imagination" to "envisage a future in which . . . the destinies of people shall nevermore be decided quickly, thrillingly, and tragically."[1] His diction is not so different from that of Januarius Jones. But the Civil War needed redeeming not merely as the prototype of trench warfare but as anesthetic, incomplete warfare, and Faulkner, at the end of a decade in which a great wave of Klan lynchings had attenuated the proper outcome of the Civil War, would come in As I Lay Dying to believe that the only way to defend his right to his art after the Great War was to develop a form of the novel that had its own reasons for inconclusiveness. In one gesture, he would absorb the lessons of the immobile, noisy, noisome trenches and marginalize them, because even to condemn the Great War was to honor the dream of a greater war, in the unfallen past or redemptive future, to suit the male fantasy of beautiful combat.

Perhaps A Fable provides the best evidence that Faulkner conceived of the Great War, by its nature as a war, as still unfinished. The book concerns a French army mutiny in May of 1918. Faulkner seems to consider it a tragic irony that

---

1. Bruce W. Wilshire, ed., *William James: The Essential Writings* (Albany, N.Y.: State University of Albany Press, 1984), 355.

by mutinying, the regiment had stopped the war; it had saved France (France? England too; the whole West; since nothing else apparently had been able to stop the Germans since the March breakthrough in front of Amiens) and this [mass execution] was to be its reward; the three thousand men who had saved France and the world, would lose their lives. . . .[2]

Ah yes, we are pleased to lament, how ironic that those who saved the world from war are killed for their trouble! Then something occurs to us: the war, without the mutiny, would be over in six months, anyway. England, France, the West, and the world were not, it happened, in mortal jeopardy. The only thing that Faulkner might have intended, as far as I can guess, by this apparent amnesia is that what the mutiny was saving Europe and the West and the world from was the *second* World War (recall that Faulkner began *A Fable* in 1943). Germany, not observing, in all the dead soldiers, ritual testimony of the unjustness of its cause, had reopened the war at the next opportunity—and had not yet been stopped.[3] The reason that not just England and France but also the West and the world were in jeopardy was the Bomb (remember that Faulkner completed the novel in 1954).

The world was Bayard Sartoris of *Flags in the Dust*, seeking climaxes in mimetic pursuit of previous—imaginary—satisfactions. Man will not only not prevail; he will not endure. The practical point of the strike in May 1918 was to prevent the final masculinization of history; but in Addie Bundren's dying—her willful, mutinous death in her own No Man's Land—Faulkner had already offered a ritual sacrifice to the same end. The Great War was muddy and inconclusive, but it resembled the Civil War in fostering a nostalgia or longing for beautiful violent climaxes; hence the resemblance of the Freikorps to the Ku Klux Klan; hence, in a word, Percy Grimm of *Light in August*, who never forgives his parents for his being born too young for the Great War, and who becomes a lyncher, instead.[4] One of the achievements of *As I Lay Dying*, despite its origin in combat envy, is that it found a way, by centering on the civilian Addie rather than the veteran Darl, to incorporate muddy undead formlessness into its form without fostering, at the same time, by the same act, the prospective nostalgia for apocalypse that would bring the world, in the year of Faulkner's death and the Cuban missile crisis, to the brink of clean and swift closure.

2. William Faulkner, *A Fable*, in *William Faulkner Novels, 1942–1954*, ed. Joseph Blotner and Noel Polk (New York: Library of America, 1994), 782.
3. See Elaine Scarry, *The Body in Pain: The Making and Unmaking of the World* (New York: Oxford University Press, 1985), for the most sophisticated discussion of the relation of dead bodies to war closure.
4. William Faulkner, *Light in August* (New York: Vintage/Random, 1990), 449–65.

DONALD M. KARTIGANER

"By It I Would Stand or Fall":
Life and Death in *As I Lay Dying*†

As I Lay Dying (1930) is a novel about making a journey in order to fulfill a promise, combining private need with family duty, lyric meditation with narrative action—conceived by a writer who has reached a moment in his career when these conflicting drives have become the terms of his own personal and professional situation. The novel, in other words, is self-reflexive in the most basic, even literal sense: the fictional characters and action mirror the writer's drama of composition, an art of tragic/comic compromise whose rewards and costs we are still learning to measure.

When Faulkner and the former Estelle Oldham Franklin returned to Oxford from their honeymoon in Pascagoula in the late summer of 1929, he was probably aware that not only his life but his writing would be taking new directions. As his letter that spring to his publisher Hal Smith, asking for a loan of $500, clearly indicates, he had entered the marriage with very mixed feelings: "I am going to be married. Both want to and have to. . . . For my honor and the sanity—I believe life—of a woman. . . . It's a situation which I engendered and permitted to ripen which has become unbearable, and I am tired of running from devilment I bring about."[1] The "running from devilment I bring about," like the reference to "bastard" children elsewhere in the letter, is likely that degree of posturing that Faulkner rarely avoided even in his most serious communications—part of the mask he never wholly dropped—yet there is no reason to doubt the conflict of desire and skepticism he felt toward marriage to Estelle. The honeymoon itself, climaxed by an apparent attempt by Estelle to drown herself in the Gulf, hardly allayed the misgivings both of them had about a relationship that had begun in childhood but was now being renewed only after her 12-year marriage to Cornell Franklin had ended.

During that summer Faulkner also read the galley proofs of *The Sound and the Fury* (1929). This too must have inspired a mixture of exhilaration and realistic reassessment. Although on the verge of publishing his fourth novel, it was difficult for Faulkner to feel optimistic about the task of reconciling the responsibilities of married life (which included two children by Estelle's first marriage) with the responsibilities of a writer. In terms of sales his situation was

† From *A Companion to William Faulkner*, ed. Richard C. Moreland (Oxford: Blackwell, 2007), pp. 429–44. Reprinted by permission of Wiley-Blackwell.
1. Joseph L. Blotner, *Faulkner: A Biography*, rev. ed. (New York: Random House, 1984), p. 240.

hardly promising. The reception of his most recently published novel, *Sartoris*, in January 1929, a radically cut version of *Flags in the Dust*, was discouraging. His attempt that spring, with marriage to Estelle looming, to write a novel that would sell had proved abortive when Smith deemed the original *Sanctuary* (1931) too sensational for publication. Moreover, Alfred Harcourt, the publisher of *Sartoris*, had expressed doubt about the salability of *The Sound and the Fury*, and did not object when Smith took it with him when he formed the firm of Cape and Smith. However impressed Faulkner may have been by the novel to which he later insisted "the shabby term Art not only can but must be applied,"[2] he must have realized that whatever he wrote in the future would have to be of a far different character.

* * *

In the fall of 1929 Faulkner and Estelle were living in the first-floor rental of Elma Meek's house on University Avenue, their first home as a married couple. He began working the night shift at the University of Mississippi Power Plant—6:00 p.m. to 6:00 a.m.—acting as supervisor to two African American men who did the work of getting coal into the boiler. Improvising a table out of a wheelbarrow in the coal bunker and working between 12 midnight and 4:00 a.m., when the need for heat at the university declined, all the while listening to the methodical hum of a dynamo on the other side of the wall, Faulkner wrote *As I Lay Dying*.

The descriptive terms for this novel were "deliberate" and "*tour de force*"—the latter always implying for Faulkner success of a lesser nature: long on virtuosity but a bit short on profundity, not to mention gallantry and magnificence. "I took this family," he said, "and subjected them to the two greatest catastrophes which man can suffer—flood and fire, that's all. That was simple *tour de force*. That was written in six weeks without changing a word because I knew from the first where that was going."[3] * * * The married man, needing to earn a living, leaves home at 5:30 p.m. He walks the mile to his power plant work place, carrying his manuscript and already writing sentences in his head (and probably passing, unacknowledged, acquaintances on the street). He performs whatever his supervisory role requires, and around midnight sits down to his wheelbarrow as the dynamo whirrs in the next room. * * * [H]e begins writing on October 25 and completes the manuscript on December 11. Presumably he doesn't bring his typewriter to the power plant, and finishes the typescript at home

2. William Faulkner, "An Introduction for *The Sound and the Fury*" in David Minter ed., *The Sound and the Fury* (New York: Norton, 1994), p. 226.
3. *Faulkner in the University: Class Conferences at the University of Virginia, 1957–58*, ed. Frederick L. Gwynn and Joseph L. Blotner (Charlottesville, VA: University of Virginia Press, 1959), p. 87.

January 12, 1930. To be sure, some words are changed, but manuscript and typescript confirm Faulkner's later claim that, of all his novels, *As I Lay Dying* required the least rewriting.

What I find particularly striking here is how the circumstances of writing, as well as how Faulkner chose to describe those circumstances, permeate the written, invest the narrowness, the elemental quality of the fictional experience, becoming its strategy and its theme. In place at the outset, waiting upon the imminent death of Addie Bundren, is the journey to Jefferson: a fixed line of narrative dictated by a woman's request made almost 30 years earlier. Fulfilling that request is her hill-country farming family, each member of which—except one, *always* except one—is reduced to a private obsession as powerful as the promise, yet inseparable from it. However delayed the progress, circuitous the route, or compromised the motive, the Bundrens are always on the way to Jefferson. "I give her my promise," Anse Bundren says repeatedly, "Her mind is set on it" (65).

The constraints of the act of writing and the novel they produce are reflected as well in the absence of much that had already become distinctive in Faulkner's work, published and unpublished—as if time and circumstance were also forcing him to abandon certain concerns he had once considered an essential part of his chosen fictional locale. One of these is race, which would always be a standard omission in his fiction about country people in the southeastern quarter of what in this novel he named Yoknapatawpha County. In a number of respects Faulkner modeled the area on his own Lafayette County, the southeast sector of which indeed had a sparse black population, unlike the northern and western sectors of richer soil and larger plantations, where the great majority of black tenant farmers was employed. Black representation in *As I Lay Dying* consists of one nameless figure, a man living on the outskirts of Jefferson who says, as the wagon with the nine-day-rotting body of Addie Bundren rolls by, " 'Great God . . . what they got in that wagon?' " (132). By the time Jewel Bundren turns to respond to the insult, he is already abreast of a white man.

Another omission is memory, and here the difference between *As I Lay Dying* and other Frenchman's Bend fiction is notable. To be sure, unlike the Sartorises and Compsons, unlike, that is, the descendants of the white planter aristocracy, the people of Frenchman's Bend do not have a multi-generational past to deal with, no proud forebears they are prepared to honor or attempt to equal. In "Father Abraham," the novel Faulkner probably began in 1926 and left unfinished until *The Hamlet* (1940), the local population recalls neither the name nor the nationality of the former great planter of the area; every outlander is simply a "frenchman." They value his large abandoned holdings only for the wood of the house they can burn for fuel and the rumor of buried gold they dream of digging up. In *As I Lay Dying*, however, Faulkner reduces the significance of memory still further. There is one "memory" beyond the lives of the current Bundrens, and it is neither a person nor an incident but a single utterance recalled only by Addie: "I could just remember how my father used to say that the reason for living was to get ready to stay dead a long time" (98). This is memory not as ignorance of the past or pragmatic use of it, but as outright dismissal: the past as merely the necessary route to the single experience that endures.

* * *

In *As I Lay Dying* Faulkner registers the difficult life of the small farmer, but he leaves out most of the dehumanizing and inequitable practices he describes at great length elsewhere. To begin with, Anse Bundren is not a tenant but a landowner, which puts him in a category of less than 30 percent of the farm population of 1930 Mississippi. His neighbor Vernon Tull is also a landowner and has paid off his mortgage. Anse's reputation when he meets Addie is that of a man with a "new house" and "a good farm," a man "forehanded" with "a good honest name" (99). The Bundrens are obviously not well off; their clothes are patched, the men are thin, Addie's coffin is made at home rather than purchased, Anse has genuine health problems as well as possibly spurious ones. But there is every indication that they make and sell a crop and feed themselves. The supper of greens they eat the night Addie dies * * * is not their typical fare. Both the Bundrens and the Tulls speak of the hardship of their lives compared with those of town folks, and prior to harvest their supply of cash is limited. Vardaman is especially conscious of what he believes town boys can have and the costliness of staples they cannot raise on the farm, like flour and sugar and coffee. But the Bundrens manage. * * * It is also clear that some of the Bundrens' frugality—waiting until the last minute before calling the doctor, using cement on Cash's leg because " 'We done bought the cement, now' pa says" (120)—are as much owing to Anse's pettiness as to genuine poverty. * * *

Of major importance, as Sylvia Jenkins Cook pointed out years ago, "No class of oppressors or exploiters exists in the book."[4] Will Varner is mentioned in *As I Lay Dying* only in his role as veterinarian, called in to tend Cash's broken leg in Peabody's absence. The Bundrens are not tenants of Varner, paying a percentage of their crop and always running the risk of ending a season in debt owing to compulsory, high-priced purchases at a company store. Nor is there any reference, as in *The Hamlet*, to the kind of implicit intimidation Varner

---

4. Sylvia J. Cook, *From Tobacco Road to Route 66: The Southern Poor White in Fiction* (Chapel Hill: University of North Carolina Press, 1976), p. 45.

wields as the owner of store, cotton gin, grist mill, and blacksmith shop. * * * Cook comments on the longstanding custom among Anse's neighbors and friends of helping him out: "In a world where charity like this exists, the question of pervasive poverty is made irrelevant."[5] This is a very different world from the Frenchman's Bend of "Father Abraham" and *The Hamlet*, where economic hardship drives men like Henry Armstid mad and Mink Snopes to murder. Above all, there is the simple fact that the great "catastrophes" of flood and fire that the Bundrens endure on the journey to Jefferson have nothing to do with their poverty but with the chance of weather and the exceptional character in the novel, Darl Bundren.

The stream-of-consciousness technique of *As I Lay Dying* also has a leaner look than its predecessor in the modern mode, *The Sound and the Fury*. Much shorter in length, the references and allusions, the twists of memory easier to follow, the interior monologues of *As I Lay Dying* * * * are keyed directly to the narrative action. Each monologue, with the significant exception of Addie's (expressed at no identifiable time) and the two monologues surrounding hers by Cora Tull and Whitfield, follows the previous one in terms of the temporal progress of the action. Whether immediately after or hours later, the monologues serve the family project, the journey, even as the individual characters do, despite the private obsessions that surface primarily in the monologues themselves.

What all this amounts to is our need to recognize that *As I Lay Dying* is a novel that strips away much of what normally goes into Faulkner's characterization of human experience, whether in the town or the country. It strips away as well a characteristic exuberance of expression present even in the darkest of his novels. The product of what he consistently described—and to a large extent his biography confirms—as a contained and controlled writing experience, answering to the new demands of marriage and family, *As I Lay Dying* * * * exhibits an almost inhuman reduction of character to the barest urges of desire and destination, reflecting a level of reality unique in Faulkner's fiction. The prominence of Addie's father's flat insistence that our lives are no more than preparation for death, whatever the form our "readiness" may take, draws the novel into consideration of the hypothesis Freud raises in *Beyond the Pleasure Principle*: "that '*the aim of all life is death.*'"[6] The death to which life drives, according to Freud and more than likely according to Addie's father, is not the higher, heavenly existence of Christian belief, but an original inanimacy, a stasis beneath being from which we have been disturbed by external stimuli.

---

5. Cook, p. 46.
6. Sigmund Freud, *Beyond the Pleasure Principle*, trans. J. Strachey, 1920 (New York: Norton, 1961), p. 32.

* * * Freud revises the dualism he always insists on as the core of psychic life by replacing the conflict between ego instincts and sexual instincts with the conflict between life and death: the forces of Eros and Thanatos. Eros is the instinct "towards change and development . . . towards progress and the production of new forms."[7] It moves outward to an external object of love, to family, to community, aiming "to establish ever greater unities and to preserve them thus— in short, to bind together."[8] Ideally it is the "instinct toward perfection at work in human beings, which has brought them to their present high level of intellectual achievement and ethical sublimation."[9] Eros is countered by the drive to destruction, "to undo connections and so to destroy things,"[1] ultimately to fulfill the basic human need to replace all psychic disturbance with former psychic calm by returning to "the quiescence of the inorganic world."[2] As for "living," it is nothing but the process of our return to inanimacy, what Freud calls the "detour," "the circuitous path . . . to death, faithfully kept to by the conservative instincts" that constitutes "the picture of the phenomena of life."[3] Those phenomena are in fact determined by the urge to die, to restore "an earlier state of things."[4]

Beyond the Pleasure Principle provides us with an illuminating perspective on this moment in Faulkner's life and career and the novel that ensues from it, as he explores the elemental matters of life and death and the emerging question of which is primary, which the source most his own. What life, now radically altered by marriage, would be his and how would it affect his work? What would he write that would be of and for that life, and yet still speak with the power of the inviolable privacy that might reflect the death that was always with him? For the first time in his published work Faulkner places country people at the center of a fiction, as if, in the manner of Wordsworth, he sees in them the opportunity to describe the most fundamental human condition. He assigns them what is for him an uncharacteristically straightforward, if lugubrious task: transporting a dead body from Frenchman's Bend to Jefferson. For the Bundrens there will be no plot that "doesn't get anywhere and has a thousand loose ends," as Faulkner's publisher claimed about *Flags in the Dust*, and might well have repeated about *The Sound and the Fury*.[5] Like Faulkner, beginning a writer's life as a married man, the Bundrens have a job to do and the novel tells the story of how they get it done.

---

7. Ibid, pp. 30–31.
8. Sigmund Freud, *An Outline of Psychoanalysis*, trans. J. Strachey, 1940 (New York: Norton, 1969), p. 5.
9. *Beyond the Pleasure Principle*, p. 36.
1. *An Outline of Psychoanalysis*, p. 5.
2. *Beyond the Pleasure Principle*, p. 56.
3. Ibid, p. 33
4. Ibid, p. 31.
5. Blotner, pp. 204–5.

But what are the compromises required to complete it, the conflicts of personal and familial loyalties? How do purpose and detour relate to each other? Is it a journey of life or death the Bundrens carry out, life or death that this novel sings?

The implications Freud draws from the possibility of a death instinct "beyond the pleasure principle" are the implications Faulkner explores in *As I Lay Dying*. He widens the net of "detours" until it enfolds virtually all the action and motive of the text, so that life and death engage each other in a reciprocity impossible to sort out into separate categories. The Bundrens are living as dying, dying as living, each drive engendering, distorting, depending on the other. If this is Eros as the paradigmatic narrative quest, it is also Eros as a long and torturous burial of the dead.

Addie Bundren is the one who enacts that reciprocal relationship with the greatest awareness, treading the paths of life and death with a deliberate and brazen simultaneity. Father, she insists, may have been right in his grim pronouncement, but "he couldn't have known he was right" (100), in fact "he could not have known what he meant himself" (101–2). Her intention is to replace her father's vision with one that "knows" it is right and what it "means" to be right. As a result she becomes the central figure of compromise in a novel of compromises, one feature of which is the terrible price they exact.

Addie's life is partly a series of joinings, the creation of "greater unities" in defiance of her father, and partly the subversion of such joinings in defiance of her husband Anse. She instigates the journey, sets in motion a purpose to be achieved, but she also undermines that journey, transforming it into detour. * * * For Addie, Eros is the means of containing death by exploiting its very destructiveness. Freud argues that the two instincts rarely if ever appear in isolation from each other. Given his theory that the inherent masochism of the death instinct can be turned outward as sadism, as aggression, the death instinct "could be pressed into the service of Eros, in that the organism was destroying some other thing . . . instead of destroying its own self."[6] Addie expands this concept by demonstrating how that aggression can serve Eros by moving toward greater unities. This is not merely the aggressive component of sexuality, but a violence that enables her to free herself, at least temporarily, from the isolation, the privacy that partakes of the original inanimacy itself. Observing her pupils, "each with his and her secret and selfish thought, and blood strange to each other blood and strange to mine," Addie thinks, "I would hate my father for having ever planted me" (98). Her retaliation against the death wish, ironically, is to make connection through

6. Sigmund Freud, *Civilization and Its Discontents*, trans. J. Strachey, 1930 (New York: Norton, 1961), p. 66.

corporal punishment: "only through the blows of the switch could my blood and their blood flow as one stream" (99). Versions of this violence characterize all her attempts at binding together. She "takes" Anse as a husband, she experiences childbirth as "aloneness . . . violated and then made whole again by the violation," but now a wholeness that includes the child, Cash: "time, Anse, love, what you will, outside the circle" (99). She discharges the "duty to the alive, to the terrible blood" (101) through adultery with the minister Whitfield, violating marriage, sanctifying sin. Finally, Addie balances accounts, "cleaning up the house afterwards" (102), by coercing sexual engagement and the pains of childbirth into matrimonial duty: Eros in its service to Addie's sense of domestic equity.

For her vengeance on Anse, however, she turns her aggression against Eros itself, or rather the form of it he represents for her. She assigns him the task of transporting her dead body to Jefferson for burial * * * [and] "My revenge would be that he would never know I was taking revenge." (100) The revenge of the journey is that Anse Bundren should not know its reason. That *is* its reason, and no other one is ever stated by Addie. The journey is Addie's decreed "detour," exemplifying death's darkest ramification, the truth "older than Anse or love," what living amounts to if it only serves to consume the path to dying. The burial ritual is wholly incidental: a long march grave-ward whose primary burden is the corpse of its meaning. That Anse Bundren, whose central commitment in life has been to emulate the stationariness of a tree or a stand of corn, should be forced to set forth on an 80-mile detour is the heart of Addie's vengeance: a quest emptied of any goal other than its secret emptiness. It is the appropriate journey for the man Addie designates as "a significant shape profoundly without life like an empty door frame" (100).

Addie calls for the journey when Cash and Darl are infants, but by the time she is ready to die, the loyalty and private needs of all the Bundrens come into play. The effect of this is to complicate immeasurably the ironies already present. * * * Cash's coffin, Jewel's horse, Dewey Dell's fetus, Vardaman's fish, Anse's teeth—they incorporate Addie, and thus keep her alive (and themselves still joined to her) in the specific forms of devotion each entails. Cash's meticulous labor on the coffin that will house her, Jewel's violent love/hate possessiveness of the horse that, as Darl surmises, is his "mother," Dewey Dell's duplication of her in impending motherhood, Vardaman's belief in her transformation into a fish, Anse's recollection of their sexual relations—these all represent Addie's continuing presence for them, at times achieving a symbolic intensity close to incarnation.

These same images, however, also refer to personal desires that lead the Bundrens away from Addie toward Jefferson and the continuation of life. The coffin embodies not only Addie but Cash's vocation of carpentry, contiguous with the tools he brings on the trip so as to begin work afterwards on Tull's barn. The horse is the prize of Jewel's private night-time labor that he plans to ride into town, accompanying yet significantly separate from the rest of the mourning family. For Dewey Dell, the fetus is the focus of the grief she has no time to expend on Addie, and that she hopes to abort, breaking the connection of motherhood. Vardaman gradually turns his attention from the fish that keeps changing forms and locations to other, more mundane shifts in identity: the buzzards that disappear at night, the toy tracks that flash in and out of sight as the train runs over them in the store window. Anse adapts desire to his need for a new wife. Sentenced by Addie, as she was by her father, to a death journey, the family carries out resistance through the dynamic of devotion and release, answering to life and death forces on the same journey, detour and purpose fueling each other in inseparable reciprocity. * * *

Purposeful action exploiting the burial journey has the sound of life facing down death's claim on it, but there remains the accumulation of loss and suffering, the awful damage that journey inflicts. Except for Anse, the personal desires of the Bundrens come to naught, and the costs of the attempts are incredibly high. Cash, his leg rebroken, swelling black through its sleeve of cement, will not be repairing Tull's barn or anything else for some time. Jewel loses his horse in Anse's trade for a new team of mules, then returns to the family to suffer severe burns on his body while saving the coffin from the fire in Gillespie's barn. Dewey Dell is not only unsuccessful at aborting the baby, but she has to pay for it by submitting to the violation of sex with the ruthless MacGowan. Vardaman finds in the buzzards, the destruction of Gillespie's barn, the fact that bananas once eaten are gone, and in the toy train new manifestations of the mutability that has traumatized him. * * *

Beyond the individual losses and suffering there is the whole enormous nine-day ordeal. Close to home are generous but skeptical neighbors who cannot penetrate the collective privacy of this family, whose actions no one fully understands. Then there is the threshold event, the nightmare river crossing, when, like the debris skimming along the surface, the Bundrens find themselves "rootless, severed from the earth, spectral above a scene of immense yet circumscribed desolation" (82). Finally, in the towns of Mottson and Jefferson they pass into increasingly less sympathetic surroundings, as onlookers grow more distant, contemptuous, always ready to invoke the law, confirmed in their sense of country people as virtually of another species.

But what of Anse? Alone among the Bundrens, he suffers no loss, either physically or psychically, and in addition to keeping his "promise" acquires all he has sought: new teeth, a new wife. His "image"—"God's will be done. . . . Now I can get them teeth" (30)—contains in its possible memory of sexual desire less of a commitment to Addie than to the sexual potency he wishes to implement again. He is able to transfer that desire to another partner with the least amount of conflict and the largest amount of equivalent satisfaction. * * * We might gather from this that Addie's revenge has been a godsend for Anse Bundren, a reversal of irony at her expense, but I believe this completely misses the point. Addie has Anse right, and his actions on the journey are perfectly typical of what she expects from him. The difference between Anse and the other Bundrens, especially Addie, is that for him there is no true reciprocity of the primary instincts at work. Anse's Eros is contrived altogether of words; it is desire unmixed with death. There is no aggression, no violence from "below"—self-destruction turned to the intruding world—from which powerful attachment, obsession might come forth. Anse's erotic movements outward betray only the speciousness of words "quick and harmless" (100), words that "don't ever fit even what they are trying to say at" (99). They do not own the power of the Bundrens' impassioned bondage (necessarily smacking of the absurdity of obsession) to their images of desire, or of Addie's adultery torn from sin "to shape and coerce the terrible blood to the forlorn echo of the dead word high in the air" (101). In short, as a "pure" Eros, Anse lacks the power Eros borrows from its foe in order to create its own costly significance. * * *

If there is a figure opposite Anse in the novel, it is not Addie and the Bundrens who follow her example into the reciprocities of life and death, but Darl Bundren, who belongs entirely to the sphere of death. His remarkable powers of vision are the gift of a virtual inanimacy-in-life from which he looks out on the world. He has no part of Eros: no desires, no images, no obsessive attachments—no palpable substitute for Addie to threaten him with too deep a devotion, or for him to transform into the cunning displacement that will urge him to Jefferson.

Addie denies him at conception— * * * and at his birth she devises the revenge of the promise that she be buried in Jefferson. Unlike her other children, there is no erotic dimension in his creation: not, as with Cash, the "answer" to the discovery that "living was terrible" (99); not, as with Jewel, the adultery that is "the duty to the alive"; not even, as with Dewey Dell and Vardaman, the obligation to clean one's house, conceiving children as payments on a debt: "now he had three children that are his and not mine" (102).

Having nothing of Eros, Darl has no neurotic need to exploit his inherent masochism in aggressive pursuits. He functions out of a perfect detachment that is the source of his exactingly objective vision that registers the world as it is, divested of desire. His narrative description of the death of Addie and the immediate responses of the Bundrens to it has the power of a passion based not on empathy but on its absence, on an indiscriminate wonder that spreads evenly among the outraged mourners: from the daughter keening across the lifeless body to the husband fumbling helplessly over the wrinkled quilt he cannot smooth over.

What Darl sees or miraculously infers is magnificent to read but in the family or society within which he exists it is not to be borne. He does not act with the violence of Addie Bundren challenging death, but he is the supreme agent of violation in the novel. He invades the people around him, not for sex but for secrets, that private, interior world, the residue of inanimacy that survives in life not as an intimation of immortality but of the death we all harbor, seek to protect and to delay. It is the inviolable self, hidden even from the family, that Darl, like Hawthorne's diabolical inquisitors, enters as through an open door. He knows the secret of Dewey Dell's pregnancy, that Jewel is not Anse's son, perhaps even that the entire journey is Addie's fabricated detour.

The vision is monstrous because it lacks even the intelligibility of malice. We wonder whether Darl is aware that he wounds in his probing questions: "I said to Dewey Dell: 'You want her to die so you can get to town: is that it?'" (24); "Your mother was a horse, but who was your father, Jewel?" (123). While at Armstid's house, as Anse provides the details of his trade with Snopes for the mules, Darl suddenly realizes that Anse has used Cash's money as part of the deal, and says, in front of Armstid and the family, "So that's what you were doing in Cash's clothes last night" (110). The public exposure of his father's theft is not a matter of filial aggression or fraternal support. Armstid observes, "He said it just like he was reading it outen the paper. Like he never give a durn himself one way or the other."

* * *

Darl's destruction of the barn is the climax of his vision and his distance from what the other Bundrens regard as reality. Setting fire to the barn is his only significant action in the novel, and yet the act seems designed less to end what for him is an absolutely meaningless journey than to provide occasion for his lyrical description of it. Although Darl uses figurative language throughout the novel, in his account of the burning barn and the rescue of the animals and coffin, his expression rises to poetic heights as well as to an extreme remoteness from the tenor of the description, an event that a farmer must regard as catastrophic. While some of the figures are apt enough, most convey not merely metaphysical strain, but a kind of irrelevance: Mack's freckles "like english peas on a plate"; the frightened cow's "tail erect and rigid as a broom nailed upright to the end of her spine"; the burning hay "like a portiere of flaming beads." Most remarkable, of course, are the figures from classical and modern art: "two figures in a Greek frieze," "the conical facade," the coffin "like a cubistic bug," and finally the allusion to theater, "the dissolving proscenium of the doorway" (126–27).

Nowhere in the description is there the slightest sense that the monologue is coming from the man who started the fire. On the contrary, the language has an autonomy to it, as if independent of the practical disaster it so brilliantly describes, as if emphasizing that all of it—the fire, the frantic effort at rescue, the journey, the very language used to register all of this momentous struggle—it is all aimless but for the original death that draws it forward, is nothing but metaphor "isolated out of all reality by the red glare" (127). Significantly, at the end of his monologue, at the peak moment of his aestheticization of detour, Darl registers the victory of Jewel. Jewel saves the coffin, "riding upon it, clinging to it," having transferred his displacement of the horse back to Addie. Perhaps compelled by the remorseless honesty of the poet or by an undeniable awareness of the power of detour, however ghostly it may appear to him, Darl acknowledges Jewel as a god "enclosed in a thin numbus of fire," the fire burning "crimson-edged holes that bloom like flowers in his undershirt" (128).

To return to the issues I raised at the beginning of this chapter, in arranging the expulsion of Darl Bundren from the novel, Faulkner is describing the expulsion of a certain kind of artistry from his work, as he moved from *The Sound and the Fury* to *As I Lay Dying*. His respect, even affection for Darl, in his extratextual comments, is clear enough: "Who can say how much of the good poetry in the world has come out of madness, and who can say just how much of superperceptivity the—a mad person might not have? . . . That maybe the madman does see more than the sane man."[7] "Madness," however, and all that it might imply for Faulkner were not what he was about in the fall of 1929. If he were going to remain a writer, he had to write: expeditiously, professionally, if possible profitably—and if not profitably then in a way that provided opportunity to earn money by other means, either by writing short stories (which he always considered, even at his best in this genre, "boiling the pot") or, as in October, 1929, by taking a job that, ostensibly, had nothing whatsoever to do with writing.

There is more to the shift marked by *As I Lay Dying*, however, than the speed with which it was written and published. He turned to the life of country people, free from the kinds of historical obsessions and race-related complexities inherent to the Southern culture

7. *Faulkner in the University*, p. 113. [See p. 189 in this Norton Critical Edition (*Editor*)].

Faulkner knew best, and free from what many would consider the major issue concerning country people: their economic plight. His purpose was to confront issues that marriage and family had thrust upon him. How does one negotiate the conflict of family obligation and personal desire? Of a privacy that seems to reach back and down into an "abject nakedness we bring here with us" (27) and a world of engagement encroaching constantly on that privacy, compelling a different kind of responsibility? Perhaps inspired by Freud's stark delineation of life and death as antagonistic instincts, Faulkner found in the journey of the Bundrens life and death forces in an inextricable interdependence that might suggest, if one knew how to read it, the possibility of achievement.

*   *   *

* * * [Darl] is expelled in the name of erotic quests: the Bundrens' to complete their mission, however compromised by ulterior motives, to get to Jefferson, to get the body into the ground, no matter its condition or scandalous treatment; Faulkner's to complete the novel, to build what Cash praises as a "tight chicken coop" rather than a court house, "shoddy" or "built well" (135), methodically pushing it out on swing-shift power-plant breaks, the novel of compromise itself compromised by the contract he and Estelle had entered into June 20, 1929.

Of the Bundrens Faulkner said that, confronted with a difficult "fate," they "pretty well coped with theirs."[8] Of his marriage he told a friend in Pascagoula, "Tom, they don't think we're gonna stick, but it is gonna stick."[9] Of *As I Lay Dying* he wrote, "I sent it to Smith and wrote him that by it I would stand or fall."[1]

8. *Lion in the Garden: Interviews with William Faulkner 1926–1962*, ed. James B. Meriwether and Michael Millgate (New York: Random House, 1968), p. 254. [See p. 187 in this Norton Critical Edition (*Editor*)].
9. Blotner, p. 243.
1. William Faulkner, "Introduction" to *Sanctuary* (New York: Random House, 1932), p. vii. [See p. 184 in this Norton Critical Edition (*Editor*)].

William Faulkner: A Chronology

1897	Born William Cuthbert Falkner on September 25, in New Albany, Mississippi, first of the four sons of Maud Butler Falkner and Murry Cuthbert Falkner. Family roots are in Ripley, MS, where in 1886 his paternal great-grandfather, William Clark Falkner—plantation owner and Confederate colonel—had taken control of the local railroad.
1902	Family moves to Oxford, MS, where his grandfather, John Falkner, is a locally prominent lawyer and politician. Father goes into business and opens a livery stable. Caroline Barr ("Mammy Callie") hired to care for the children.
1903	Meets and sometimes plays with Lida Estelle Oldham (b. 1896), whom in 1929 he will marry.
1909–15	Works in father's livery stable when off from school. Starts to draw and write, and to read authors like Twain, Shakespeare, Conrad, Balzac, and Melville. Begins to fall in love with Estelle. Friendship with law student Phil Stone, his first literary mentor.
1918	Estelle engaged to Cornell Franklin, a lawyer, but is ready to elope with young "Falkner" anyway. Families block their marriage and she weds Franklin, by whom she will have two children. Visits Phil Stone at Yale that spring, and in July joins the Royal Air Force in Toronto. Enlists under the name "Faulkner." Discharged in December before finishing training.
1919–24	Writes poetry, publishes some of it, and briefly attends the University of Mississippi in his hometown. Called "Count No 'Count" by fellow students who find him pretentious. Visits New York, returns to job as postmaster at the university. Develops friendship with Sherwood Anderson in New Orleans, where he writes for local magazines. First book: *The Marble Faun*, poems, published December 1924.
1925	Begins work on novel *Mayday* (later *Soldier's Pay*). In July sails to Europe on freighter; travels through Italy and

Switzerland to Paris, then briefly to England. Returns in December.

1926   *Soldier's Pay.* Parents shocked at sexual content. Begins work on the Yoknapatawpha cycle with both the unfinished *Father Abraham*, which contains the germ of his Snopes novels, and *Flags in the Dust*, drawing upon family history.

1927–28   *Mosquitoes.* Estelle returns to Oxford after beginning divorce proceedings. *Flags in the Dust* rejected. His career at an impasse, writes *The Sound and the Fury*, working without plan or design in a state of never-to-be-recovered ecstasy.

1929   Publishes both *Sartoris*, a revised and cut version of *Flags in the Dust*, and *The Sound and the Fury.* Marries Estelle. Works on early version of *Sanctuary*, rejected as too scandalous to publish without fear of prosecution. In the fall, writes *As I Lay Dying* while working as a nighttime supervisor at the University of Mississippi power plant.

1930   Purchases rundown antebellum Oxford house and names it Rowan Oak. *As I Lay Dying.*

1931   Revised but no less scandalous *Sanctuary* appears. *These 13*, a collection of stories. Daughter Alabama born in January, dies after nine days. Faulkner drinking heavily.

1932   *Light in August.* Goes to California to write for Metro-Goldwyn-Mayer. Will work on-and-off in the movie industry, especially for the director Howard Hawks, until 1951. Father Murry Falkner dies.

1933   *A Green Bough*, poetry. Daughter Jill born in June.

1934   *Doctor Martino and Other Stories.*

1935   *Pylon.* Brother Dean killed in plane crash. Faulkner assumes financial responsibility for Dean's widow and unborn child. Begins intermittent, fifteen-year relationship with Hawks's secretary, Meta Doherty Carpenter.

1936   *Absalom, Absalom!*

1938   *The Unvanquished*, a novel stitched together from a series of heavily revised magazine stories about a boy's experiences during the Civil War and after. Book sold to Hollywood, though never filmed, and Faulkner buys a farm with the proceeds.

1939   *The Wild Palms.* Appears on the cover of *Time.* Elected to the National Institute of Arts and Letters.

1940   *The Hamlet*, episodic first novel in the Snopes trilogy, again drawing on earlier published material. Caroline

Barr dies; Faulkner gives the eulogy at her funeral and will dedicate *Go Down, Moses* to her, his cycle of stories about the black and white descendants of the same planter.

1942–46   *Go Down, Moses and Other Stories.* Spends much of World War II in Hollywood, working on such classic films as *The Big Sleep* and *Mildred Pierce* among others. Drinks heavily and notes that all his books with the exception of *Sanctuary* have fallen out of print. Begins to work with the critic Malcolm Cowley on a selection from his work.

1946   Cowley publishes *The Portable Faulkner*, including Faulkner's new appendix to *The Sound and the Fury*, "Compson: 1699–1945." *The Sound and the Fury* and *As I Lay Dying* republished in a single volume by the Modern Library.

1948   *Intruder in the Dust.* Sells film rights for $50,000. Elected to the American Academy of Arts and Letters.

1949   *Knight's Gambit,* a volume of detective stories. Movie of *Intruder in the Dust* released, with its premiere held in Oxford.

1950   In May, receives the Howells Medal for Fiction from the American Academy of Arts and Letters. *Collected Stories of William Faulkner* (National Book Award). November: announcement of the Nobel Prize, travels to Sweden for prize ceremony.

1951   *Requiem for a Nun.*

1952–53   Hospitalized several times in Paris, Memphis, and New York for riding- and drinking-related injuries.

1954   *A Fable* (Pulitzer Prize and National Book Award). Travels in Europe. Daughter Jill marries Paul D. Summers Jr.; they settle in Charlottesville, VA.

1955   *Big Woods,* a collection of hunting stories. Increasingly involved in the civil rights movement, and advocates school integration.

1957–59   *The Town,* second novel of the Snopes trilogy. Teaches at the University of Virginia and buys a house there to be near Jill and his new grandchildren. Enjoys fox hunting but rides recklessly and is often hurt in falls. *The Mansion,* final Snopes novel.

1960   Mother Maud Butler Falkner dies. Divides time between Oxford and Charlottesville.

1962   Gold Medal for Fiction from the National Institute of Arts and Letters. Hospitalized several times, his riding injuries exacerbated by his drinking. *The Reivers* (Pulitzer Prize), a comic novel about a horse theft, published in June. Faulkner dies of a heart attack on July 6, and is buried in Oxford.

1972   Death of Estelle Faulkner.

Selected Bibliography

• Indicates works included or excerpted in this Norton Critical Edition.

Biographical and Historical

Blotner, Joseph. *Faulkner: A Biography.* 1 vol. Rev. ed., New York: Random House, 1984.

Blotner, Joseph, ed. *Selected Letters of William Faulkner.* New York: Random House, 1977.

• Blotner, Joseph, and Frederick L. Gwynn. *Faulkner in the University.* Charlottesville, VA: University of Virginia Press, 1959.

Cowley, Malcolm. *The Faulkner-Cowley File: Letters and Memories, 1944–1962.* New York: Viking, 1966.

Doyle, Don H. *Faulkner's County: The Historical Roots of Yoknapatawpha.* Chapel Hill: University of North Carolina Press, 2001.

• Gray, Richard, *The Life of William Faulkner.* Oxford, England: Blackwell, 1994.

• Meriwether, James B. ed. *Essays, Speeches, and Public Letters by William Faulkner.* New York: Random House, 1965.

• Meriwether, James B., and Michael Millgate, eds. *Lion in the Garden: Interviews with William Faulkner 1926–1962.* New York: Random House, 1968.

Sensibar, Judith L. *Faulkner and Love: The Women Who Shaped His Art.* New Haven and London: Yale University Press, 2009.

Williamson, Joel. *William Faulkner and Southern History.* Oxford, England: Oxford University Press, 1993.

Reference and Collections

Bassett, John. *William Faulkner: The Critical Heritage.* London: Routledge and Kegan Paul, 1975.

Brown, Calvin S. *A Glossary of Faulkner's South.* New Haven: Yale University Press, 1976.

Claridge, Henry. *William Faulkner: Critical Assessments.* 4 vols. East Sussex: Helm Information, 1999.

Cox, Dianne L. *William Faulkner's* As I Lay Dying: *A Critical Casebook.* New York: Garland, 1985.

Hamblin, Robert W., and Charles A. Peek. *A William Faulkner Encyclopedia.* Westport, CT: Greenwood, 1999.

Inge, Thomas M. *William Faulkner: The Contemporary Reviews.* Cambridge: Cambridge University Press, 1995.

Kirk, Robert W. *Faulkner's People.* Berkeley and Los Angeles: University of California Press, 1963.

Luce, Dianne C. *Annotations to* As I Lay Dying. New York and London: Garland, 1990.

• Moreland, Richard C. *A Companion to William Faulkner.* Oxford, England: Blackwell, 2007.

Peek, Charles A., and Robert W. Hamblin. *A Companion to Faulkner Studies.* Westport, CT: Greenwood, 2004.

Warren, Robert Penn, ed. *Faulkner: A Collection of Critical Essays.* Englewood Cliffs, NJ: Prentice Hall, 1966.

Weinstein, Philip M., ed. *The Cambridge Companion to William Faulkner.* Cambridge: Cambridge University Press, 1995.

Books about Faulkner

Atkinson, Ted. *Faulkner and the Great Depression.* Athens: University of Georgia Press, 2006.

Baker, Houston A. Jr. *I Don't Hate the South: Reflections on Faulkner, Family, and the South.* New York and Oxford: Oxford University Press, 2007.

• Bleikasten, André. *Faulkner's* As I Lay Dying: Trans. Roger Little. Bloomington: Indiana University Press, 1973.

———. *The Ink of Melancholy.* Bloomington: Indiana University Press, 1990.

• Brooks, Cleanth. *William Faulkner: The Yoknapatawpha Country.* New Haven: Yale University Press, 1963.

Clarke, Deborah. *Robbing the Mother: Women in Faulkner.* Jackson: University Press of Mississippi, 1994.

• Coindreau, Maurice Edgar. *The Time of William Faulkner.* Ed. and chiefly trans. by George McMillan Reeves. Columbia, South Carolina: University of South Carolina Press, 1971.

Davis, Thadious. *Faulkner's 'Negro': Art and the Southern Context.* Baton Rouge: Louisiana State University Press, 1983.

Fowler, Doreen. *Faulkner: The Return of the Repressed.* Charlottesville: University of Virginia Press, 1997.

Glissant, Edouard. *Faulkner, Mississippi.* (1996) Trans. Barbara Lewis and Thomas C. Spear. New York: Farrar Straus & Giroux, 1999.

Gwin, Minrose C. *The Feminine and Faulkner: Reading (Beyond) Sexual Difference.* Knoxville: University of Tennessee Press, 1990.

Howe, Irving. *William Faulkner.* Chicago: University of Chicago Press, 1951.

Irwin, John. *Doubling and Incest/Repetition and Revenge: A Speculative Reading of Faulkner.* Baltimore: Johns Hopkins University Press, 1975.

Jehlen, Myra. *Class and Character in Faulkner's South.* New York: Columbia University Press, 1976.

Kartiganer, Donald M. *The Fragile Thread: The Meaning of Form in Faulkner's Novels.* Amherst: University of Massachusetts Press, 1979.

Kinney, Arthur F. *Faulkner's Narrative Poetics: Style as Vision.* Amherst: University of Massachusetts Press, 1978.

Matthews, John T. *The Play of Faulkner's Language.* Ithaca: Cornell University Press, 1982.

Millgate, Michael. *The Achievement of William Faulkner.* New York: Random House, 1966.

Minter, David M. *William Faulkner: His Life and Work.* Baltimore: Johns Hopkins University Press, 1980.

Polk, Noel. *Children of the Dark House: Text and Context in Faulkner.* Jackson: University Press of Mississippi, 1996.

Roberts, Diane. *Faulkner and Southern Womanhood.* Athens: University of Georgia Press, 1994.

• Ross, Stephen M. *Fiction's Inexhaustible Voice: Speech and Writing in Faulkner.* Athens: University of Georgia Press, 1989.

• Sundquist, Eric. *Faulkner: The House Divided*. Baltimore: Johns Hopkins University Press, 1983.
• Vickery, Olga W. *The Novels of William Faulkner*. Baton Rouge: Louisiana State University Press, 1959.
 Wadlington, Warwick. *Reading Faulknerian Tragedy*. Ithaca: Cornell University Press, 1987.
 ————. As I Lay Dying: *Stories Out of Stories*. New York: Twayne, 1992.
 Weinstein, Philip M. *Faulkner's Subject: A Cosmos No One Owns*. Cambridge: Cambridge University Press, 1992.

Articles

Essays reprinted in this Norton Critical Edition are not included in the list below.

Bergman, Jill. "'this was the answer to it': Sexuality and Maternity in *As I Lay Dying*." *Mississippi Quarterly* 49.3 (Summer 1996): 393–407.
Blaine, Diana York. "The Abjection of Addie and Other Myths of the Maternal in *As I Lay Dying*." *Mississippi Quarterly* 47.3 (1994): 419–39.
Blotner, Joseph. "*As I Lay Dying*: Christian Lore and Irony." *Twentieth Century Literature* 3 (April 1957): 11–19.
Collins, Carvel. "The Pairing of *The Sound and the Fury* and *As I Lay Dying*." *Princeton University Library Chronicle* 18 (Spring 1957): 114–23.
Douglas, Harold J., and Robert Daniel. "Faulkner and the Puritanism of the South." *Tennessee Studies in Literature* 2 (1957): 1–13.
Garrett, George Palmer. "Some Revisions in *As I Lay Dying*." *Modern Language Notes* 73.6 (June 1958): 414–17.
Hale, Dorothy J. "*As I Lay Dying's* Heterogeneous Discourse." *Novel* 23.1 (Fall 1989): 5–23.
Hustis, Harriet. "The Tangled Web We Weave: Faulkner Scholarship and the Significance of Addie Bundren's Monologue." *Faulkner Journal* 12.1 (Fall 1996): 3–21.
Kincaid, Nanci. "As me and Addie lay dying." *Southern Review* 30.3 (Summer 1994): 582–95.
LeCercle-Sweet, Ann. "The Chip and the Chink: The Dying of the I in *As I Lay Dying*." *Faulkner Journal* 2.1 (Fall 1986): 46–61.
Lester, Cheryl. "As They Lay Dying: Rural Depopulation and Social Dislocation as a Structure of Feeling." *Faulkner Journal* 21.1/2 (Fall 2005/2006): 28–50.
Matthews, John T. "*As I Lay Dying* in the Machine Age." *Boundary 2*, 19.1 (Spring 1992): 69–94.
Peek, Charles A. "'A-laying there, right up to my door': As American *As I Lay Dying*." In *Faulkner in America*. Ed. Joseph R. Urgo and Ann J. Abadie. Jackson, MS: University Press of Mississippi, 2001, 116–35.
Porter, Carolyn. "Symbolic Fathers and Dead Mothers: A Feminist Approach to Faulkner." In *Faulkner and Psychology*. Ed. Donald M. Kartiganer and Ann J. Abadie. Jackson: University Press of Mississippi, 1994, 78–122.
Rippetoe, Rita. "Unstained Shirt, Stained Character: Anse Bundren Reread." *Mississippi Quarterly* 54.3 (Summer 2001): 313–25.
Schroeder, Patricia R. "The Comic World of *As I Lay Dying*." In *Faulkner and Humor*. Ed. Doreen Fowler and Ann J. Abadie. Jackson, MS: University Press of Mississippi, 1986, 34–46.
Simon, John K. "'What are you Laughing at, Darl?' Madness and Humor in *As I Lay Dying*." *College English* 25 (November 1963): 104–10.
Waid, Candace. "Burying the Regional Mother: Faulkner's Road to Race through the Visual Arts." *Faulkner Journal* 23.1 (Fall 2007): 37–93.

Wasiolek, Edward. "*As I Lay Dying*: Distortion in the Slow Eddy of Current Opinion." *Critique* 3 (Spring–Fall 1959): 15–23.

Willis, Susan. "Learning from the Banana." *American Quarterly* 39.4 (Winter 1987): 586–600.

Wood, Amy Louise. "Feminine Rebellion and Mimicry in Faulkner's *As I Lay Dying*." *Faulkner Journal* 9.1/2 (1993/4): 99–112.

Three periodicals specialize in Faulkner studies: the *Faulkner Journal*; the *Mississippi Quarterly*, which regularly devotes a special issue to Faulkner's work; and the volume drawn each year from the "Faulkner and Yoknapatawpha" conference held every summer at the University of Mississippi (e.g., *Faulkner and Humor*, above). The most comprehensive website is "William Faulkner on the Web."